Faker.

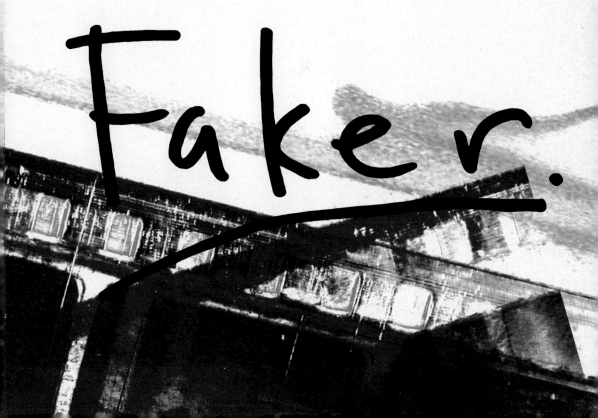

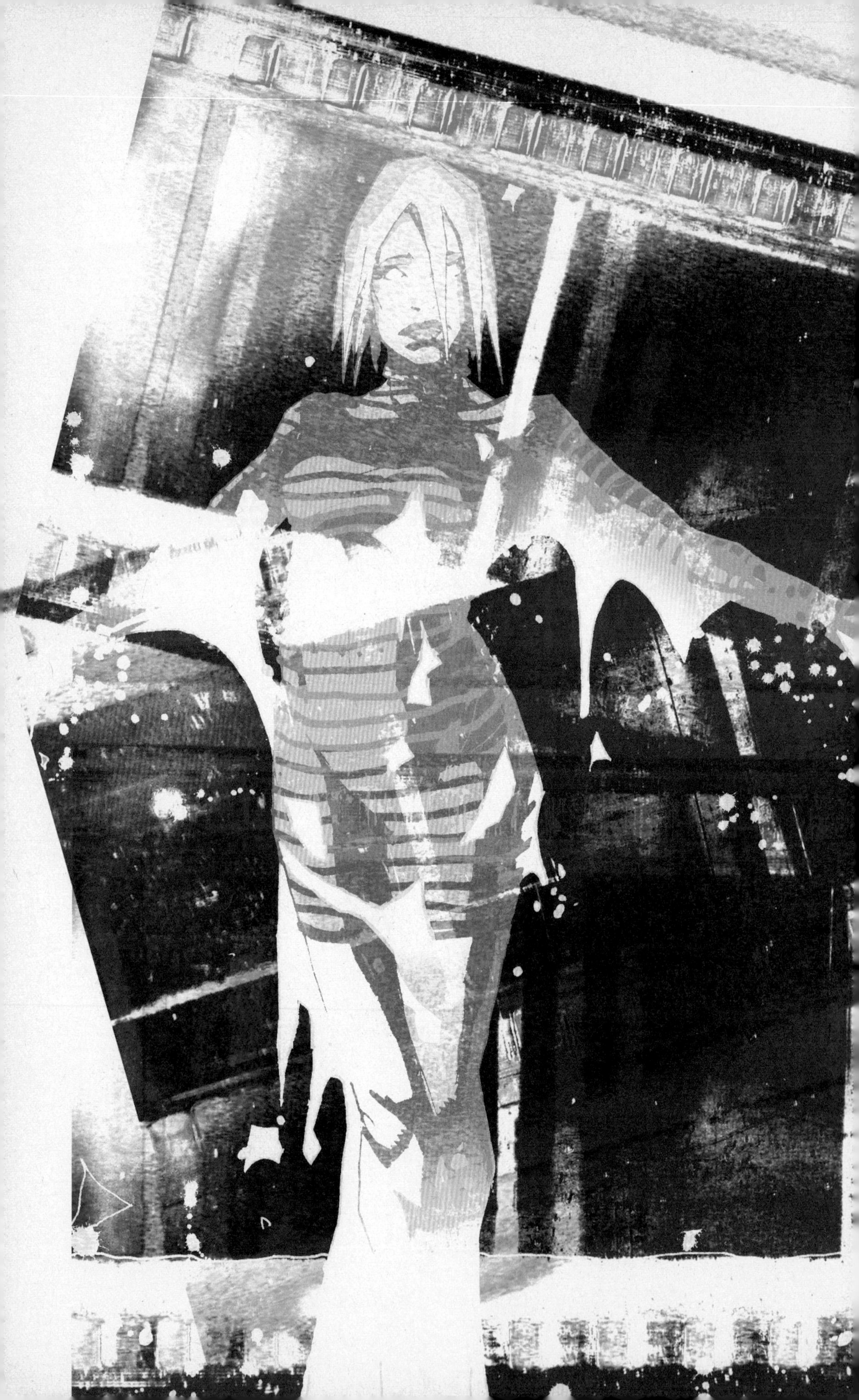

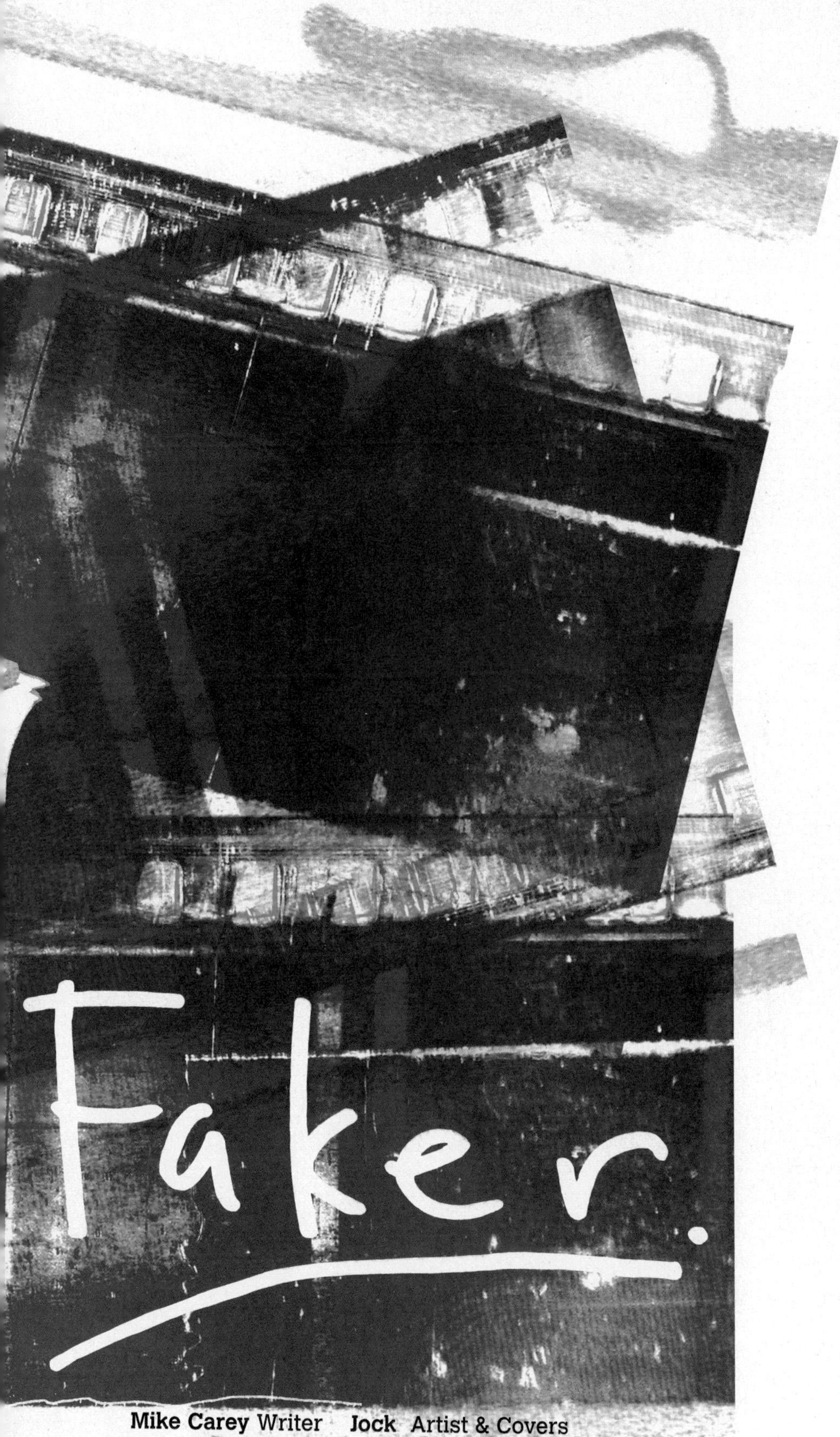

Faker.

Mike Carey Writer **Jock** Artist & Covers
Clem Robins Letterer **Lee Loughridge** Colorist
Faker created by Carey and Jock

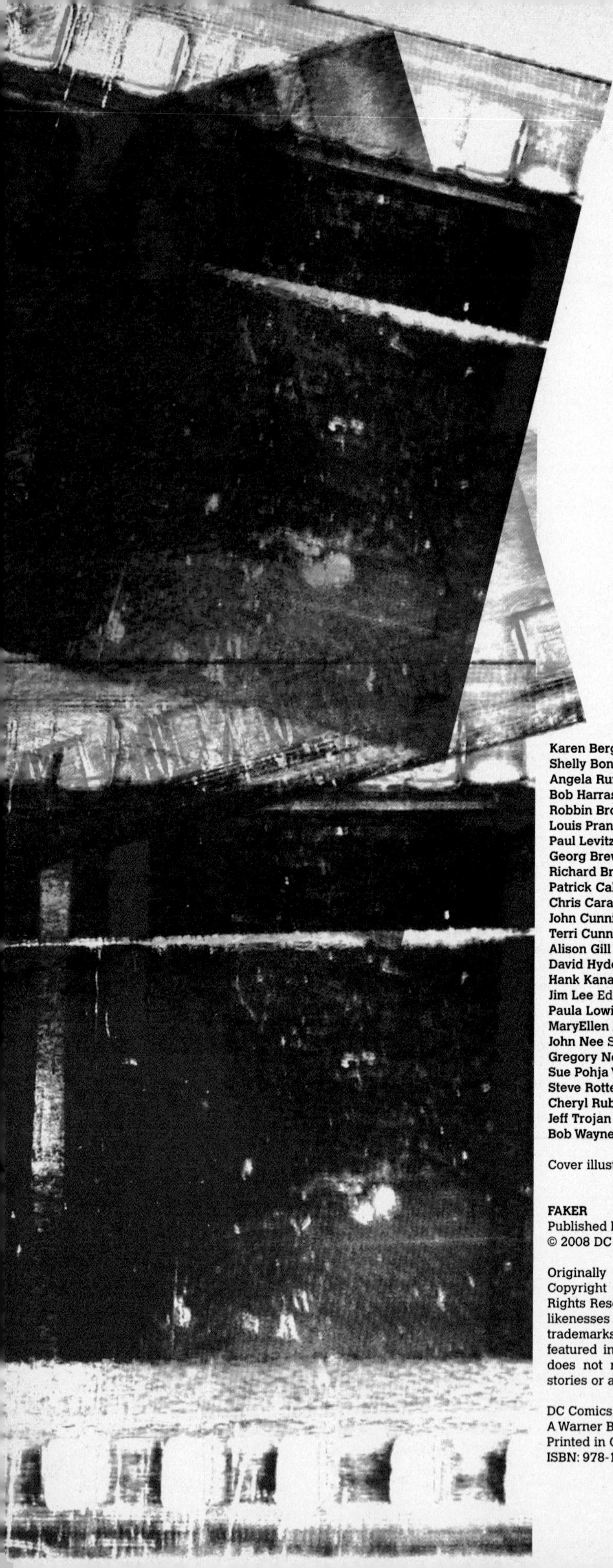

Karen Berger Senior VP-Executive Editor
Shelly Bond Editor-original series
Angela Rufino Assistant Editor-original series
Bob Harras Editor-collected edition
Robbin Brosterman Senior Art Director
Louis Prandi Art Director
Paul Levitz President & Publisher
Georg Brewer VP-Design & DC Direct Creative
Richard Bruning Senior VP-Creative Director
Patrick Caldon Executive VP-Finance & Operations
Chris Caramalis VP-Finance
John Cunningham VP-Marketing
Terri Cunningham VP-Managing Editor
Alison Gill VP-Manufacturing
David Hyde VP-Publicity
Hank Kanalz VP-General Manager, WildStorm
Jim Lee Editorial Director-WildStorm
Paula Lowitt Senior VP-Business & Legal Affairs
MaryEllen McLaughlin VP-Advertising & Custom Publishing
John Nee Senior VP-Business Development
Gregory Noveck Senior VP-Creative Affairs
Sue Pohja VP-Book Trade Sales
Steve Rotterdam Senior VP-Sales & Marketing
Cheryl Rubin Senior VP-Brand Management
Jeff Trojan VP-Business Development, DC Direct
Bob Wayne VP-Sales

Cover illustration and logo by **Jock**

FAKER

DC Comics, 1700 Broadway, New York, NY 10019
A Warner Bros. Entertainment Company.
Printed in Canada. First Printing.
ISBN: 978-1-4012-1663-4

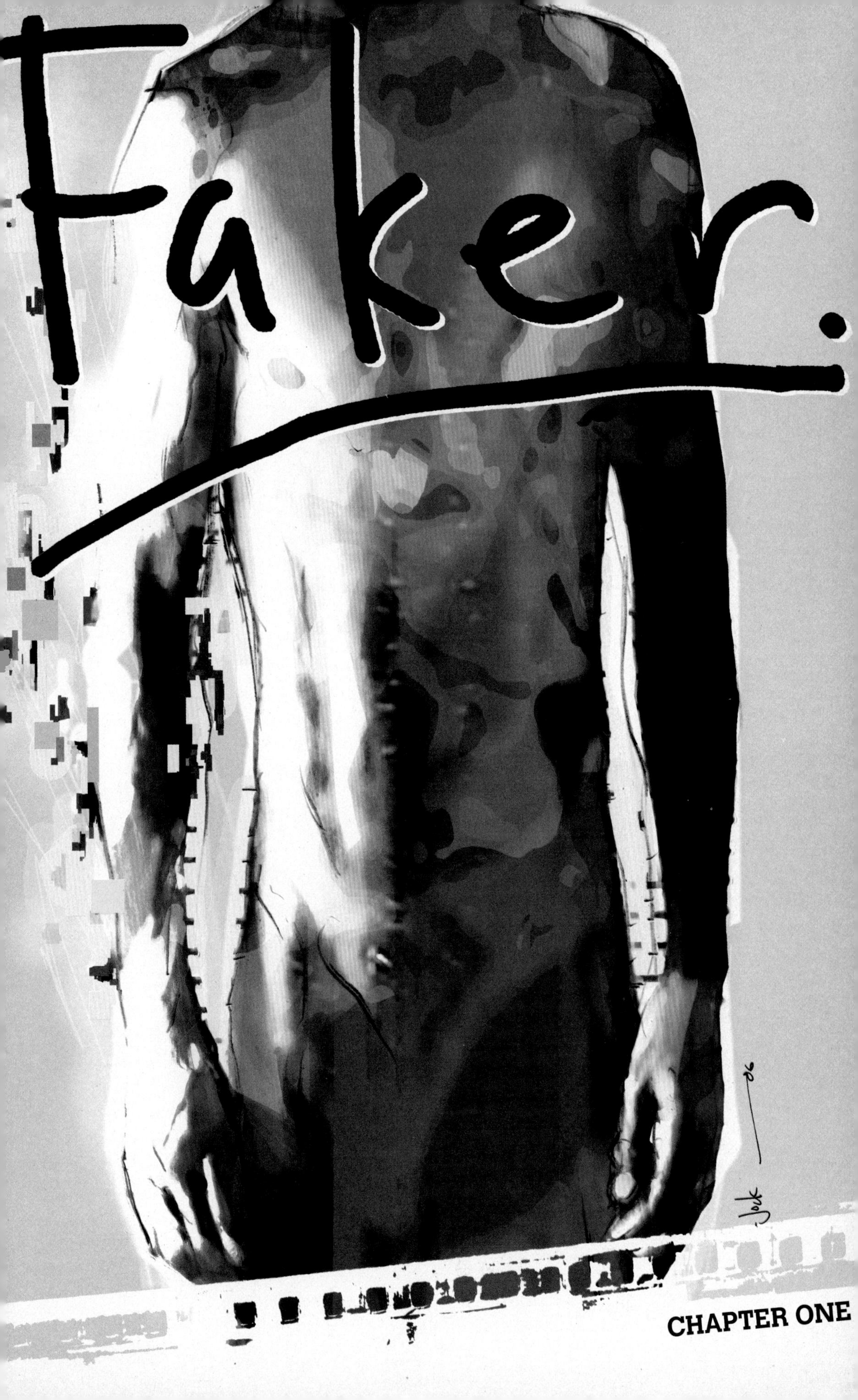
Faker.
Jock 06
CHAPTER ONE

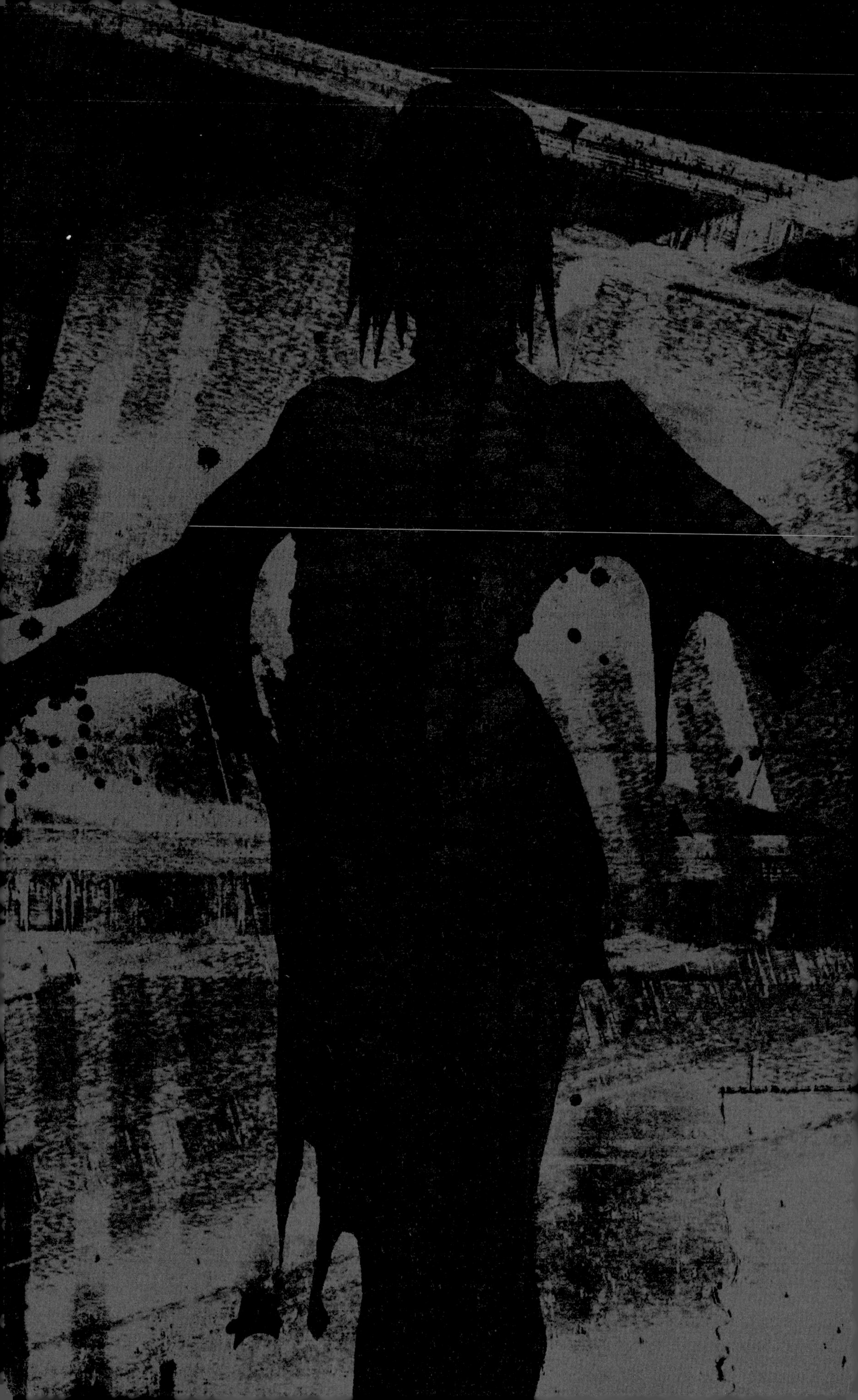

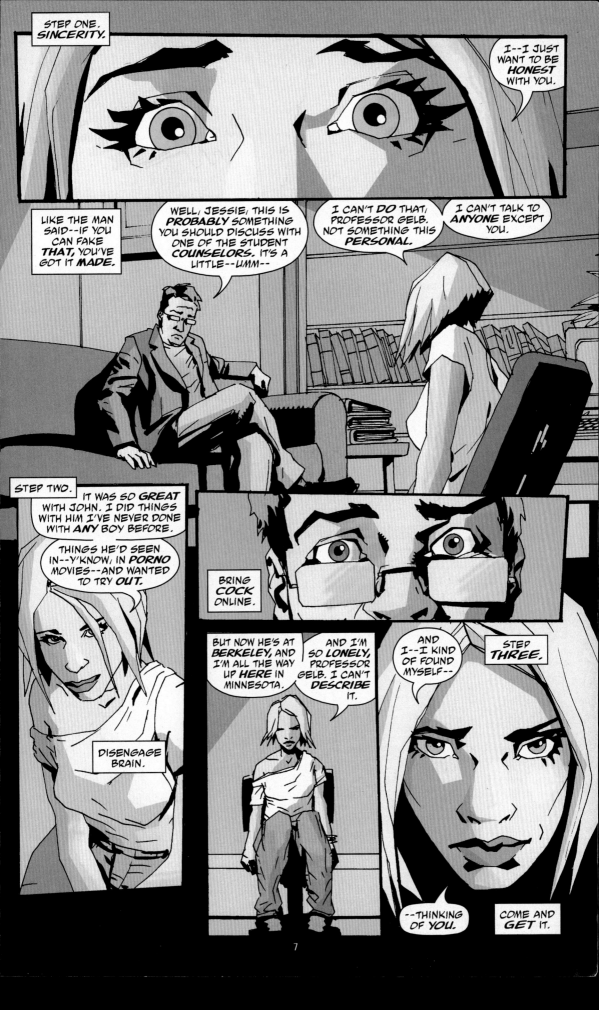

STEP ONE. SINCERITY.

I--I JUST WANT TO BE *HONEST* WITH YOU.

LIKE THE MAN SAID--IF YOU CAN FAKE *THAT*, YOU'VE GOT IT *MADE*.

WELL, JESSIE, THIS IS *PROBABLY* SOMETHING YOU SHOULD DISCUSS WITH ONE OF THE STUDENT *COUNSELORS*. IT'S A LITTLE--*UMM*--

I CAN'T *DO* THAT, PROFESSOR GELB. NOT SOMETHING THIS *PERSONAL*.

I CAN'T TALK TO *ANYONE* EXCEPT YOU.

STEP TWO.

IT WAS SO *GREAT* WITH JOHN. I DID THINGS WITH HIM I'VE NEVER DONE WITH *ANY* BOY BEFORE.

THINGS HE'D SEEN IN--Y'KNOW, IN *PORNO* MOVIES--AND WANTED TO TRY *OUT*.

BRING *COCK* ONLINE.

DISENGAGE BRAIN.

BUT NOW HE'S AT *BERKELEY*, AND I'M ALL THE WAY UP *HERE* IN MINNESOTA.

AND I'M SO *LONELY*, PROFESSOR GELB. I CAN'T *DESCRIBE* IT.

AND I--I KIND OF FOUND MYSELF--

STEP *THREE*.

--THINKING OF *YOU*.

COME AND *GET* IT.

7

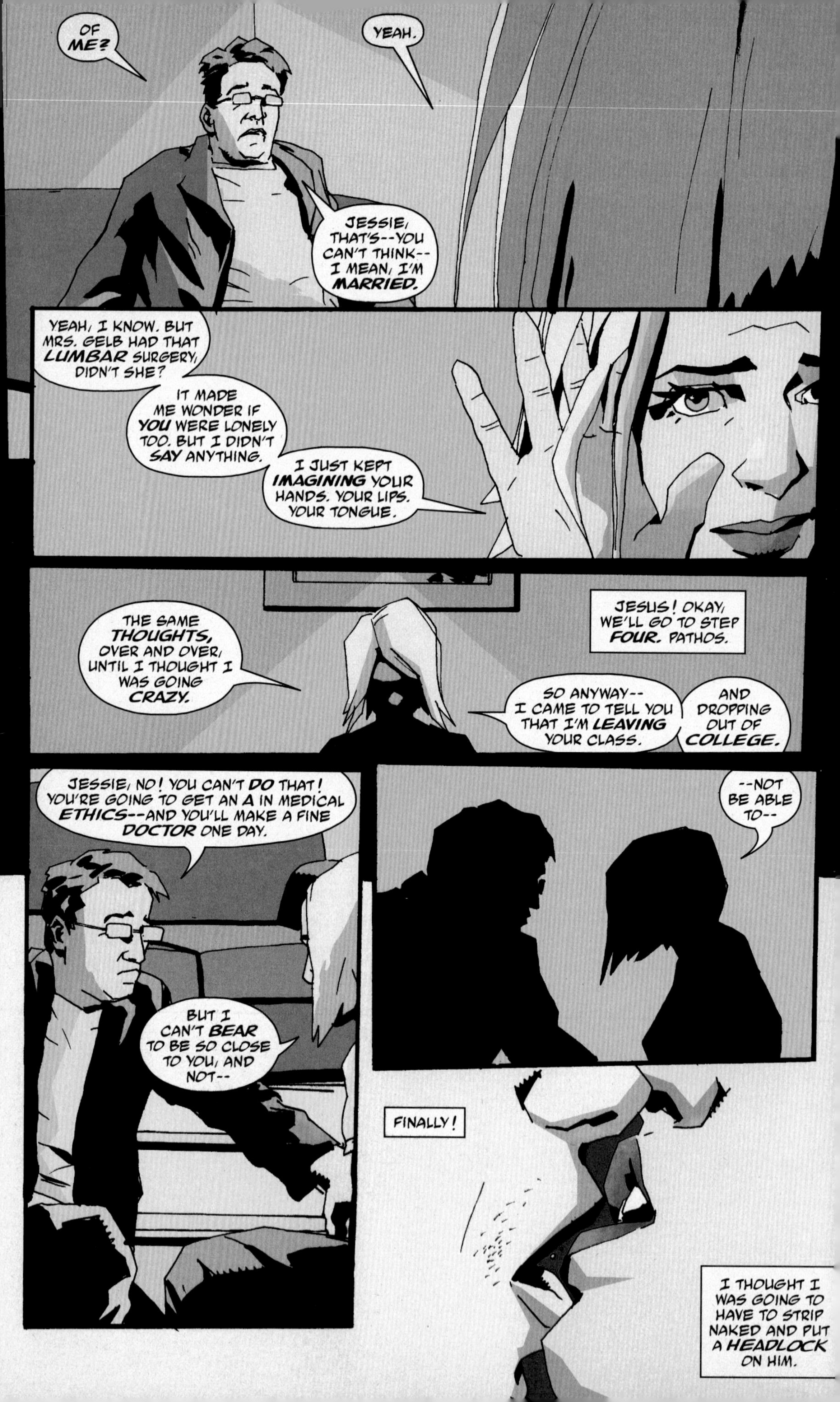
OF ME?
YEAH.
JESSIE, THAT'S--YOU CAN'T THINK-- I MEAN, I'M MARRIED.
YEAH, I KNOW. BUT MRS. GELB HAD THAT LUMBAR SURGERY, DIDN'T SHE?
IT MADE ME WONDER IF YOU WERE LONELY TOO. BUT I DIDN'T SAY ANYTHING.
I JUST KEPT IMAGINING YOUR HANDS. YOUR LIPS. YOUR TONGUE.
THE SAME THOUGHTS, OVER AND OVER, UNTIL I THOUGHT I WAS GOING CRAZY.
JESUS! OKAY, WE'LL GO TO STEP FOUR. PATHOS.
SO ANYWAY-- I CAME TO TELL YOU THAT I'M LEAVING YOUR CLASS.
AND DROPPING OUT OF COLLEGE.
JESSIE, NO! YOU CAN'T DO THAT! YOU'RE GOING TO GET AN A IN MEDICAL ETHICS--AND YOU'LL MAKE A FINE DOCTOR ONE DAY.
BUT I CAN'T BEAR TO BE SO CLOSE TO YOU, AND NOT--
--NOT BE ABLE TO--
FINALLY!
I THOUGHT I WAS GOING TO HAVE TO STRIP NAKED AND PUT A HEADLOCK ON HIM.

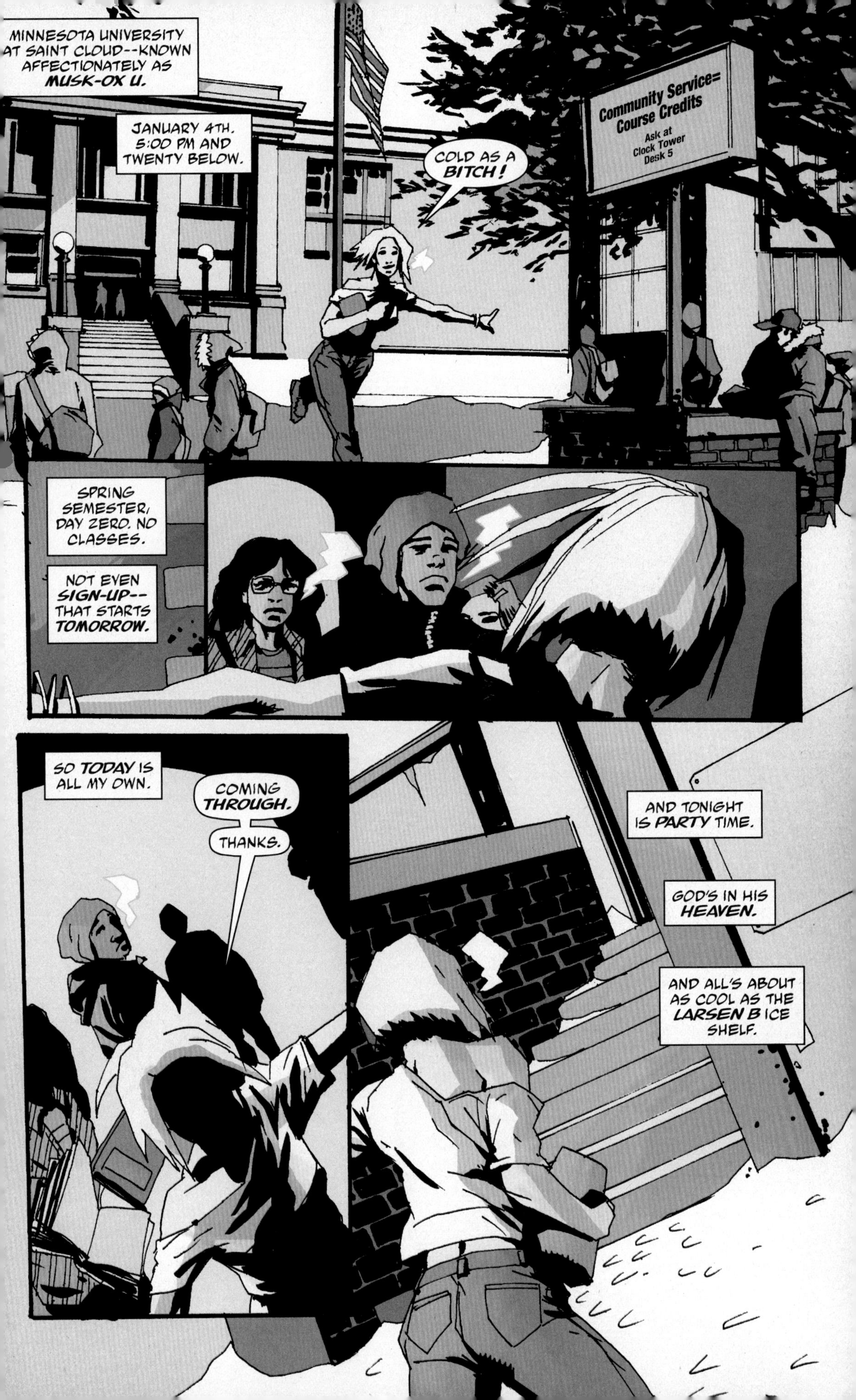
MINNESOTA UNIVERSITY AT SAINT CLOUD--KNOWN AFFECTIONATELY AS MUSK-OX U.
JANUARY 4TH. 5:00 PM AND TWENTY BELOW.
COLD AS A BITCH!
Community Service= Course Credits
Ask at Clock Tower Desk 5
SPRING SEMESTER, DAY ZERO. NO CLASSES.
NOT EVEN SIGN-UP-- THAT STARTS TOMORROW.
SO TODAY IS ALL MY OWN.
COMING THROUGH.
THANKS.
AND TONIGHT IS PARTY TIME.
GOD'S IN HIS HEAVEN.
AND ALL'S ABOUT AS COOL AS THE LARSEN B ICE SHELF.

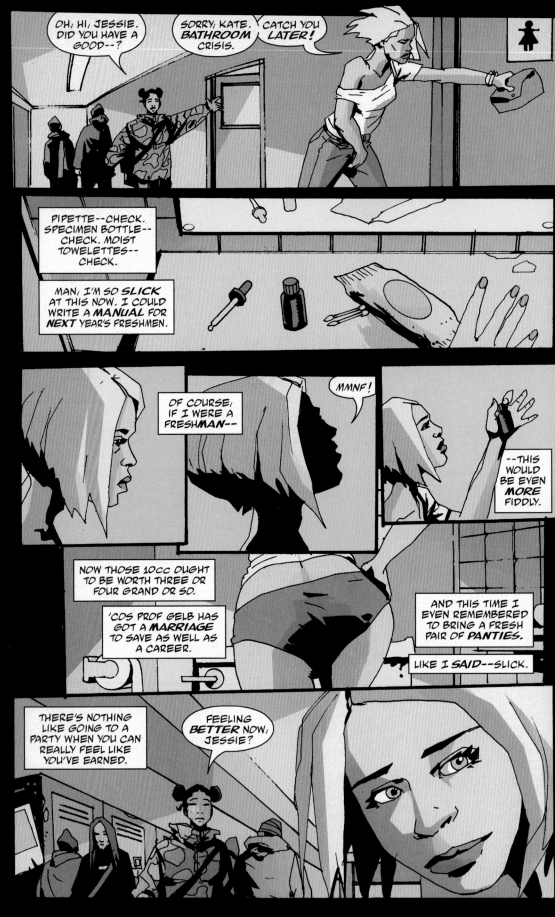

OH, HI, JESSIE. DID YOU HAVE A GOOD--?

SORRY, KATE. *BATHROOM* CRISIS. CATCH YOU *LATER!*

PIPETTE--CHECK. SPECIMEN BOTTLE-- CHECK. MOIST TOWELETTES-- CHECK.

MAN, I'M SO *SLICK* AT THIS NOW. I COULD WRITE A *MANUAL* FOR *NEXT* YEAR'S FRESHMEN.

OF COURSE, IF I WERE A *FRESHMAN*--

MMNF!

--THIS WOULD BE EVEN *MORE* FIDDLY.

NOW THOSE 10CC OUGHT TO BE WORTH THREE OR FOUR GRAND OR SO.

'COS PROF GELB HAS GOT A *MARRIAGE* TO SAVE AS WELL AS A CAREER.

AND THIS TIME I EVEN REMEMBERED TO BRING A FRESH PAIR OF *PANTIES.*

LIKE I *SAID*--SLICK.

THERE'S NOTHING LIKE GOING TO A PARTY WHEN YOU CAN REALLY FEEL LIKE YOU'VE EARNED.

FEELING *BETTER* NOW, JESSIE?

10

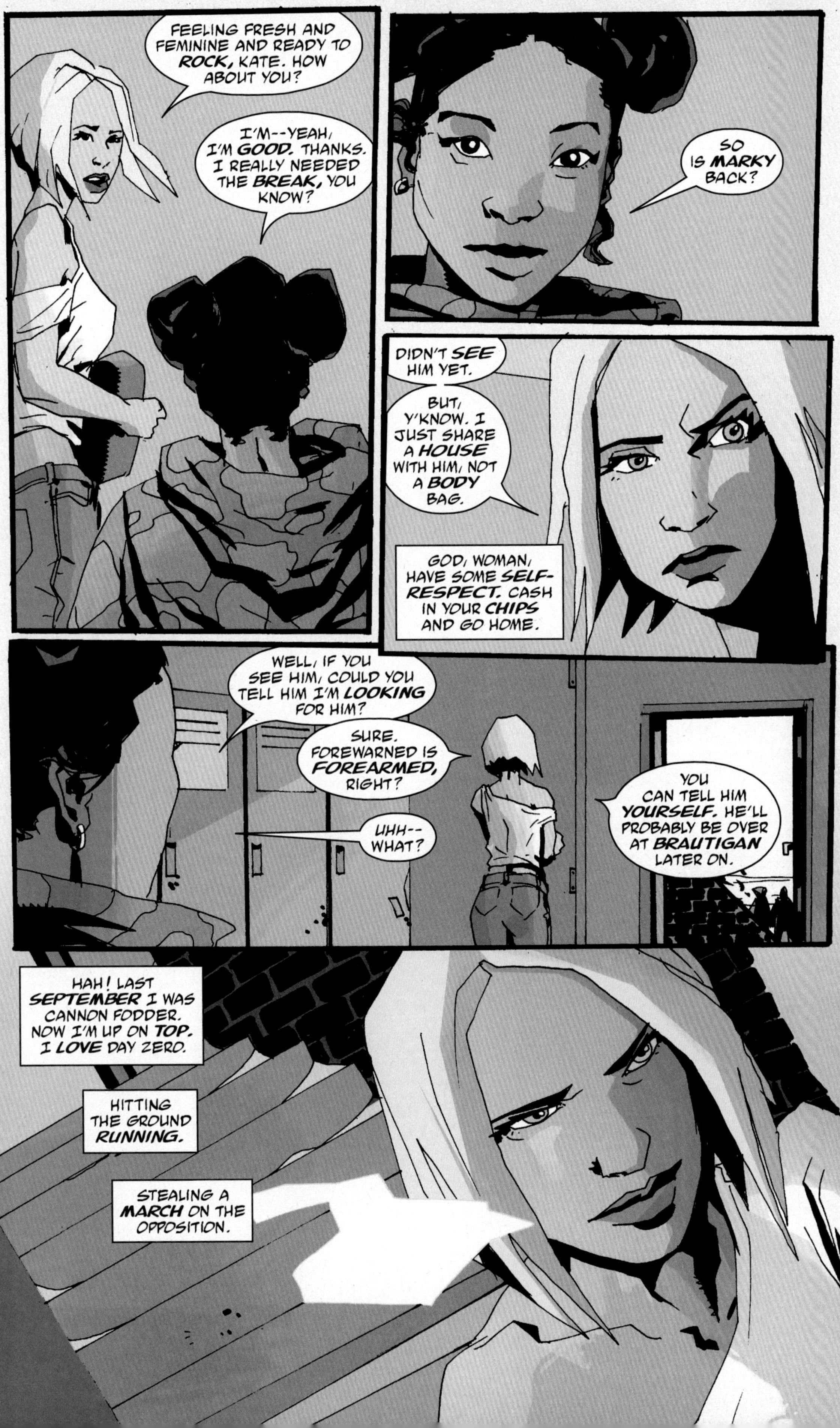
FEELING FRESH AND FEMININE AND READY TO ROCK, KATE. HOW ABOUT YOU?
I'M--YEAH, I'M GOOD. THANKS. I REALLY NEEDED THE BREAK, YOU KNOW?
SO IS MARKY BACK?
DIDN'T SEE HIM YET.
BUT, Y'KNOW. I JUST SHARE A HOUSE WITH HIM, NOT A BODY BAG.
GOD, WOMAN, HAVE SOME SELF-RESPECT. CASH IN YOUR CHIPS AND GO HOME.
WELL, IF YOU SEE HIM, COULD YOU TELL HIM I'M LOOKING FOR HIM?
SURE. FOREWARNED IS FOREARMED, RIGHT?
UHH--WHAT?
YOU CAN TELL HIM YOURSELF. HE'LL PROBABLY BE OVER AT BRAUTIGAN LATER ON.
HAH! LAST SEPTEMBER I WAS CANNON FODDER. NOW I'M UP ON TOP. I LOVE DAY ZERO.
HITTING THE GROUND RUNNING.
STEALING A MARCH ON THE OPPOSITION.

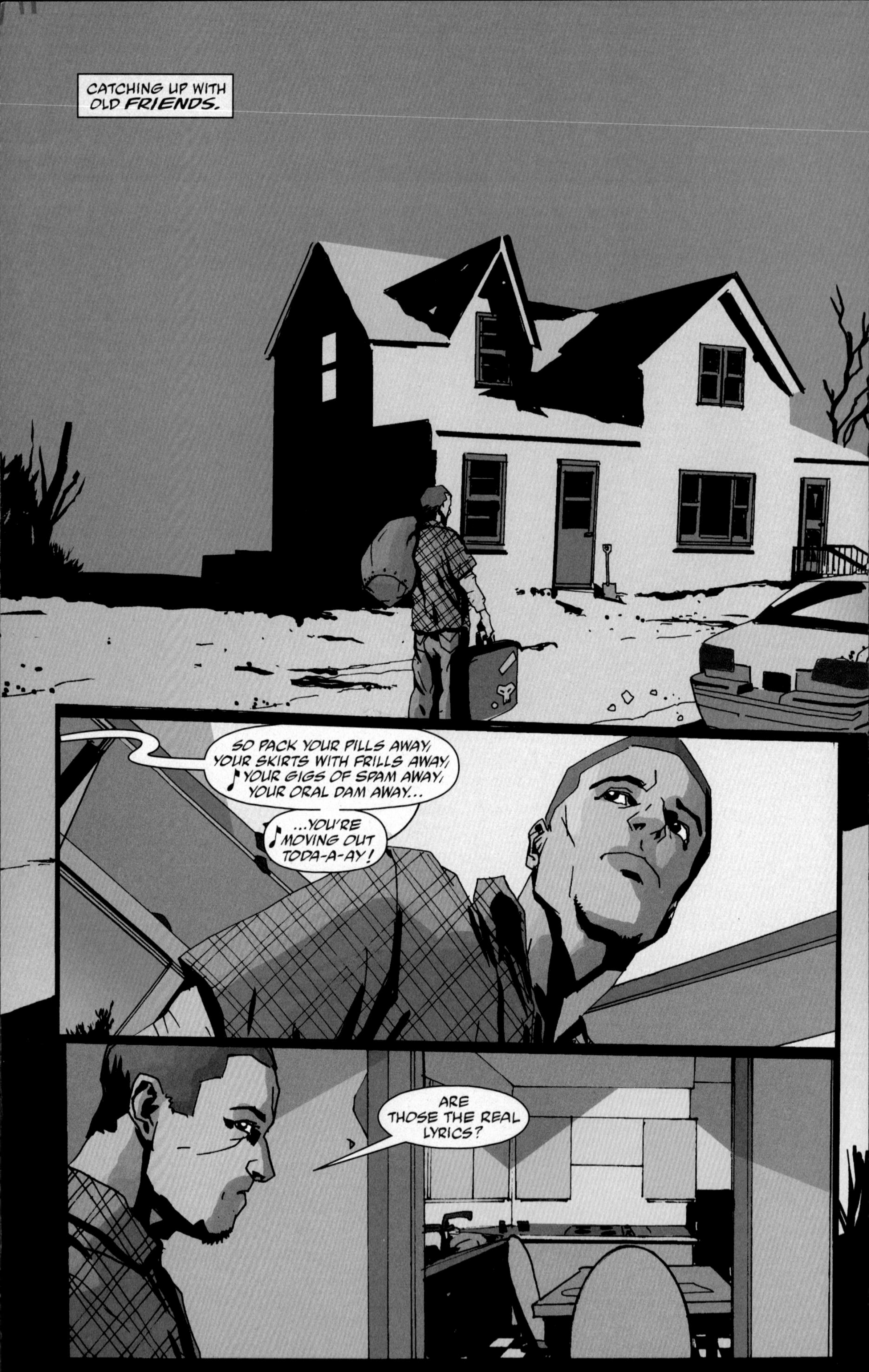
CATCHING UP WITH OLD FRIENDS.
SO PACK YOUR PILLS AWAY, YOUR SKIRTS WITH FRILLS AWAY, ♪ YOUR GIGS OF SPAM AWAY, YOUR ORAL DAM AWAY...
...YOU'RE ♪ MOVING OUT TODA-A-AY!
ARE THOSE THE REAL LYRICS?

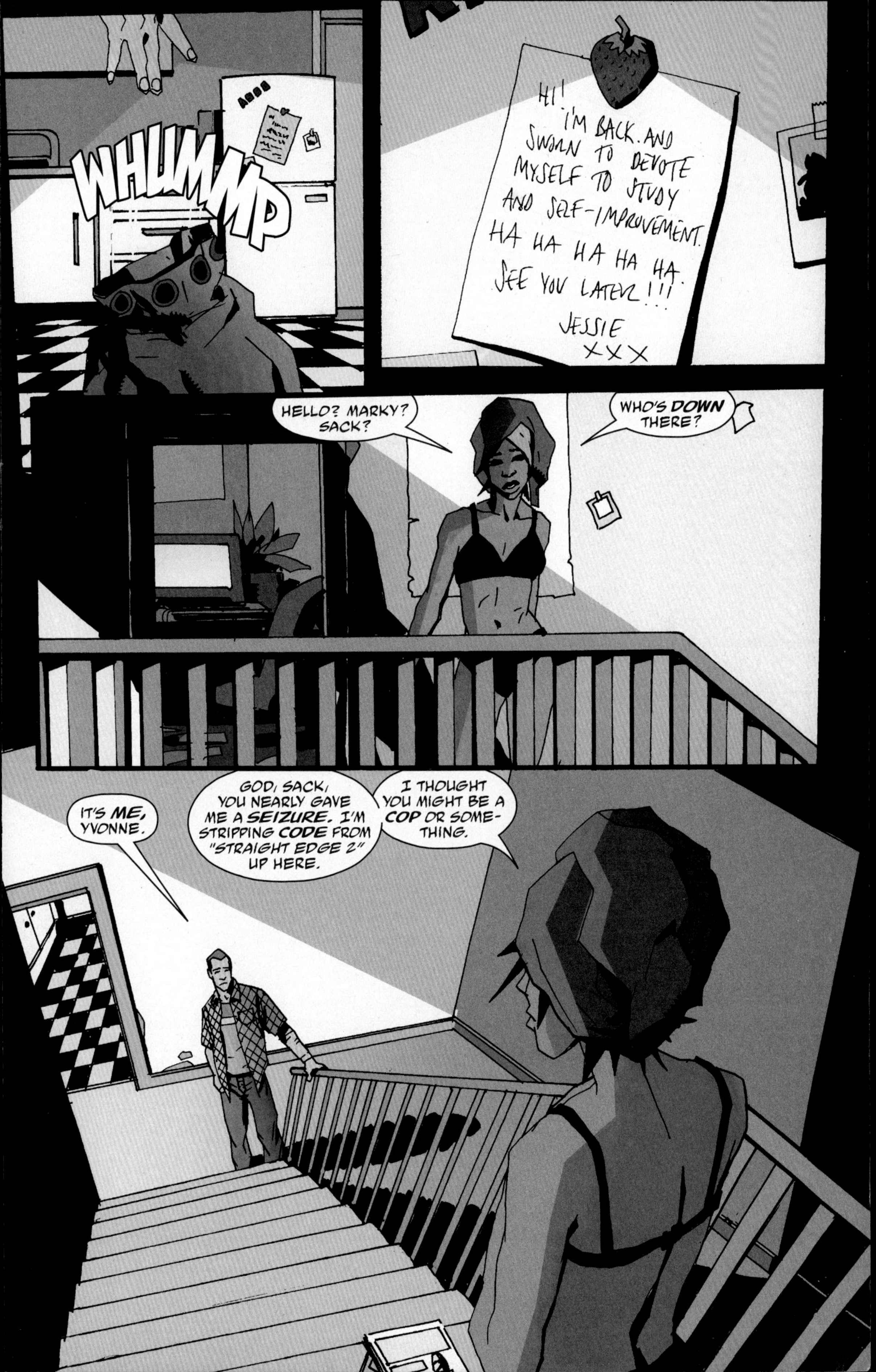
WHUMMP
HI! I'M BACK. AND SWORN TO DEVOTE MYSELF TO STUDY AND SELF-IMPROVEMENT. HA HA HA HA HA. SEE YOU LATER!!! JESSIE XXX
HELLO? MARKY? SACK?
WHO'S **DOWN** THERE?
IT'S **ME,** YVONNE.
GOD, SACK, YOU NEARLY GAVE ME A **SEIZURE.** I'M STRIPPING **CODE** FROM "STRAIGHT EDGE 2" UP HERE.
I THOUGHT YOU MIGHT BE A **COP** OR SOME-THING.

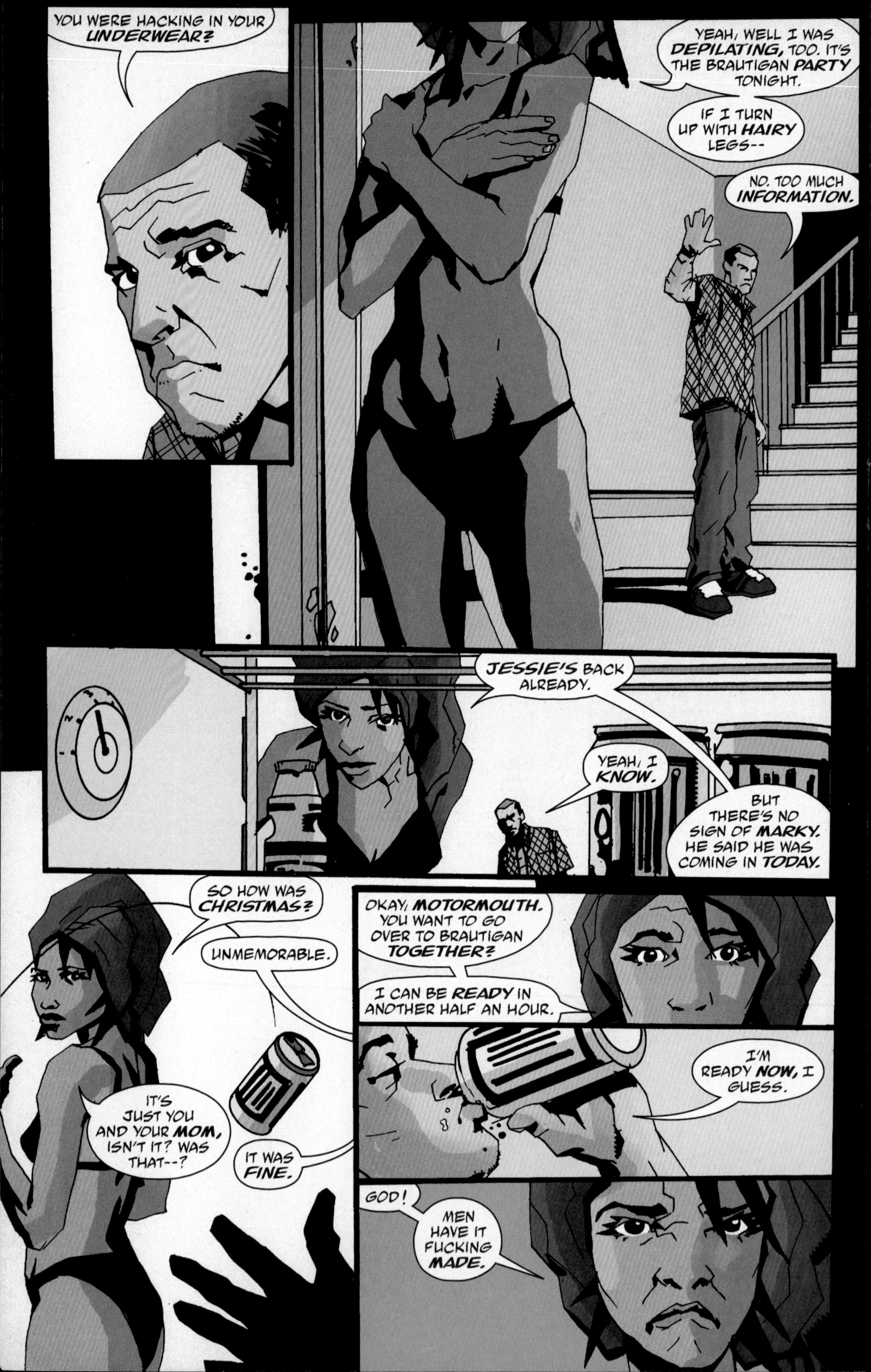
YOU WERE HACKING IN YOUR UNDERWEAR?
YEAH, WELL I WAS DEPILATING, TOO. IT'S THE BRAUTIGAN PARTY TONIGHT.
IF I TURN UP WITH HAIRY LEGS--
NO. TOO MUCH INFORMATION.
JESSIE'S BACK ALREADY.
YEAH, I KNOW.
BUT THERE'S NO SIGN OF MARKY. HE SAID HE WAS COMING IN TODAY.
SO HOW WAS CHRISTMAS?
UNMEMORABLE.
IT'S JUST YOU AND YOUR MOM, ISN'T IT? WAS THAT--?
IT WAS FINE.
OKAY, MOTORMOUTH. YOU WANT TO GO OVER TO BRAUTIGAN TOGETHER?
I CAN BE READY IN ANOTHER HALF AN HOUR.
I'M READY NOW, I GUESS.
GOD!
MEN HAVE IT FUCKING MADE.

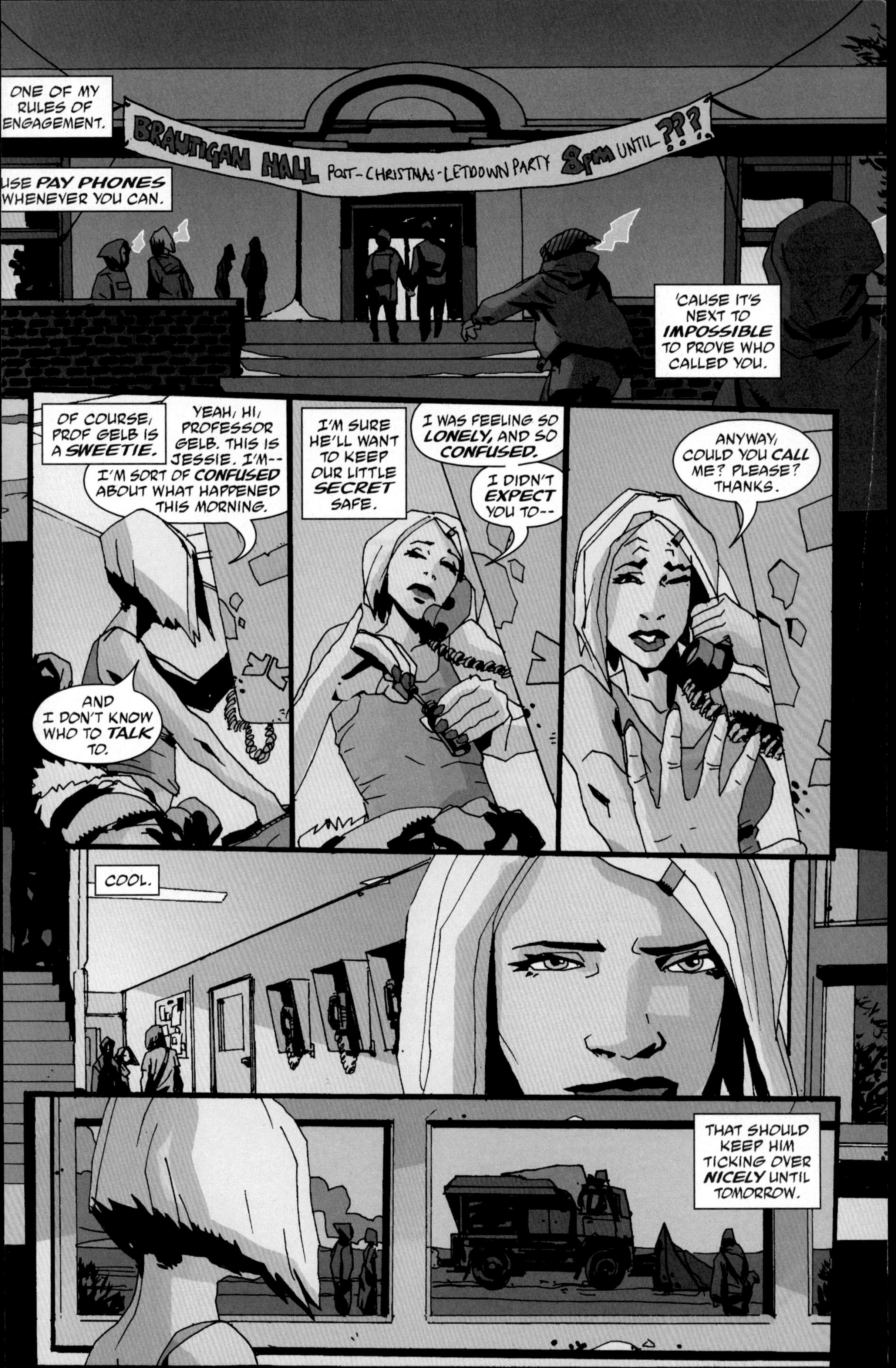
ONE OF MY RULES OF ENGAGEMENT.
BRAUTIGAN HALL POST-CHRISTMAS-LETDOWN PARTY 8pm UNTIL ???
USE PAY PHONES WHENEVER YOU CAN.
'CAUSE IT'S NEXT TO IMPOSSIBLE TO PROVE WHO CALLED YOU.
OF COURSE, PROF GELB IS A SWEETIE.
YEAH, HI, PROFESSOR GELB. THIS IS JESSIE. I'M--
I'M SORT OF CONFUSED ABOUT WHAT HAPPENED THIS MORNING.
AND I DON'T KNOW WHO TO TALK TO.
I'M SURE HE'LL WANT TO KEEP OUR LITTLE SECRET SAFE.
I WAS FEELING SO LONELY, AND SO CONFUSED.
I DIDN'T EXPECT YOU TO--
ANYWAY, COULD YOU CALL ME? PLEASE? THANKS.
COOL.
THAT SHOULD KEEP HIM TICKING OVER NICELY UNTIL TOMORROW.

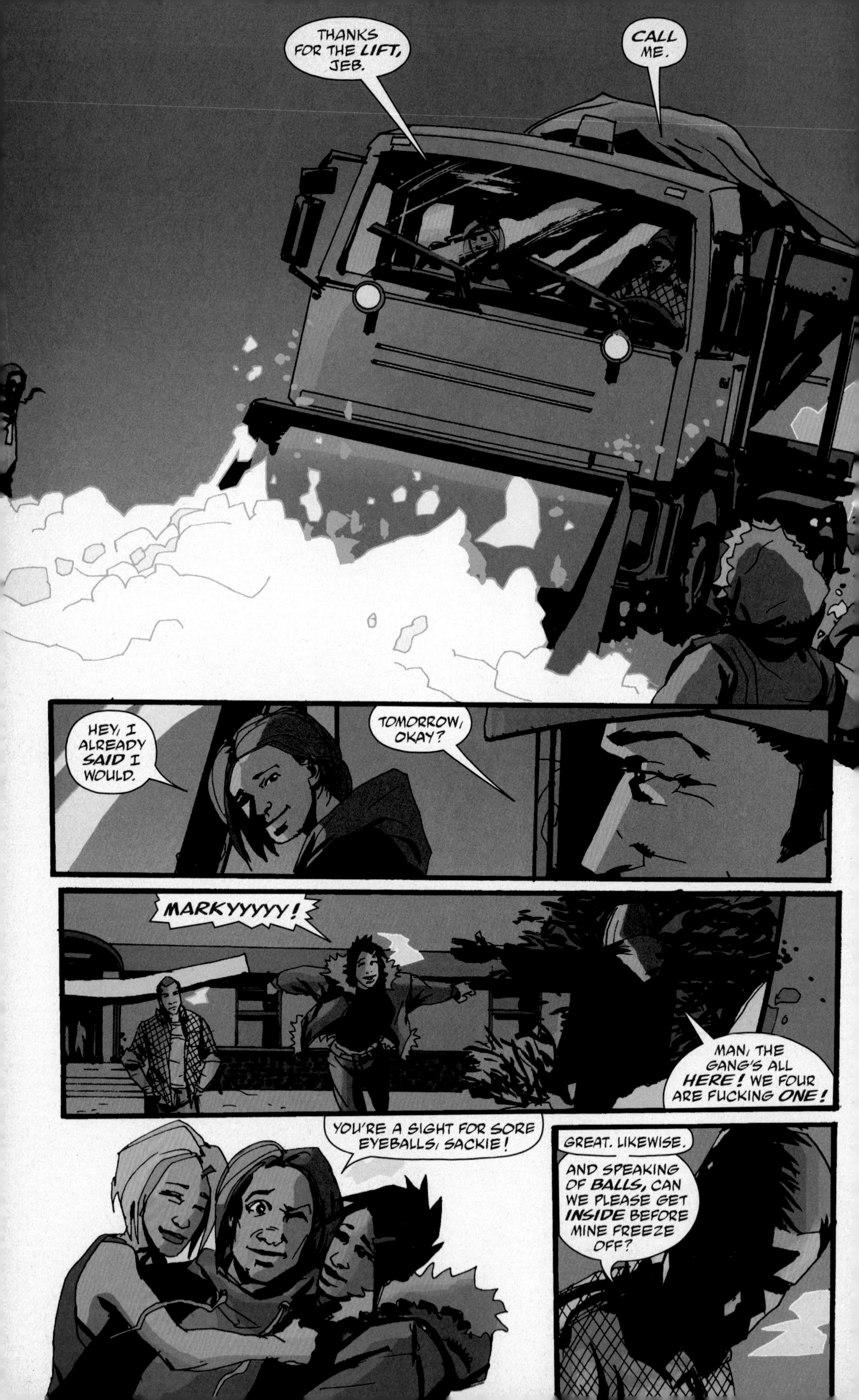
THANKS FOR THE LIFT, JEB.
CALL ME.
HEY, I ALREADY SAID I WOULD.
TOMORROW, OKAY?
MARKYYYYY!
MAN, THE GANG'S ALL HERE! WE FOUR ARE FUCKING ONE!
YOU'RE A SIGHT FOR SORE EYEBALLS, SACKIE!
GREAT. LIKEWISE.
AND SPEAKING OF BALLS, CAN WE PLEASE GET INSIDE BEFORE MINE FREEZE OFF?

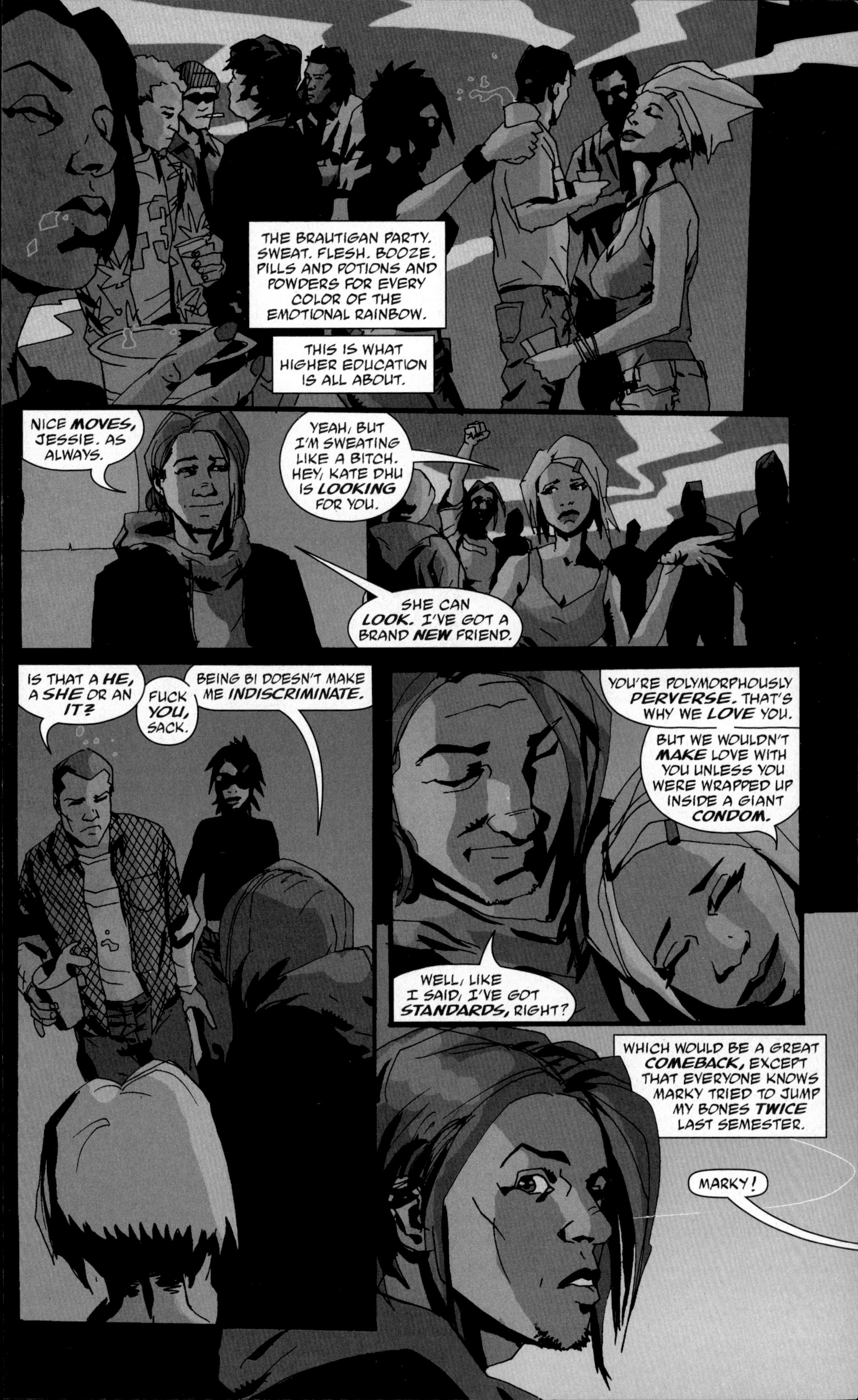
THE BRAUTIGAN PARTY. SWEAT. FLESH. BOOZE. PILLS AND POTIONS AND POWDERS FOR EVERY COLOR OF THE EMOTIONAL RAINBOW.
THIS IS WHAT HIGHER EDUCATION IS ALL ABOUT.
NICE MOVES, JESSIE. AS ALWAYS.
YEAH, BUT I'M SWEATING LIKE A BITCH. HEY, KATE DHU IS LOOKING FOR YOU.
SHE CAN LOOK. I'VE GOT A BRAND NEW FRIEND.
IS THAT A HE, A SHE OR AN IT?
FUCK YOU, SACK.
BEING BI DOESN'T MAKE ME INDISCRIMINATE.
YOU'RE POLYMORPHOUSLY PERVERSE. THAT'S WHY WE LOVE YOU.
BUT WE WOULDN'T MAKE LOVE WITH YOU UNLESS YOU WERE WRAPPED UP INSIDE A GIANT CONDOM.
WELL, LIKE I SAID, I'VE GOT STANDARDS, RIGHT?
WHICH WOULD BE A GREAT COMEBACK, EXCEPT THAT EVERYONE KNOWS MARKY TRIED TO JUMP MY BONES TWICE LAST SEMESTER.
MARKY!

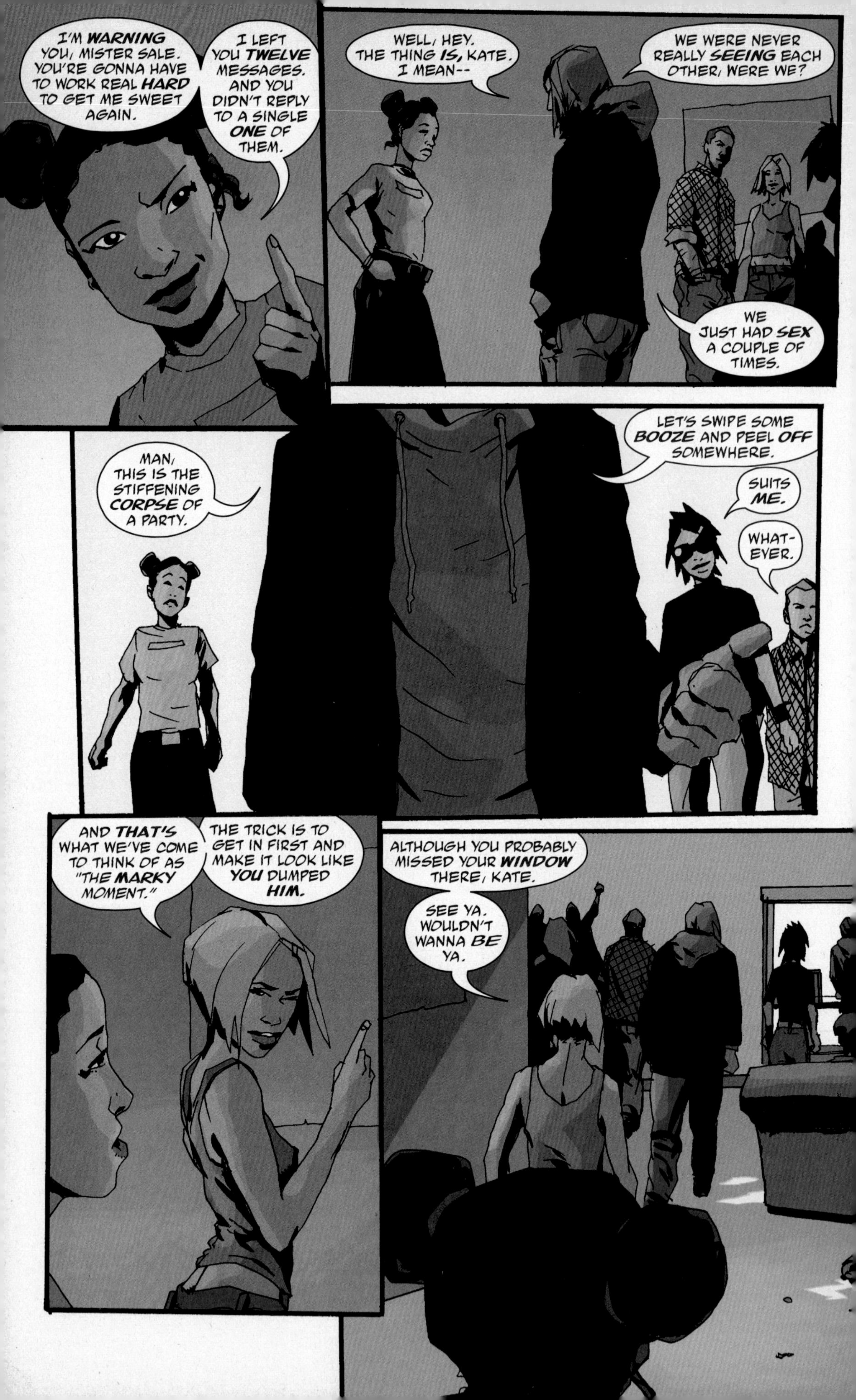
I'M WARNING YOU, MISTER SALE. YOU'RE GONNA HAVE TO WORK REAL HARD TO GET ME SWEET AGAIN.
I LEFT YOU TWELVE MESSAGES. AND YOU DIDN'T REPLY TO A SINGLE ONE OF THEM.
WELL, HEY. THE THING IS, KATE. I MEAN--
WE WERE NEVER REALLY SEEING EACH OTHER, WERE WE?
WE JUST HAD SEX A COUPLE OF TIMES.
MAN, THIS IS THE STIFFENING CORPSE OF A PARTY.
LET'S SWIPE SOME BOOZE AND PEEL OFF SOMEWHERE.
SUITS ME.
WHAT-EVER.
AND THAT'S WHAT WE'VE COME TO THINK OF AS "THE MARKY MOMENT."
THE TRICK IS TO GET IN FIRST AND MAKE IT LOOK LIKE YOU DUMPED HIM.
ALTHOUGH YOU PROBABLY MISSED YOUR WINDOW THERE, KATE.
SEE YA. WOULDN'T WANNA BE YA.

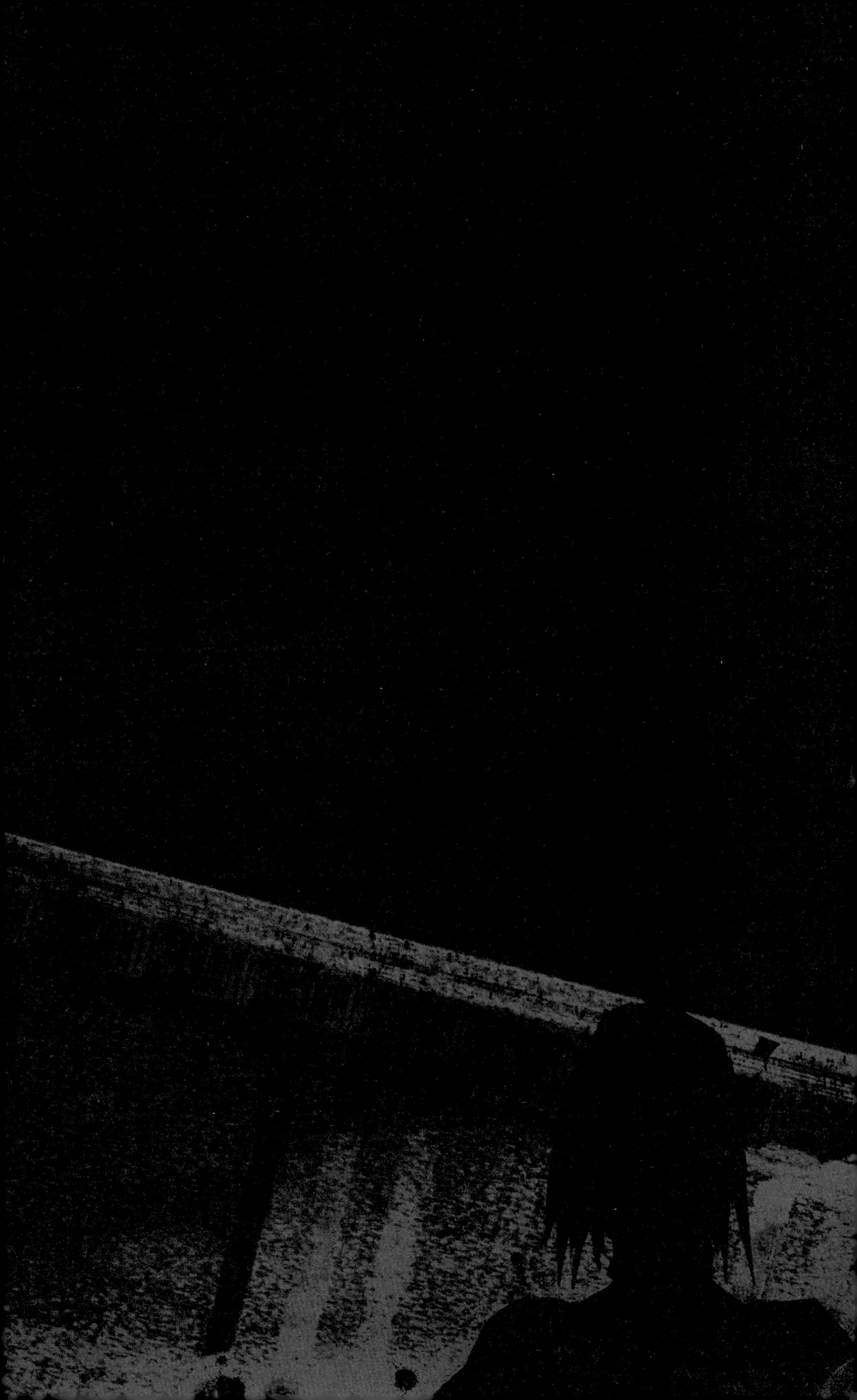

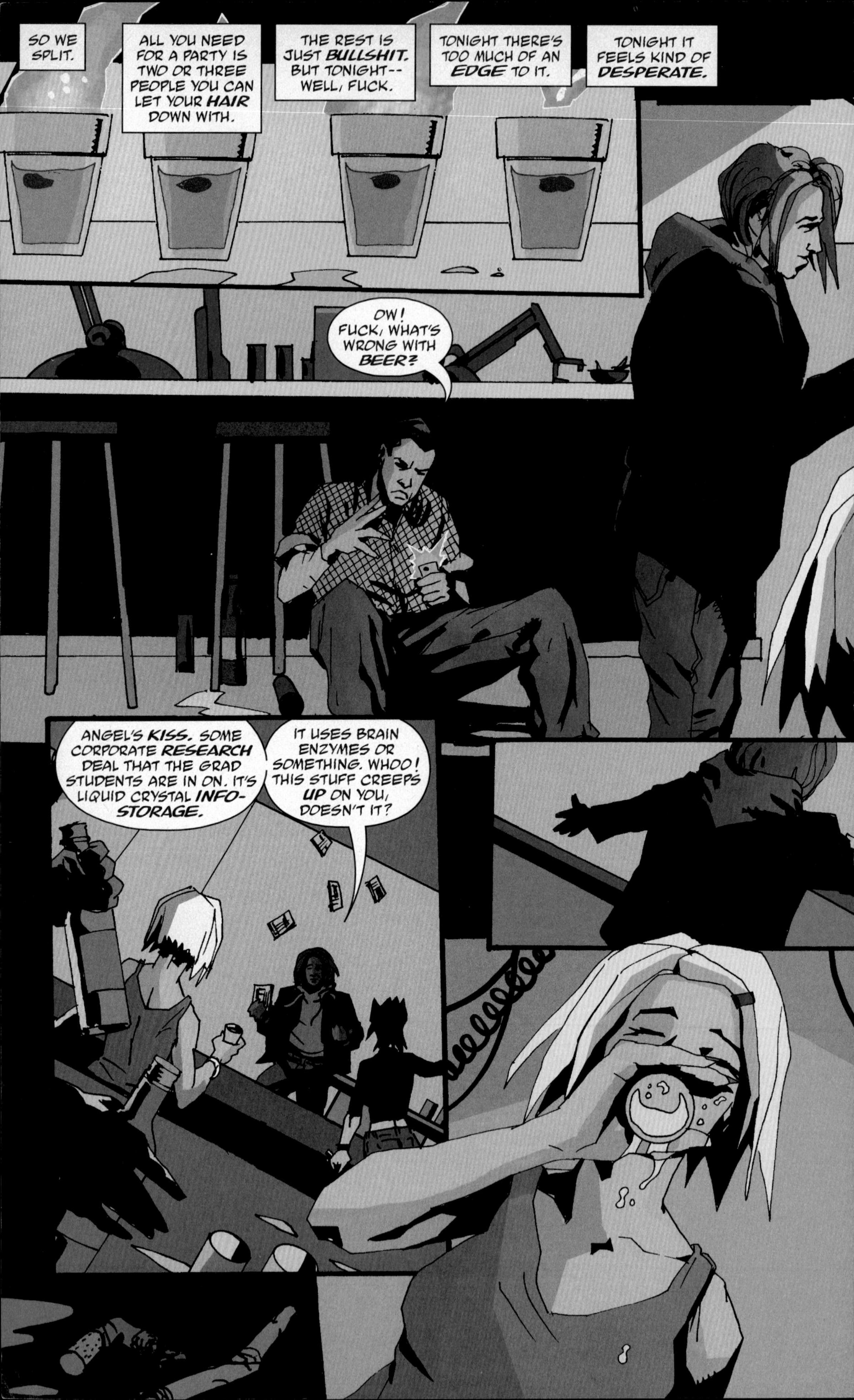
SO WE SPLIT.
ALL YOU NEED FOR A PARTY IS TWO OR THREE PEOPLE YOU CAN LET YOUR HAIR DOWN WITH.
THE REST IS JUST BULLSHIT. BUT TONIGHT-- WELL, FUCK.
TONIGHT THERE'S TOO MUCH OF AN EDGE TO IT.
TONIGHT IT FEELS KIND OF DESPERATE.
OW! FUCK, WHAT'S WRONG WITH BEER?
ANGEL'S KISS. SOME CORPORATE RESEARCH DEAL THAT THE GRAD STUDENTS ARE IN ON. IT'S LIQUID CRYSTAL INFO-STORAGE.
IT USES BRAIN ENZYMES OR SOMETHING. WHOO! THIS STUFF CREEPS UP ON YOU, DOESN'T IT?

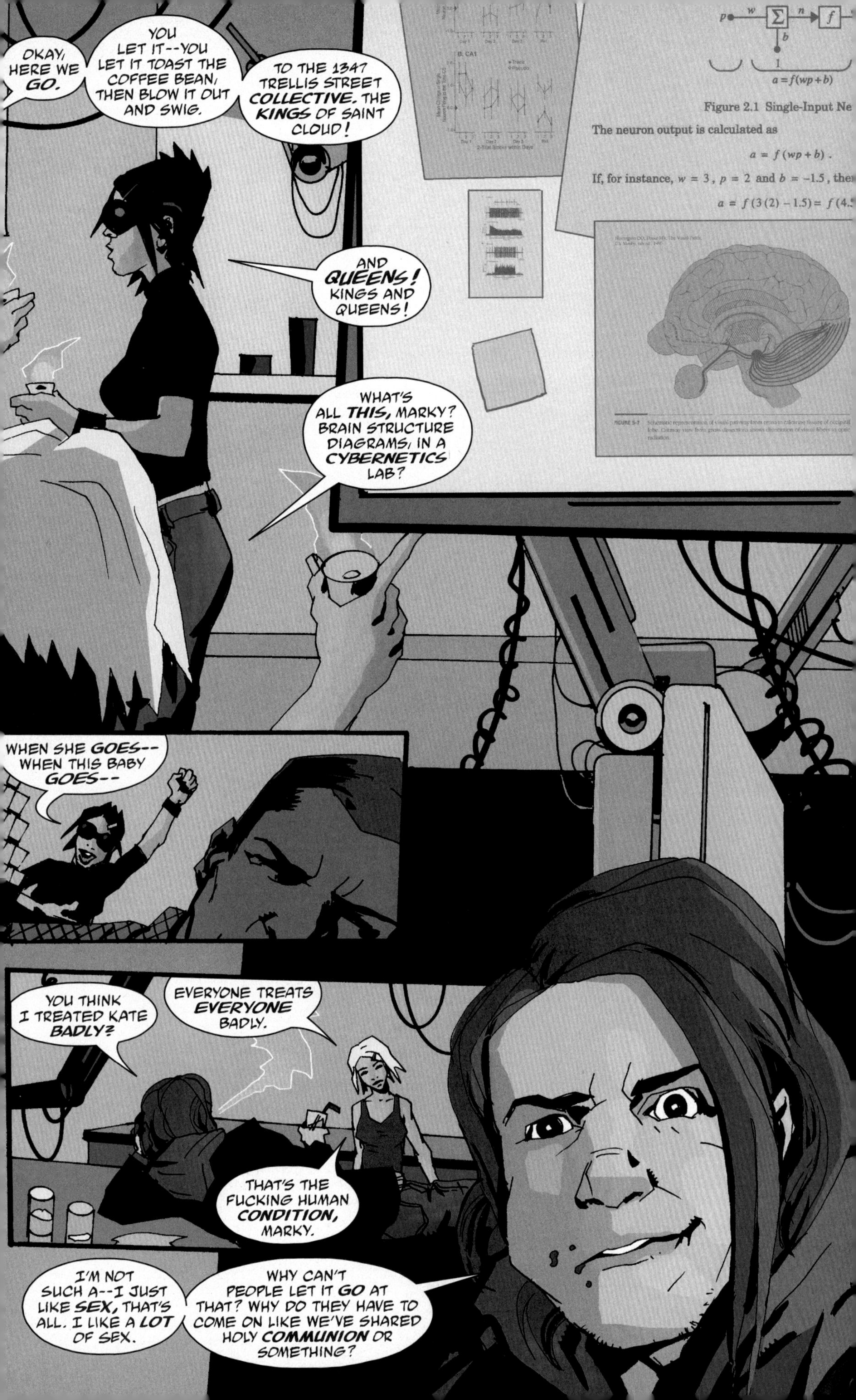

OKAY, HERE WE GO.
YOU LET IT--YOU LET IT TOAST THE COFFEE BEAN, THEN BLOW IT OUT AND SWIG.
TO THE 1347 TRELLIS STREET COLLECTIVE. THE KINGS OF SAINT CLOUD!
The neuron output is calculated as
AND QUEENS! KINGS AND QUEENS!
WHAT'S ALL THIS, MARKY? BRAIN STRUCTURE DIAGRAMS, IN A CYBERNETICS LAB?
WHEN SHE GOES--WHEN THIS BABY GOES--
YOU THINK I TREATED KATE BADLY?
EVERYONE TREATS EVERYONE BADLY.
THAT'S THE FUCKING HUMAN CONDITION, MARKY.
I'M NOT SUCH A--I JUST LIKE SEX, THAT'S ALL. I LIKE A LOT OF SEX.
WHY CAN'T PEOPLE LET IT GO AT THAT? WHY DO THEY HAVE TO COME ON LIKE WE'VE SHARED HOLY COMMUNION OR SOMETHING?

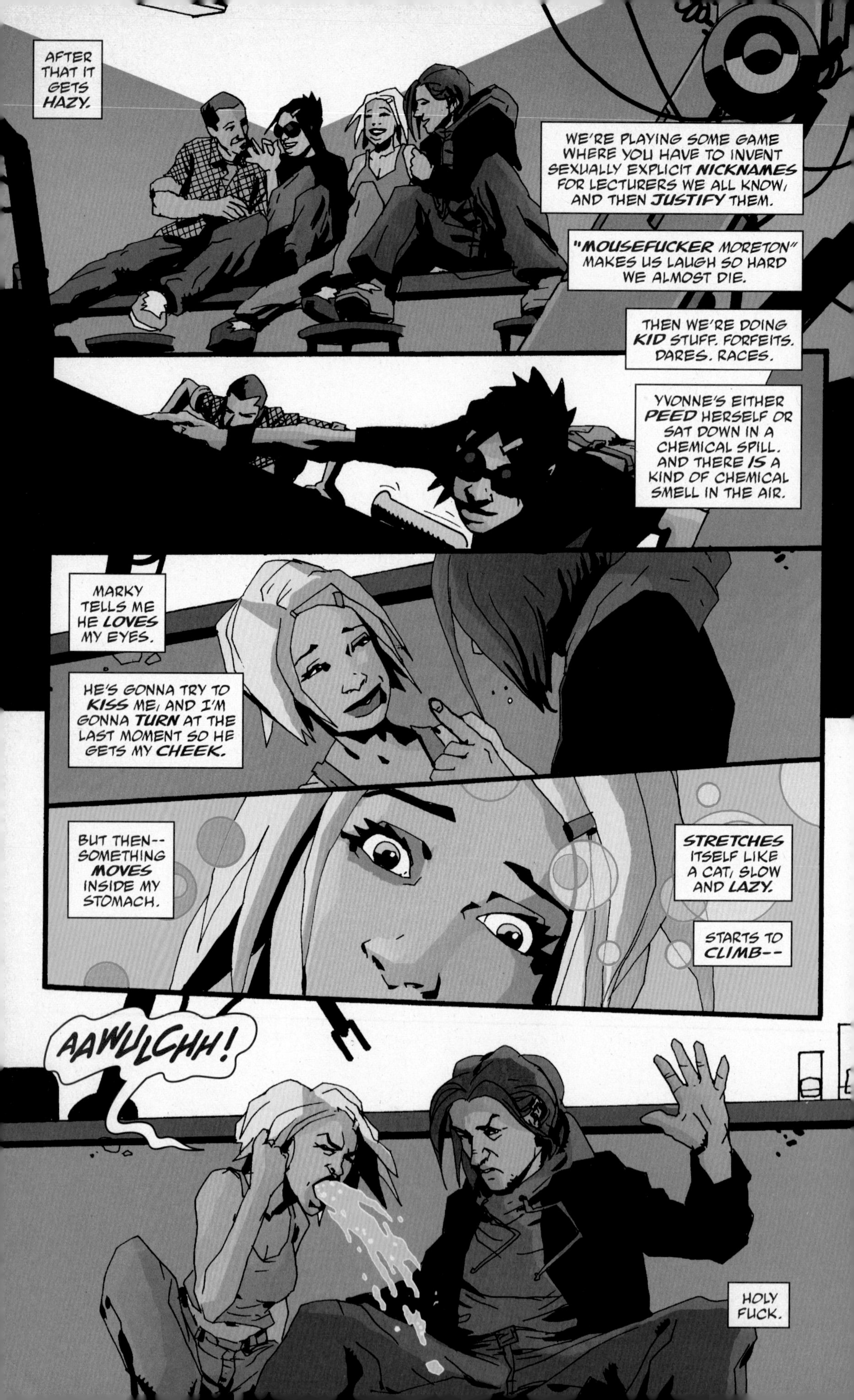

AFTER THAT IT GETS HAZY.
WE'RE PLAYING SOME GAME WHERE YOU HAVE TO INVENT SEXUALLY EXPLICIT NICKNAMES FOR LECTURERS WE ALL KNOW, AND THEN JUSTIFY THEM.
"MOUSEFUCKER MORETON" MAKES US LAUGH SO HARD WE ALMOST DIE.
THEN WE'RE DOING KID STUFF. FORFEITS. DARES. RACES.
YVONNE'S EITHER PEED HERSELF OR SAT DOWN IN A CHEMICAL SPILL. AND THERE IS A KIND OF CHEMICAL SMELL IN THE AIR.
MARKY TELLS ME HE LOVES MY EYES.
HE'S GONNA TRY TO KISS ME, AND I'M GONNA TURN AT THE LAST MOMENT SO HE GETS MY CHEEK.
BUT THEN-- SOMETHING MOVES INSIDE MY STOMACH.
STRETCHES ITSELF LIKE A CAT, SLOW AND LAZY.
STARTS TO CLIMB--
AAWULCHH!
HOLY FUCK.

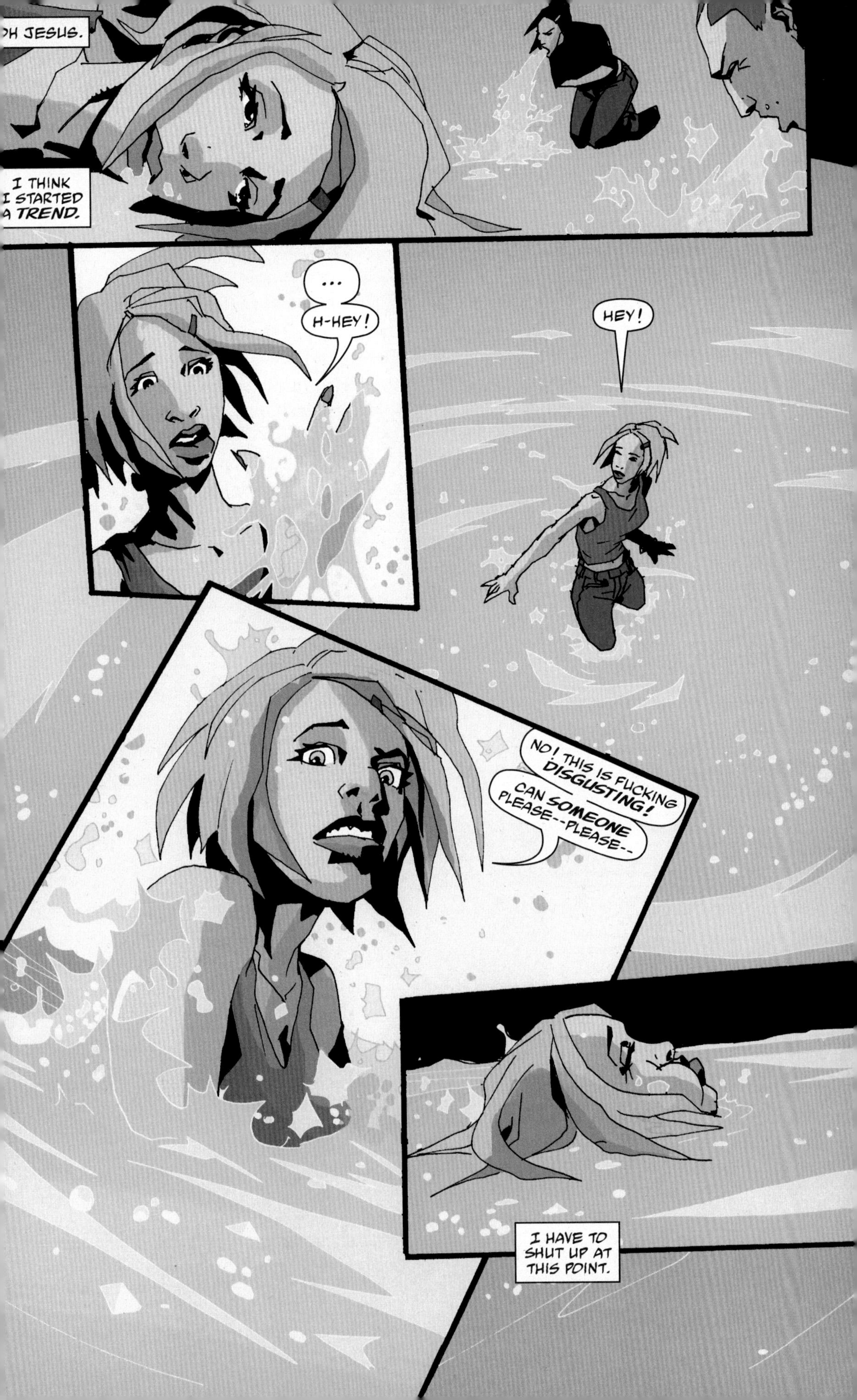
OH JESUS.
I THINK I STARTED A TREND.
...
H-HEY!
HEY!
NO! THIS IS FUCKING DISGUSTING!
CAN SOMEONE PLEASE--PLEASE--
I HAVE TO SHUT UP AT THIS POINT.

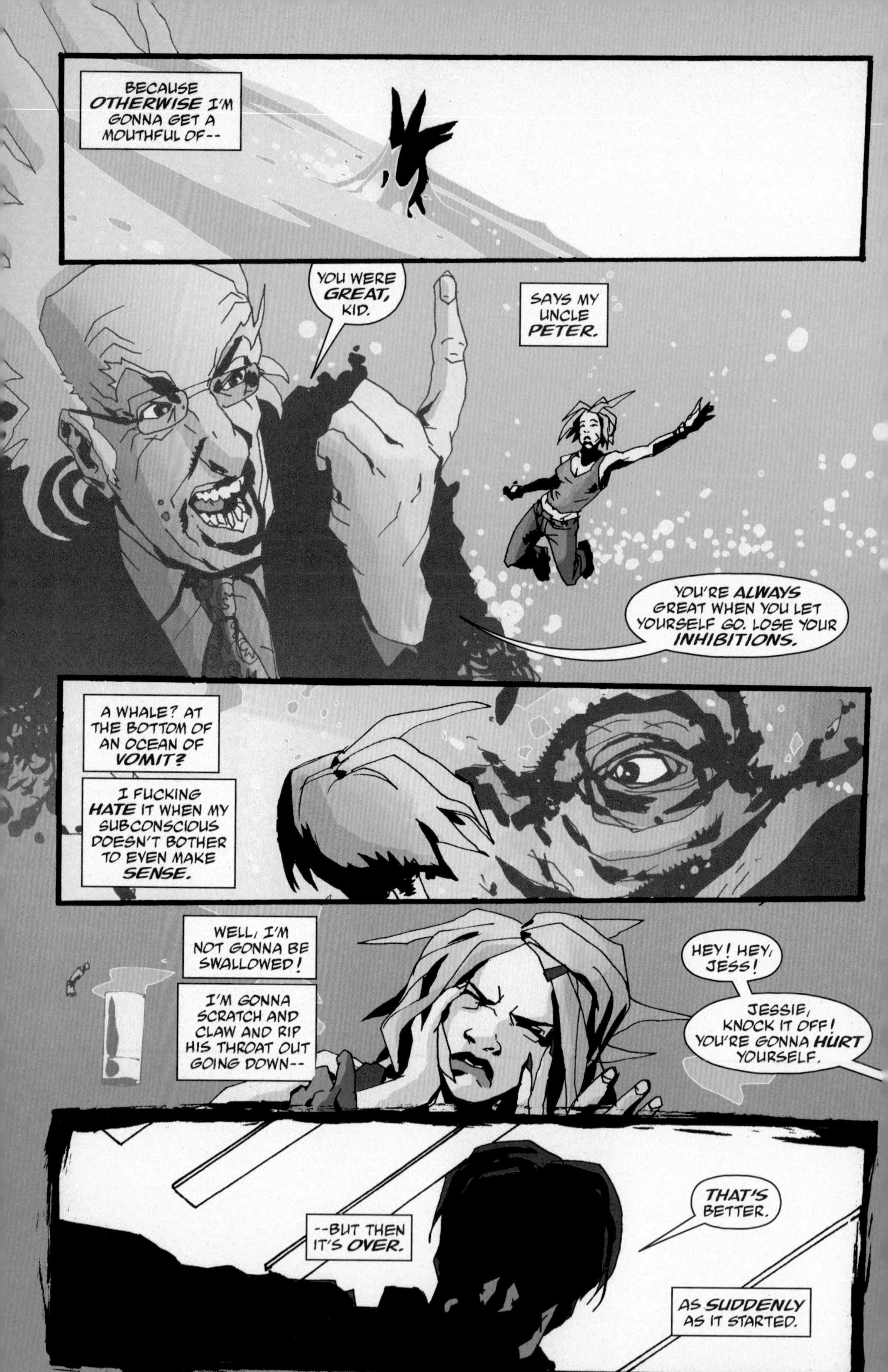
BECAUSE OTHERWISE I'M GONNA GET A MOUTHFUL OF--
YOU WERE GREAT, KID.
SAYS MY UNCLE PETER.
YOU'RE ALWAYS GREAT WHEN YOU LET YOURSELF GO. LOSE YOUR INHIBITIONS.
A WHALE? AT THE BOTTOM OF AN OCEAN OF VOMIT?
I FUCKING HATE IT WHEN MY SUBCONSCIOUS DOESN'T BOTHER TO EVEN MAKE SENSE.
WELL, I'M NOT GONNA BE SWALLOWED!
I'M GONNA SCRATCH AND CLAW AND RIP HIS THROAT OUT GOING DOWN--
HEY! HEY, JESS!
JESSIE, KNOCK IT OFF! YOU'RE GONNA HURT YOURSELF.
--BUT THEN IT'S OVER.
THAT'S BETTER.
AS SUDDENLY AS IT STARTED.

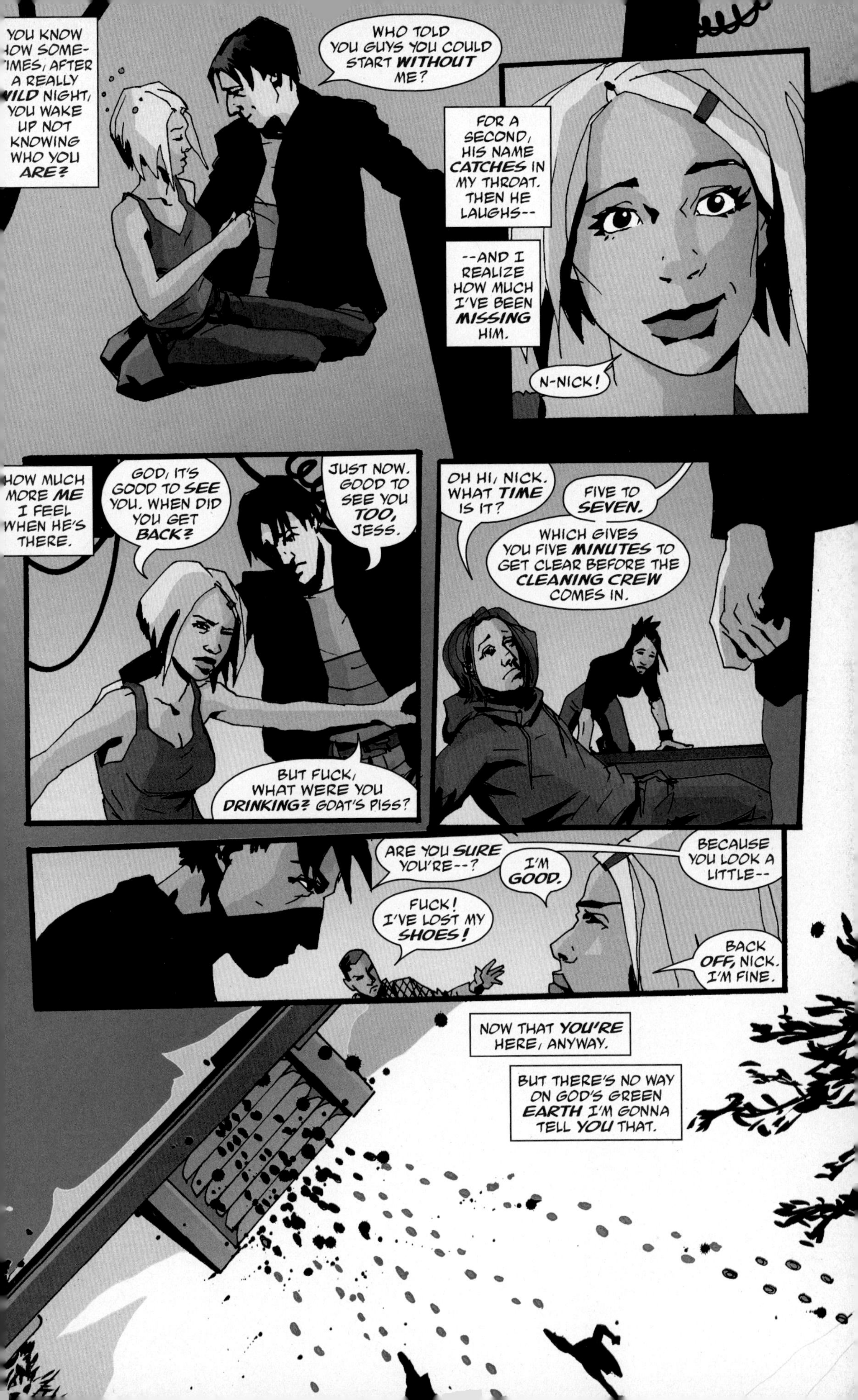
YOU KNOW HOW SOMETIMES, AFTER A REALLY WILD NIGHT, YOU WAKE UP NOT KNOWING WHO YOU ARE?
WHO TOLD YOU GUYS YOU COULD START WITHOUT ME?
FOR A SECOND, HIS NAME CATCHES IN MY THROAT. THEN HE LAUGHS--
--AND I REALIZE HOW MUCH I'VE BEEN MISSING HIM.
N-NICK!
HOW MUCH MORE ME I FEEL WHEN HE'S THERE.
GOD, IT'S GOOD TO SEE YOU. WHEN DID YOU GET BACK?
JUST NOW. GOOD TO SEE YOU TOO, JESS.
BUT FUCK, WHAT WERE YOU DRINKING? GOAT'S PISS?
OH HI, NICK. WHAT TIME IS IT?
FIVE TO SEVEN.
WHICH GIVES YOU FIVE MINUTES TO GET CLEAR BEFORE THE CLEANING CREW COMES IN.
ARE YOU SURE YOU'RE--?
I'M GOOD.
BECAUSE YOU LOOK A LITTLE--
FUCK! I'VE LOST MY SHOES!
BACK OFF, NICK. I'M FINE.
NOW THAT YOU'RE HERE, ANYWAY.
BUT THERE'S NO WAY ON GOD'S GREEN EARTH I'M GONNA TELL YOU THAT.

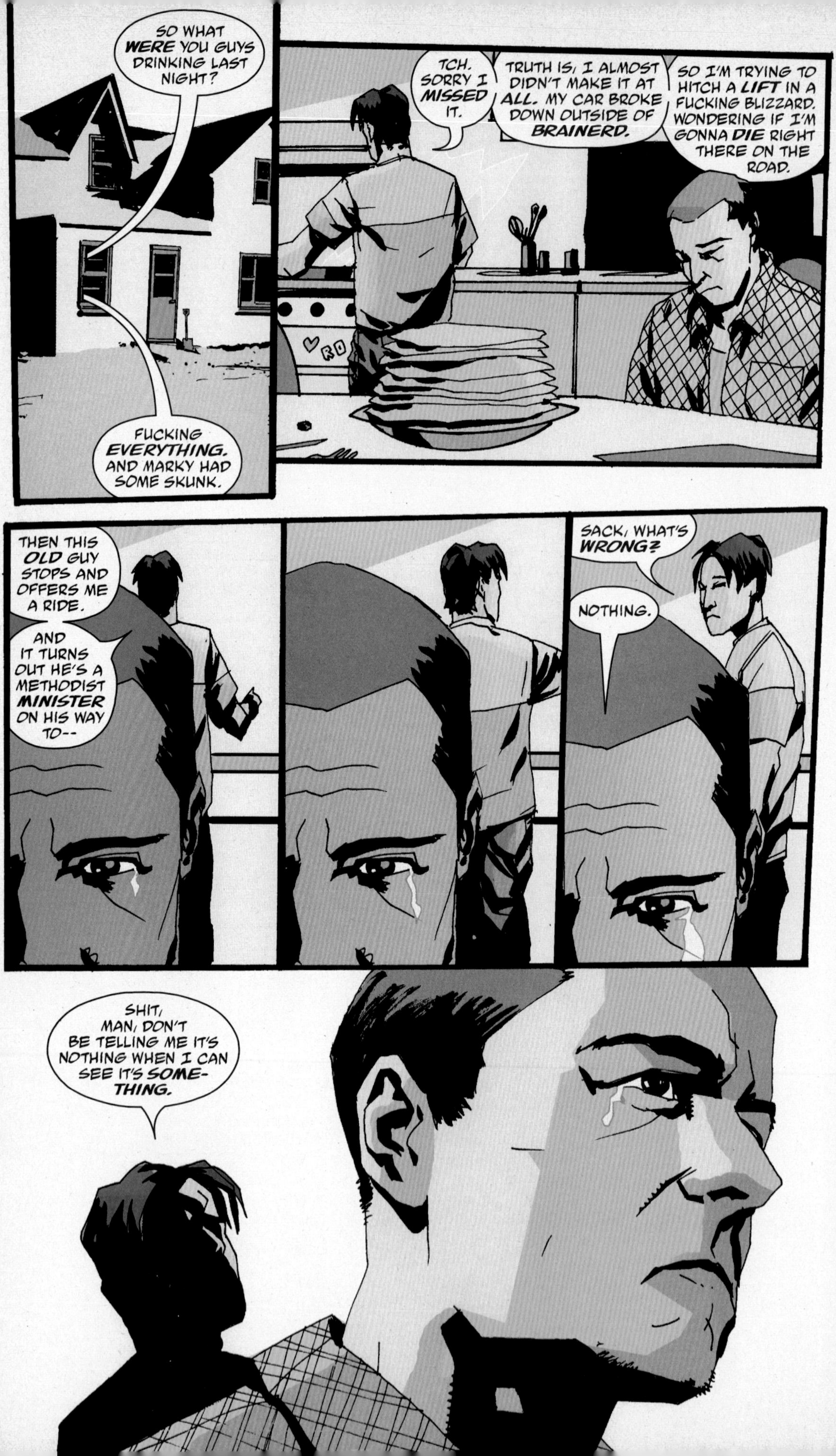
SO WHAT WERE YOU GUYS DRINKING LAST NIGHT?
FUCKING EVERYTHING. AND MARKY HAD SOME SKUNK.
TCH. SORRY I MISSED IT.
TRUTH IS, I ALMOST DIDN'T MAKE IT AT ALL. MY CAR BROKE DOWN OUTSIDE OF BRAINERD.
SO I'M TRYING TO HITCH A LIFT IN A FUCKING BLIZZARD. WONDERING IF I'M GONNA DIE RIGHT THERE ON THE ROAD.
THEN THIS OLD GUY STOPS AND OFFERS ME A RIDE.
AND IT TURNS OUT HE'S A METHODIST MINISTER ON HIS WAY TO--
SACK, WHAT'S WRONG?
NOTHING.
SHIT, MAN, DON'T BE TELLING ME IT'S NOTHING WHEN I CAN SEE IT'S SOMETHING.

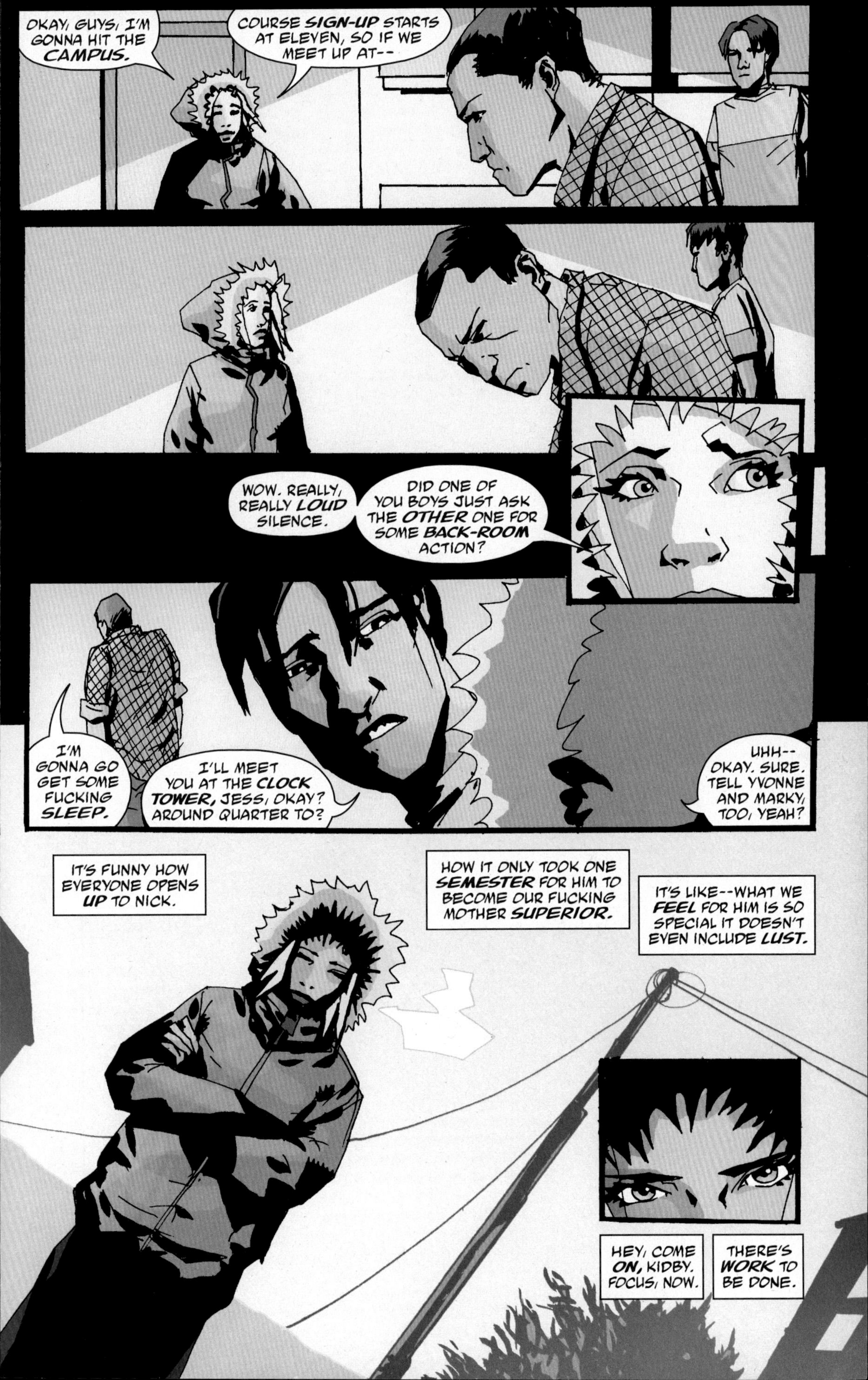
OKAY, GUYS, I'M GONNA HIT THE CAMPUS.
COURSE SIGN-UP STARTS AT ELEVEN, SO IF WE MEET UP AT--
WOW. REALLY, REALLY LOUD SILENCE.
DID ONE OF YOU BOYS JUST ASK THE OTHER ONE FOR SOME BACK-ROOM ACTION?
I'M GONNA GO GET SOME FUCKING SLEEP.
I'LL MEET YOU AT THE CLOCK TOWER, JESS, OKAY? AROUND QUARTER TO?
UHH--OKAY. SURE. TELL YVONNE AND MARKY, TOO, YEAH?
IT'S FUNNY HOW EVERYONE OPENS UP TO NICK.
HOW IT ONLY TOOK ONE SEMESTER FOR HIM TO BECOME OUR FUCKING MOTHER SUPERIOR.
IT'S LIKE--WHAT WE FEEL FOR HIM IS SO SPECIAL IT DOESN'T EVEN INCLUDE LUST.
HEY, COME ON, KIDBY. FOCUS, NOW.
THERE'S WORK TO BE DONE.

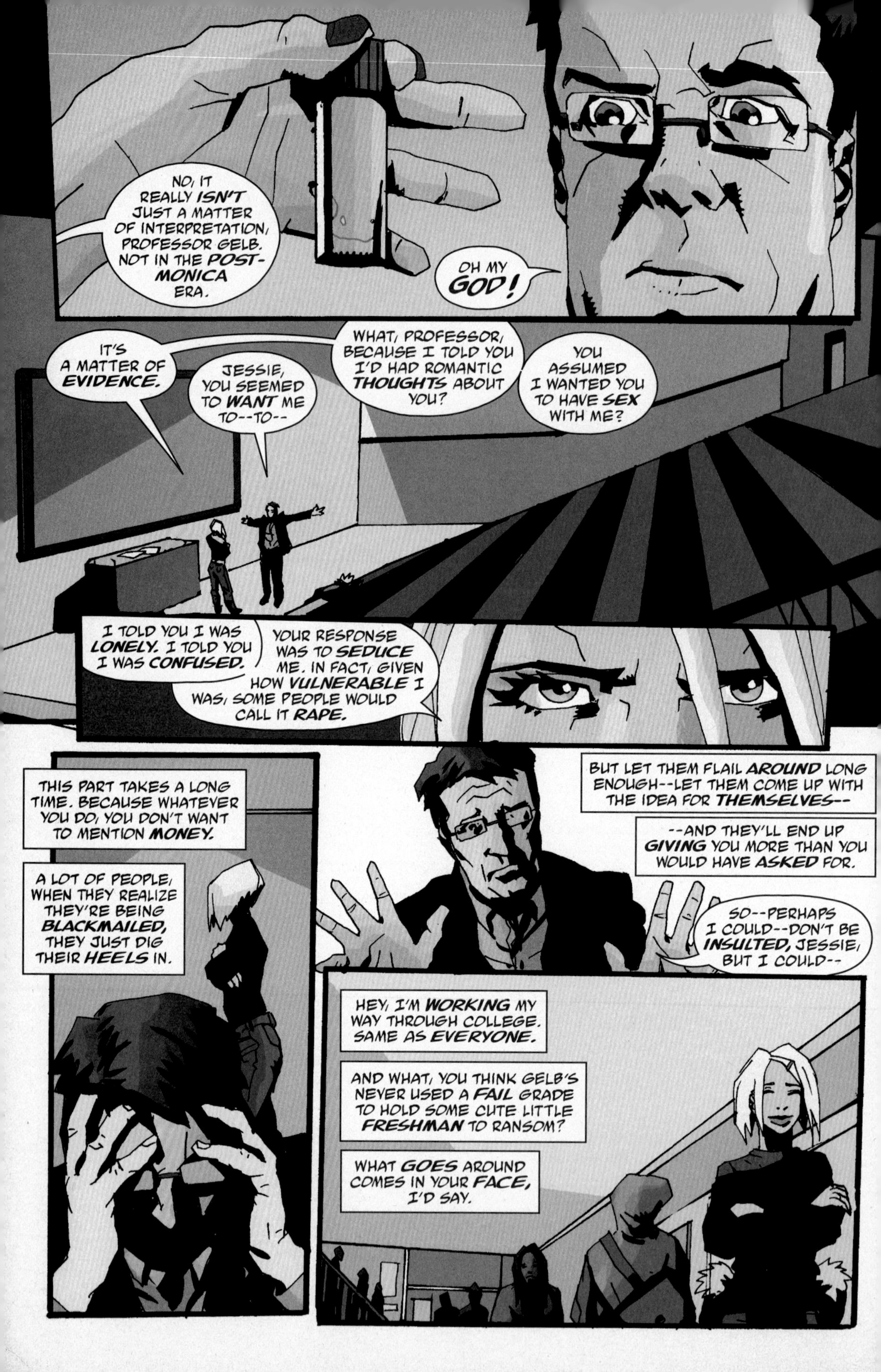
NO, IT REALLY ISN'T JUST A MATTER OF INTERPRETATION, PROFESSOR GELB. NOT IN THE POST-MONICA ERA.
OH MY GOD!
IT'S A MATTER OF EVIDENCE.
JESSIE, YOU SEEMED TO WANT ME TO--TO--
WHAT, PROFESSOR, BECAUSE I TOLD YOU I'D HAD ROMANTIC THOUGHTS ABOUT YOU?
YOU ASSUMED I WANTED YOU TO HAVE SEX WITH ME?
I TOLD YOU I WAS LONELY. I TOLD YOU I WAS CONFUSED.
YOUR RESPONSE WAS TO SEDUCE ME. IN FACT, GIVEN HOW VULNERABLE I WAS, SOME PEOPLE WOULD CALL IT RAPE.
THIS PART TAKES A LONG TIME. BECAUSE WHATEVER YOU DO, YOU DON'T WANT TO MENTION MONEY.
A LOT OF PEOPLE, WHEN THEY REALIZE THEY'RE BEING BLACKMAILED, THEY JUST DIG THEIR HEELS IN.
BUT LET THEM FLAIL AROUND LONG ENOUGH--LET THEM COME UP WITH THE IDEA FOR THEMSELVES--
--AND THEY'LL END UP GIVING YOU MORE THAN YOU WOULD HAVE ASKED FOR.
SO--PERHAPS I COULD--DON'T BE INSULTED, JESSIE, BUT I COULD--
HEY, I'M WORKING MY WAY THROUGH COLLEGE. SAME AS EVERYONE.
AND WHAT, YOU THINK GELB'S NEVER USED A FAIL GRADE TO HOLD SOME CUTE LITTLE FRESHMAN TO RANSOM?
WHAT GOES AROUND COMES IN YOUR FACE, I'D SAY.

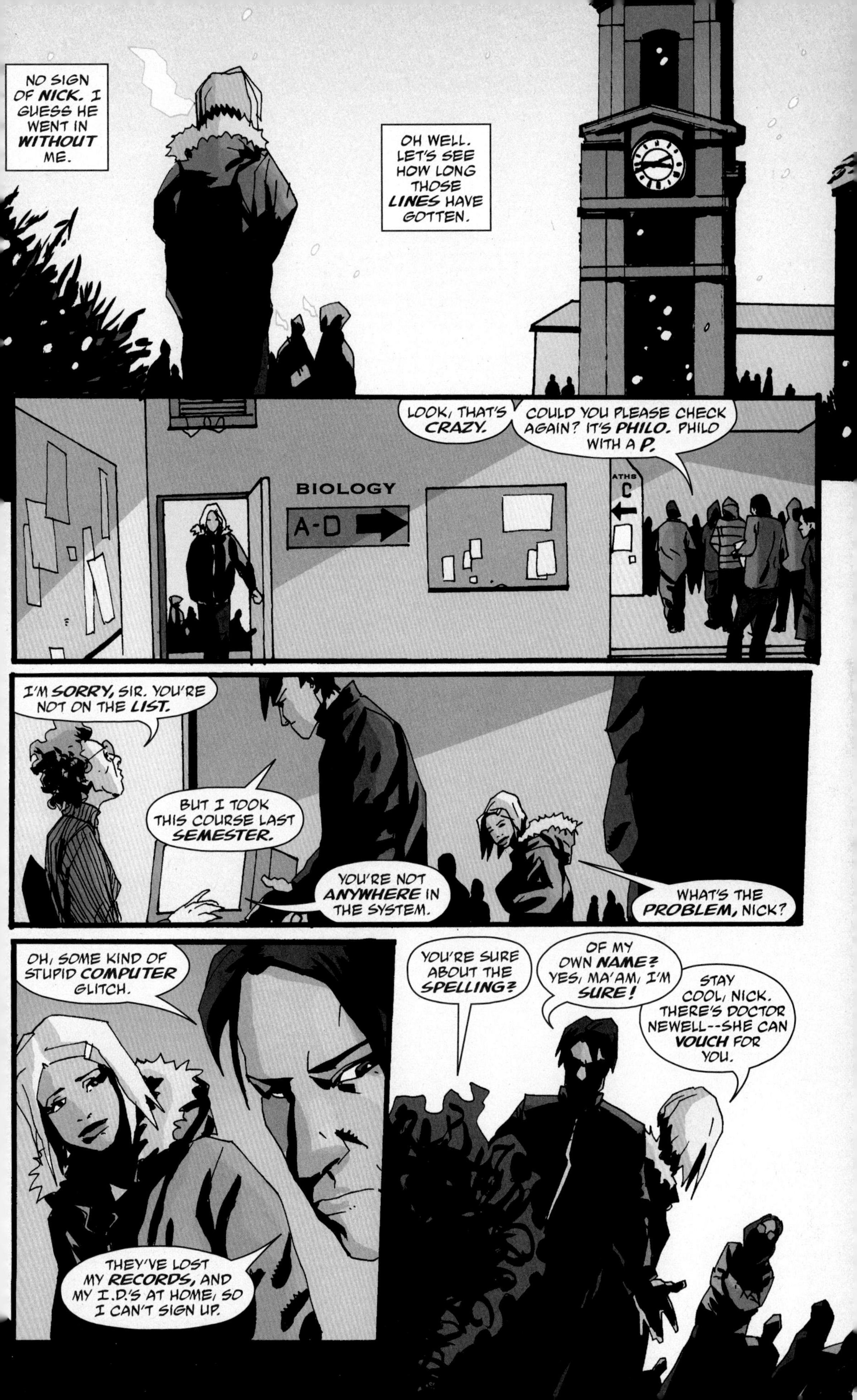
NO SIGN OF NICK. I GUESS HE WENT IN WITHOUT ME.
OH WELL. LET'S SEE HOW LONG THOSE LINES HAVE GOTTEN.
BIOLOGY
A-D
LOOK, THAT'S CRAZY.
COULD YOU PLEASE CHECK AGAIN? IT'S PHILO. PHILO WITH A P.
I'M SORRY, SIR. YOU'RE NOT ON THE LIST.
BUT I TOOK THIS COURSE LAST SEMESTER.
YOU'RE NOT ANYWHERE IN THE SYSTEM.
WHAT'S THE PROBLEM, NICK?
OH, SOME KIND OF STUPID COMPUTER GLITCH.
THEY'VE LOST MY RECORDS, AND MY I.D.'S AT HOME, SO I CAN'T SIGN UP.
YOU'RE SURE ABOUT THE SPELLING?
OF MY OWN NAME? YES, MA'AM, I'M SURE!
STAY COOL, NICK. THERE'S DOCTOR NEWELL--SHE CAN VOUCH FOR YOU.

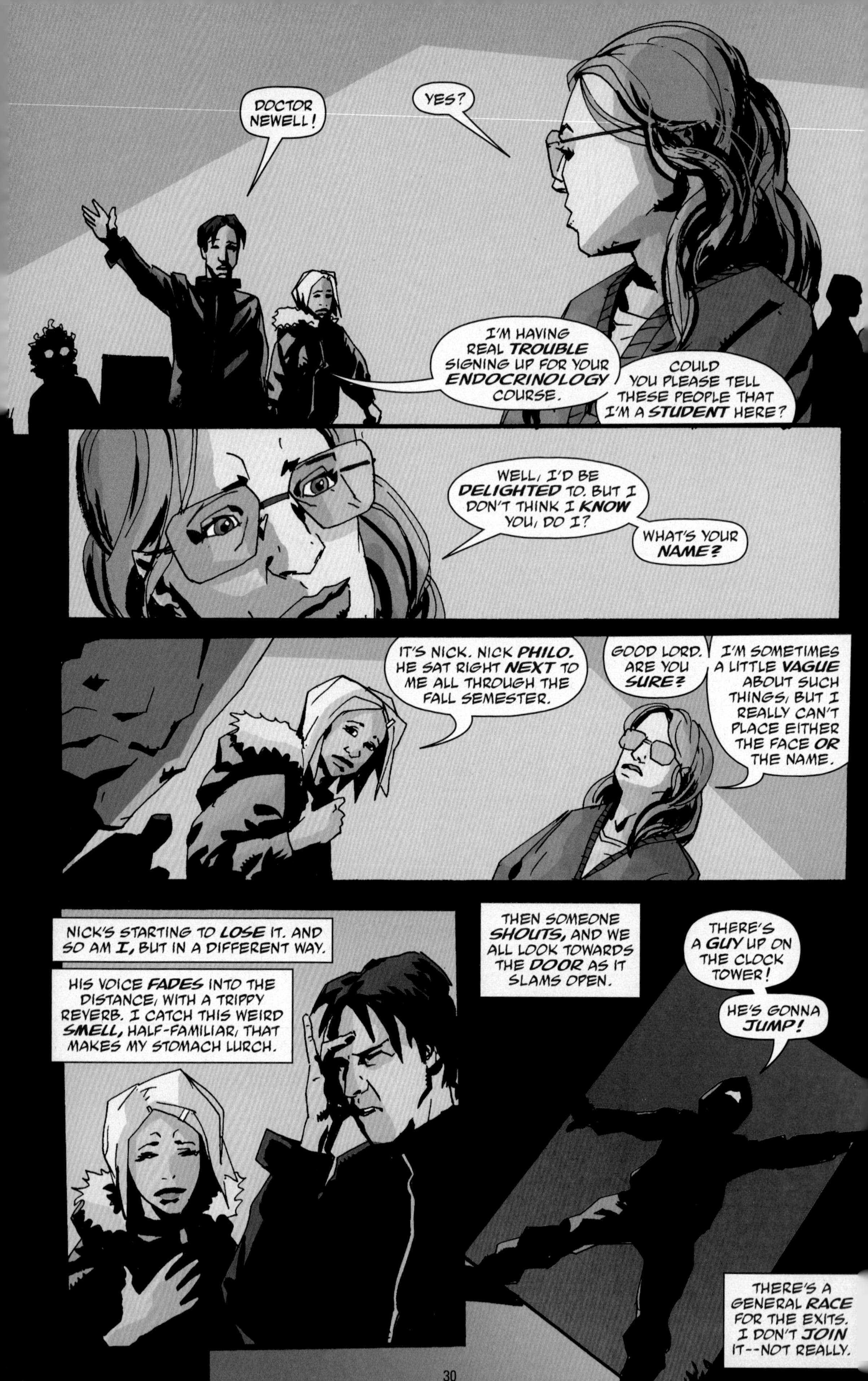
DOCTOR NEWELL!
YES?
I'M HAVING REAL TROUBLE SIGNING UP FOR YOUR ENDOCRINOLOGY COURSE.
COULD YOU PLEASE TELL THESE PEOPLE THAT I'M A STUDENT HERE?
WELL, I'D BE DELIGHTED TO. BUT I DON'T THINK I KNOW YOU, DO I?
WHAT'S YOUR NAME?
IT'S NICK. NICK PHILO. HE SAT RIGHT NEXT TO ME ALL THROUGH THE FALL SEMESTER.
GOOD LORD. ARE YOU SURE?
I'M SOMETIMES A LITTLE VAGUE ABOUT SUCH THINGS, BUT I REALLY CAN'T PLACE EITHER THE FACE OR THE NAME.
NICK'S STARTING TO LOSE IT. AND SO AM I, BUT IN A DIFFERENT WAY.
HIS VOICE FADES INTO THE DISTANCE, WITH A TRIPPY REVERB. I CATCH THIS WEIRD SMELL, HALF-FAMILIAR, THAT MAKES MY STOMACH LURCH.
THEN SOMEONE SHOUTS, AND WE ALL LOOK TOWARDS THE DOOR AS IT SLAMS OPEN.
THERE'S A GUY UP ON THE CLOCK TOWER!
HE'S GONNA JUMP!
THERE'S A GENERAL RACE FOR THE EXITS. I DON'T JOIN IT--NOT REALLY.

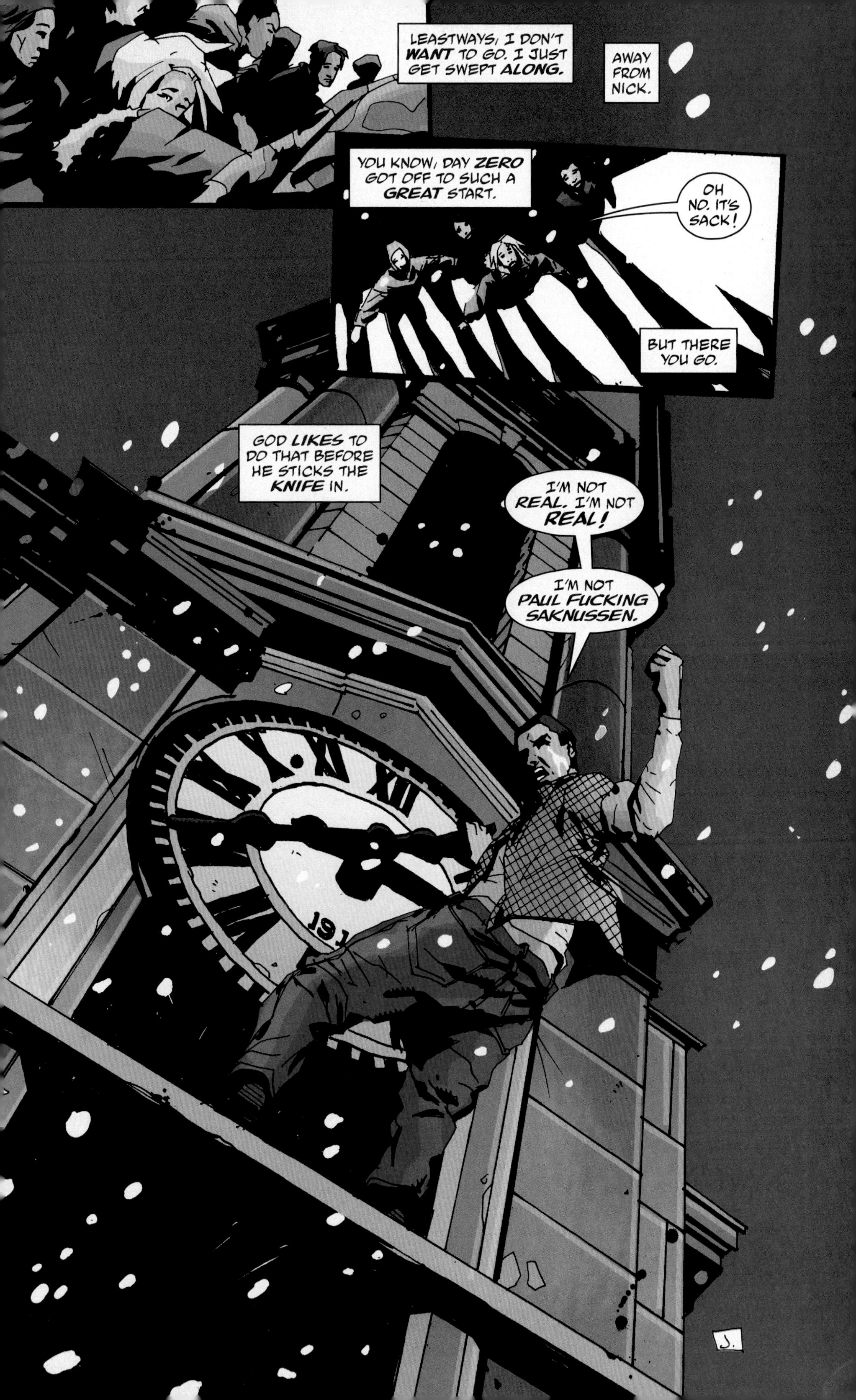
LEASTWAYS, I DON'T WANT TO GO. I JUST GET SWEPT ALONG.
AWAY FROM NICK.
YOU KNOW, DAY ZERO GOT OFF TO SUCH A GREAT START.
OH NO. IT'S SACK!
BUT THERE YOU GO.
GOD LIKES TO DO THAT BEFORE HE STICKS THE KNIFE IN.
I'M NOT REAL. I'M NOT REAL!
I'M NOT PAUL FUCKING SAKNUSSEN.
J.

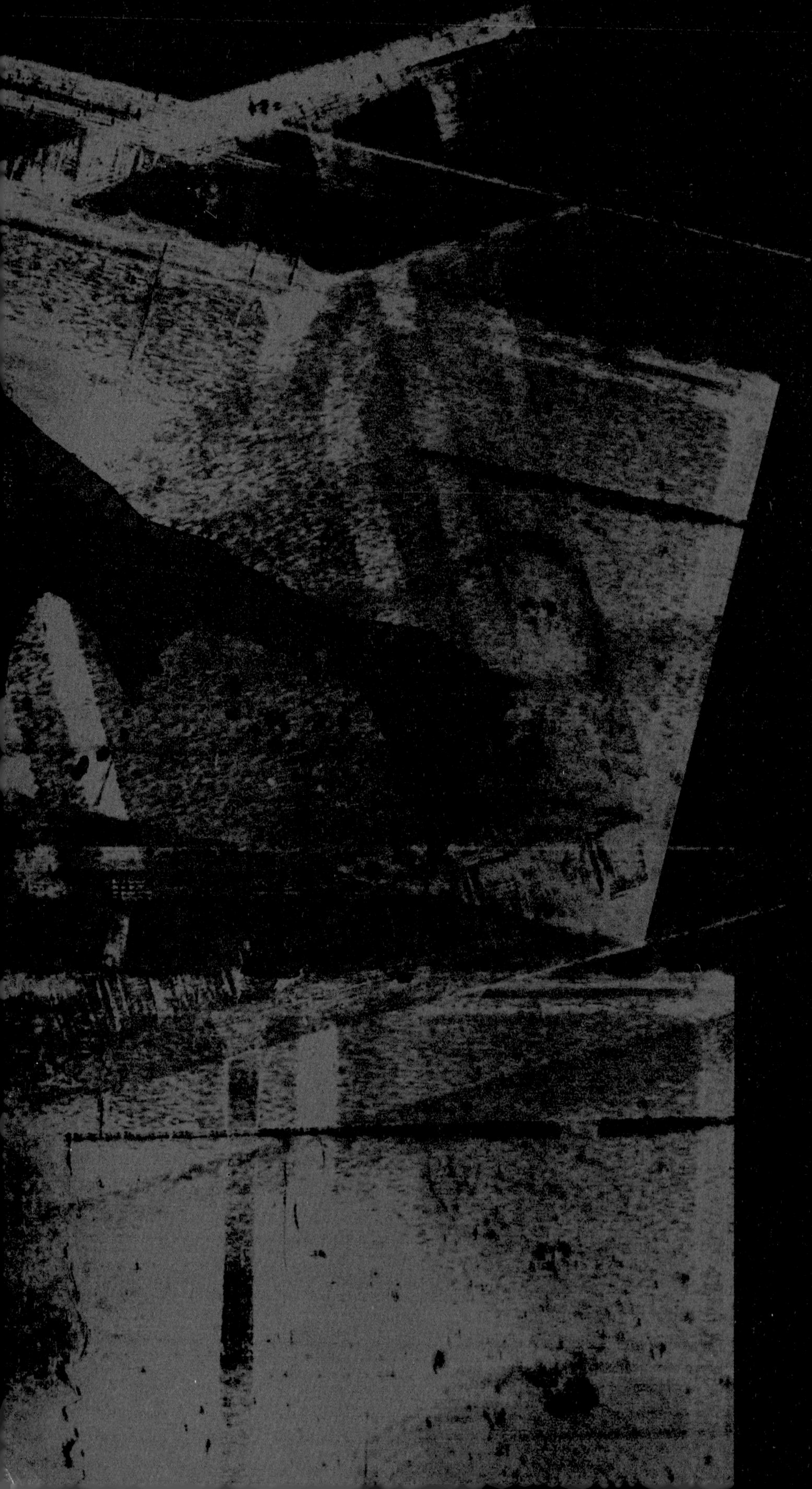

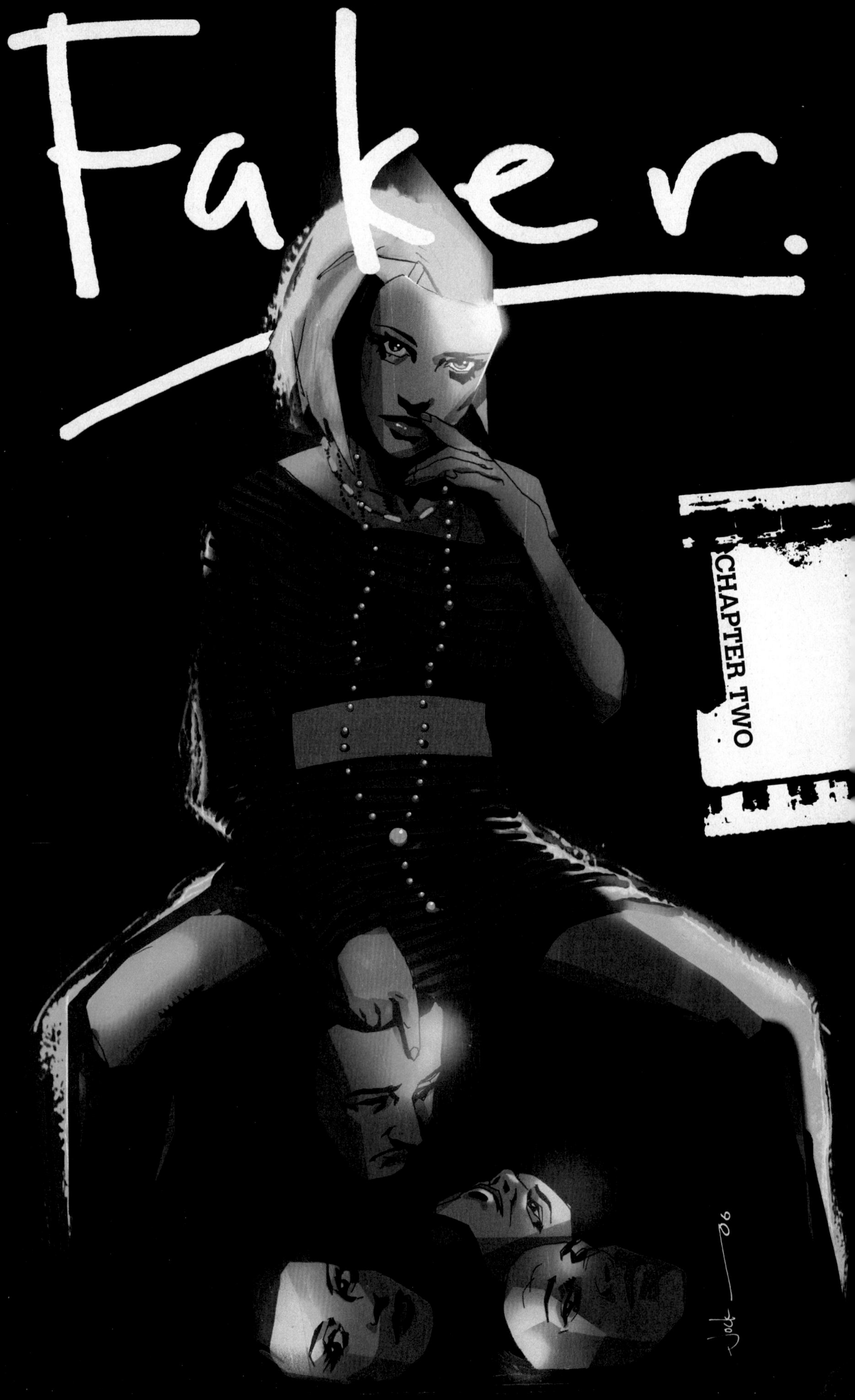
Faker.
CHAPTER TWO
Jock 06

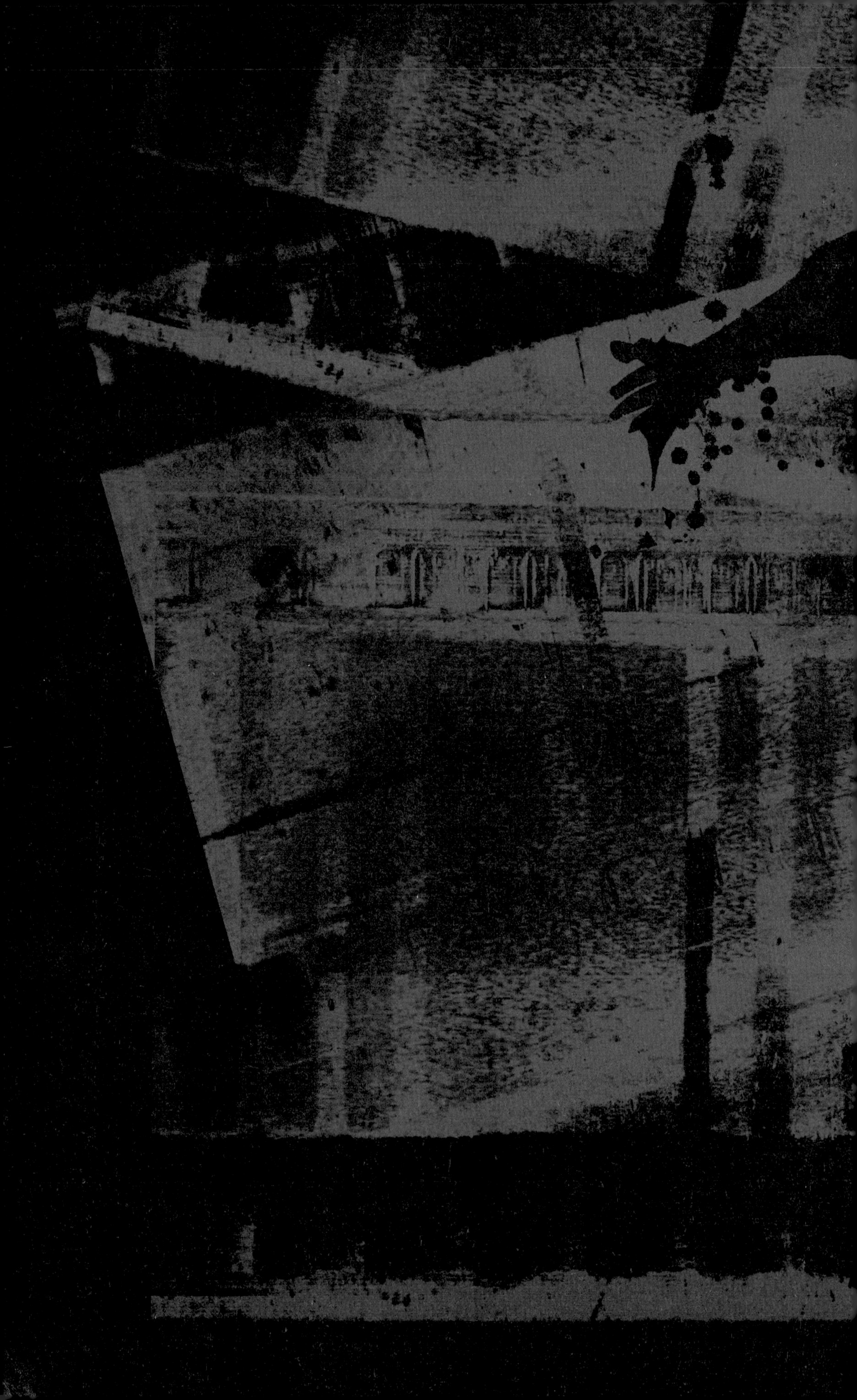

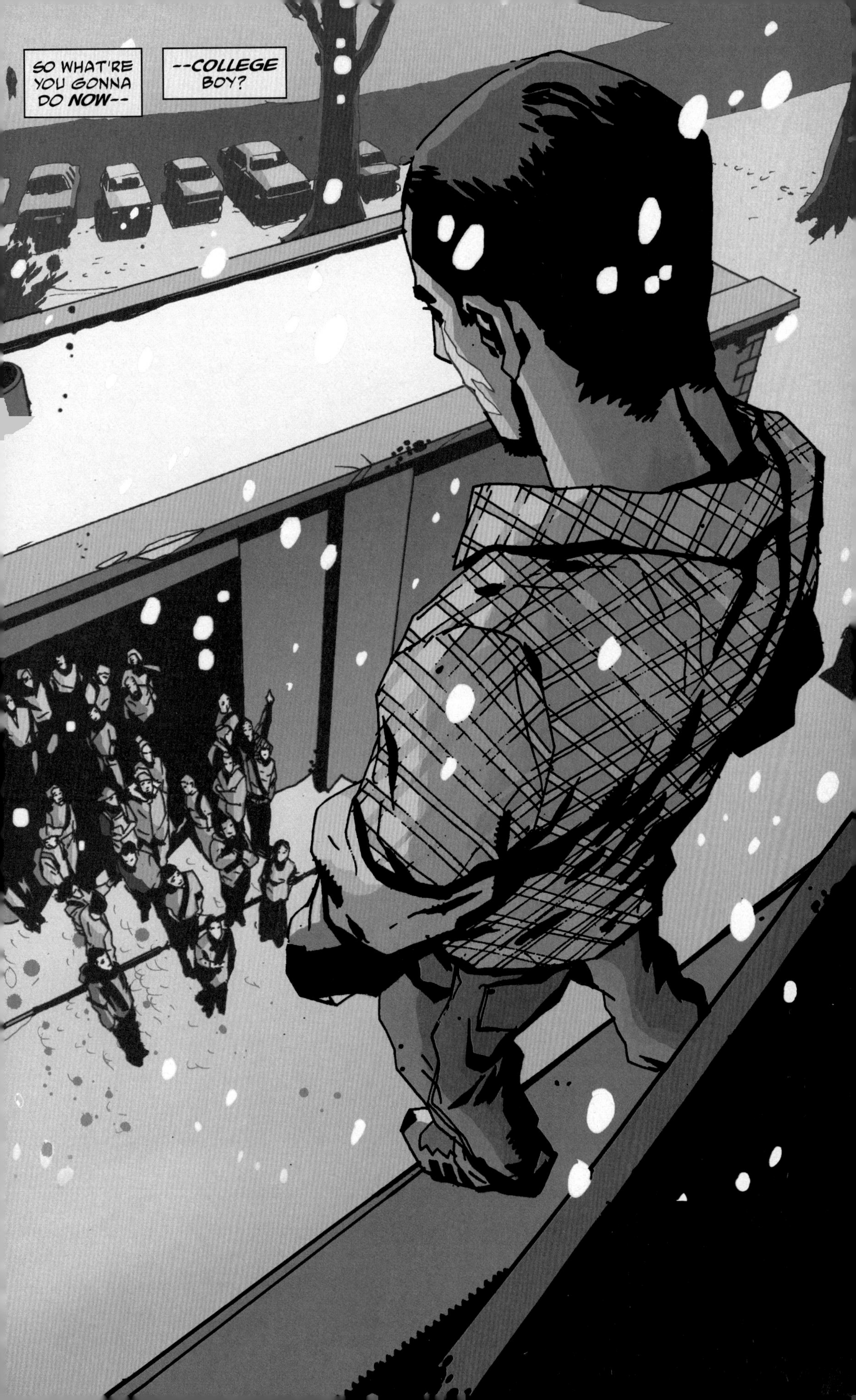
SO WHAT'RE YOU GONNA DO **NOW**--
--**COLLEGE** BOY?

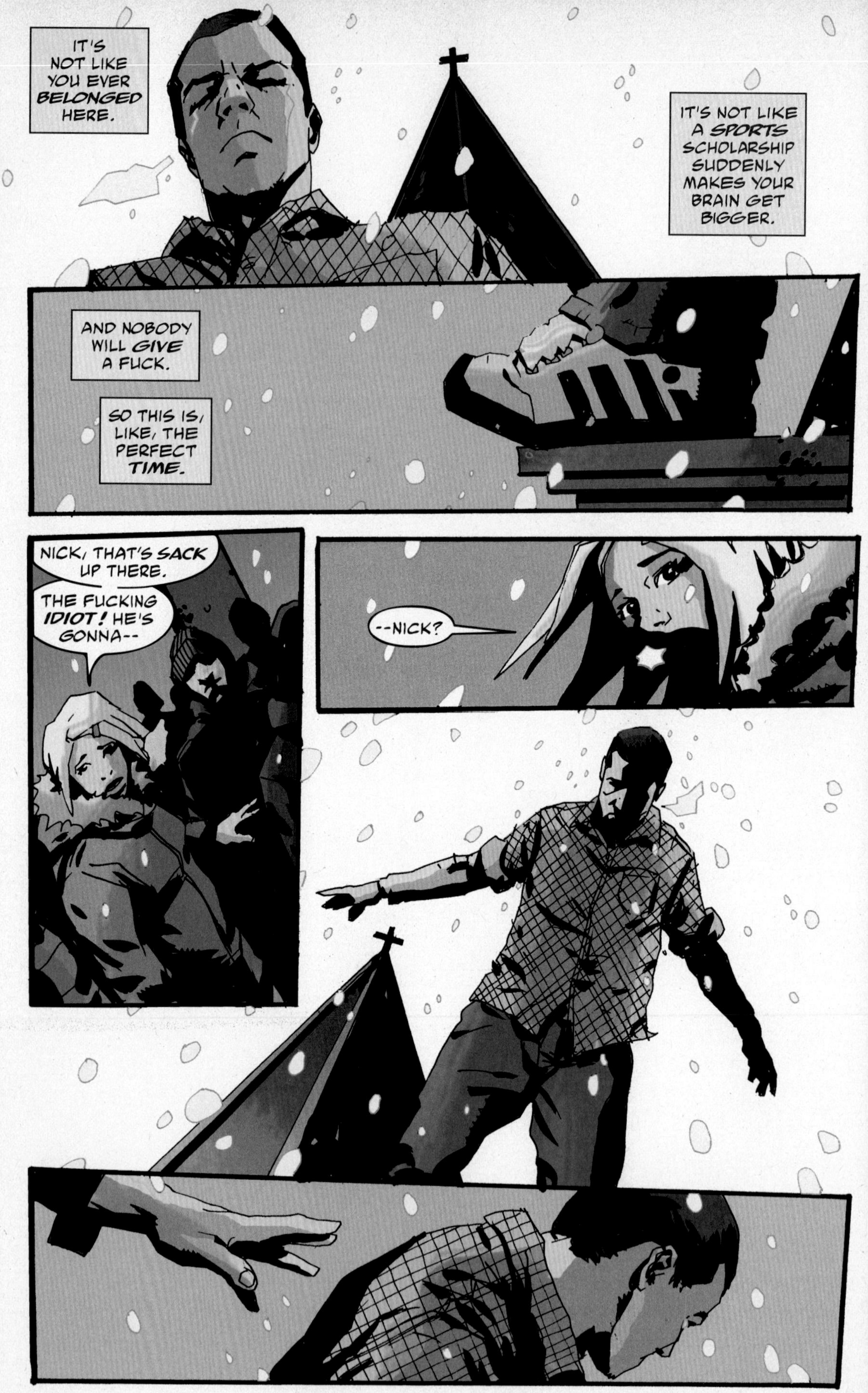
IT'S NOT LIKE YOU EVER BELONGED HERE.
IT'S NOT LIKE A SPORTS SCHOLARSHIP SUDDENLY MAKES YOUR BRAIN GET BIGGER.
AND NOBODY WILL GIVE A FUCK.
SO THIS IS, LIKE, THE PERFECT TIME.
NICK, THAT'S SACK UP THERE.
THE FUCKING IDIOT! HE'S GONNA--
--NICK?

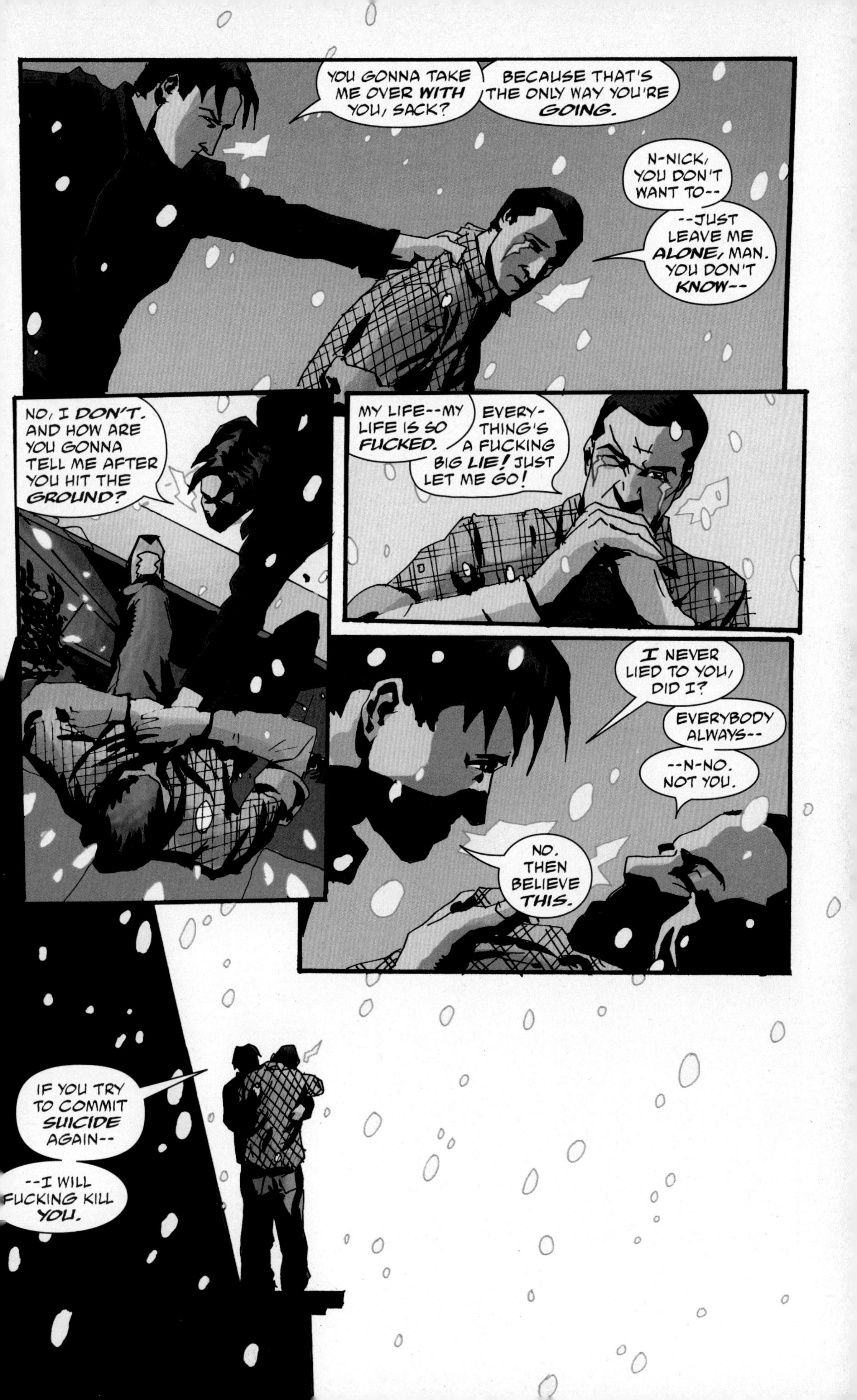
YOU GONNA TAKE ME OVER WITH YOU, SACK?
BECAUSE THAT'S THE ONLY WAY YOU'RE GOING.
N-NICK, YOU DON'T WANT TO--
--JUST LEAVE ME ALONE, MAN. YOU DON'T KNOW--
NO, I DON'T. AND HOW ARE YOU GONNA TELL ME AFTER YOU HIT THE GROUND?
MY LIFE--MY LIFE IS SO FUCKED.
EVERY-THING'S A FUCKING BIG LIE! JUST LET ME GO!
I NEVER LIED TO YOU, DID I?
EVERYBODY ALWAYS--
--N-NO. NOT YOU.
NO. THEN BELIEVE THIS.
IF YOU TRY TO COMMIT SUICIDE AGAIN--
--I WILL FUCKING KILL YOU.

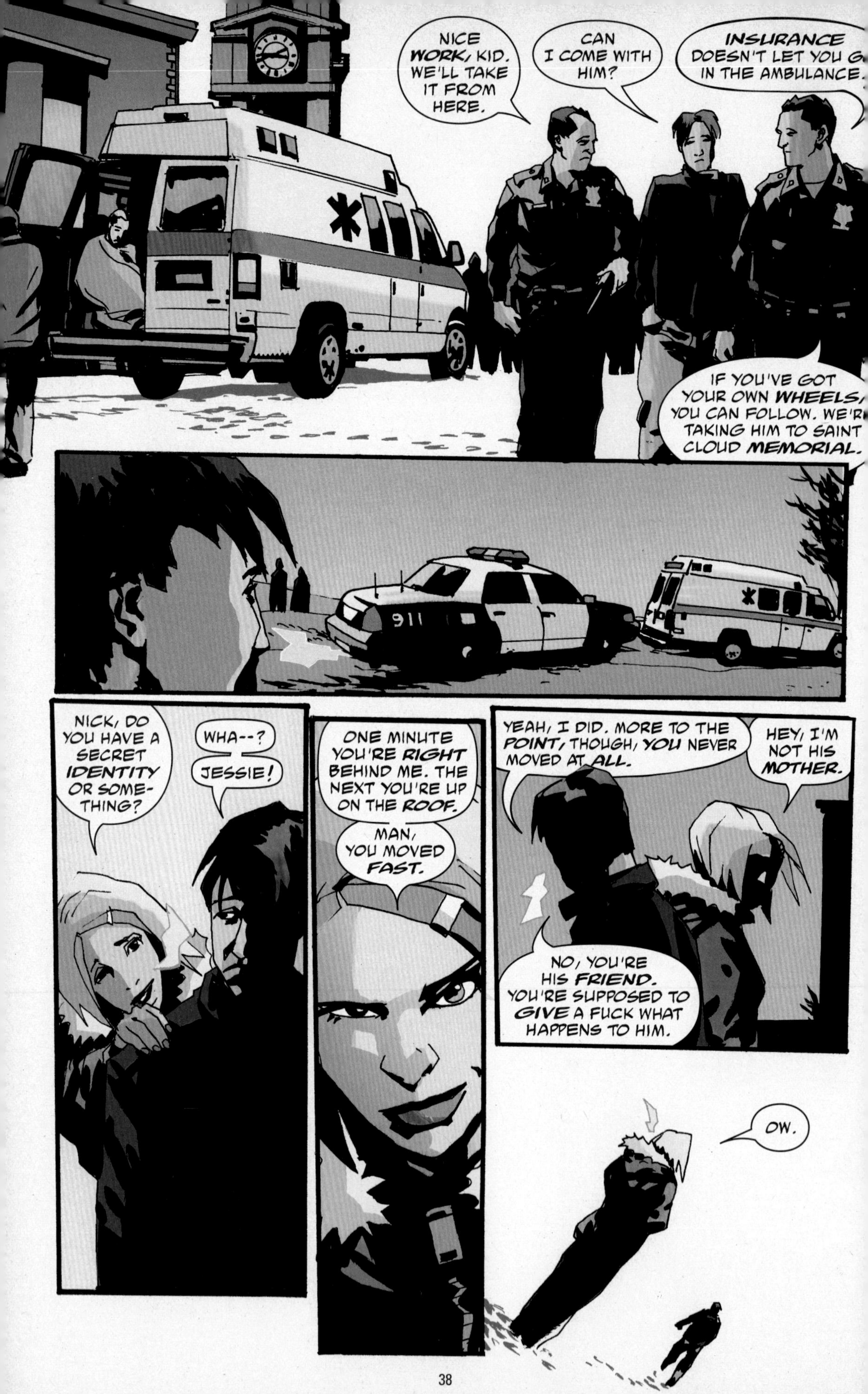
NICE WORK, KID. WE'LL TAKE IT FROM HERE.
CAN I COME WITH HIM?
INSURANCE DOESN'T LET YOU G IN THE AMBULANCE.
IF YOU'VE GOT YOUR OWN WHEELS, YOU CAN FOLLOW. WE'R TAKING HIM TO SAINT CLOUD MEMORIAL.
911
NICK, DO YOU HAVE A SECRET IDENTITY OR SOME-THING?
WHA--?
JESSIE!
ONE MINUTE YOU'RE RIGHT BEHIND ME. THE NEXT YOU'RE UP ON THE ROOF.
MAN, YOU MOVED FAST.
YEAH, I DID. MORE TO THE POINT, THOUGH, YOU NEVER MOVED AT ALL.
HEY, I'M NOT HIS MOTHER.
NO, YOU'RE HIS FRIEND. YOU'RE SUPPOSED TO GIVE A FUCK WHAT HAPPENS TO HIM.
OW.

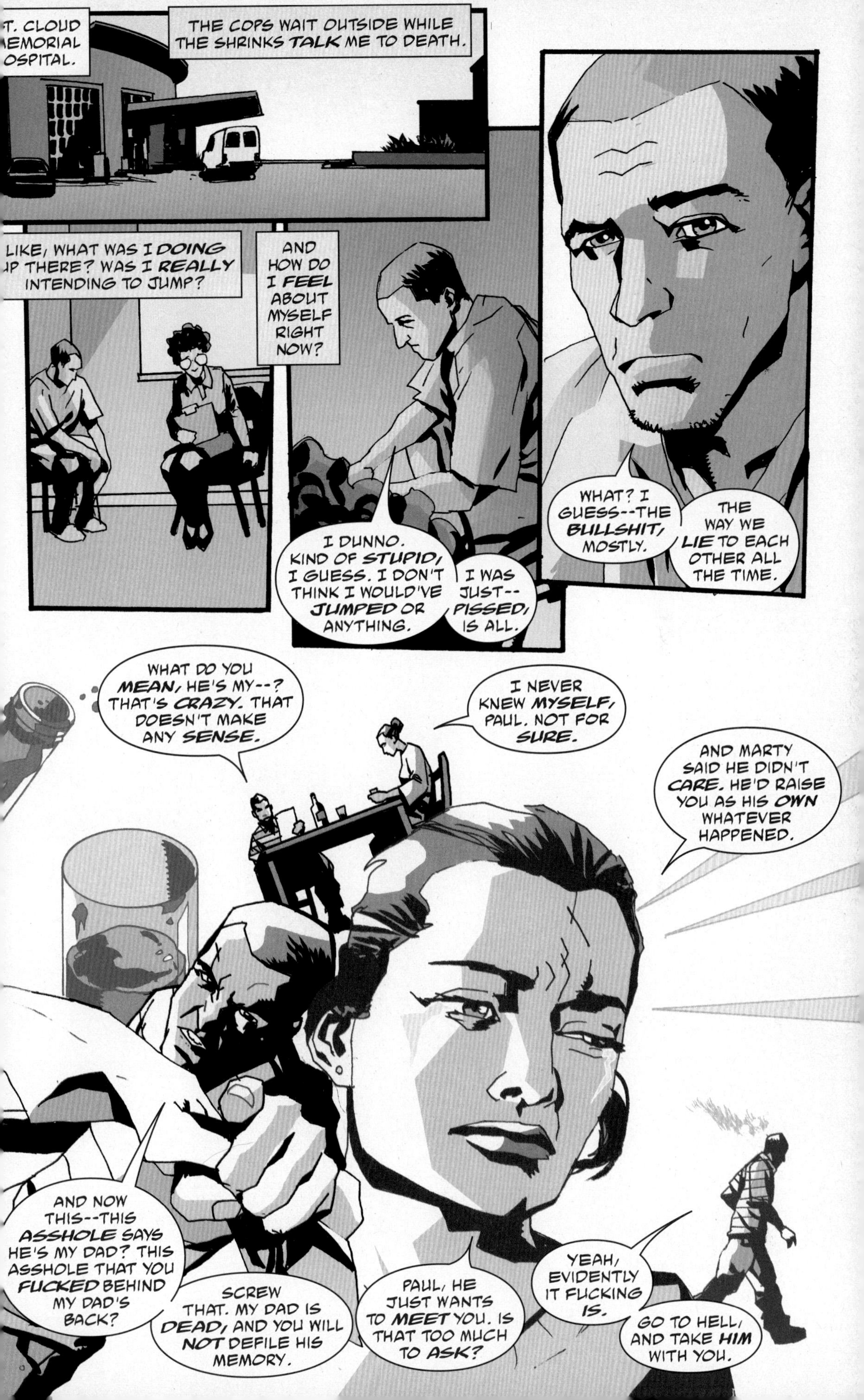
T. CLOUD
EMORIAL
OSPITAL.
THE COPS WAIT OUTSIDE WHILE THE SHRINKS TALK ME TO DEATH.
LIKE, WHAT WAS I DOING
P THERE? WAS I REALLY
INTENDING TO JUMP?
AND HOW DO I FEEL ABOUT MYSELF RIGHT NOW?
I DUNNO. KIND OF STUPID, I GUESS. I DON'T THINK I WOULD'VE JUMPED OR ANYTHING.
I WAS JUST-- PISSED, IS ALL.
WHAT? I GUESS--THE BULLSHIT, MOSTLY.
THE WAY WE LIE TO EACH OTHER ALL THE TIME.
WHAT DO YOU MEAN, HE'S MY--? THAT'S CRAZY. THAT DOESN'T MAKE ANY SENSE.
I NEVER KNEW MYSELF, PAUL. NOT FOR SURE.
AND MARTY SAID HE DIDN'T CARE. HE'D RAISE YOU AS HIS OWN WHATEVER HAPPENED.
AND NOW THIS--THIS ASSHOLE SAYS HE'S MY DAD? THIS ASSHOLE THAT YOU FUCKED BEHIND MY DAD'S BACK?
SCREW THAT. MY DAD IS DEAD, AND YOU WILL NOT DEFILE HIS MEMORY.
PAUL, HE JUST WANTS TO MEET YOU. IS THAT TOO MUCH TO ASK?
YEAH, EVIDENTLY IT FUCKING IS.
GO TO HELL, AND TAKE HIM WITH YOU.

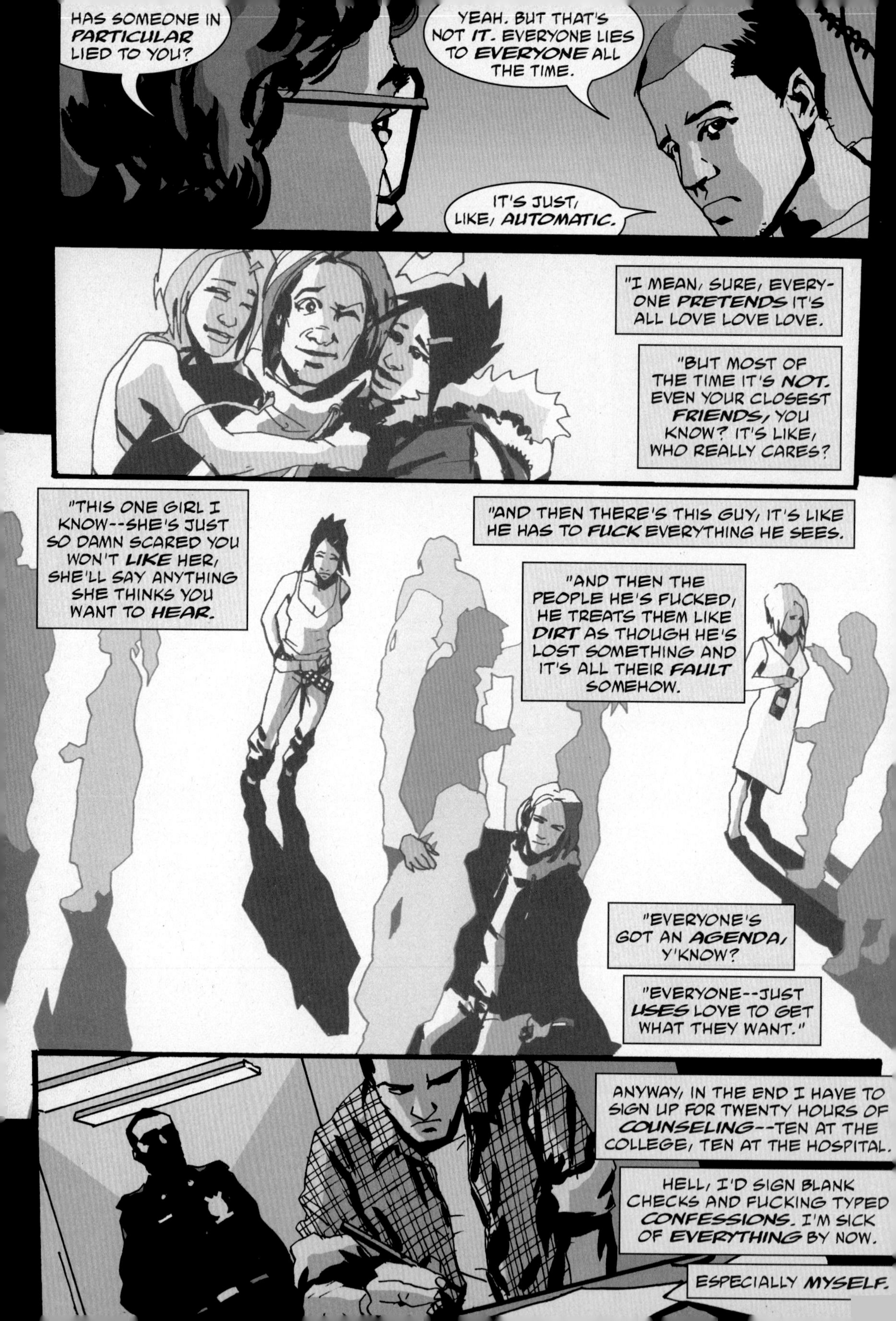
HAS SOMEONE IN PARTICULAR LIED TO YOU?
YEAH. BUT THAT'S NOT IT. EVERYONE LIES TO EVERYONE ALL THE TIME.
IT'S JUST, LIKE, AUTOMATIC.
"I MEAN, SURE, EVERYONE PRETENDS IT'S ALL LOVE LOVE LOVE.
"BUT MOST OF THE TIME IT'S NOT. EVEN YOUR CLOSEST FRIENDS, YOU KNOW? IT'S LIKE, WHO REALLY CARES?
"THIS ONE GIRL I KNOW--SHE'S JUST SO DAMN SCARED YOU WON'T LIKE HER, SHE'LL SAY ANYTHING SHE THINKS YOU WANT TO HEAR.
"AND THEN THERE'S THIS GUY, IT'S LIKE HE HAS TO FUCK EVERYTHING HE SEES.
"AND THEN THE PEOPLE HE'S FUCKED, HE TREATS THEM LIKE DIRT AS THOUGH HE'S LOST SOMETHING AND IT'S ALL THEIR FAULT SOMEHOW.
"EVERYONE'S GOT AN AGENDA, Y'KNOW?
"EVERYONE--JUST USES LOVE TO GET WHAT THEY WANT."
ANYWAY, IN THE END I HAVE TO SIGN UP FOR TWENTY HOURS OF COUNSELING--TEN AT THE COLLEGE, TEN AT THE HOSPITAL.
HELL, I'D SIGN BLANK CHECKS AND FUCKING TYPED CONFESSIONS. I'M SICK OF EVERYTHING BY NOW.
ESPECIALLY MYSELF.

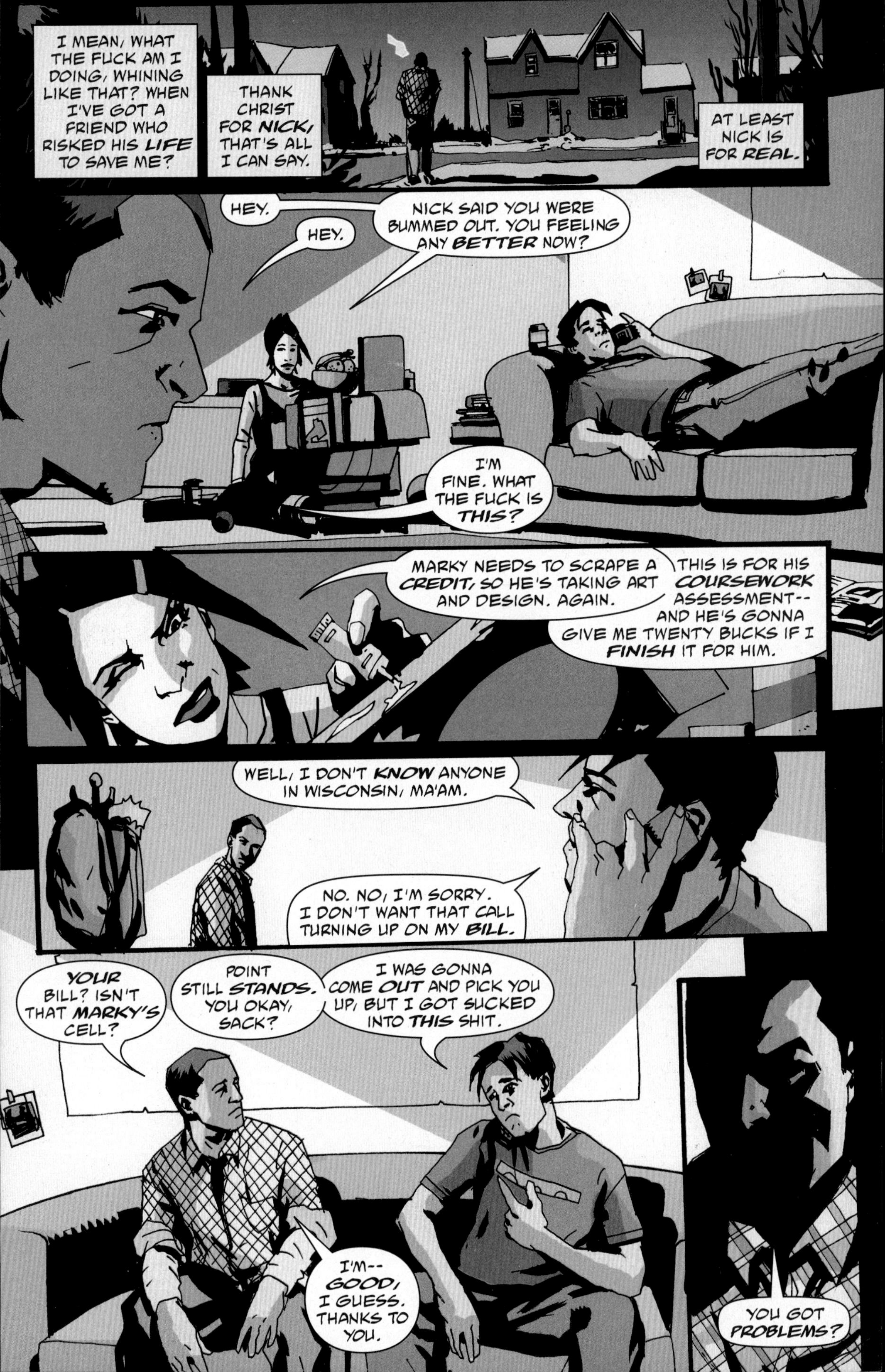
I MEAN, WHAT THE FUCK AM I DOING, WHINING LIKE THAT? WHEN I'VE GOT A FRIEND WHO RISKED HIS LIFE TO SAVE ME?
THANK CHRIST FOR NICK, THAT'S ALL I CAN SAY.
AT LEAST NICK IS FOR REAL.
HEY.
HEY.
NICK SAID YOU WERE BUMMED OUT. YOU FEELING ANY BETTER NOW?
I'M FINE. WHAT THE FUCK IS THIS?
MARKY NEEDS TO SCRAPE A CREDIT, SO HE'S TAKING ART AND DESIGN. AGAIN.
THIS IS FOR HIS COURSEWORK ASSESSMENT-- AND HE'S GONNA GIVE ME TWENTY BUCKS IF I FINISH IT FOR HIM.
WELL, I DON'T KNOW ANYONE IN WISCONSIN, MA'AM.
NO. NO, I'M SORRY. I DON'T WANT THAT CALL TURNING UP ON MY BILL.
YOUR BILL? ISN'T THAT MARKY'S CELL?
POINT STILL STANDS. YOU OKAY, SACK?
I WAS GONNA COME OUT AND PICK YOU UP, BUT I GOT SUCKED INTO THIS SHIT.
I'M-- GOOD, I GUESS. THANKS TO YOU.
YOU GOT PROBLEMS?

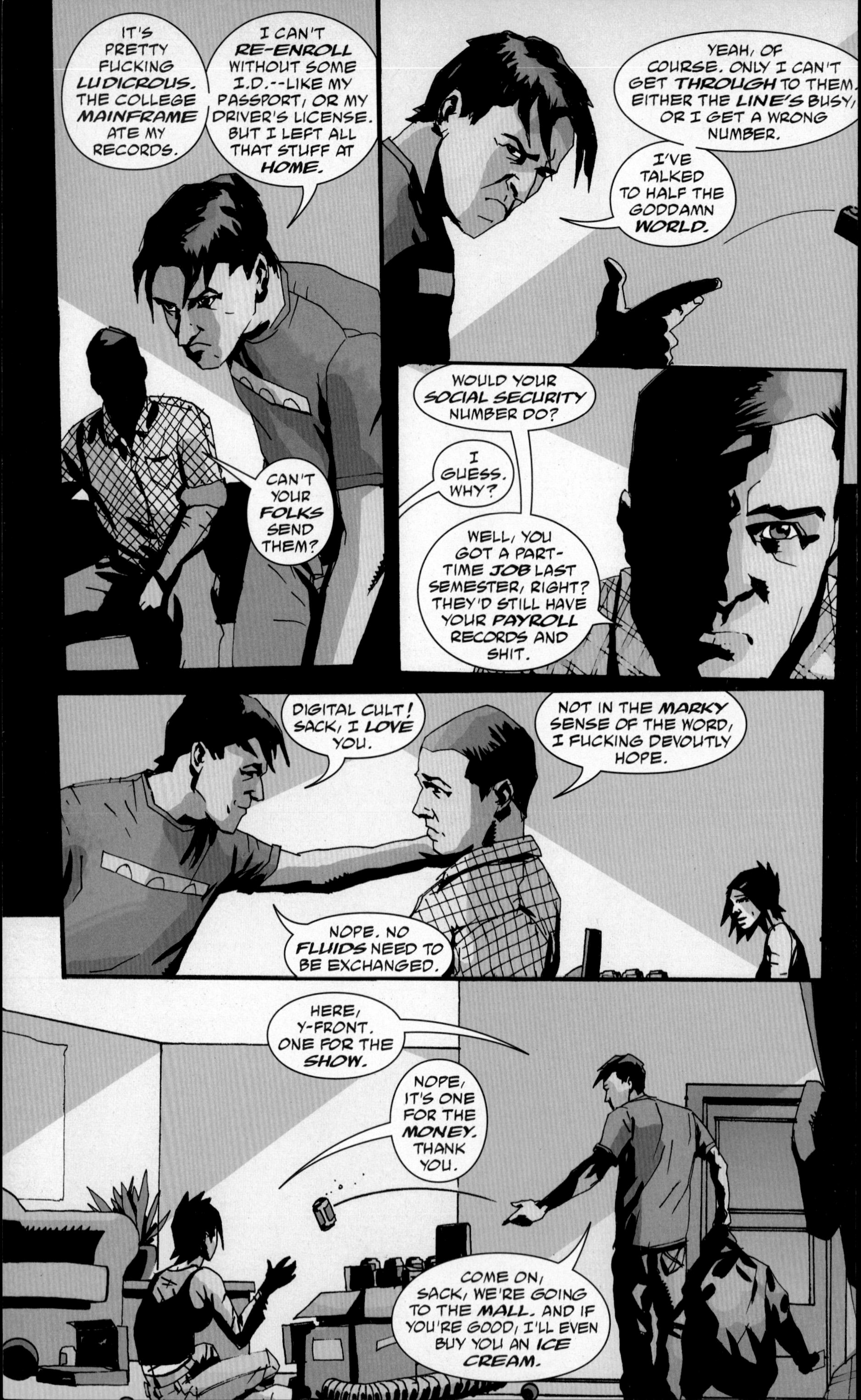
IT'S PRETTY FUCKING LUDICROUS. THE COLLEGE MAINFRAME ATE MY RECORDS.
I CAN'T RE-ENROLL WITHOUT SOME I.D.--LIKE MY PASSPORT, OR MY DRIVER'S LICENSE. BUT I LEFT ALL THAT STUFF AT HOME.
CAN'T YOUR FOLKS SEND THEM?
YEAH, OF COURSE. ONLY I CAN'T GET THROUGH TO THEM. EITHER THE LINE'S BUSY, OR I GET A WRONG NUMBER.
I'VE TALKED TO HALF THE GODDAMN WORLD.
WOULD YOUR SOCIAL SECURITY NUMBER DO?
I GUESS. WHY?
WELL, YOU GOT A PART-TIME JOB LAST SEMESTER, RIGHT? THEY'D STILL HAVE YOUR PAYROLL RECORDS AND SHIT.
DIGITAL CULT! SACK, I LOVE YOU.
NOT IN THE MARKY SENSE OF THE WORD, I FUCKING DEVOUTLY HOPE.
NOPE. NO FLUIDS NEED TO BE EXCHANGED.
HERE, Y-FRONT. ONE FOR THE SHOW.
NOPE, IT'S ONE FOR THE MONEY. THANK YOU.
COME ON, SACK, WE'RE GOING TO THE MALL. AND IF YOU'RE GOOD, I'LL EVEN BUY YOU AN ICE CREAM.

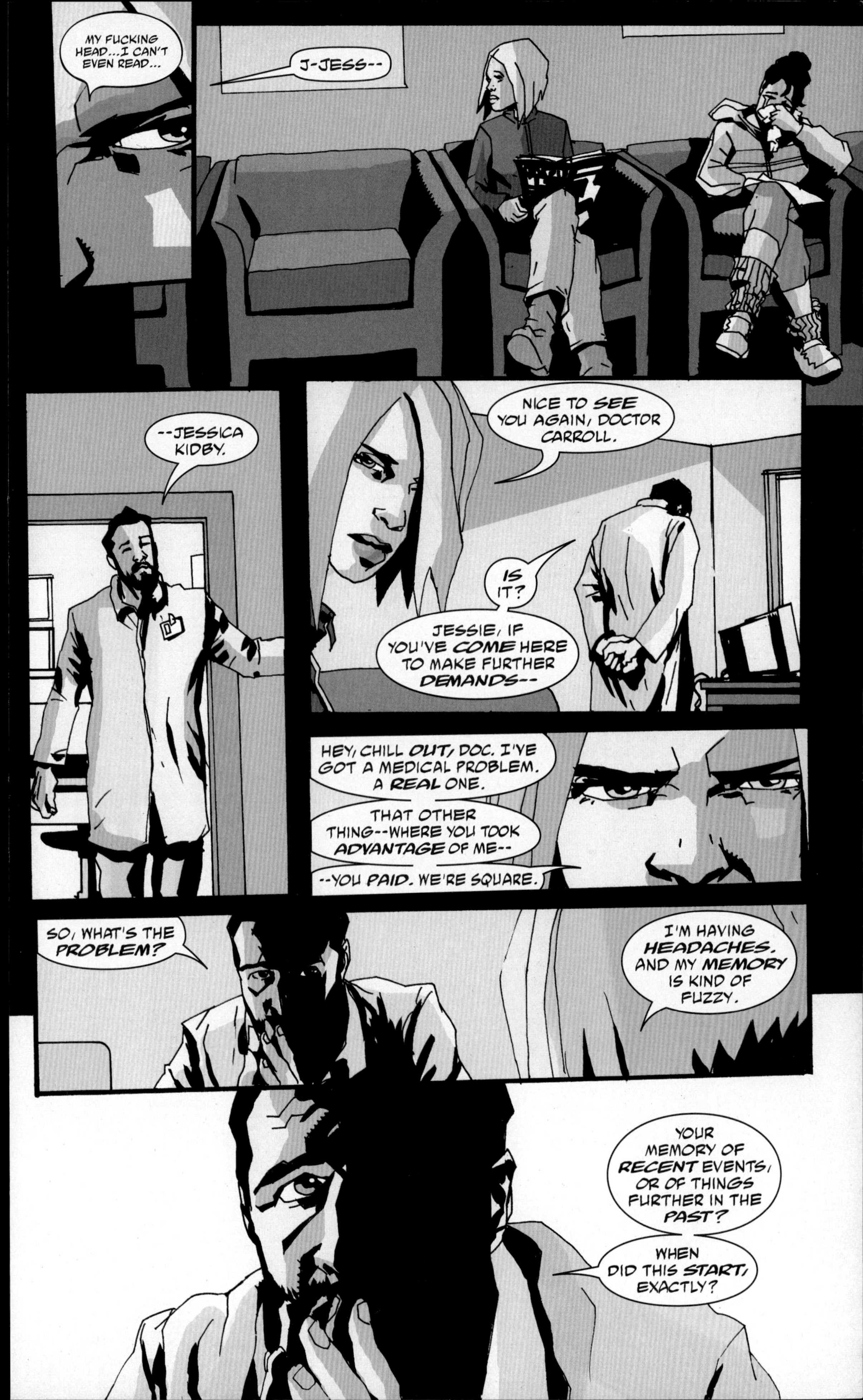
MY FUCKING HEAD...I CAN'T EVEN READ...
J-JESS--
--JESSICA KIDBY.
NICE TO SEE YOU AGAIN, DOCTOR CARROLL.
IS IT?
JESSIE, IF YOU'VE COME HERE TO MAKE FURTHER DEMANDS--
HEY, CHILL OUT, DOC. I'VE GOT A MEDICAL PROBLEM. A REAL ONE.
THAT OTHER THING--WHERE YOU TOOK ADVANTAGE OF ME--
--YOU PAID. WE'RE SQUARE.
SO, WHAT'S THE PROBLEM?
I'M HAVING HEADACHES. AND MY MEMORY IS KIND OF FUZZY.
YOUR MEMORY OF RECENT EVENTS, OR OF THINGS FURTHER IN THE PAST?
WHEN DID THIS START, EXACTLY?

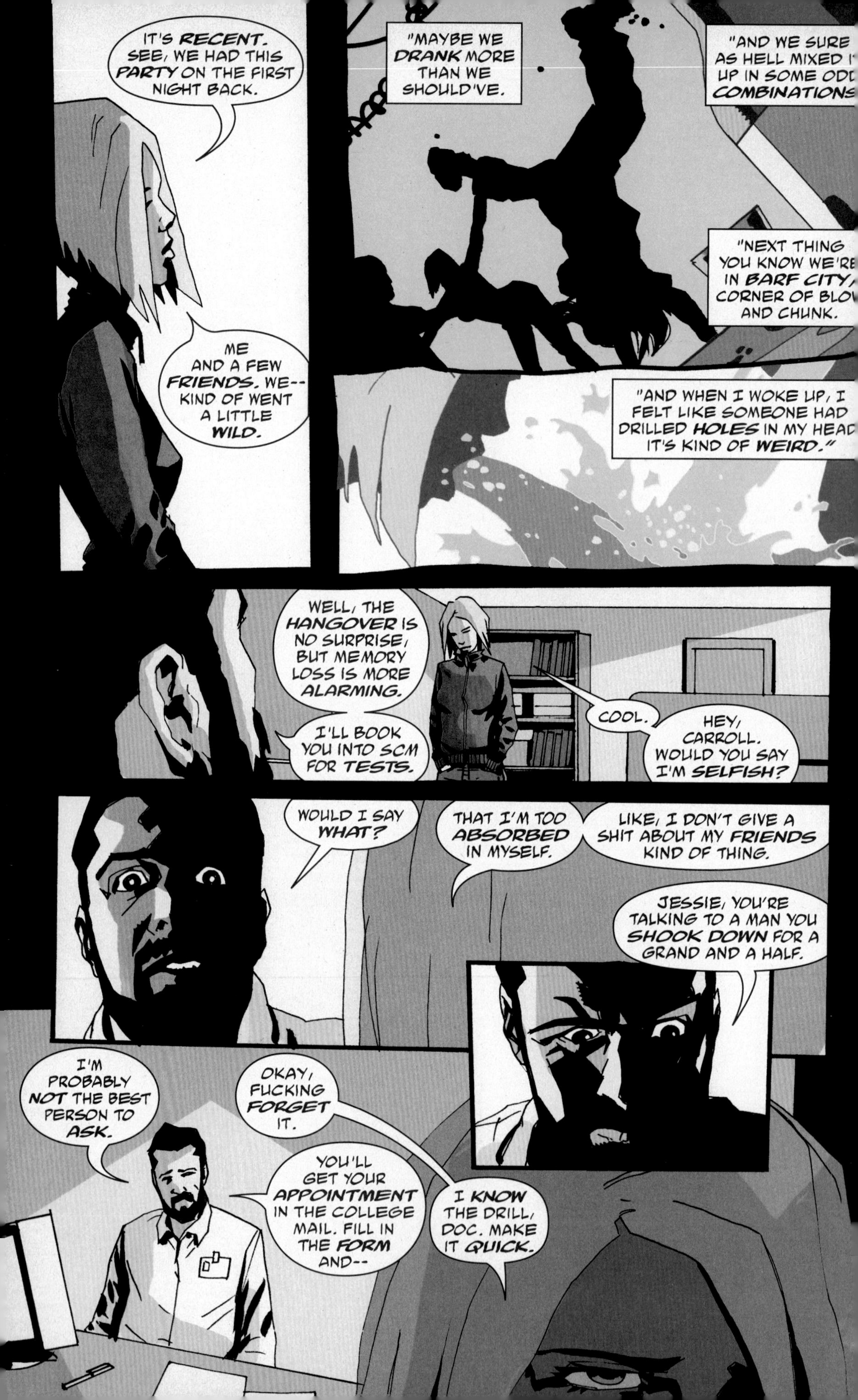
IT'S RECENT. SEE, WE HAD THIS PARTY ON THE FIRST NIGHT BACK.
ME AND A FEW FRIENDS. WE-- KIND OF WENT A LITTLE WILD.
"MAYBE WE DRANK MORE THAN WE SHOULD'VE.
"AND WE SURE AS HELL MIXED I UP IN SOME ODD COMBINATIONS
"NEXT THING YOU KNOW WE'RE IN BARF CITY, CORNER OF BLO AND CHUNK.
"AND WHEN I WOKE UP, I FELT LIKE SOMEONE HAD DRILLED HOLES IN MY HEAD IT'S KIND OF WEIRD."
WELL, THE HANGOVER IS NO SURPRISE, BUT MEMORY LOSS IS MORE ALARMING.
I'LL BOOK YOU INTO SCM FOR TESTS.
COOL.
HEY, CARROLL. WOULD YOU SAY I'M SELFISH?
WOULD I SAY WHAT?
THAT I'M TOO ABSORBED IN MYSELF.
LIKE, I DON'T GIVE A SHIT ABOUT MY FRIENDS KIND OF THING.
JESSIE, YOU'RE TALKING TO A MAN YOU SHOOK DOWN FOR A GRAND AND A HALF.
I'M PROBABLY NOT THE BEST PERSON TO ASK.
OKAY, FUCKING FORGET IT.
YOU'LL GET YOUR APPOINTMENT IN THE COLLEGE MAIL. FILL IN THE FORM AND--
I KNOW THE DRILL, DOC. MAKE IT QUICK.

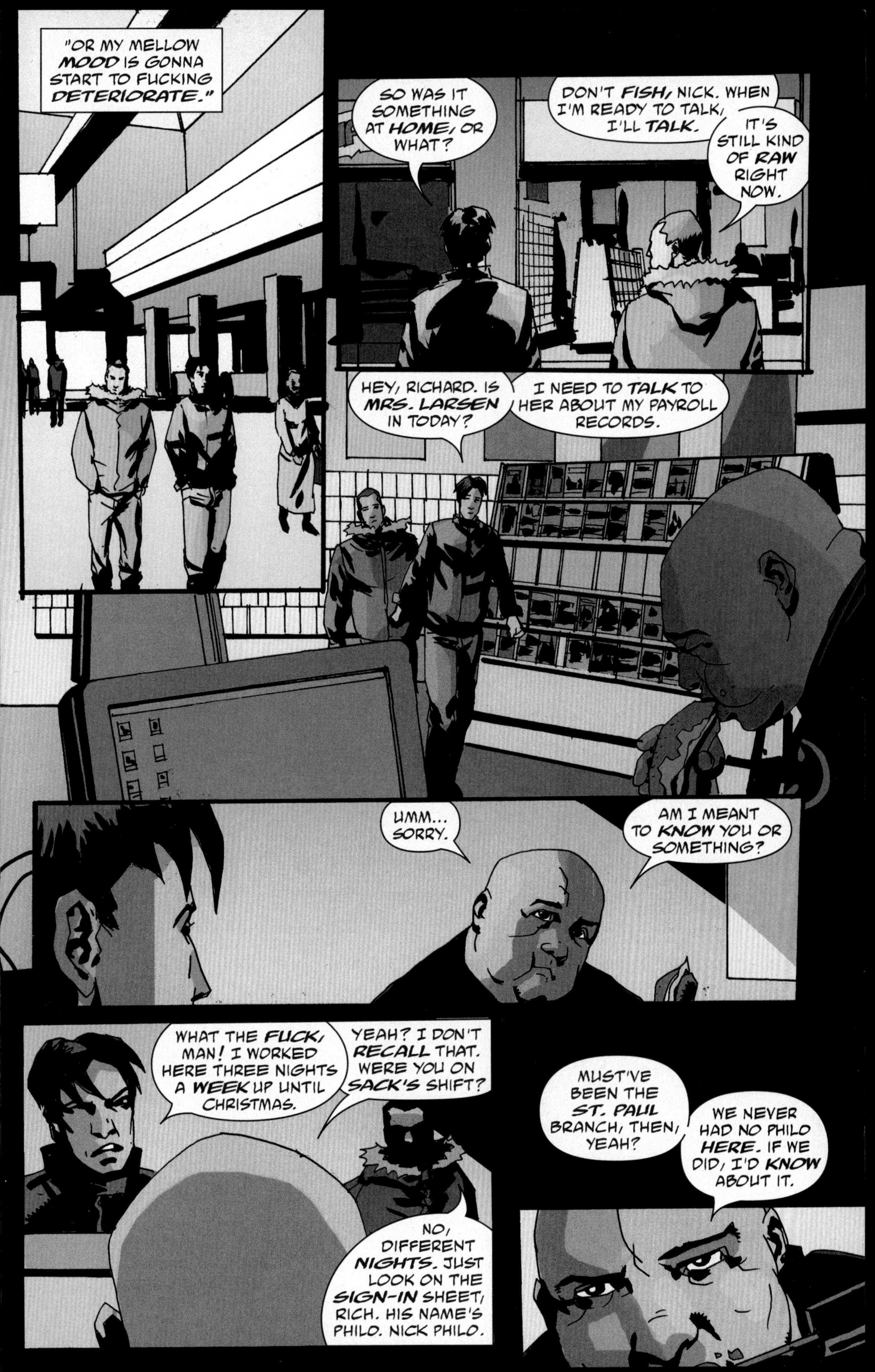
"OR MY MELLOW MOOD IS GONNA START TO FUCKING DETERIORATE."
SO WAS IT SOMETHING AT HOME, OR WHAT?
DON'T FISH, NICK. WHEN I'M READY TO TALK, I'LL TALK.
IT'S STILL KIND OF RAW RIGHT NOW.
HEY, RICHARD. IS MRS. LARSEN IN TODAY?
I NEED TO TALK TO HER ABOUT MY PAYROLL RECORDS.
UMM... SORRY.
AM I MEANT TO KNOW YOU OR SOMETHING?
WHAT THE FUCK, MAN! I WORKED HERE THREE NIGHTS A WEEK UP UNTIL CHRISTMAS.
YEAH? I DON'T RECALL THAT. WERE YOU ON SACK'S SHIFT?
NO, DIFFERENT NIGHTS. JUST LOOK ON THE SIGN-IN SHEET, RICH. HIS NAME'S PHILO. NICK PHILO.
MUST'VE BEEN THE ST. PAUL BRANCH, THEN, YEAH?
WE NEVER HAD NO PHILO HERE. IF WE DID, I'D KNOW ABOUT IT.

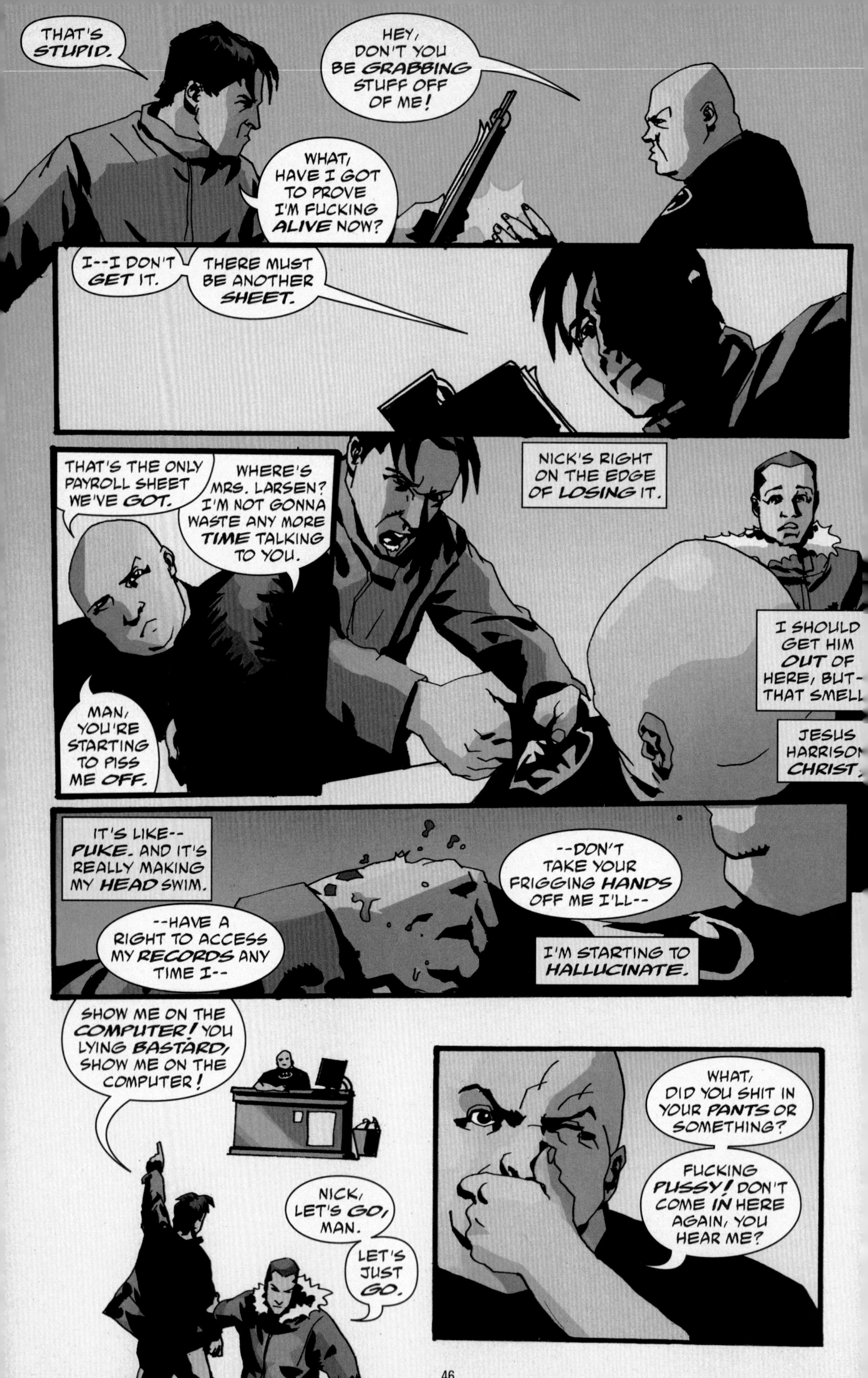
THAT'S STUPID.
HEY, DON'T YOU BE GRABBING STUFF OFF OF ME!
WHAT, HAVE I GOT TO PROVE I'M FUCKING ALIVE NOW?
I--I DON'T GET IT.
THERE MUST BE ANOTHER SHEET.
THAT'S THE ONLY PAYROLL SHEET WE'VE GOT.
WHERE'S MRS. LARSEN? I'M NOT GONNA WASTE ANY MORE TIME TALKING TO YOU.
NICK'S RIGHT ON THE EDGE OF LOSING IT.
MAN, YOU'RE STARTING TO PISS ME OFF.
I SHOULD GET HIM OUT OF HERE, BUT-- THAT SMELL
JESUS HARRISON CHRIST.
IT'S LIKE-- PUKE. AND IT'S REALLY MAKING MY HEAD SWIM.
--HAVE A RIGHT TO ACCESS MY RECORDS ANY TIME I--
--DON'T TAKE YOUR FRIGGING HANDS OFF ME I'LL--
I'M STARTING TO HALLUCINATE.
SHOW ME ON THE COMPUTER! YOU LYING BASTARD, SHOW ME ON THE COMPUTER!
NICK, LET'S GO, MAN.
LET'S JUST GO.
WHAT, DID YOU SHIT IN YOUR PANTS OR SOMETHING?
FUCKING PUSSY! DON'T COME IN HERE AGAIN, YOU HEAR ME?

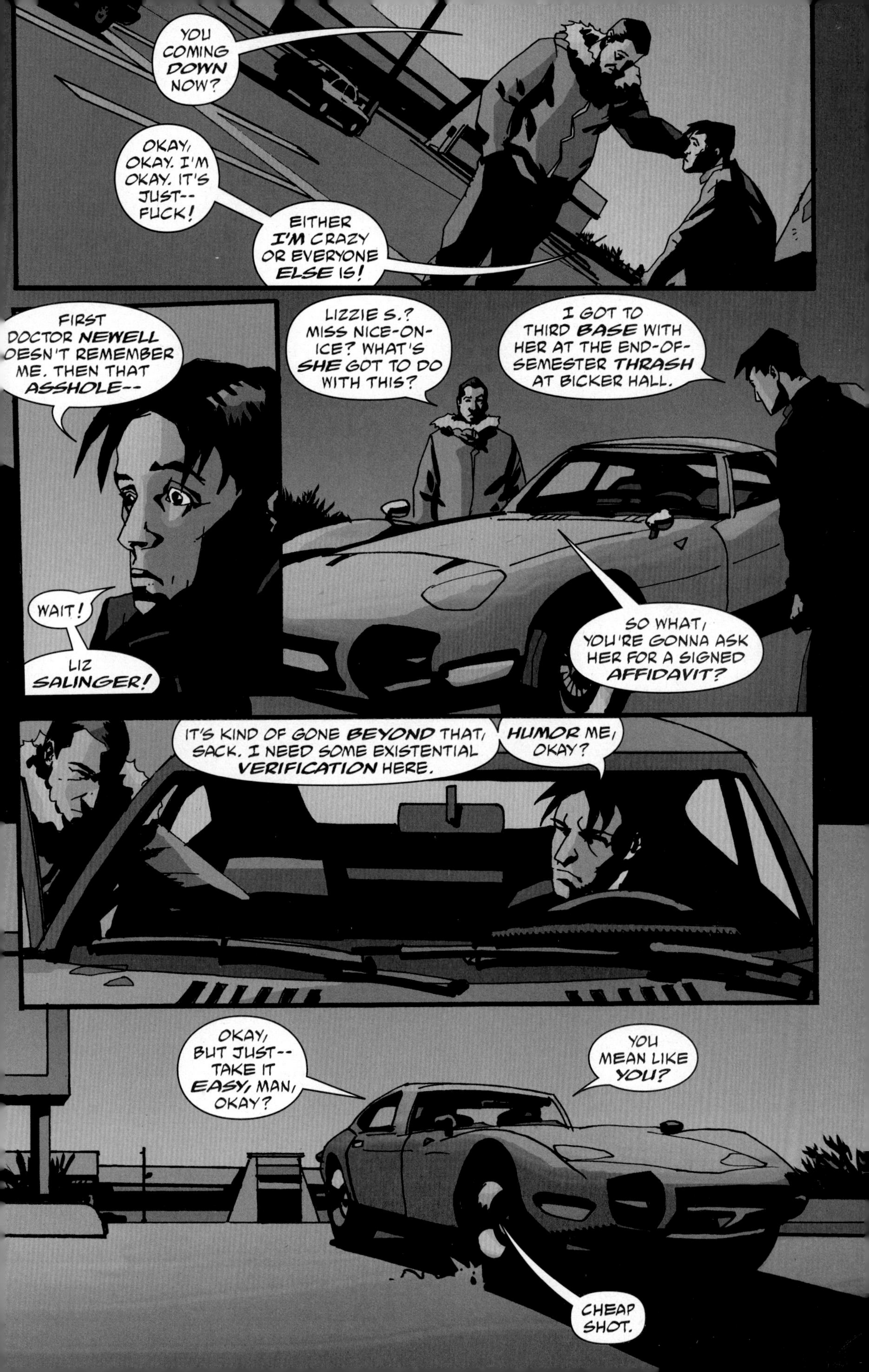
YOU COMING DOWN NOW?
OKAY, OKAY. I'M OKAY. IT'S JUST-- FUCK!
EITHER I'M CRAZY OR EVERYONE ELSE IS!
FIRST DOCTOR NEWELL DOESN'T REMEMBER ME. THEN THAT ASSHOLE--
WAIT!
LIZ SALINGER!
LIZZIE S.? MISS NICE-ON-ICE? WHAT'S SHE GOT TO DO WITH THIS?
I GOT TO THIRD BASE WITH HER AT THE END-OF-SEMESTER THRASH AT BICKER HALL.
SO WHAT, YOU'RE GONNA ASK HER FOR A SIGNED AFFIDAVIT?
IT'S KIND OF GONE BEYOND THAT, SACK. I NEED SOME EXISTENTIAL VERIFICATION HERE.
HUMOR ME, OKAY?
OKAY, BUT JUST-- TAKE IT EASY, MAN, OKAY?
YOU MEAN LIKE YOU?
CHEAP SHOT.

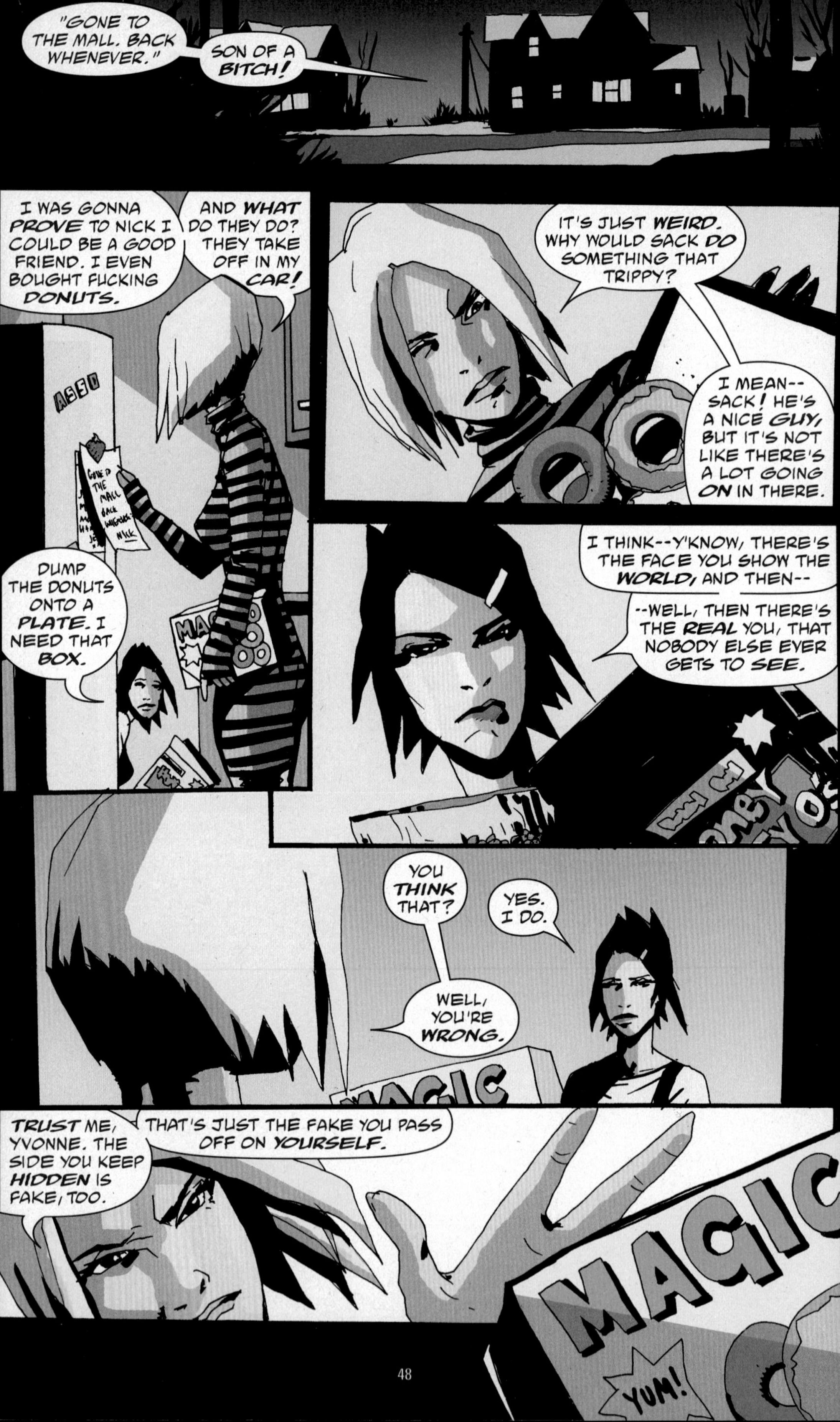
"GONE TO THE MALL. BACK WHENEVER."
SON OF A BITCH!
I WAS GONNA PROVE TO NICK I COULD BE A GOOD FRIEND. I EVEN BOUGHT FUCKING DONUTS.
AND WHAT DO THEY DO? THEY TAKE OFF IN MY CAR!
DUMP THE DONUTS ONTO A PLATE. I NEED THAT BOX.
MAGIC
IT'S JUST WEIRD. WHY WOULD SACK DO SOMETHING THAT TRIPPY?
I MEAN-- SACK! HE'S A NICE GUY, BUT IT'S NOT LIKE THERE'S A LOT GOING ON IN THERE.
I THINK--Y'KNOW, THERE'S THE FACE YOU SHOW THE WORLD, AND THEN--
--WELL, THEN THERE'S THE REAL YOU, THAT NOBODY ELSE EVER GETS TO SEE.
YOU THINK THAT?
YES. I DO.
WELL, YOU'RE WRONG.
MAGIC
TRUST ME, YVONNE. THE SIDE YOU KEEP HIDDEN IS FAKE, TOO.
THAT'S JUST THE FAKE YOU PASS OFF ON YOURSELF.
MAGIC
YUM!

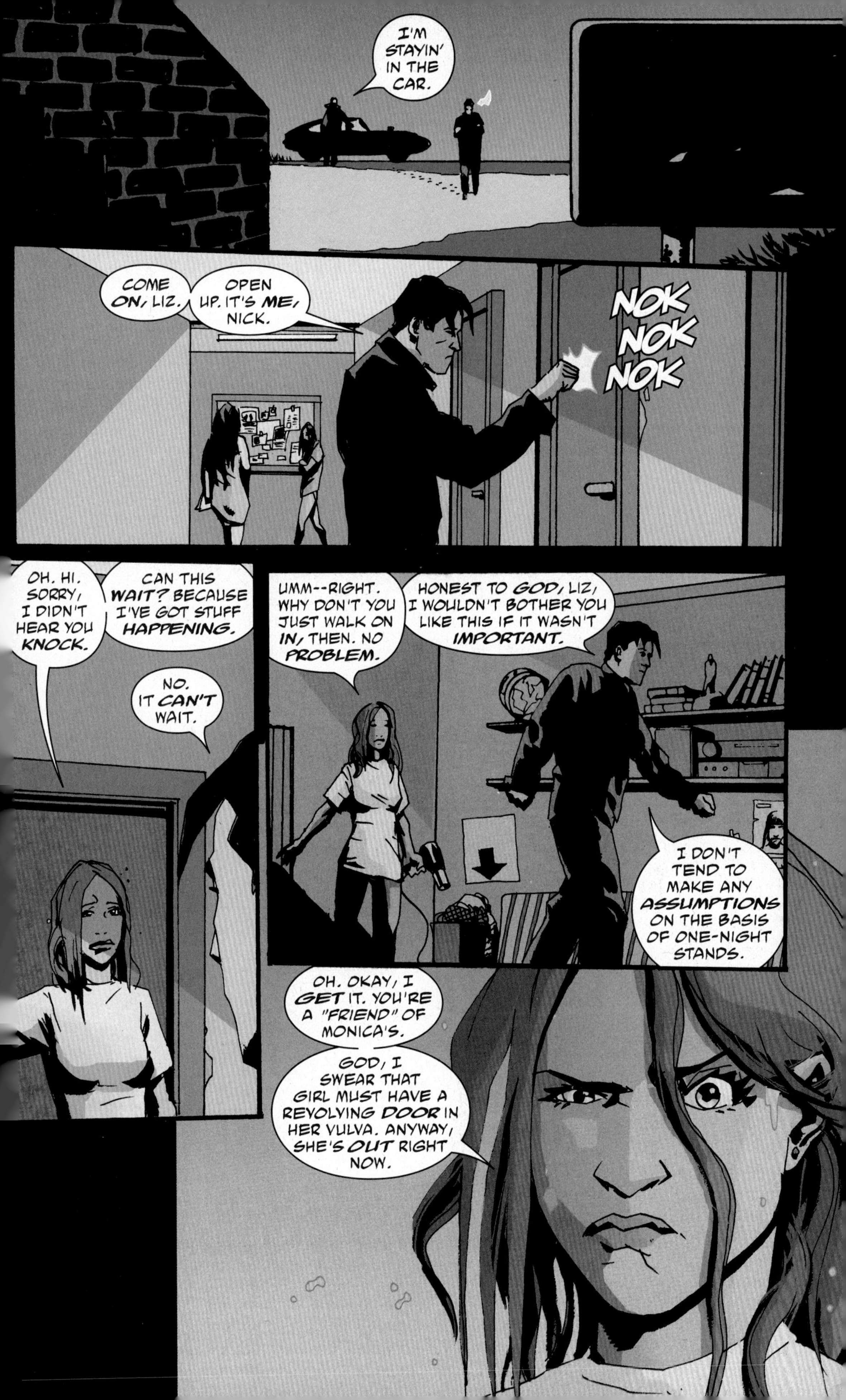
I'M STAYIN' IN THE CAR.
COME ON, LIZ.
OPEN UP. IT'S ME, NICK.
NOK NOK NOK
OH. HI. SORRY, I DIDN'T HEAR YOU KNOCK.
CAN THIS WAIT? BECAUSE I'VE GOT STUFF HAPPENING.
NO. IT CAN'T WAIT.
UMM--RIGHT. WHY DON'T YOU JUST WALK ON IN, THEN. NO PROBLEM.
HONEST TO GOD, LIZ, I WOULDN'T BOTHER YOU LIKE THIS IF IT WASN'T IMPORTANT.
I DON'T TEND TO MAKE ANY ASSUMPTIONS ON THE BASIS OF ONE-NIGHT STANDS.
OH. OKAY, I GET IT. YOU'RE A "FRIEND" OF MONICA'S.
GOD, I SWEAR THAT GIRL MUST HAVE A REVOLVING DOOR IN HER VULVA. ANYWAY, SHE'S OUT RIGHT NOW.

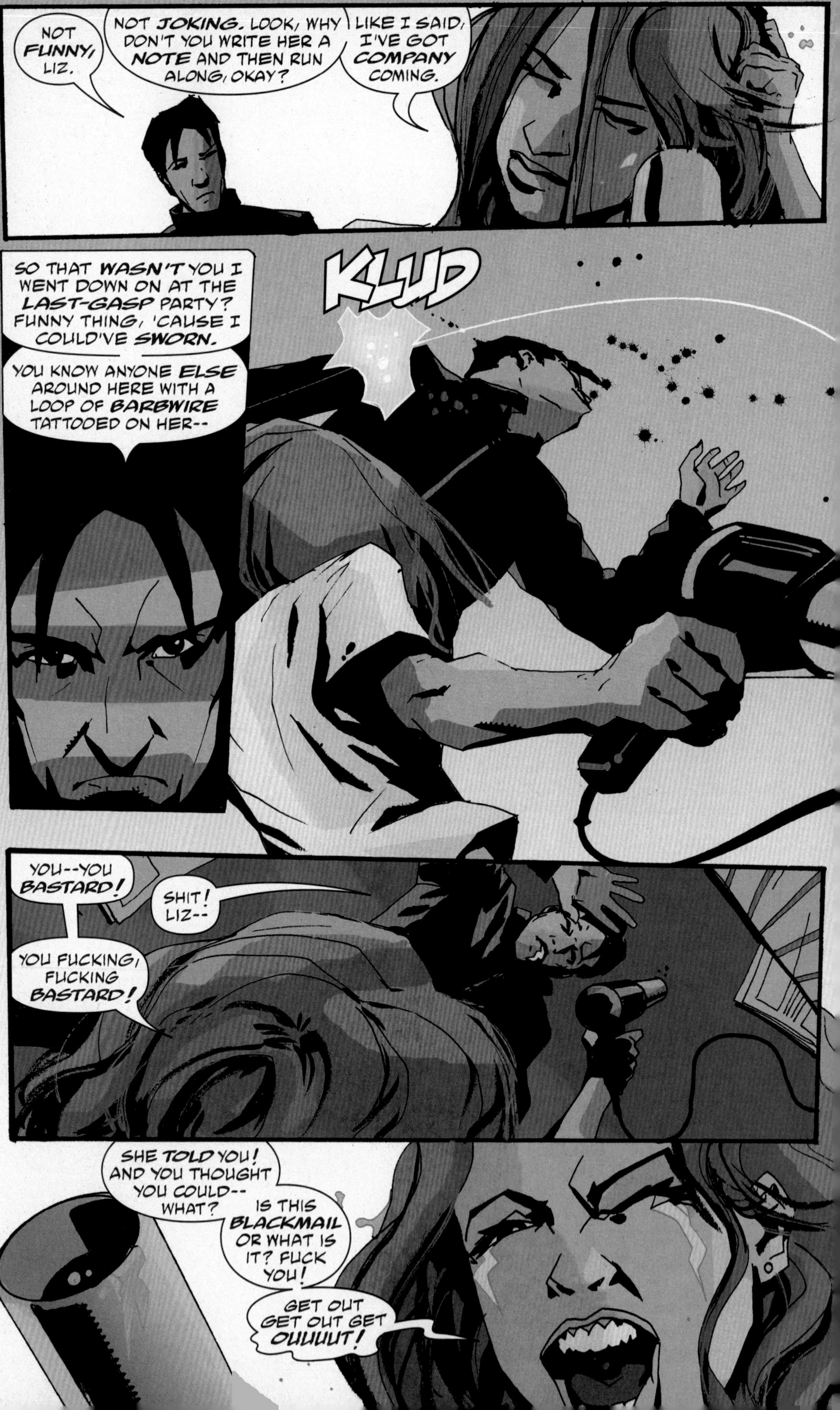
NOT FUNNY, LIZ.
NOT JOKING. LOOK, WHY DON'T YOU WRITE HER A NOTE AND THEN RUN ALONG, OKAY?
LIKE I SAID, I'VE GOT COMPANY COMING.
SO THAT WASN'T YOU I WENT DOWN ON AT THE LAST-GASP PARTY? FUNNY THING, 'CAUSE I COULD'VE SWORN.
YOU KNOW ANYONE ELSE AROUND HERE WITH A LOOP OF BARBWIRE TATTOOED ON HER--
KLUD
YOU--YOU BASTARD!
SHIT! LIZ--
YOU FUCKING, FUCKING BASTARD!
SHE TOLD YOU! AND YOU THOUGHT YOU COULD-- WHAT?
IS THIS BLACKMAIL OR WHAT IS IT? FUCK YOU!
GET OUT GET OUT GET OUUUUT!

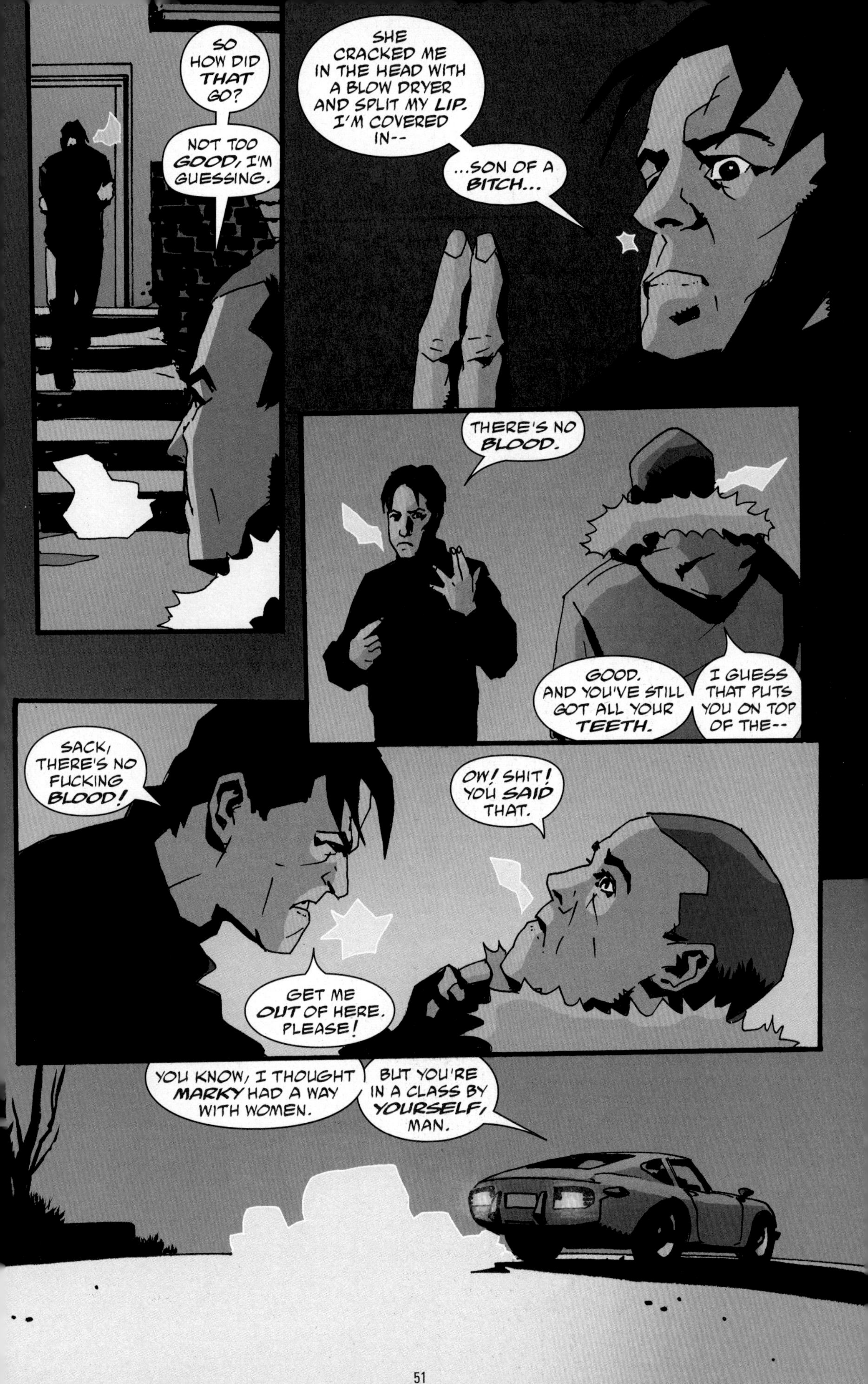
SO HOW DID THAT GO?
NOT TOO GOOD, I'M GUESSING.
SHE CRACKED ME IN THE HEAD WITH A BLOW DRYER AND SPLIT MY LIP. I'M COVERED IN--
...SON OF A BITCH...
THERE'S NO BLOOD.
GOOD. AND YOU'VE STILL GOT ALL YOUR TEETH.
I GUESS THAT PUTS YOU ON TOP OF THE--
SACK, THERE'S NO FUCKING BLOOD!
OW! SHIT! YOU SAID THAT.
GET ME OUT OF HERE. PLEASE!
YOU KNOW, I THOUGHT MARKY HAD A WAY WITH WOMEN.
BUT YOU'RE IN A CLASS BY YOURSELF, MAN.

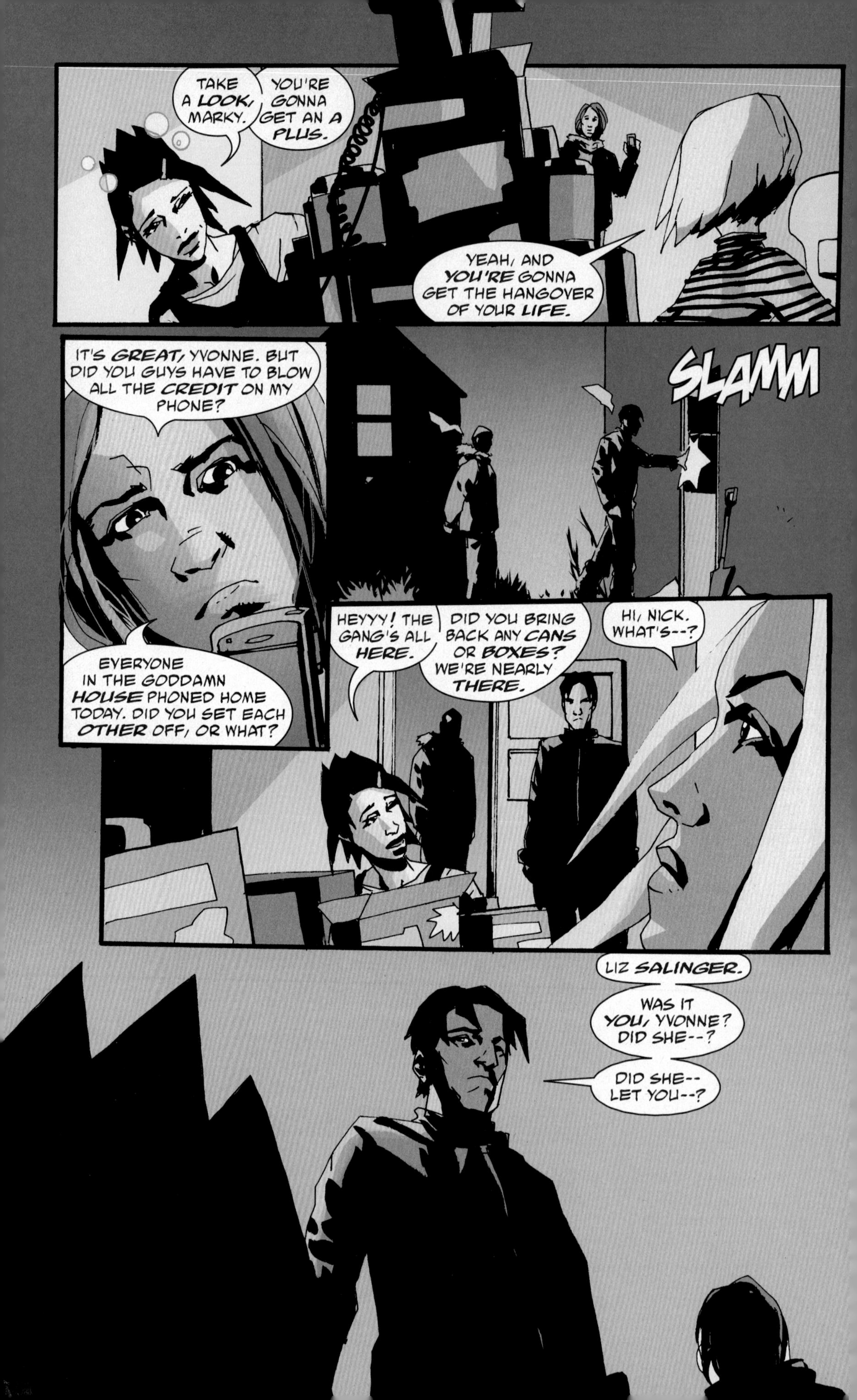
TAKE A LOOK, MARKY.
YOU'RE GONNA GET AN A PLUS.
YEAH, AND YOU'RE GONNA GET THE HANGOVER OF YOUR LIFE.
IT'S GREAT, YVONNE. BUT DID YOU GUYS HAVE TO BLOW ALL THE CREDIT ON MY PHONE?
SLAMM
EVERYONE IN THE GODDAMN HOUSE PHONED HOME TODAY. DID YOU SET EACH OTHER OFF, OR WHAT?
HEYYY! THE GANG'S ALL HERE.
DID YOU BRING BACK ANY CANS OR BOXES? WE'RE NEARLY THERE.
HI, NICK. WHAT'S--?
LIZ SALINGER.
WAS IT YOU, YVONNE? DID SHE--?
DID SHE-- LET YOU--?

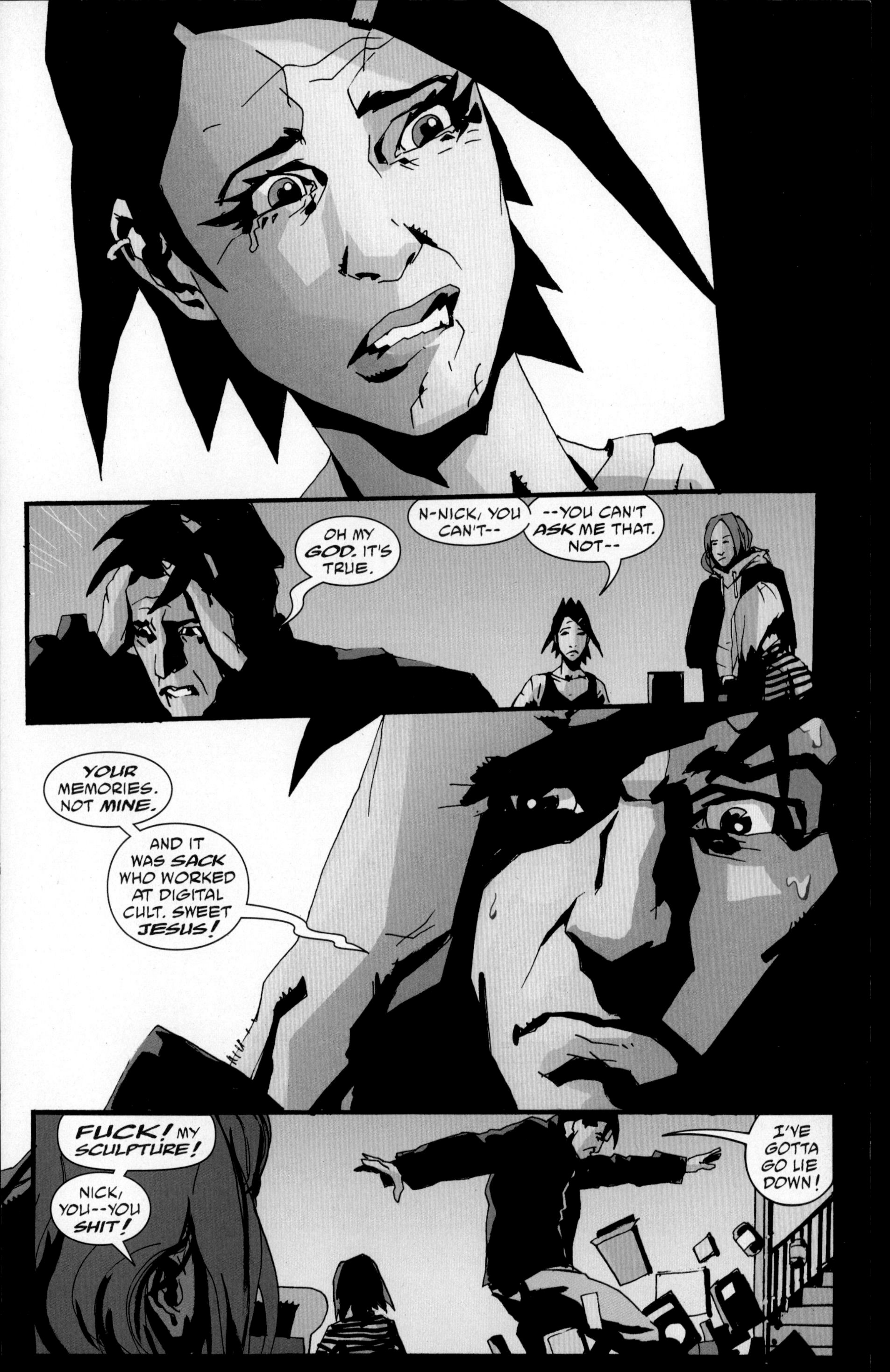
OH MY GOD. IT'S TRUE.
N-NICK, YOU CAN'T--
--YOU CAN'T ASK ME THAT. NOT--
YOUR MEMORIES. NOT MINE.
AND IT WAS SACK WHO WORKED AT DIGITAL CULT. SWEET JESUS!
FUCK! MY SCULPTURE!
NICK, YOU--YOU SHIT!
I'VE GOTTA GO LIE DOWN!

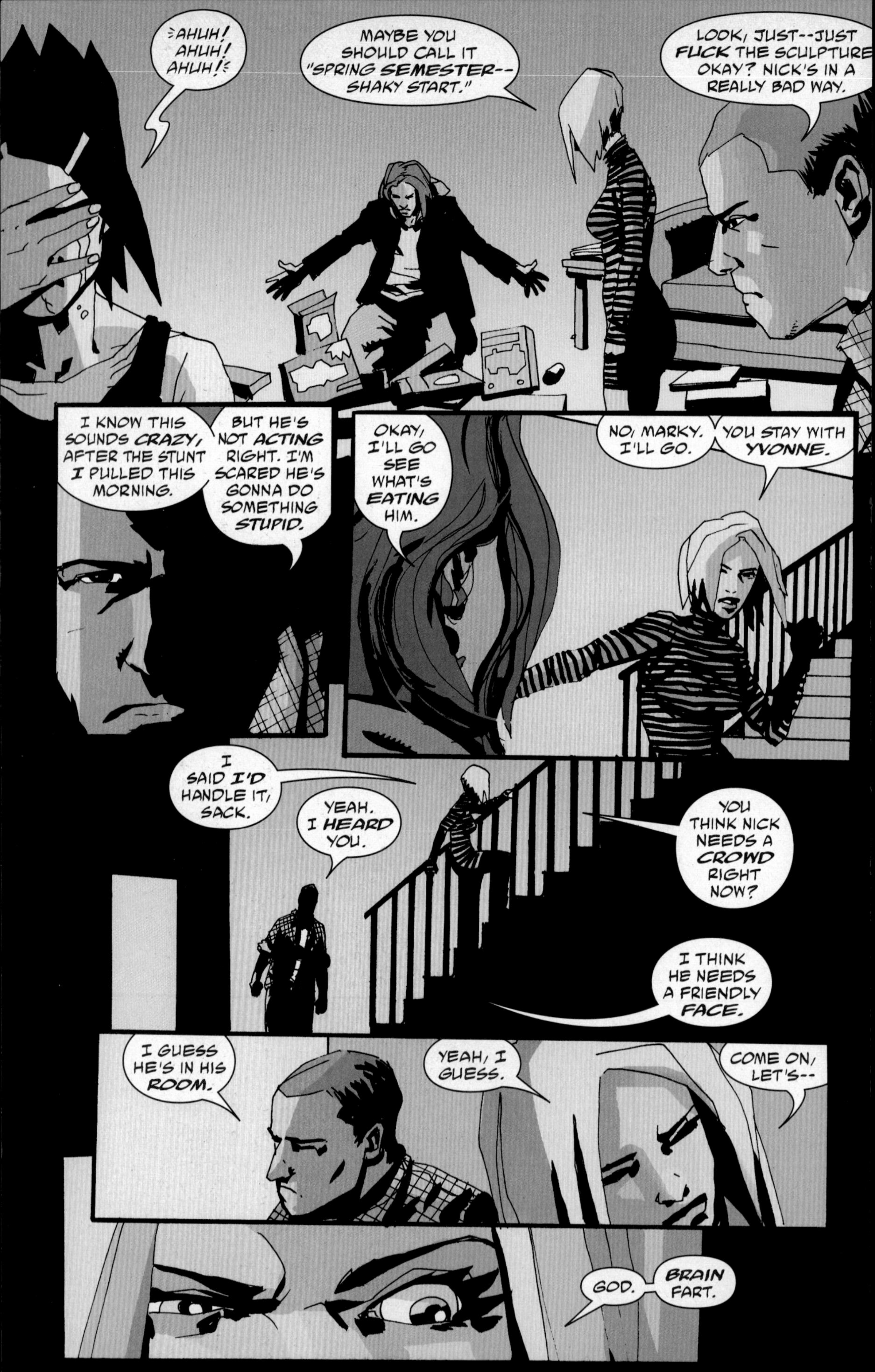
AHUH! AHUH! AHUH!
MAYBE YOU SHOULD CALL IT "SPRING SEMESTER--SHAKY START."
LOOK, JUST--JUST FUCK THE SCULPTURE OKAY? NICK'S IN A REALLY BAD WAY.
I KNOW THIS SOUNDS CRAZY, AFTER THE STUNT I PULLED THIS MORNING.
BUT HE'S NOT ACTING RIGHT. I'M SCARED HE'S GONNA DO SOMETHING STUPID.
OKAY, I'LL GO SEE WHAT'S EATING HIM.
NO, MARKY. I'LL GO.
YOU STAY WITH YVONNE.
I SAID I'D HANDLE IT, SACK.
YEAH. I HEARD YOU.
YOU THINK NICK NEEDS A CROWD RIGHT NOW?
I THINK HE NEEDS A FRIENDLY FACE.
I GUESS HE'S IN HIS ROOM.
YEAH, I GUESS.
COME ON, LET'S--
GOD.
BRAIN FART.

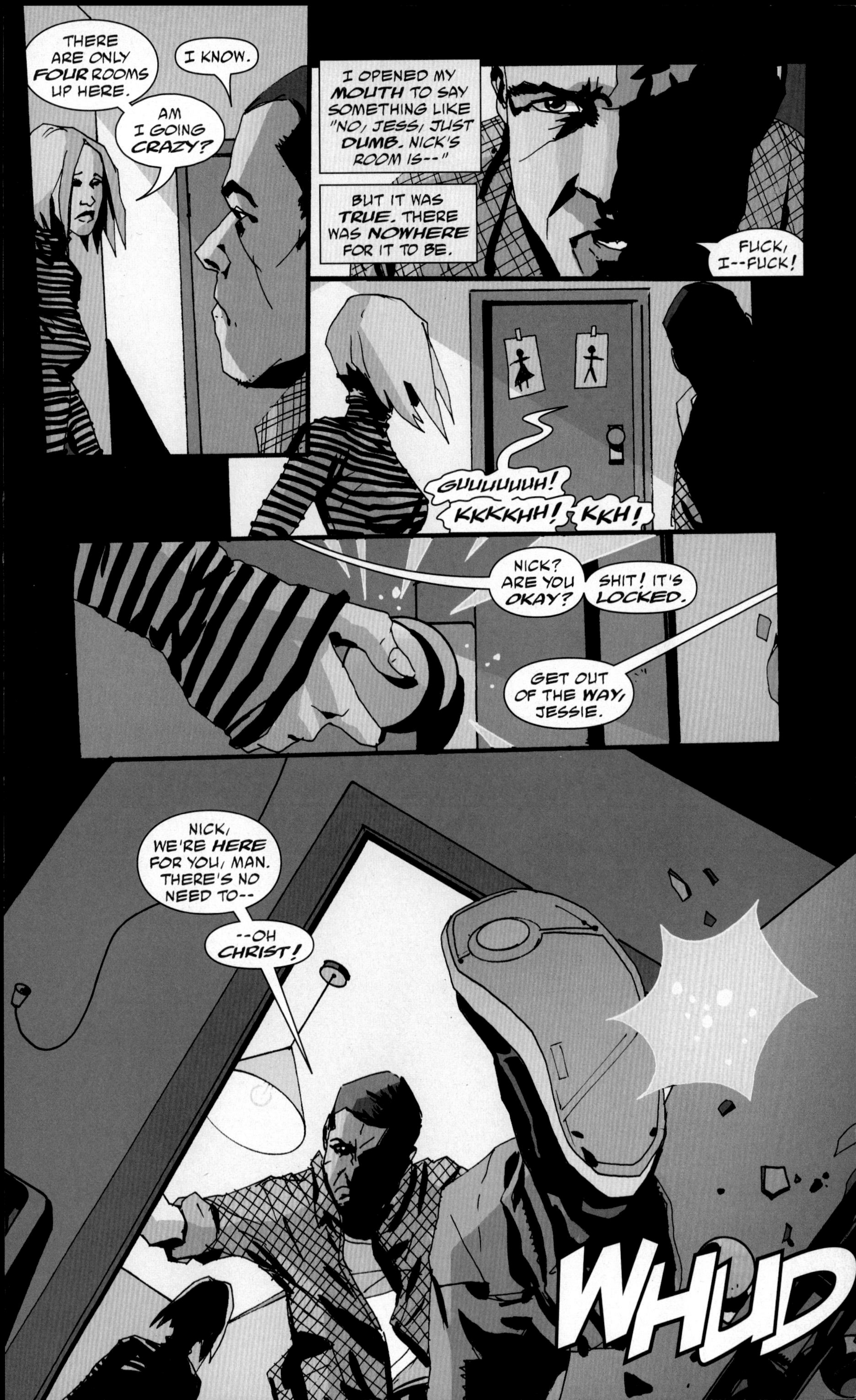
THERE ARE ONLY FOUR ROOMS UP HERE.
I KNOW.
AM I GOING CRAZY?
I OPENED MY MOUTH TO SAY SOMETHING LIKE "NO, JESS, JUST DUMB. NICK'S ROOM IS--"
BUT IT WAS TRUE. THERE WAS NOWHERE FOR IT TO BE.
FUCK, I--FUCK!
GUUUUUUH! KKKKHH! KKH!
NICK? ARE YOU OKAY?
SHIT! IT'S LOCKED.
GET OUT OF THE WAY, JESSIE.
NICK, WE'RE HERE FOR YOU, MAN. THERE'S NO NEED TO--
--OH CHRIST!
WHUD

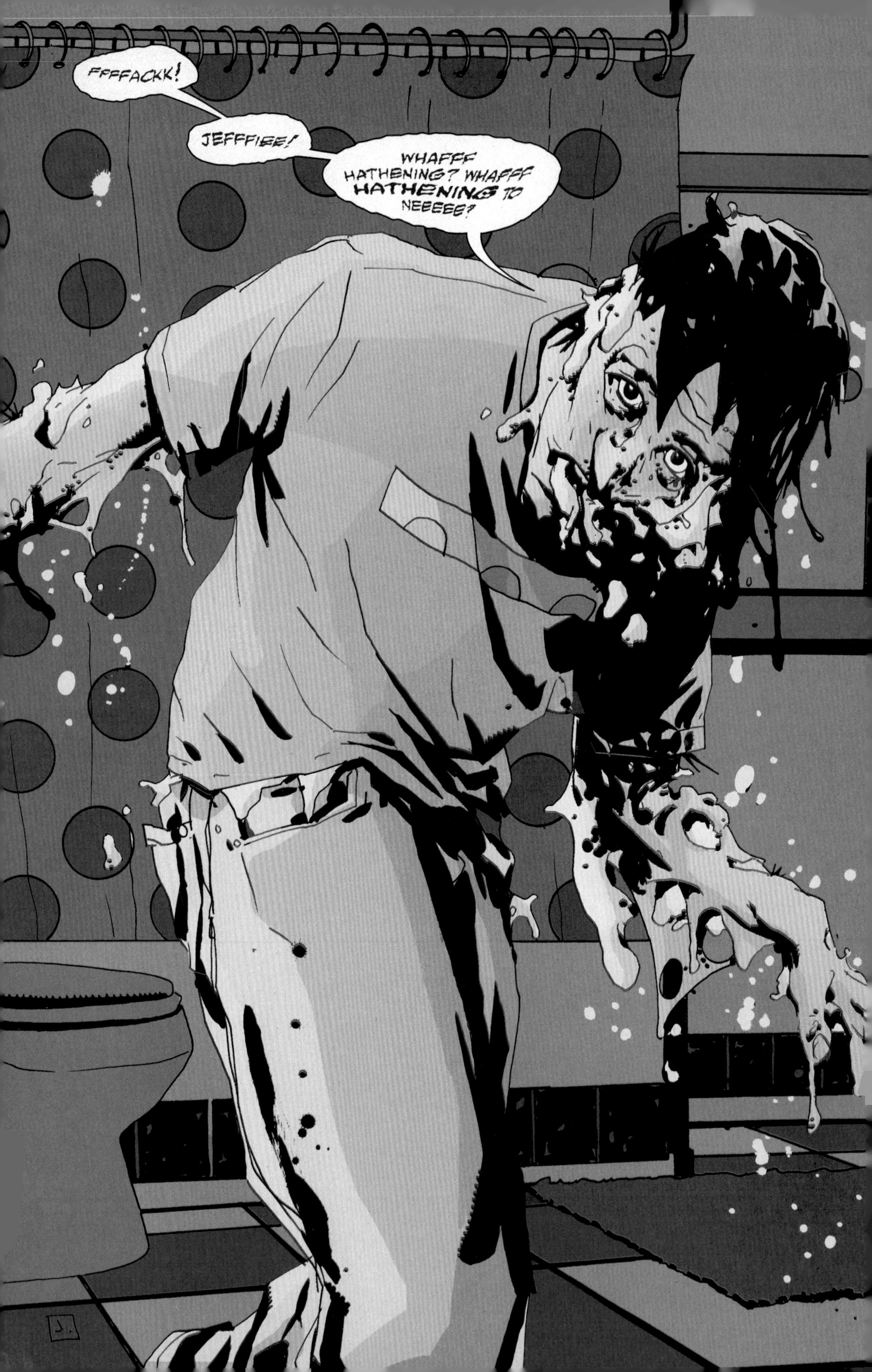
FFFFACKK!
JEFFFIEE!
WHAFFF HATHENING? WHAFFF HATHENING TO NEEEEEE?

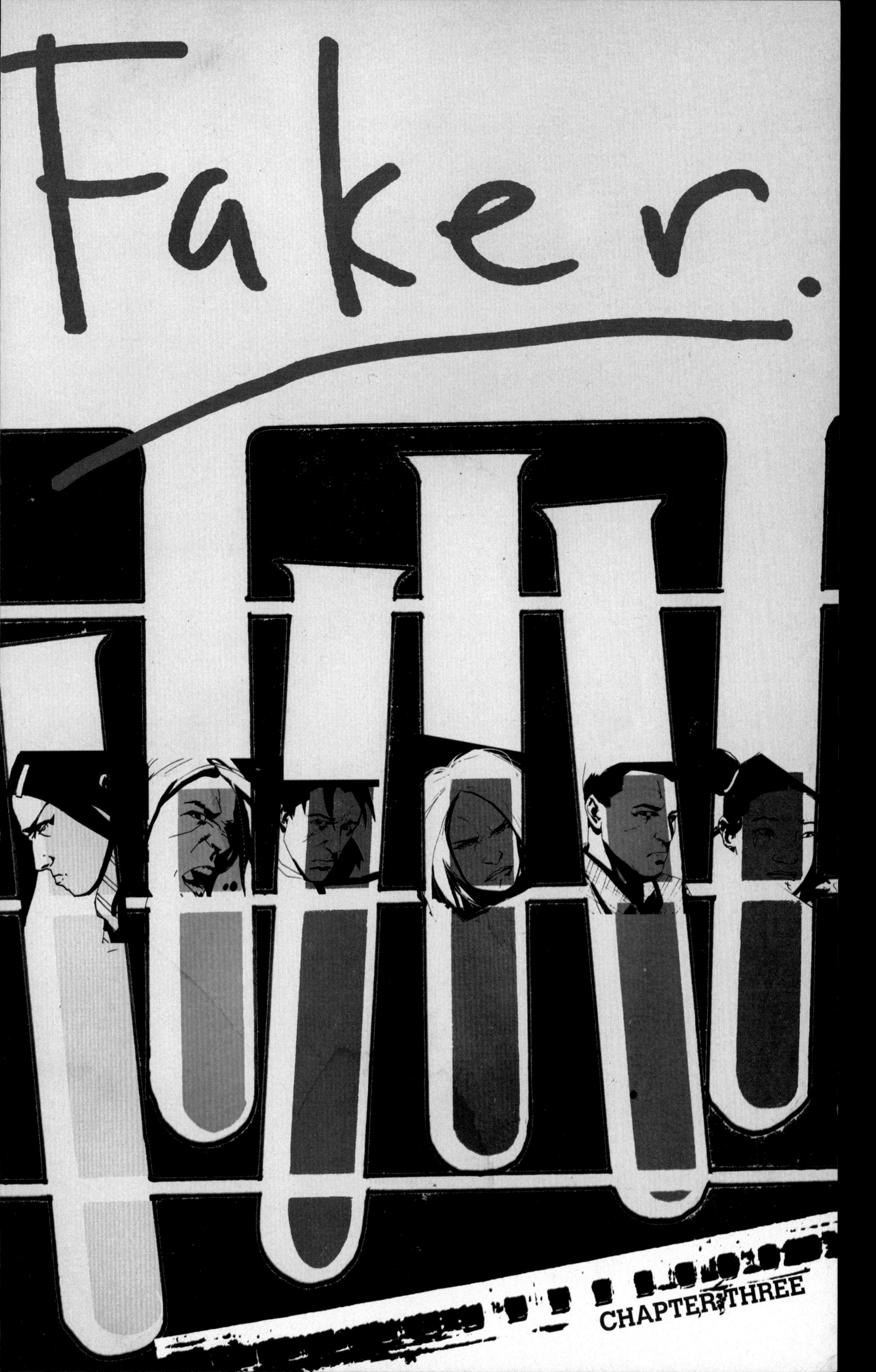
Faker.
CHAPTER THREE

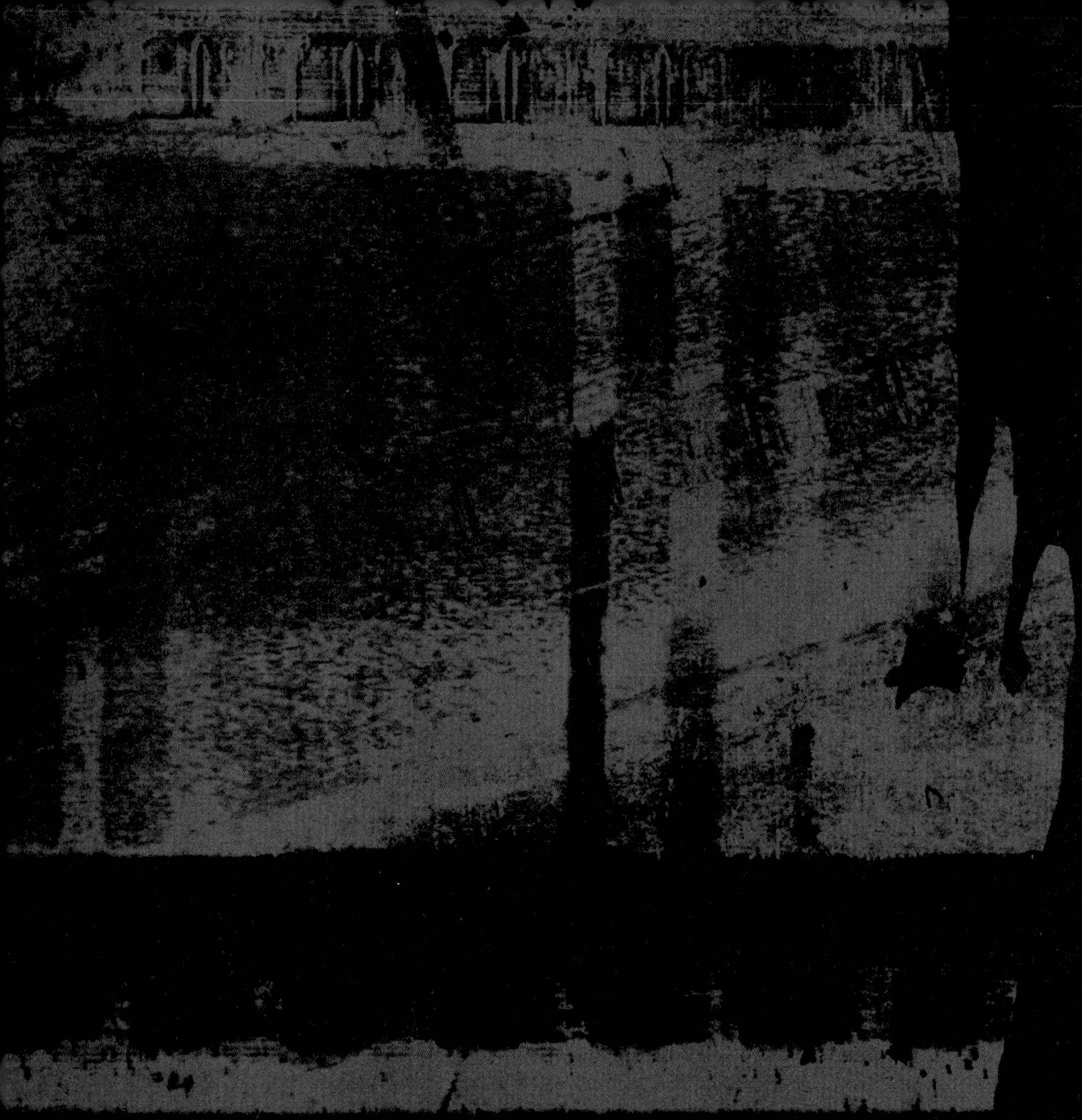

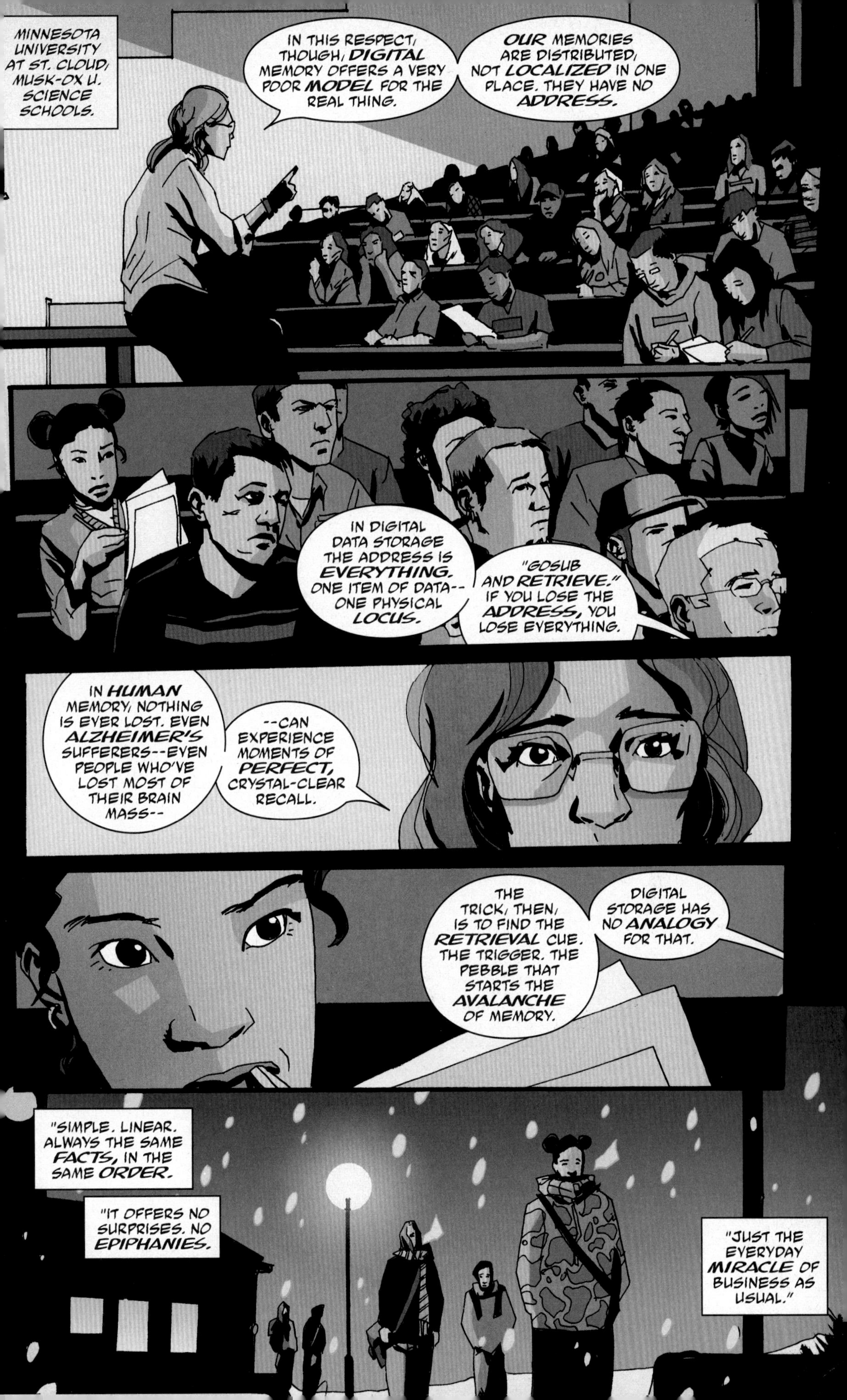
MINNESOTA UNIVERSITY AT ST. CLOUD, MUSK-OX U. SCIENCE SCHOOLS.
IN THIS RESPECT, THOUGH, DIGITAL MEMORY OFFERS A VERY POOR MODEL FOR THE REAL THING.
OUR MEMORIES ARE DISTRIBUTED, NOT LOCALIZED IN ONE PLACE. THEY HAVE NO ADDRESS.
IN DIGITAL DATA STORAGE THE ADDRESS IS EVERYTHING. ONE ITEM OF DATA-- ONE PHYSICAL LOCUS.
"GOSUB AND RETRIEVE." IF YOU LOSE THE ADDRESS, YOU LOSE EVERYTHING.
IN HUMAN MEMORY, NOTHING IS EVER LOST. EVEN ALZHEIMER'S SUFFERERS--EVEN PEOPLE WHO'VE LOST MOST OF THEIR BRAIN MASS--
--CAN EXPERIENCE MOMENTS OF PERFECT, CRYSTAL-CLEAR RECALL.
THE TRICK, THEN, IS TO FIND THE RETRIEVAL CUE. THE TRIGGER. THE PEBBLE THAT STARTS THE AVALANCHE OF MEMORY.
DIGITAL STORAGE HAS NO ANALOGY FOR THAT.
"SIMPLE. LINEAR. ALWAYS THE SAME FACTS, IN THE SAME ORDER.
"IT OFFERS NO SURPRISES. NO EPIPHANIES.
"JUST THE EVERYDAY MIRACLE OF BUSINESS AS USUAL."

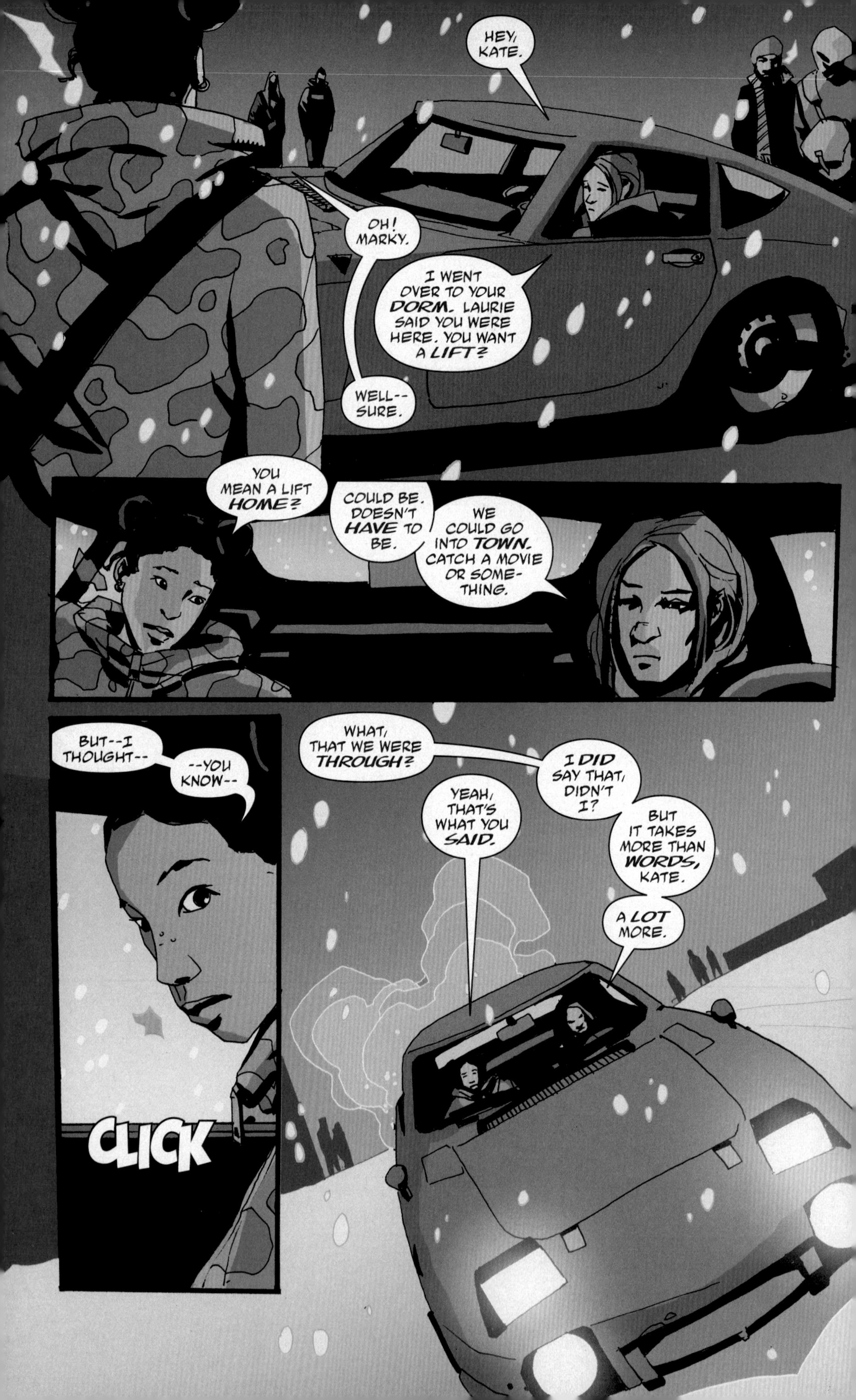
HEY, KATE.
OH! MARKY.
I WENT OVER TO YOUR DORM. LAURIE SAID YOU WERE HERE. YOU WANT A LIFT?
WELL-- SURE.
YOU MEAN A LIFT HOME?
COULD BE. DOESN'T HAVE TO BE.
WE COULD GO INTO TOWN. CATCH A MOVIE OR SOME-THING.
BUT--I THOUGHT--
--YOU KNOW--
CLICK
WHAT, THAT WE WERE THROUGH?
I DID SAY THAT, DIDN'T I?
YEAH, THAT'S WHAT YOU SAID.
BUT IT TAKES MORE THAN WORDS, KATE.
A LOT MORE.

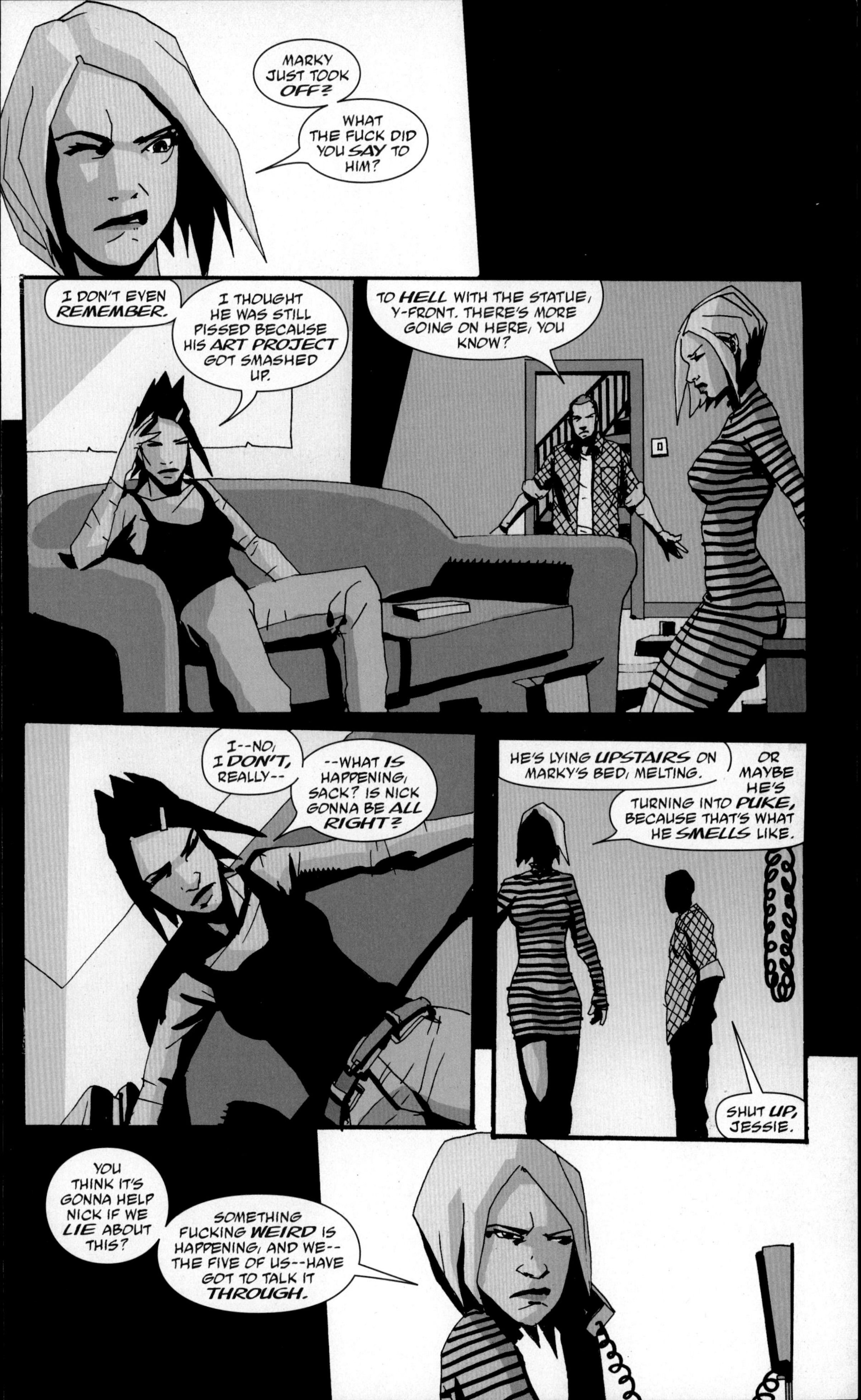
MARKY JUST TOOK OFF?
WHAT THE FUCK DID YOU SAY TO HIM?
I DON'T EVEN REMEMBER.
I THOUGHT HE WAS STILL PISSED BECAUSE HIS ART PROJECT GOT SMASHED UP.
TO HELL WITH THE STATUE, Y-FRONT. THERE'S MORE GOING ON HERE, YOU KNOW?
I--NO, I DON'T, REALLY--
--WHAT IS HAPPENING, SACK? IS NICK GONNA BE ALL RIGHT?
HE'S LYING UPSTAIRS ON MARKY'S BED, MELTING.
OR MAYBE HE'S TURNING INTO PUKE, BECAUSE THAT'S WHAT HE SMELLS LIKE.
SHUT UP, JESSIE.
YOU THINK IT'S GONNA HELP NICK IF WE LIE ABOUT THIS?
SOMETHING FUCKING WEIRD IS HAPPENING, AND WE--THE FIVE OF US--HAVE GOT TO TALK IT THROUGH.

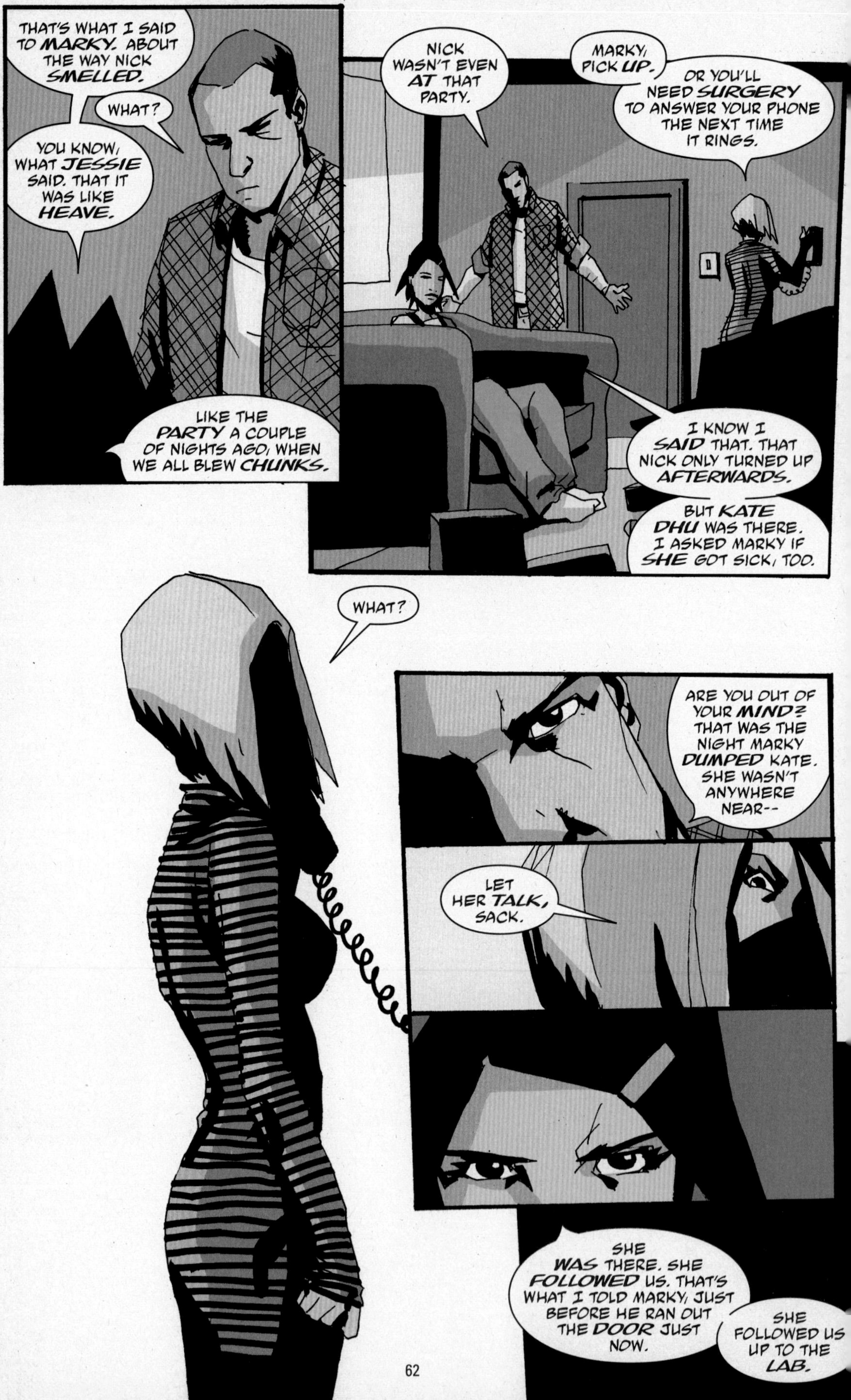
THAT'S WHAT I SAID TO MARKY. ABOUT THE WAY NICK SMELLED.
WHAT?
YOU KNOW, WHAT JESSIE SAID. THAT IT WAS LIKE HEAVE.
LIKE THE PARTY A COUPLE OF NIGHTS AGO, WHEN WE ALL BLEW CHUNKS.
NICK WASN'T EVEN AT THAT PARTY.
MARKY, PICK UP.
OR YOU'LL NEED SURGERY TO ANSWER YOUR PHONE THE NEXT TIME IT RINGS.
I KNOW I SAID THAT. THAT NICK ONLY TURNED UP AFTERWARDS.
BUT KATE DHU WAS THERE. I ASKED MARKY IF SHE GOT SICK, TOO.
WHAT?
ARE YOU OUT OF YOUR MIND? THAT WAS THE NIGHT MARKY DUMPED KATE. SHE WASN'T ANYWHERE NEAR--
LET HER TALK, SACK.
SHE WAS THERE. SHE FOLLOWED US. THAT'S WHAT I TOLD MARKY, JUST BEFORE HE RAN OUT THE DOOR JUST NOW.
SHE FOLLOWED US UP TO THE LAB.

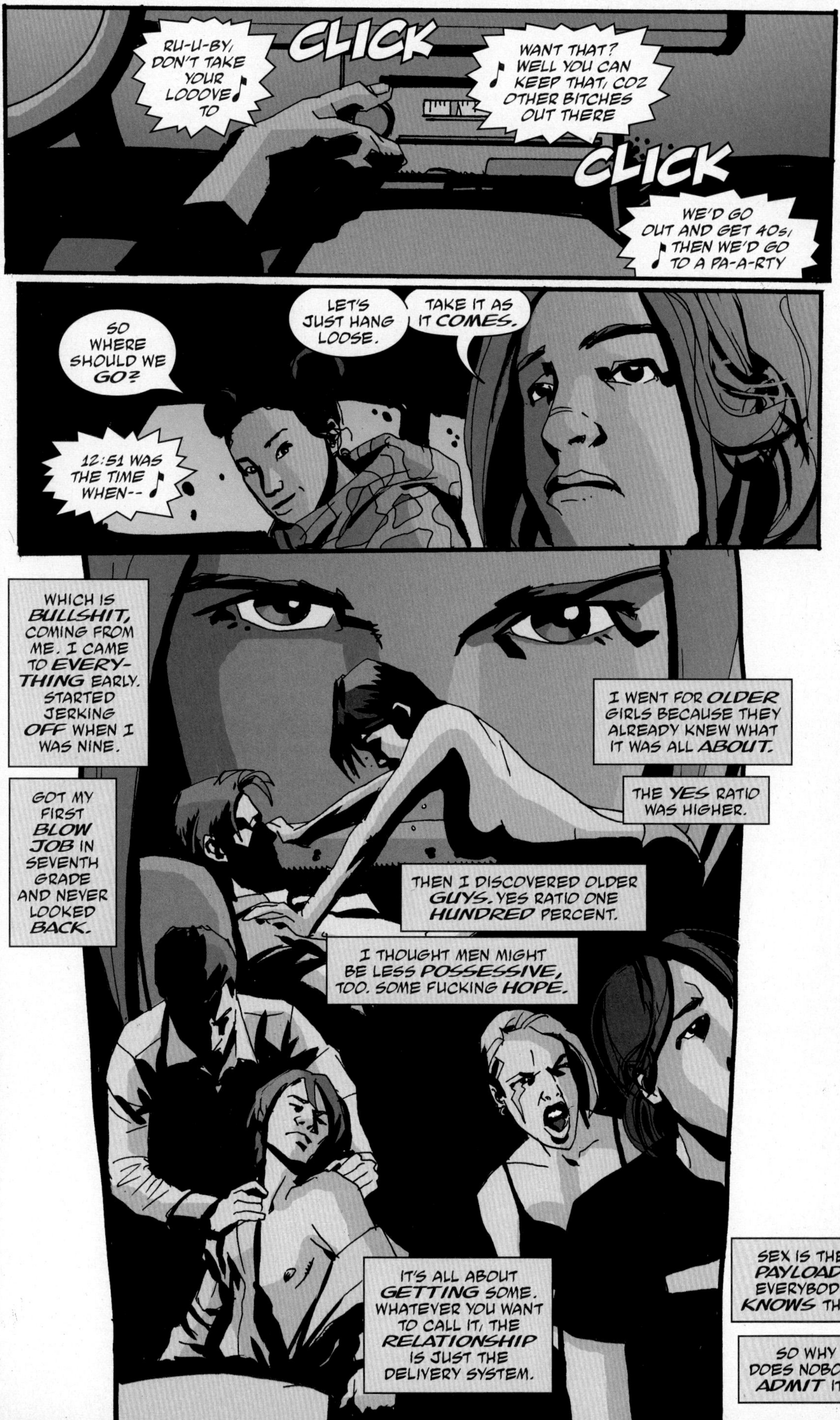
RU-U-BY, DON'T TAKE YOUR LOOOVE TO ♪
CLICK
♪ WANT THAT? WELL YOU CAN KEEP THAT, COZ OTHER BITCHES OUT THERE
CLICK
WE'D GO OUT AND GET 40s, ♪ THEN WE'D GO ♪ TO A PA-A-RTY
SO WHERE SHOULD WE GO?
LET'S JUST HANG LOOSE.
TAKE IT AS IT COMES.
12:51 WAS THE TIME WHEN-- ♪
WHICH IS BULLSHIT, COMING FROM ME. I CAME TO EVERYTHING EARLY. STARTED JERKING OFF WHEN I WAS NINE.
I WENT FOR OLDER GIRLS BECAUSE THEY ALREADY KNEW WHAT IT WAS ALL ABOUT.
GOT MY FIRST BLOW JOB IN SEVENTH GRADE AND NEVER LOOKED BACK.
THE YES RATIO WAS HIGHER.
THEN I DISCOVERED OLDER GUYS. YES RATIO ONE HUNDRED PERCENT.
I THOUGHT MEN MIGHT BE LESS POSSESSIVE, TOO. SOME FUCKING HOPE.
IT'S ALL ABOUT GETTING SOME. WHATEVER YOU WANT TO CALL IT, THE RELATIONSHIP IS JUST THE DELIVERY SYSTEM.
SEX IS THE PAYLOAD. EVERYBODY KNOWS THAT.
SO WHY DOES NOBODY ADMIT IT?

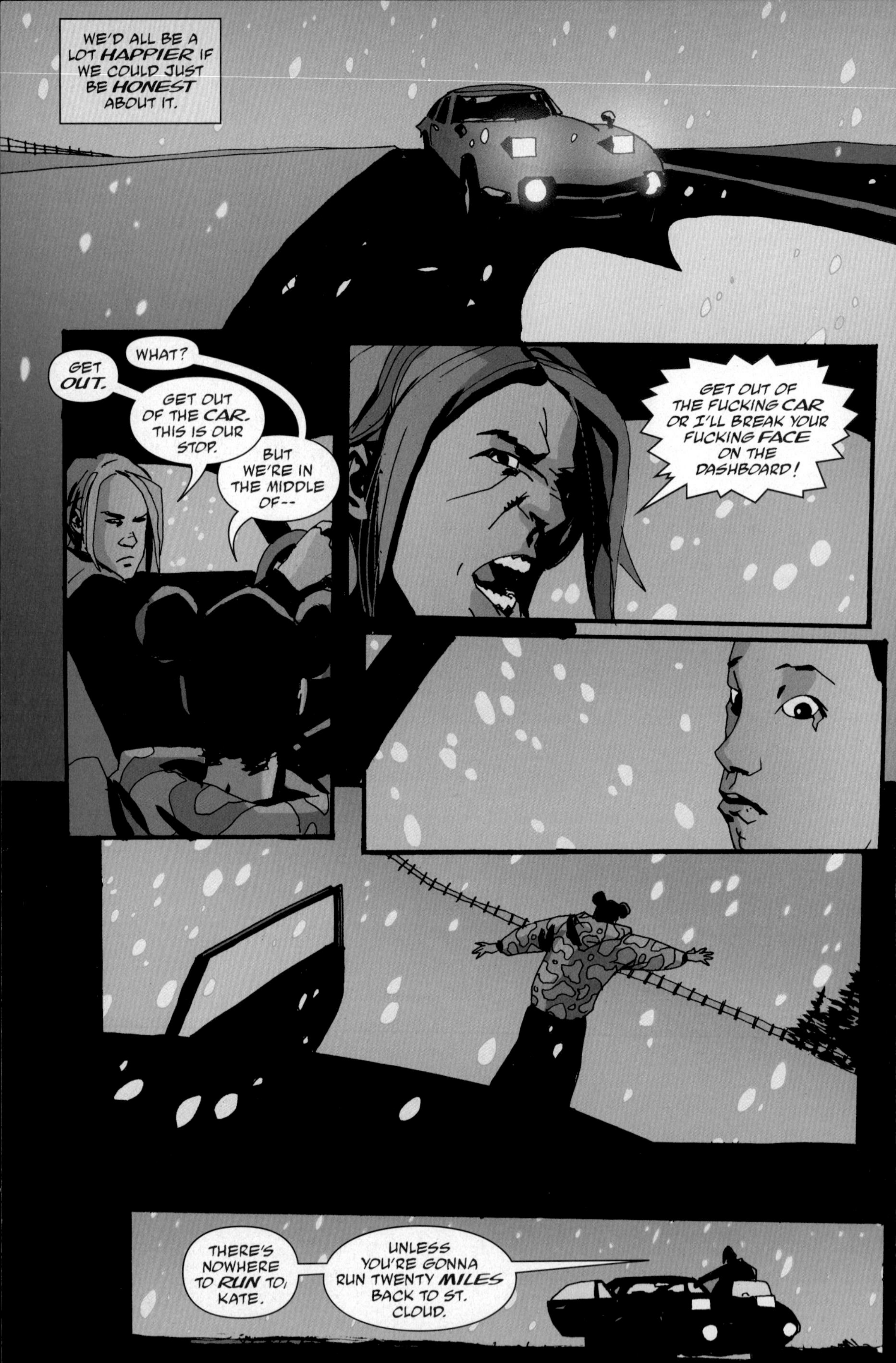
WE'D ALL BE A LOT HAPPIER IF WE COULD JUST BE HONEST ABOUT IT.
WHAT?
GET OUT.
GET OUT OF THE CAR. THIS IS OUR STOP.
BUT WE'RE IN THE MIDDLE OF--
GET OUT OF THE FUCKING CAR OR I'LL BREAK YOUR FUCKING FACE ON THE DASHBOARD!
THERE'S NOWHERE TO RUN TO, KATE.
UNLESS YOU'RE GONNA RUN TWENTY MILES BACK TO ST. CLOUD.

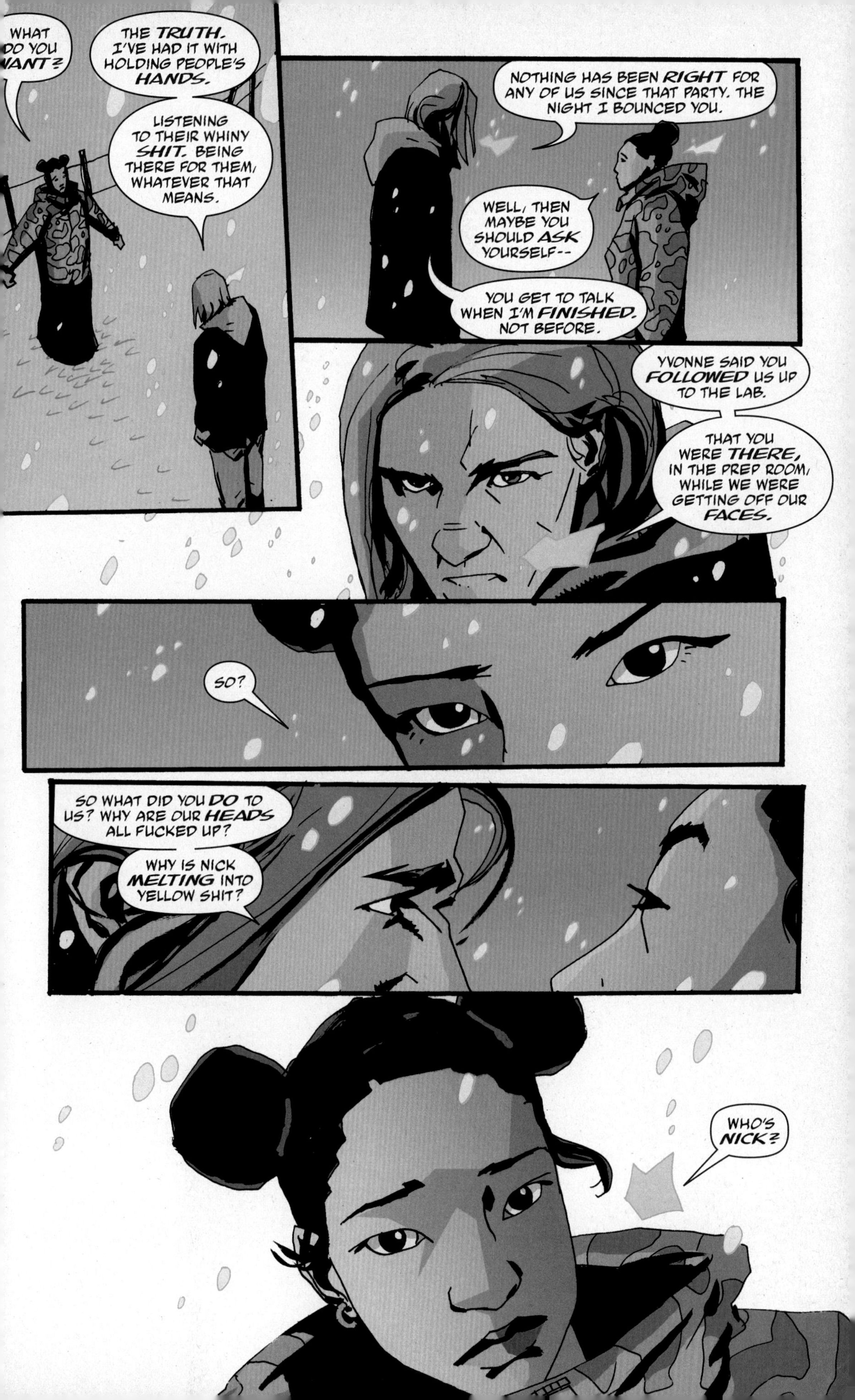
WHAT DO YOU WANT?
THE TRUTH. I'VE HAD IT WITH HOLDING PEOPLE'S HANDS.
LISTENING TO THEIR WHINY SHIT. BEING THERE FOR THEM, WHATEVER THAT MEANS.
NOTHING HAS BEEN RIGHT FOR ANY OF US SINCE THAT PARTY. THE NIGHT I BOUNCED YOU.
WELL, THEN MAYBE YOU SHOULD ASK YOURSELF--
YOU GET TO TALK WHEN I'M FINISHED. NOT BEFORE.
YVONNE SAID YOU FOLLOWED US UP TO THE LAB.
THAT YOU WERE THERE, IN THE PREP ROOM, WHILE WE WERE GETTING OFF OUR FACES.
SO?
SO WHAT DID YOU DO TO US? WHY ARE OUR HEADS ALL FUCKED UP?
WHY IS NICK MELTING INTO YELLOW SHIT?
WHO'S NICK?

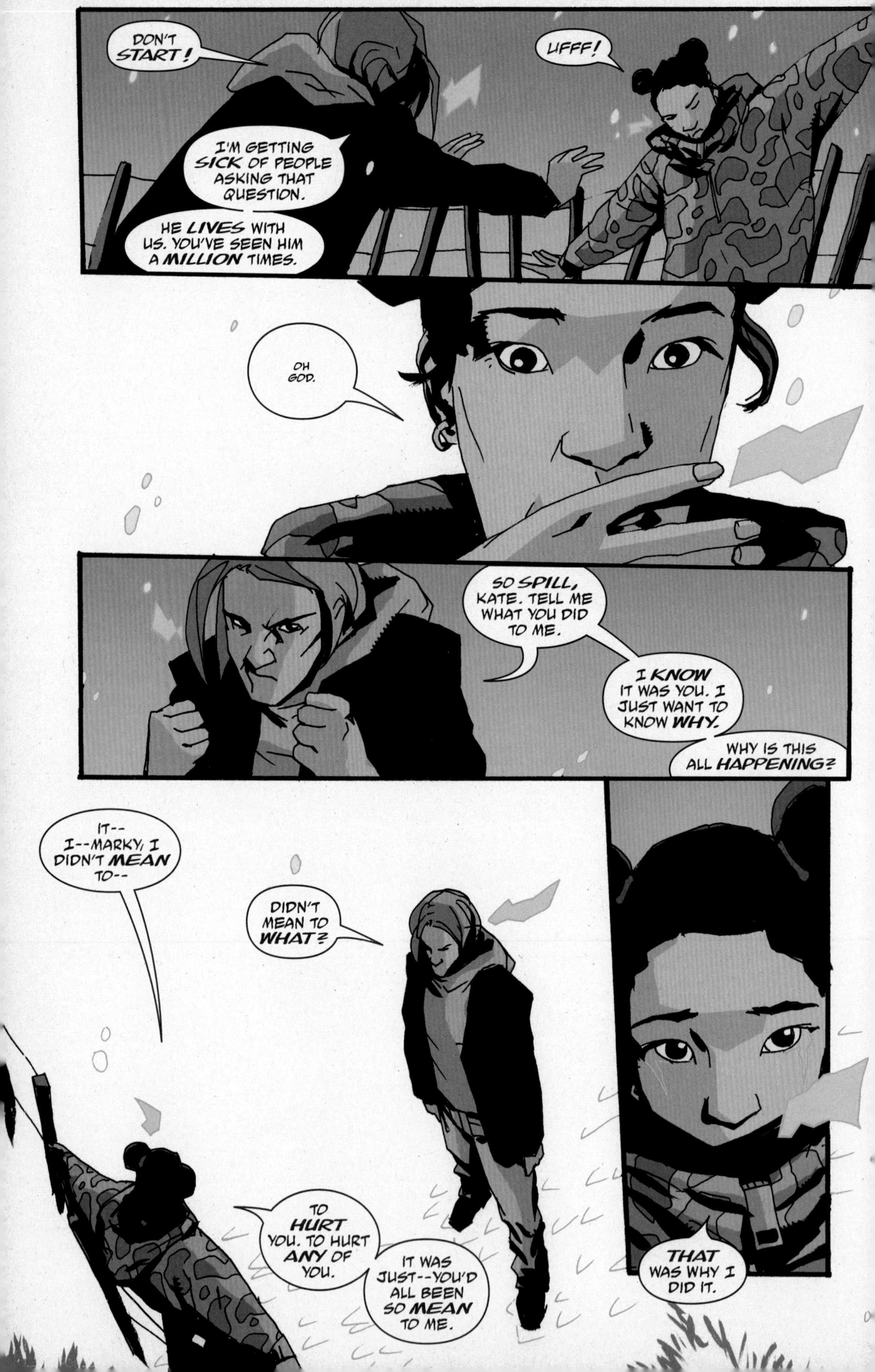
DON'T START!
UFFF!
I'M GETTING SICK OF PEOPLE ASKING THAT QUESTION.
HE LIVES WITH US. YOU'VE SEEN HIM A MILLION TIMES.
OH GOD.
SO SPILL, KATE. TELL ME WHAT YOU DID TO ME.
I KNOW IT WAS YOU. I JUST WANT TO KNOW WHY.
WHY IS THIS ALL HAPPENING?
IT-- I--MARKY, I DIDN'T MEAN TO--
DIDN'T MEAN TO WHAT?
TO HURT YOU. TO HURT ANY OF YOU.
IT WAS JUST--YOU'D ALL BEEN SO MEAN TO ME.
THAT WAS WHY I DID IT.

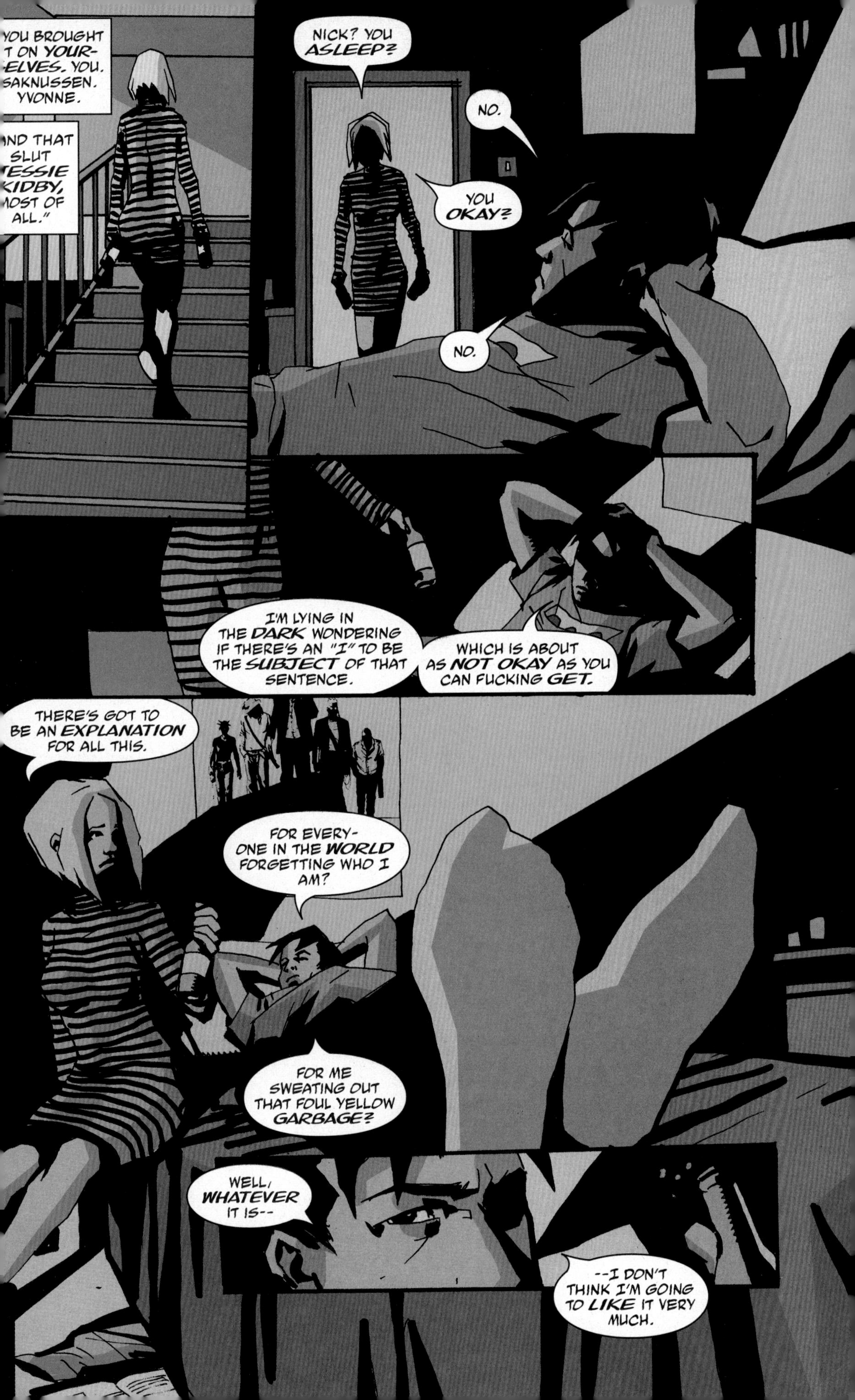
YOU BROUGHT
T ON YOUR-
ELVES. YOU.
SAKNUSSEN.
YVONNE.
ND THAT
SLUT
TESSIE
KIDBY,
MOST OF
ALL."
NICK? YOU ASLEEP?
NO.
YOU OKAY?
NO.
I'M LYING IN THE DARK WONDERING IF THERE'S AN "I" TO BE THE SUBJECT OF THAT SENTENCE.
WHICH IS ABOUT AS NOT OKAY AS YOU CAN FUCKING GET.
THERE'S GOT TO BE AN EXPLANATION FOR ALL THIS.
FOR EVERY-ONE IN THE WORLD FORGETTING WHO I AM?
FOR ME SWEATING OUT THAT FOUL YELLOW GARBAGE?
WELL, WHATEVER IT IS--
--I DON'T THINK I'M GOING TO LIKE IT VERY MUCH.

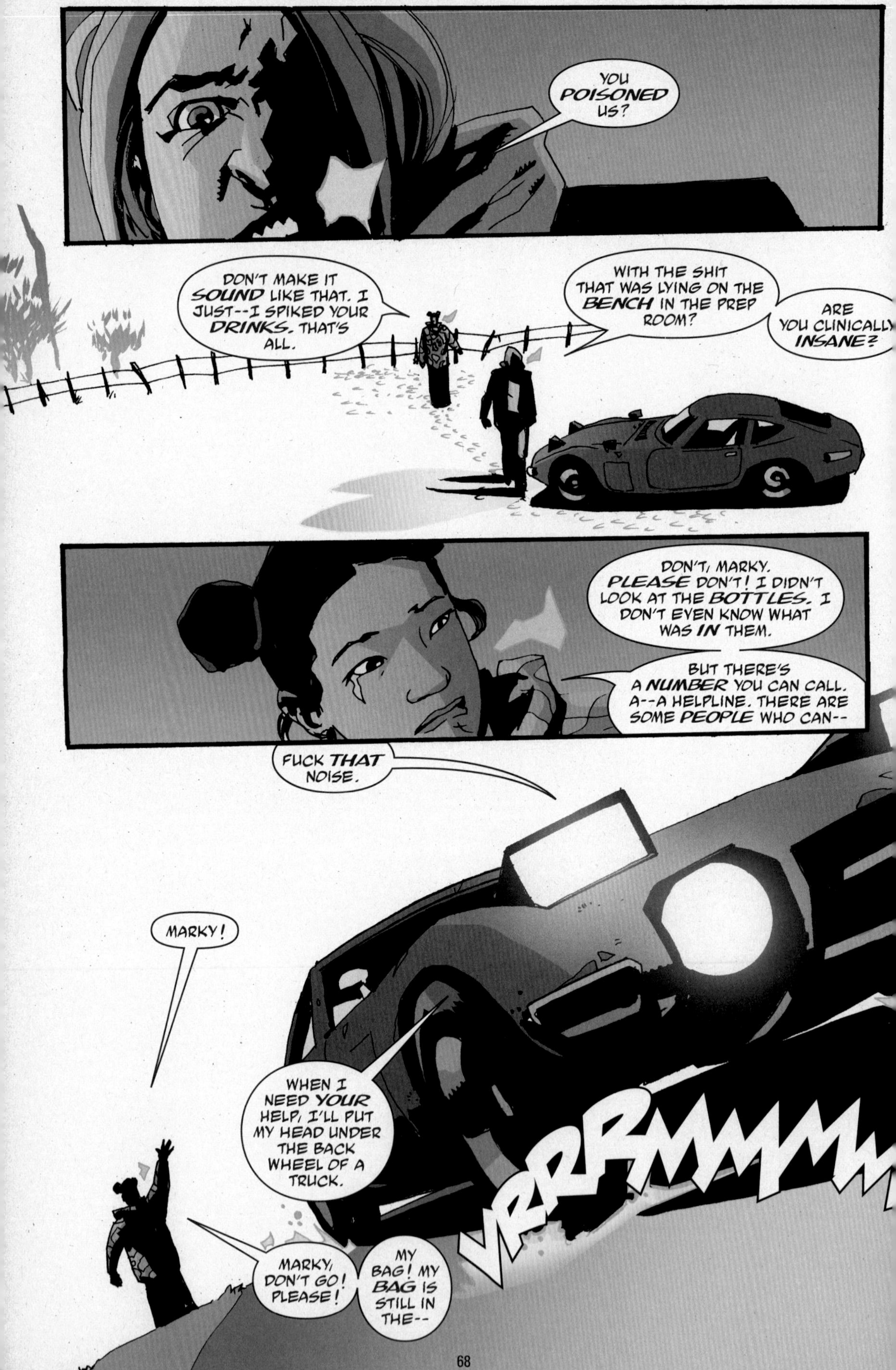
YOU POISONED US?
DON'T MAKE IT SOUND LIKE THAT. I JUST--I SPIKED YOUR DRINKS. THAT'S ALL.
WITH THE SHIT THAT WAS LYING ON THE BENCH IN THE PREP ROOM?
ARE YOU CLINICALLY INSANE?
DON'T, MARKY. PLEASE DON'T! I DIDN'T LOOK AT THE BOTTLES. I DON'T EVEN KNOW WHAT WAS IN THEM.
BUT THERE'S A NUMBER YOU CAN CALL. A--A HELPLINE. THERE ARE SOME PEOPLE WHO CAN--
FUCK THAT NOISE.
MARKY!
WHEN I NEED YOUR HELP, I'LL PUT MY HEAD UNDER THE BACK WHEEL OF A TRUCK.
MARKY, DON'T GO! PLEASE!
MY BAG! MY BAG IS STILL IN THE--
VRRRMMMM

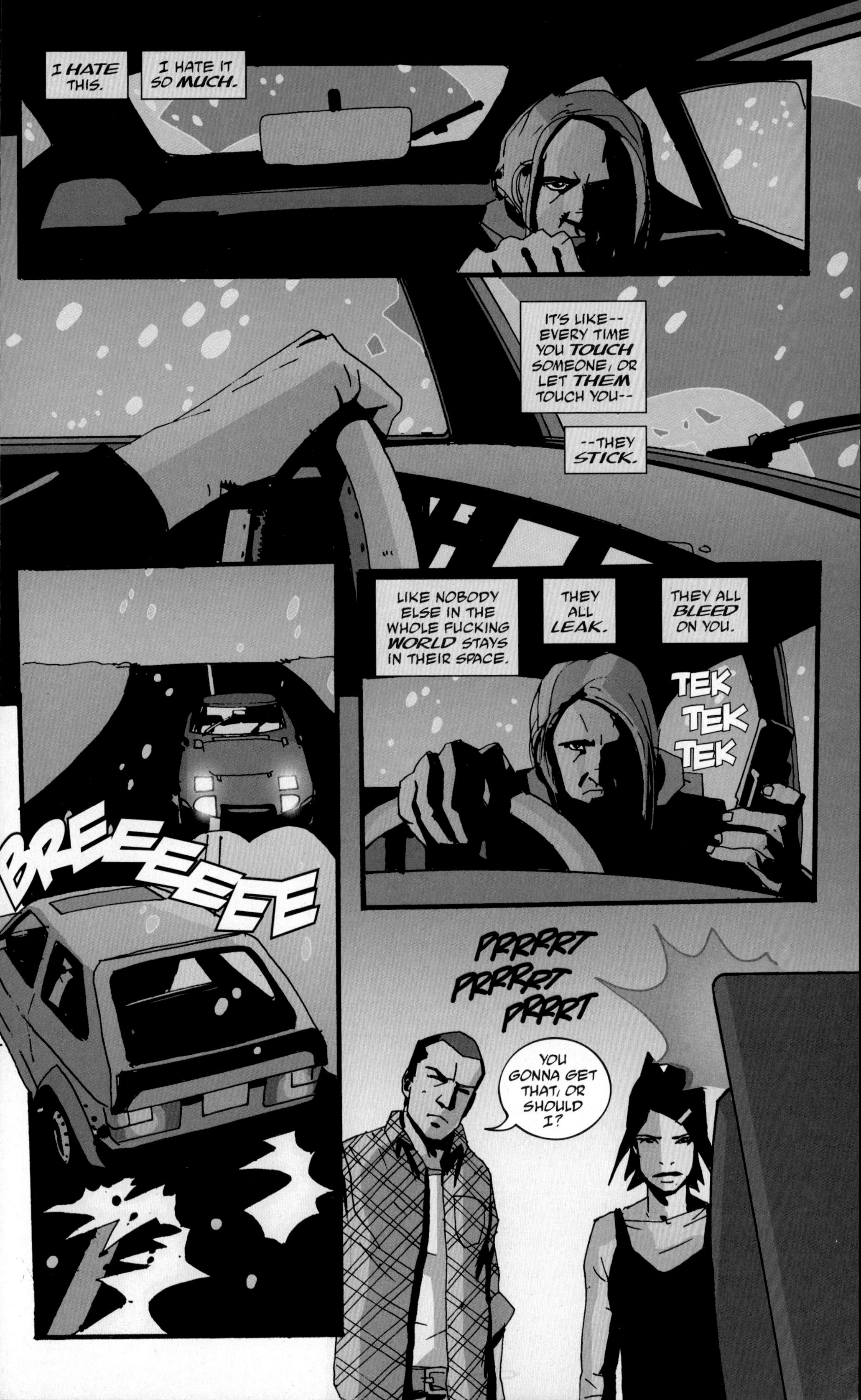

I HATE THIS.
I HATE IT SO MUCH.
IT'S LIKE-- EVERY TIME YOU TOUCH SOMEONE, OR LET THEM TOUCH YOU--
--THEY STICK.
LIKE NOBODY ELSE IN THE WHOLE FUCKING WORLD STAYS IN THEIR SPACE.
THEY ALL LEAK.
THEY ALL BLEED ON YOU.
TEK TEK TEK
BREEEEEE
PRRRRT PRRRRT PRRRT
YOU GONNA GET THAT, OR SHOULD I?

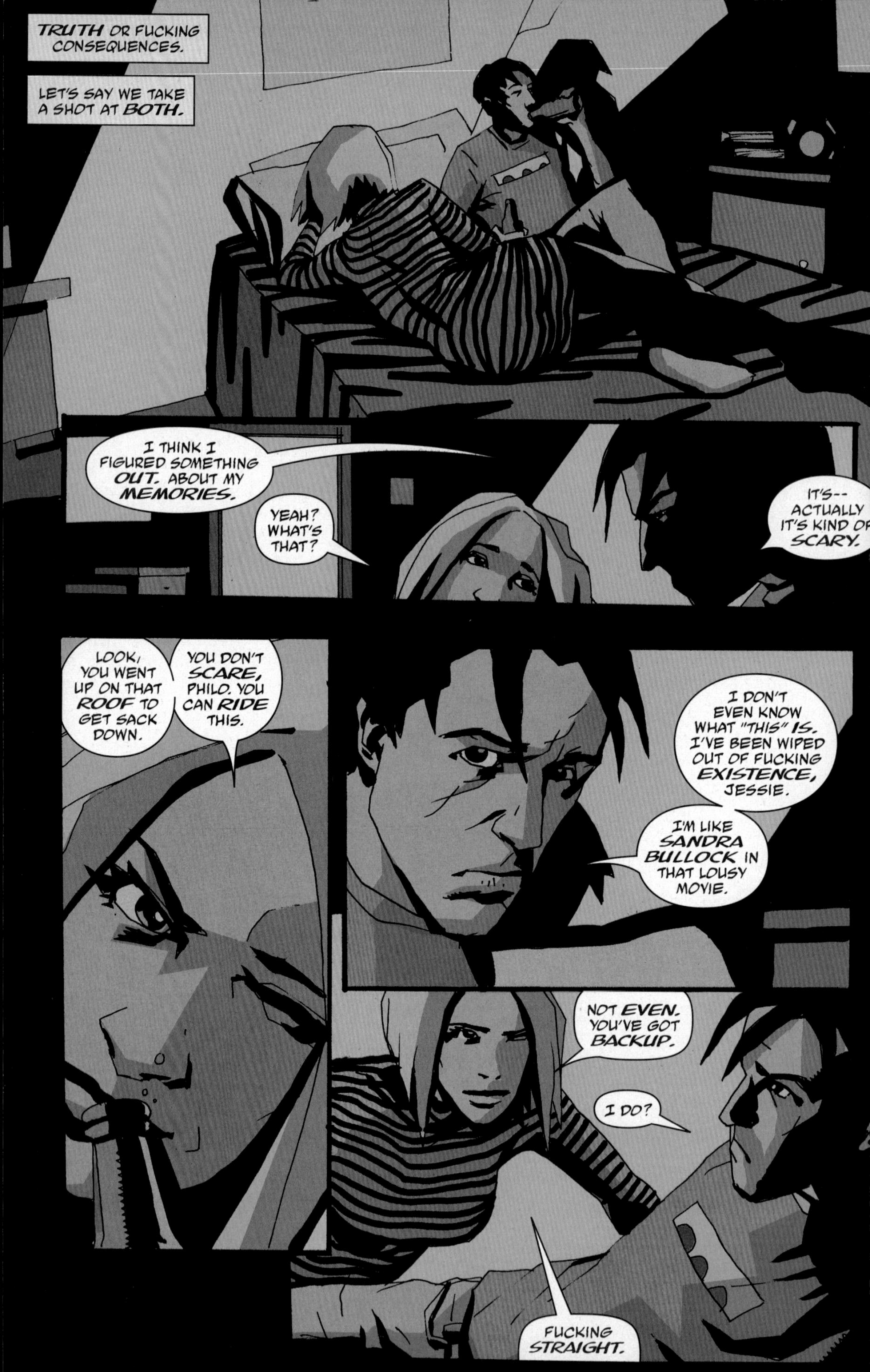
TRUTH OR FUCKING CONSEQUENCES.
LET'S SAY WE TAKE A SHOT AT BOTH.
I THINK I FIGURED SOMETHING OUT. ABOUT MY MEMORIES.
YEAH? WHAT'S THAT?
IT'S-- ACTUALLY IT'S KIND OF SCARY.
LOOK, YOU WENT UP ON THAT ROOF TO GET SACK DOWN.
YOU DON'T SCARE, PHILO. YOU CAN RIDE THIS.
I DON'T EVEN KNOW WHAT "THIS" IS. I'VE BEEN WIPED OUT OF FUCKING EXISTENCE, JESSIE.
I'M LIKE SANDRA BULLOCK IN THAT LOUSY MOVIE.
NOT EVEN. YOU'VE GOT BACKUP.
I DO?
FUCKING STRAIGHT.

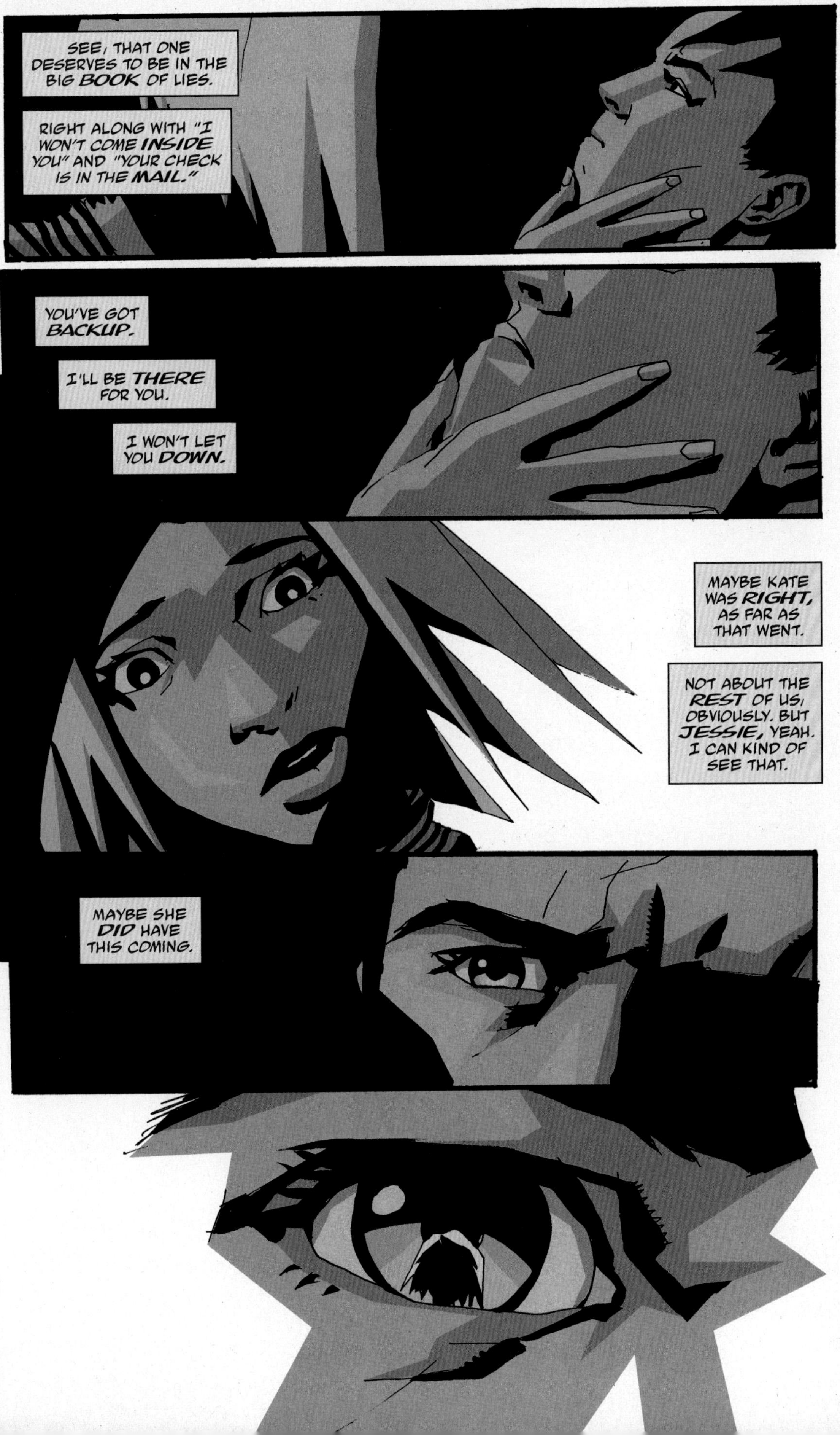
SEE, THAT ONE DESERVES TO BE IN THE BIG BOOK OF LIES.
RIGHT ALONG WITH "I WON'T COME INSIDE YOU" AND "YOUR CHECK IS IN THE MAIL."
YOU'VE GOT BACKUP.
I'LL BE THERE FOR YOU.
I WON'T LET YOU DOWN.
MAYBE KATE WAS RIGHT, AS FAR AS THAT WENT.
NOT ABOUT THE REST OF US, OBVIOUSLY. BUT JESSIE, YEAH. I CAN KIND OF SEE THAT.
MAYBE SHE DID HAVE THIS COMING.

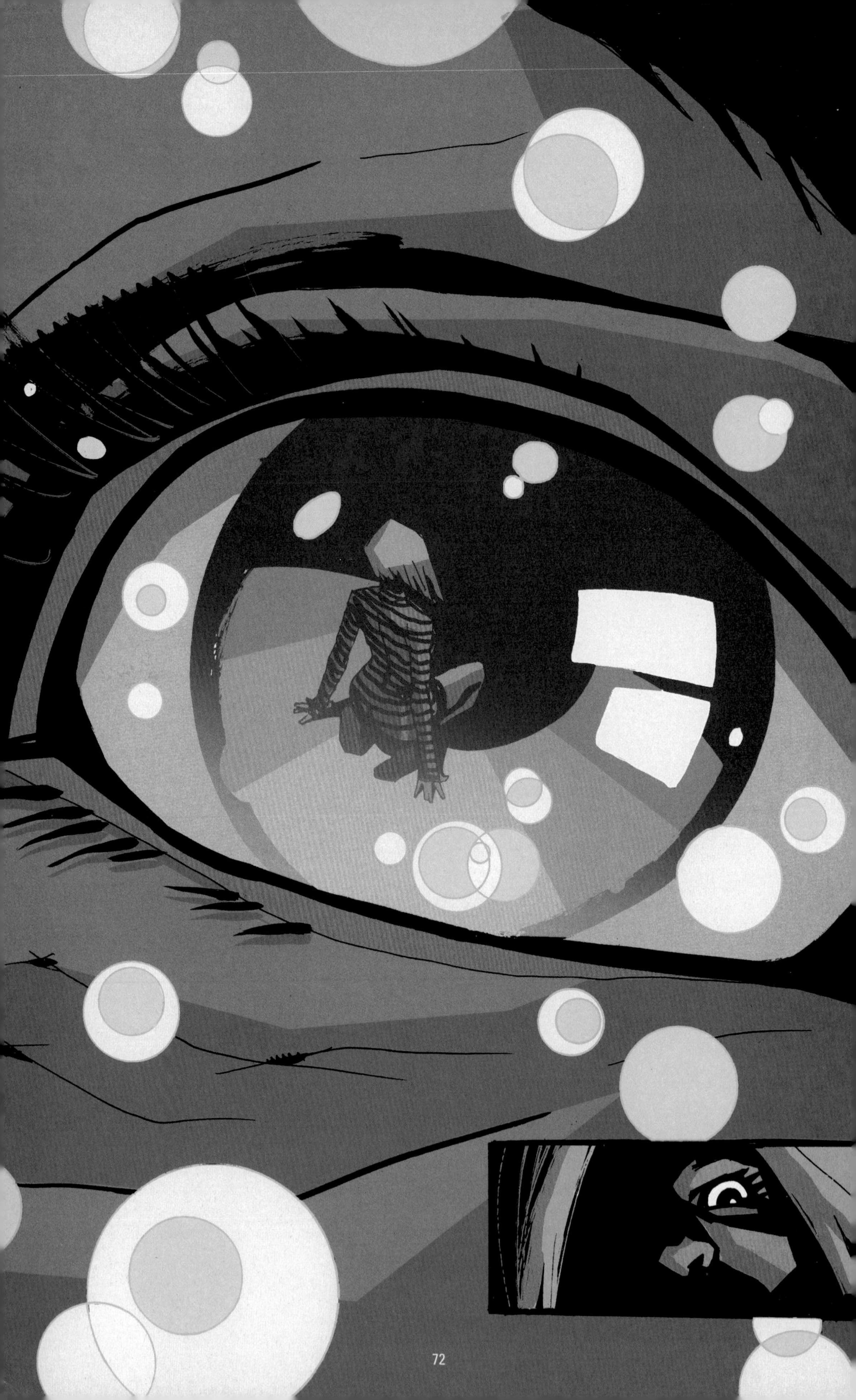

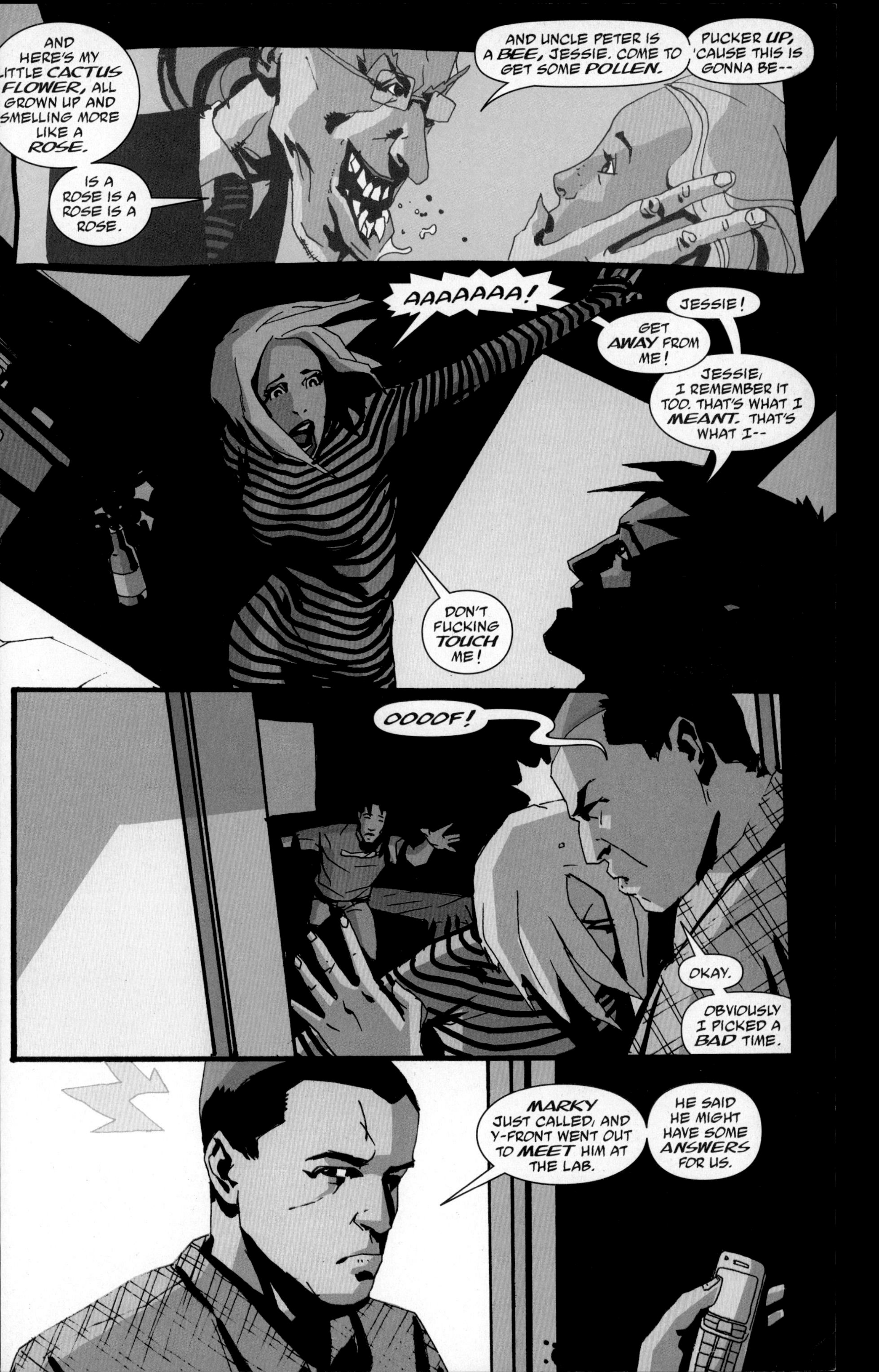
AND HERE'S MY LITTLE CACTUS FLOWER, ALL GROWN UP AND SMELLING MORE LIKE A ROSE.
IS A ROSE IS A ROSE IS A ROSE.
AND UNCLE PETER IS A BEE, JESSIE. COME TO GET SOME POLLEN.
PUCKER UP, 'CAUSE THIS IS GONNA BE--
AAAAAAA!
JESSIE!
GET AWAY FROM ME!
JESSIE, I REMEMBER IT TOO. THAT'S WHAT I MEANT. THAT'S WHAT I--
DON'T FUCKING TOUCH ME!
OOOOF!
OKAY.
OBVIOUSLY I PICKED A BAD TIME.
MARKY JUST CALLED, AND Y-FRONT WENT OUT TO MEET HIM AT THE LAB.
HE SAID HE MIGHT HAVE SOME ANSWERS FOR US.

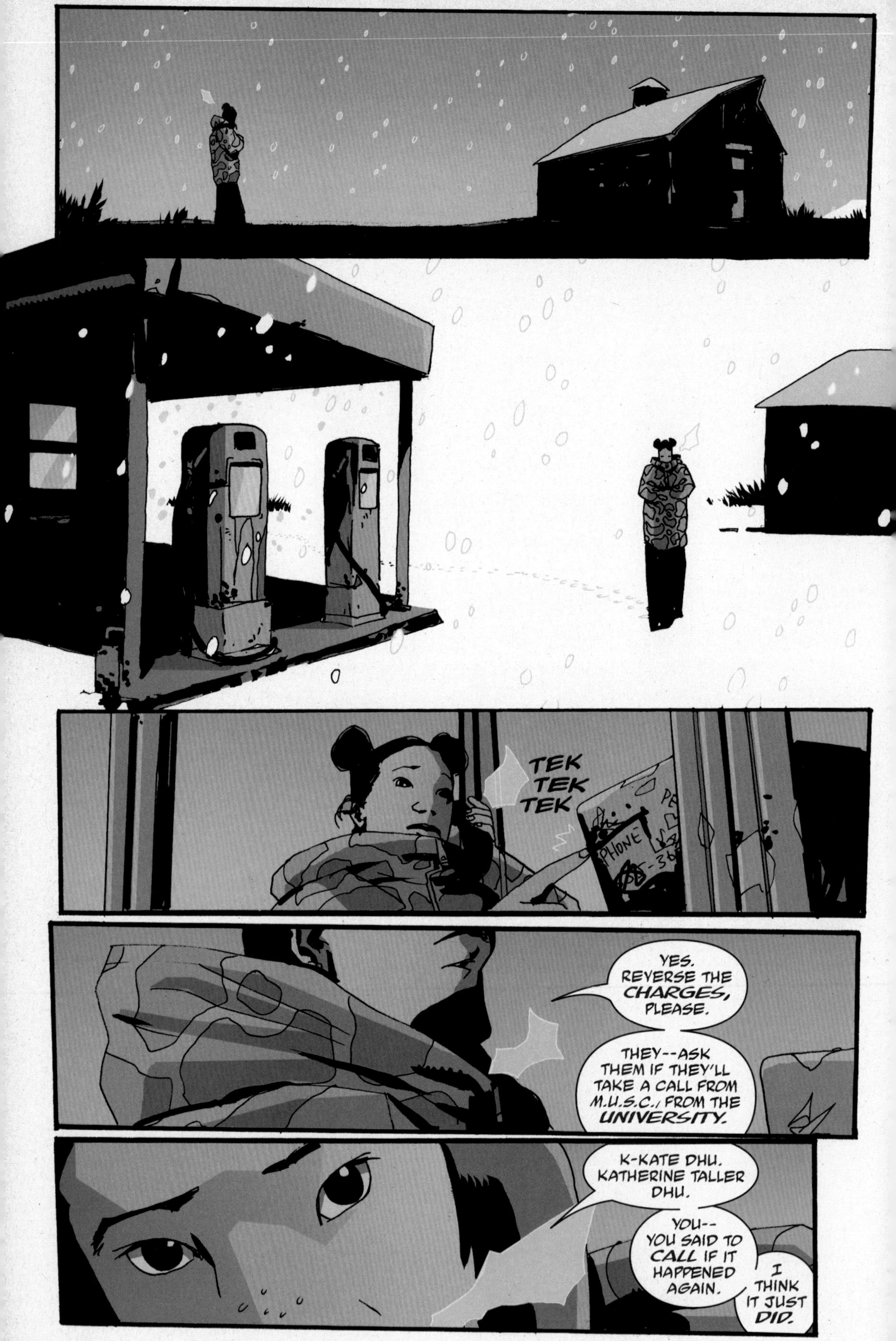
TEK
TEK
TEK
PHONE
YES. REVERSE THE CHARGES, PLEASE.
THEY--ASK THEM IF THEY'LL TAKE A CALL FROM M.U.S.C., FROM THE UNIVERSITY.
K-KATE DHU. KATHERINE TALLER DHU.
YOU-- YOU SAID TO CALL IF IT HAPPENED AGAIN.
I THINK IT JUST DID.

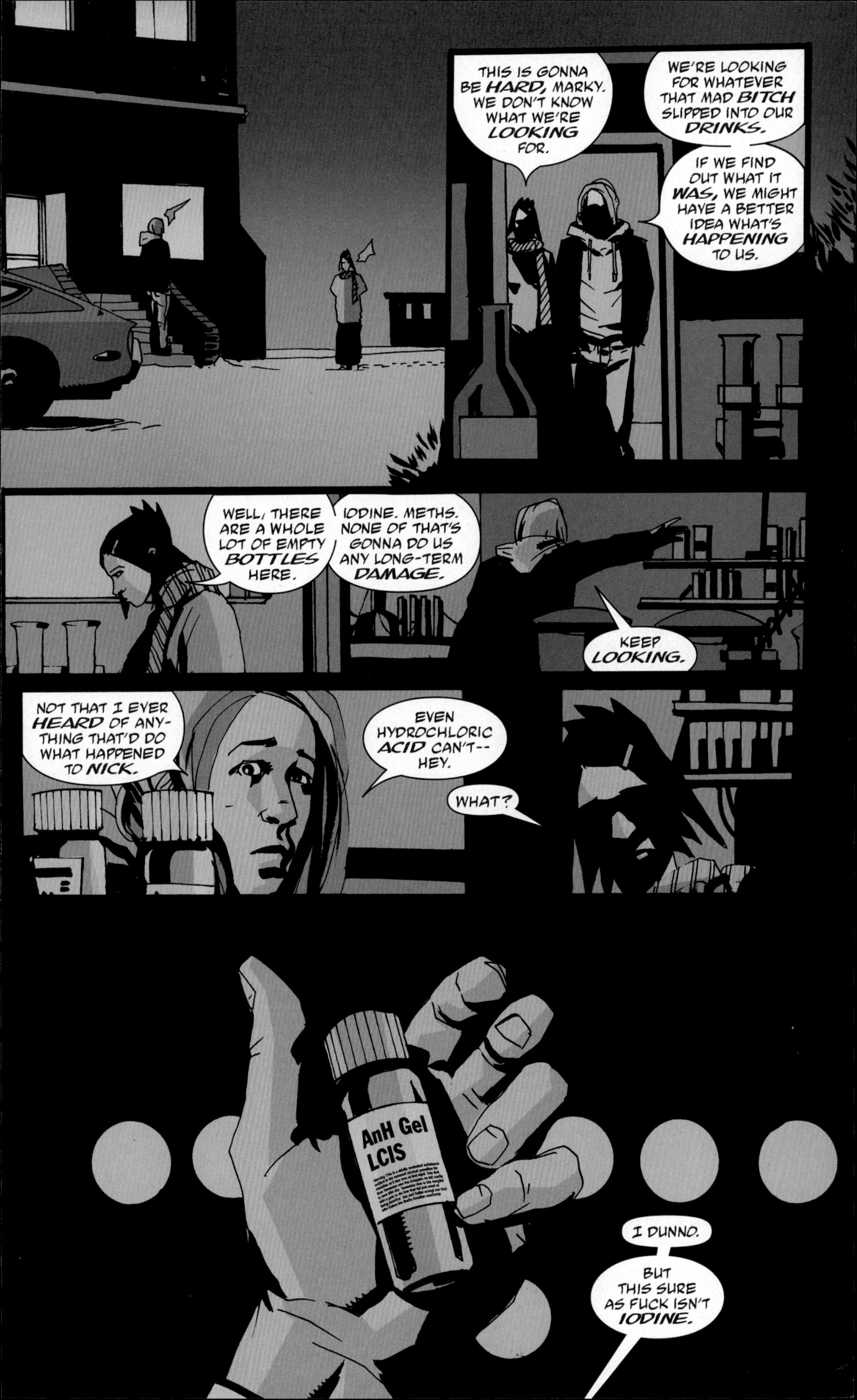
THIS IS GONNA BE HARD, MARKY. WE DON'T KNOW WHAT WE'RE LOOKING FOR.
WE'RE LOOKING FOR WHATEVER THAT MAD BITCH SLIPPED INTO OUR DRINKS.
IF WE FIND OUT WHAT IT WAS, WE MIGHT HAVE A BETTER IDEA WHAT'S HAPPENING TO US.
WELL, THERE ARE A WHOLE LOT OF EMPTY BOTTLES HERE.
IODINE. METHS. NONE OF THAT'S GONNA DO US ANY LONG-TERM DAMAGE.
KEEP LOOKING.
NOT THAT I EVER HEARD OF ANY-THING THAT'D DO WHAT HAPPENED TO NICK.
EVEN HYDROCHLORIC ACID CAN'T-- HEY.
WHAT?
AnH Gel
LCIS
I DUNNO.
BUT THIS SURE AS FUCK ISN'T IODINE.

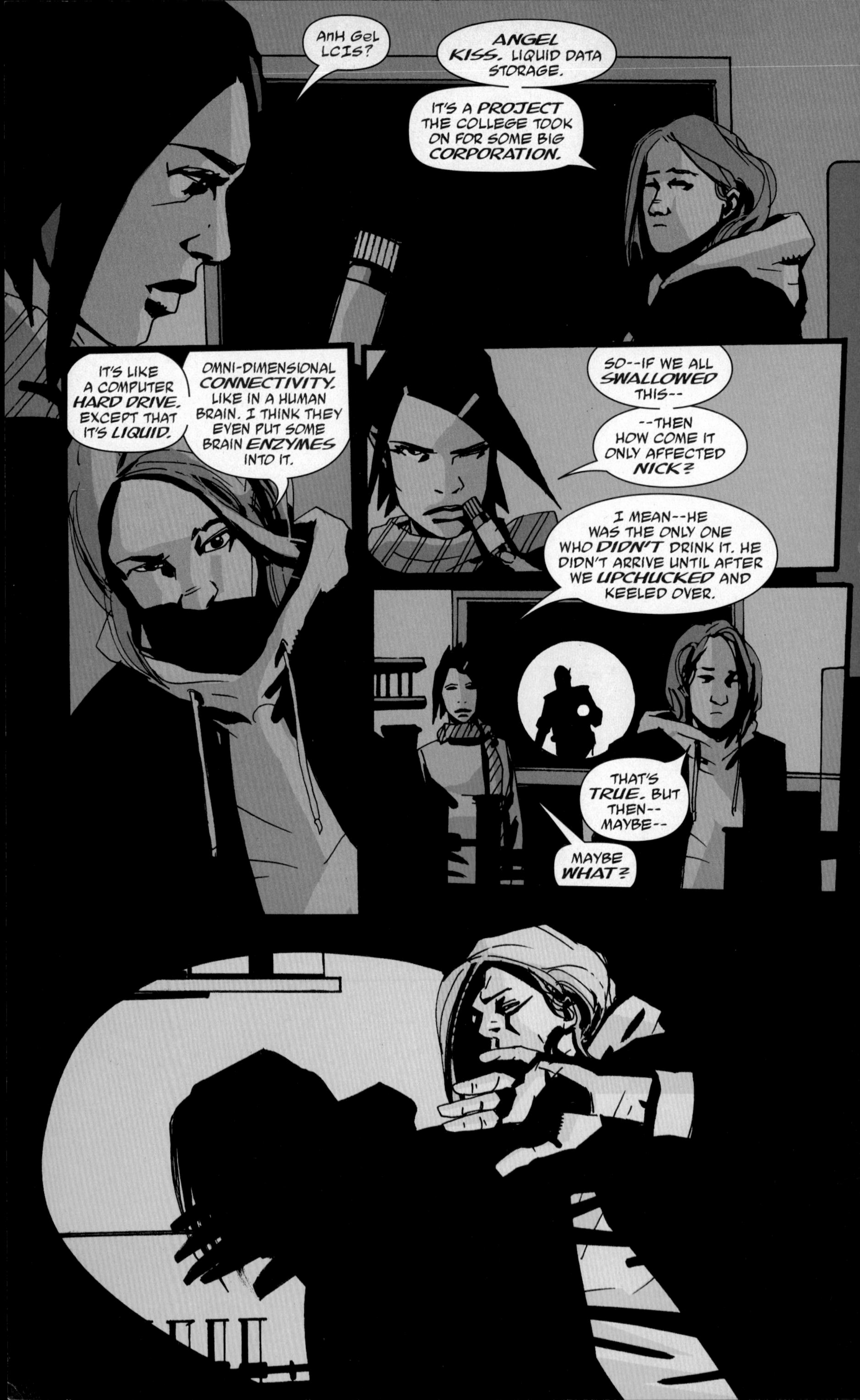
AnH Gel LCIS?
ANGEL KISS. LIQUID DATA STORAGE.
IT'S A PROJECT THE COLLEGE TOOK ON FOR SOME BIG CORPORATION.
IT'S LIKE A COMPUTER HARD DRIVE. EXCEPT THAT IT'S LIQUID.
OMNI-DIMENSIONAL CONNECTIVITY. LIKE IN A HUMAN BRAIN. I THINK THEY EVEN PUT SOME BRAIN ENZYMES INTO IT.
SO--IF WE ALL SWALLOWED THIS--
--THEN HOW COME IT ONLY AFFECTED NICK?
I MEAN--HE WAS THE ONLY ONE WHO DIDN'T DRINK IT. HE DIDN'T ARRIVE UNTIL AFTER WE UPCHUCKED AND KEELED OVER.
THAT'S TRUE. BUT THEN-- MAYBE--
MAYBE WHAT?

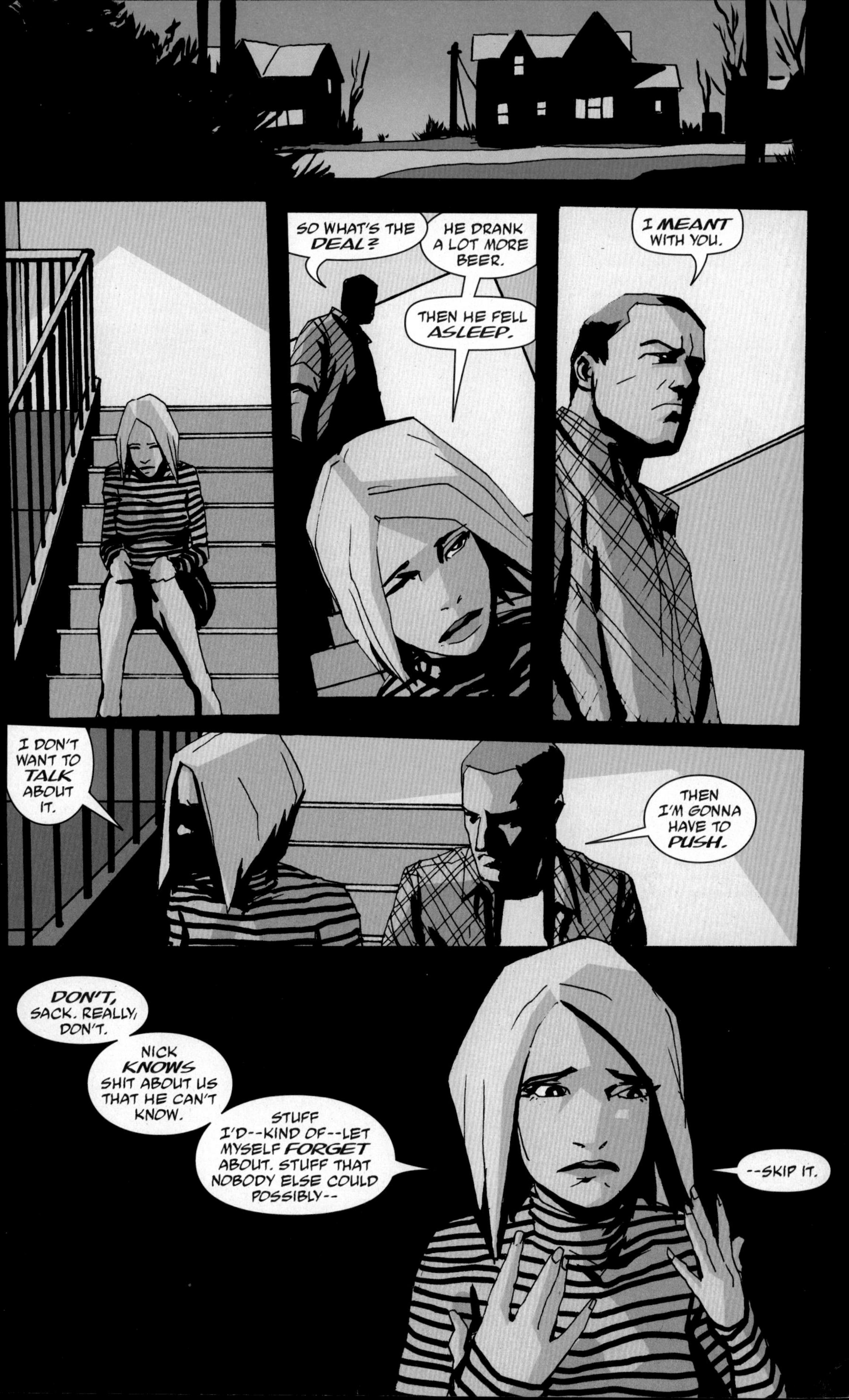

SO WHAT'S THE DEAL?
HE DRANK A LOT MORE BEER.
THEN HE FELL ASLEEP.
I MEANT WITH YOU.
I DON'T WANT TO TALK ABOUT IT.
THEN I'M GONNA HAVE TO PUSH.
DON'T, SACK. REALLY, DON'T.
NICK KNOWS SHIT ABOUT US THAT HE CAN'T KNOW.
STUFF I'D--KIND OF--LET MYSELF FORGET ABOUT. STUFF THAT NOBODY ELSE COULD POSSIBLY--
--SKIP IT.

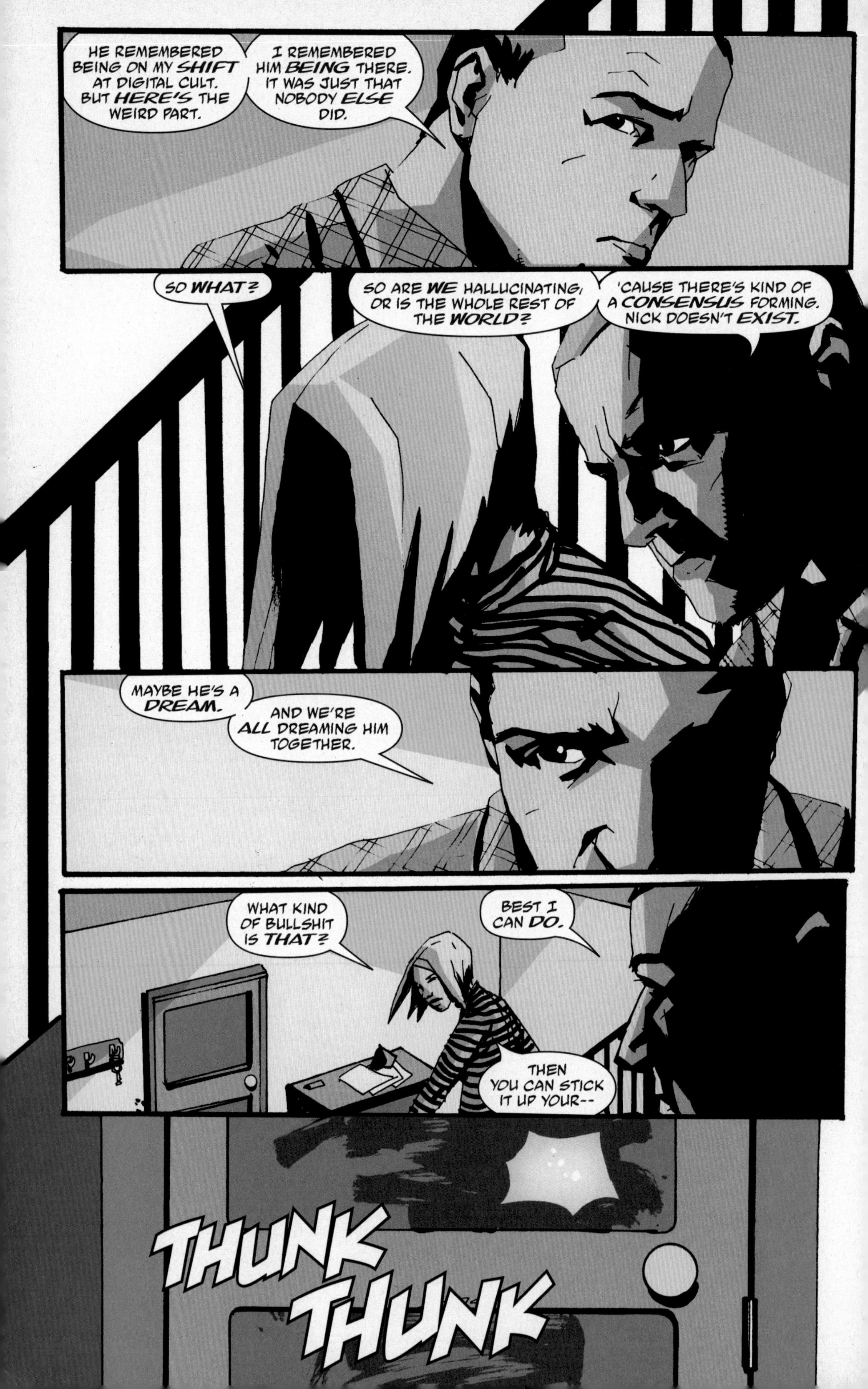
HE REMEMBERED BEING ON MY SHIFT AT DIGITAL CULT. BUT HERE'S THE WEIRD PART.
I REMEMBERED HIM BEING THERE. IT WAS JUST THAT NOBODY ELSE DID.
SO WHAT?
SO ARE WE HALLUCINATING, OR IS THE WHOLE REST OF THE WORLD?
'CAUSE THERE'S KIND OF A CONSENSUS FORMING. NICK DOESN'T EXIST.
MAYBE HE'S A DREAM.
AND WE'RE ALL DREAMING HIM TOGETHER.
WHAT KIND OF BULLSHIT IS THAT?
BEST I CAN DO.
THEN YOU CAN STICK IT UP YOUR--
THUNK
THUNK

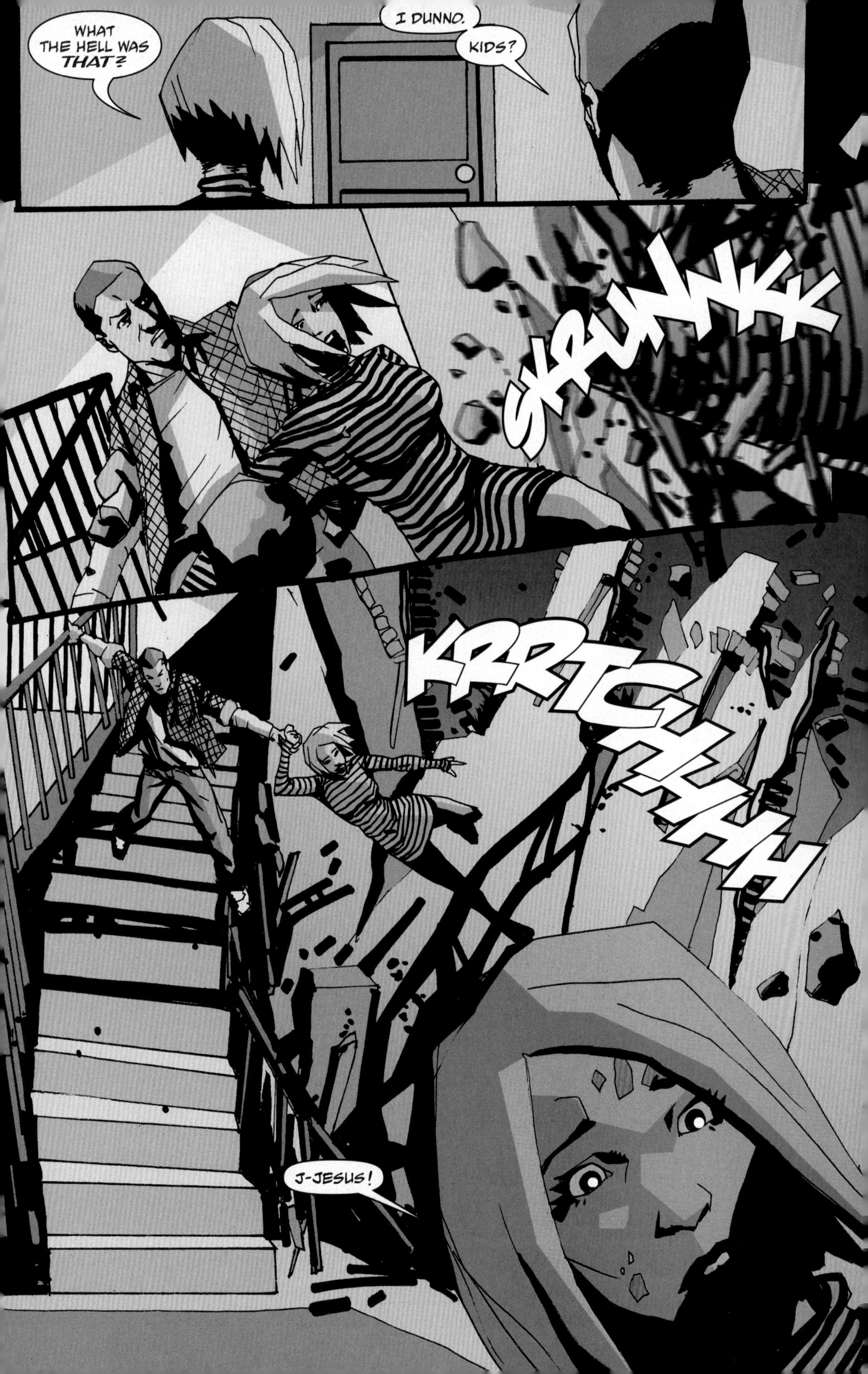
WHAT THE HELL WAS THAT?
I DUNNO.
KIDS?
SKRUNKK
KRRTCHHHH
J-JESUS!

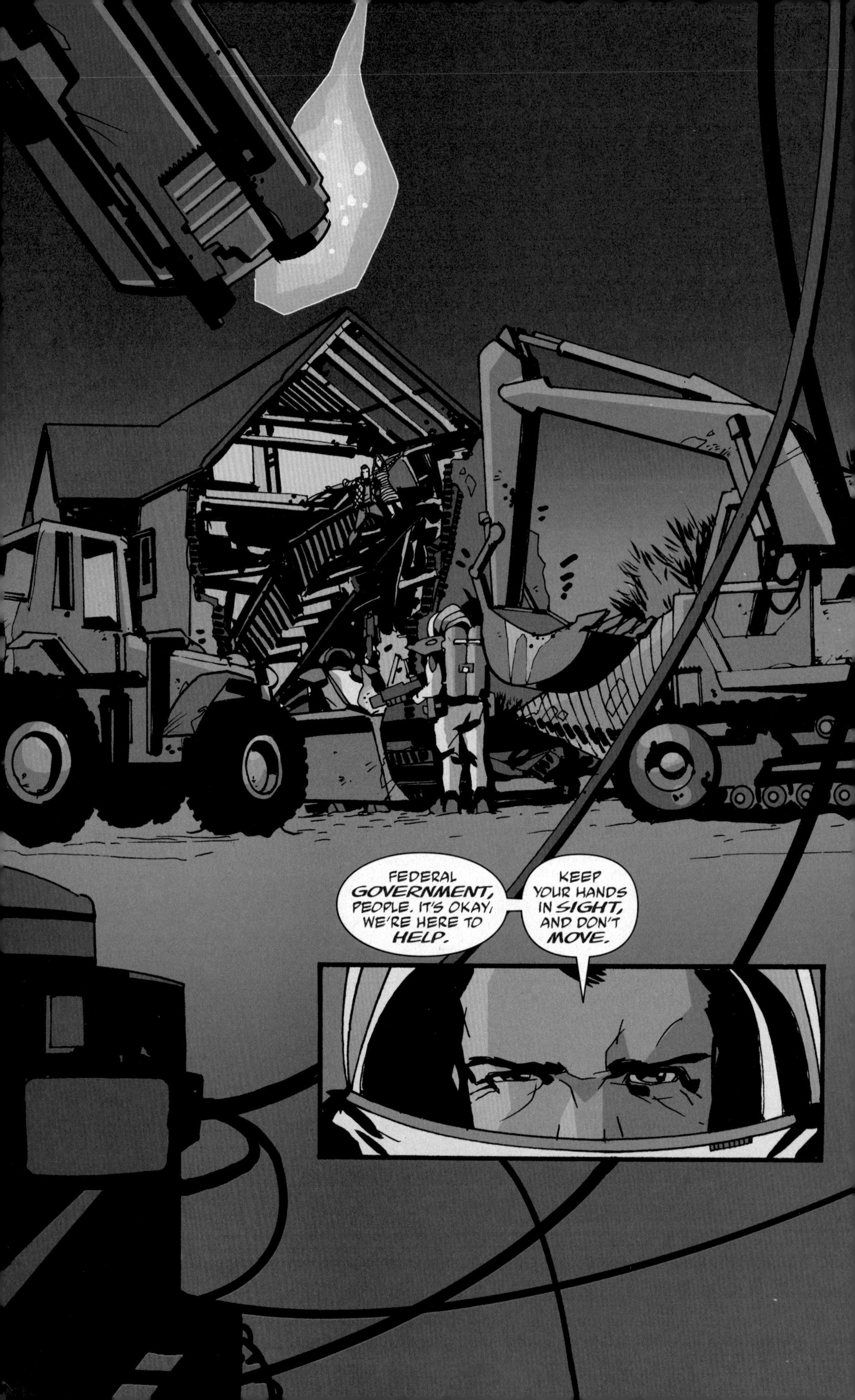
FEDERAL GOVERNMENT, PEOPLE. IT'S OKAY, WE'RE HERE TO HELP.
KEEP YOUR HANDS IN SIGHT, AND DON'T MOVE.

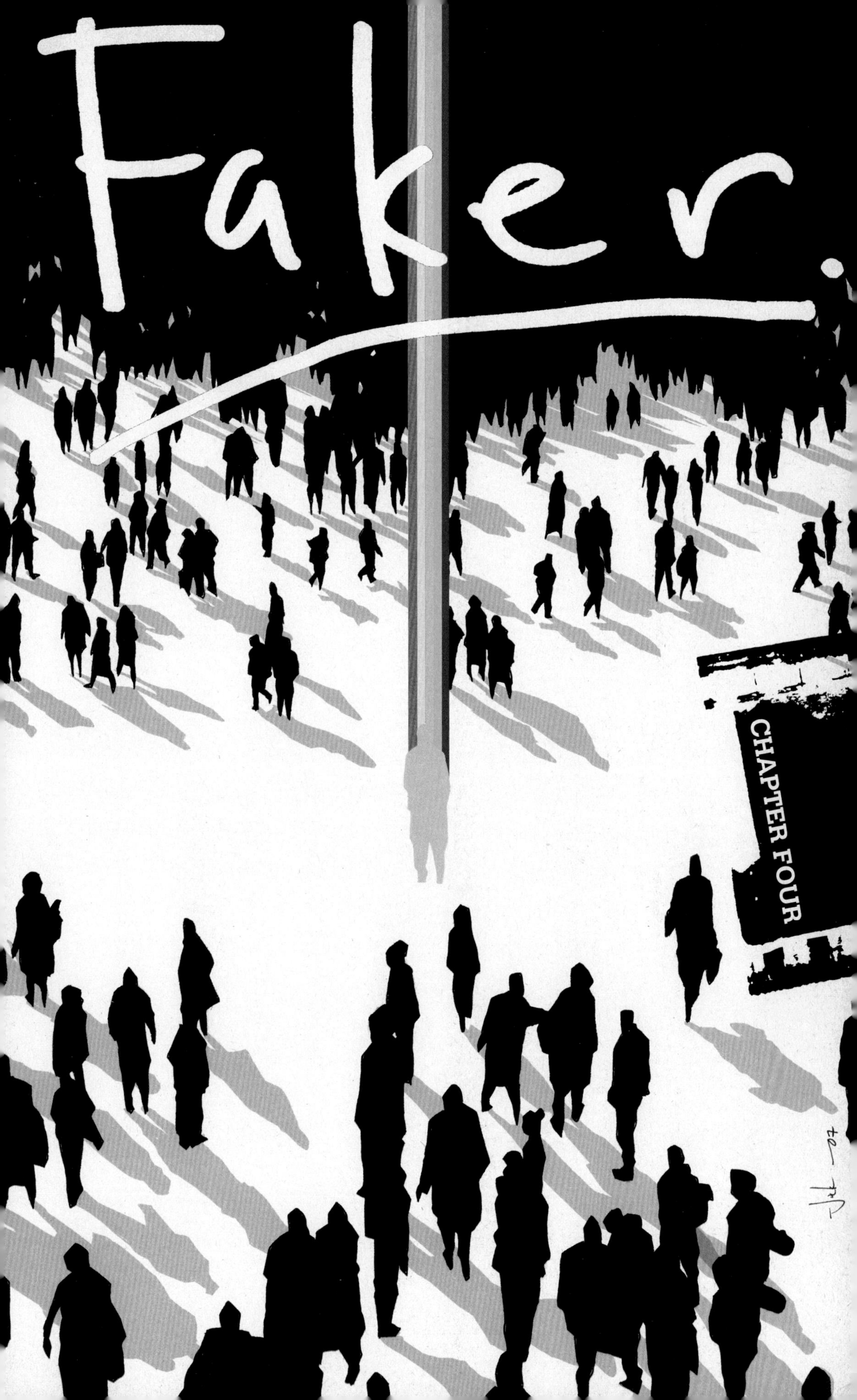
Faker.
CHAPTER FOUR

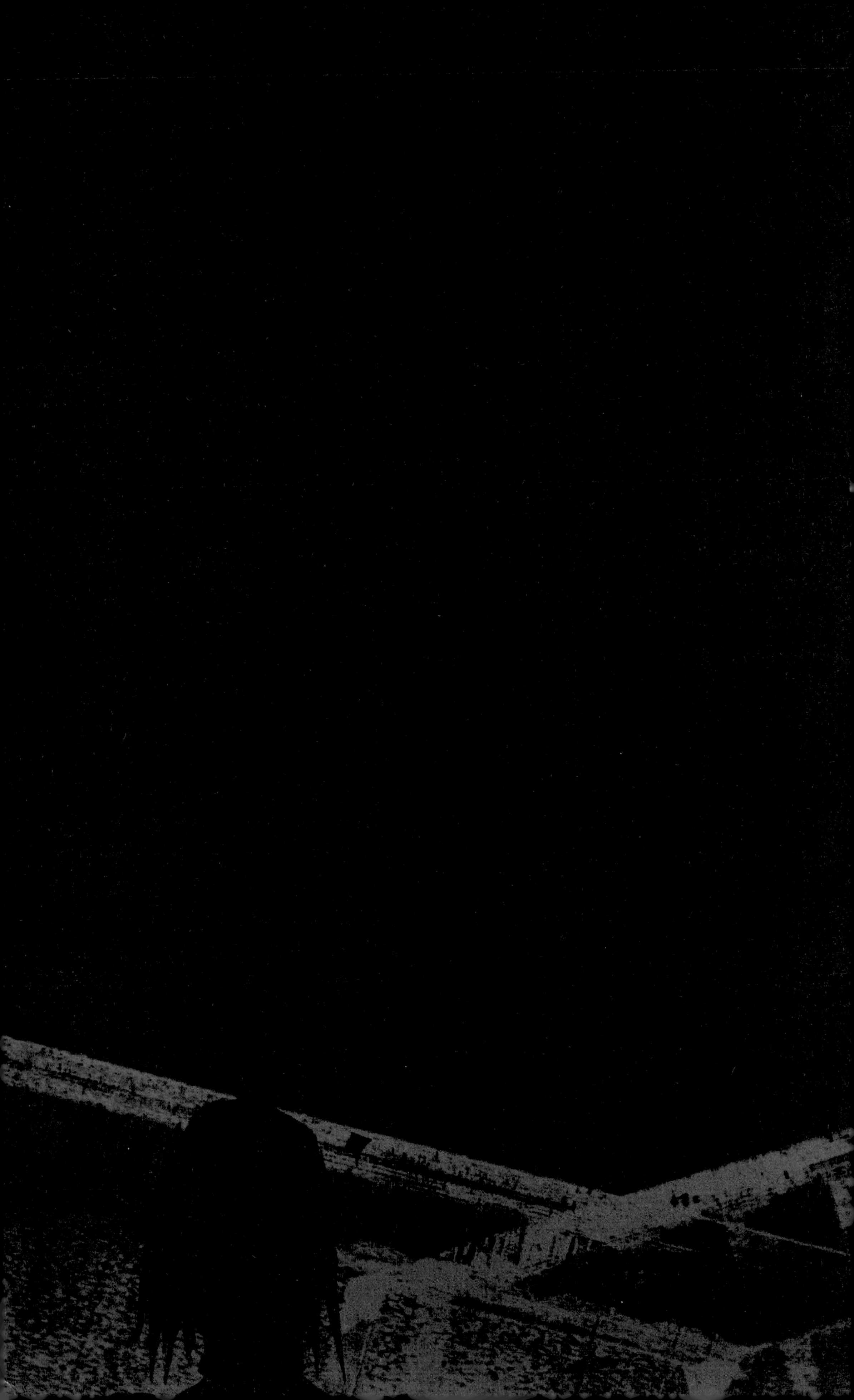

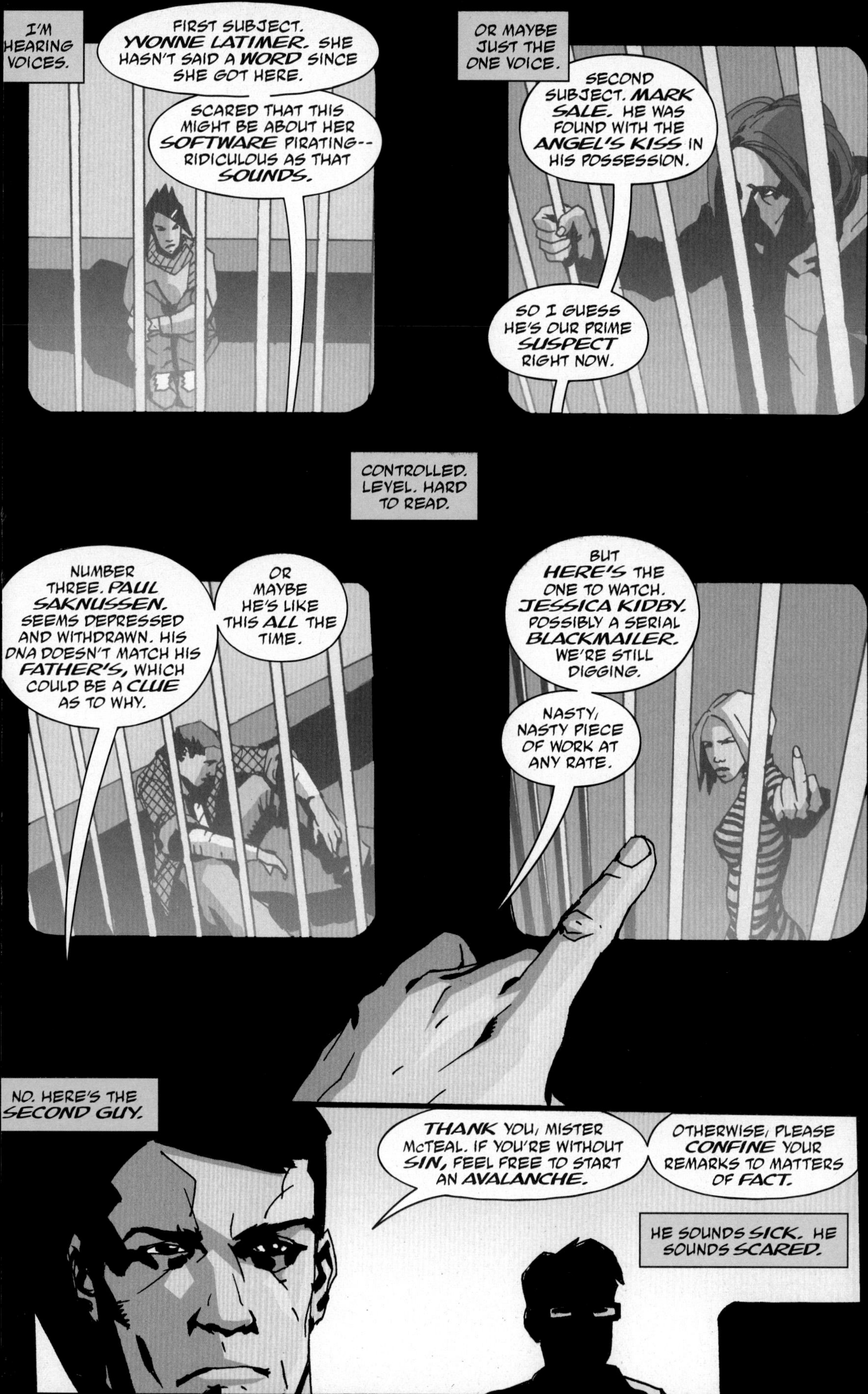
I'M HEARING VOICES.
FIRST SUBJECT. YVONNE LATIMER. SHE HASN'T SAID A WORD SINCE SHE GOT HERE.
SCARED THAT THIS MIGHT BE ABOUT HER SOFTWARE PIRATING-- RIDICULOUS AS THAT SOUNDS.
OR MAYBE JUST THE ONE VOICE.
SECOND SUBJECT. MARK SALE. HE WAS FOUND WITH THE ANGEL'S KISS IN HIS POSSESSION.
SO I GUESS HE'S OUR PRIME SUSPECT RIGHT NOW.
CONTROLLED. LEVEL. HARD TO READ.
NUMBER THREE. PAUL SAKNUSSEN. SEEMS DEPRESSED AND WITHDRAWN. HIS DNA DOESN'T MATCH HIS FATHER'S, WHICH COULD BE A CLUE AS TO WHY.
OR MAYBE HE'S LIKE THIS ALL THE TIME.
BUT HERE'S THE ONE TO WATCH. JESSICA KIDBY. POSSIBLY A SERIAL BLACKMAILER. WE'RE STILL DIGGING.
NASTY, NASTY PIECE OF WORK AT ANY RATE.
NO. HERE'S THE SECOND GUY.
THANK YOU, MISTER McTEAL. IF YOU'RE WITHOUT SIN, FEEL FREE TO START AN AVALANCHE.
OTHERWISE, PLEASE CONFINE YOUR REMARKS TO MATTERS OF FACT.
HE SOUNDS SICK. HE SOUNDS SCARED.

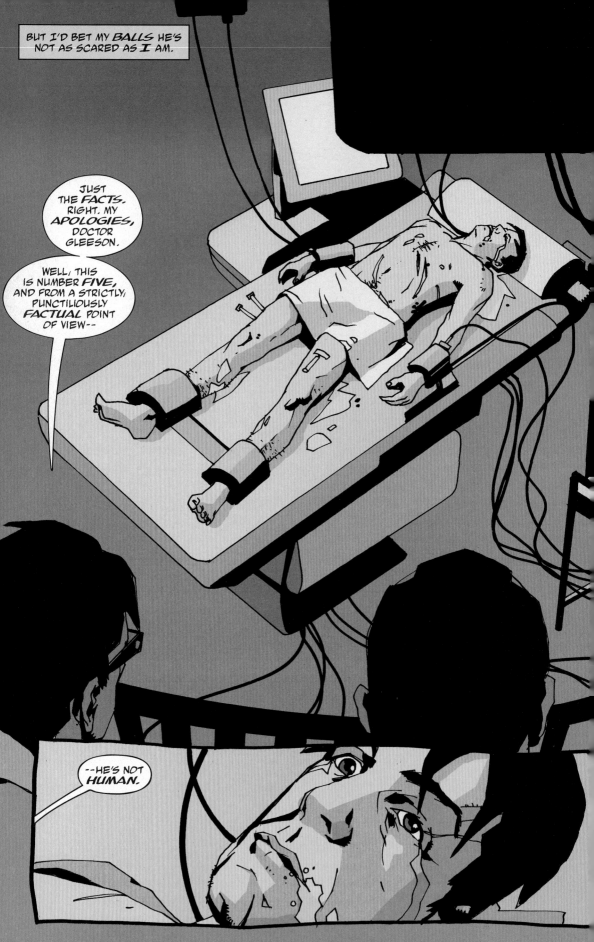

BUT I'D BET MY *BALLS* HE'S NOT AS SCARED AS *I* AM.

JUST THE *FACTS*, RIGHT. MY *APOLOGIES*, DOCTOR GLEESON.

WELL, THIS IS NUMBER *FIVE*, AND FROM A STRICTLY, PUNCTILIOUSLY *FACTUAL* POINT OF VIEW--

--HE'S NOT *HUMAN*.

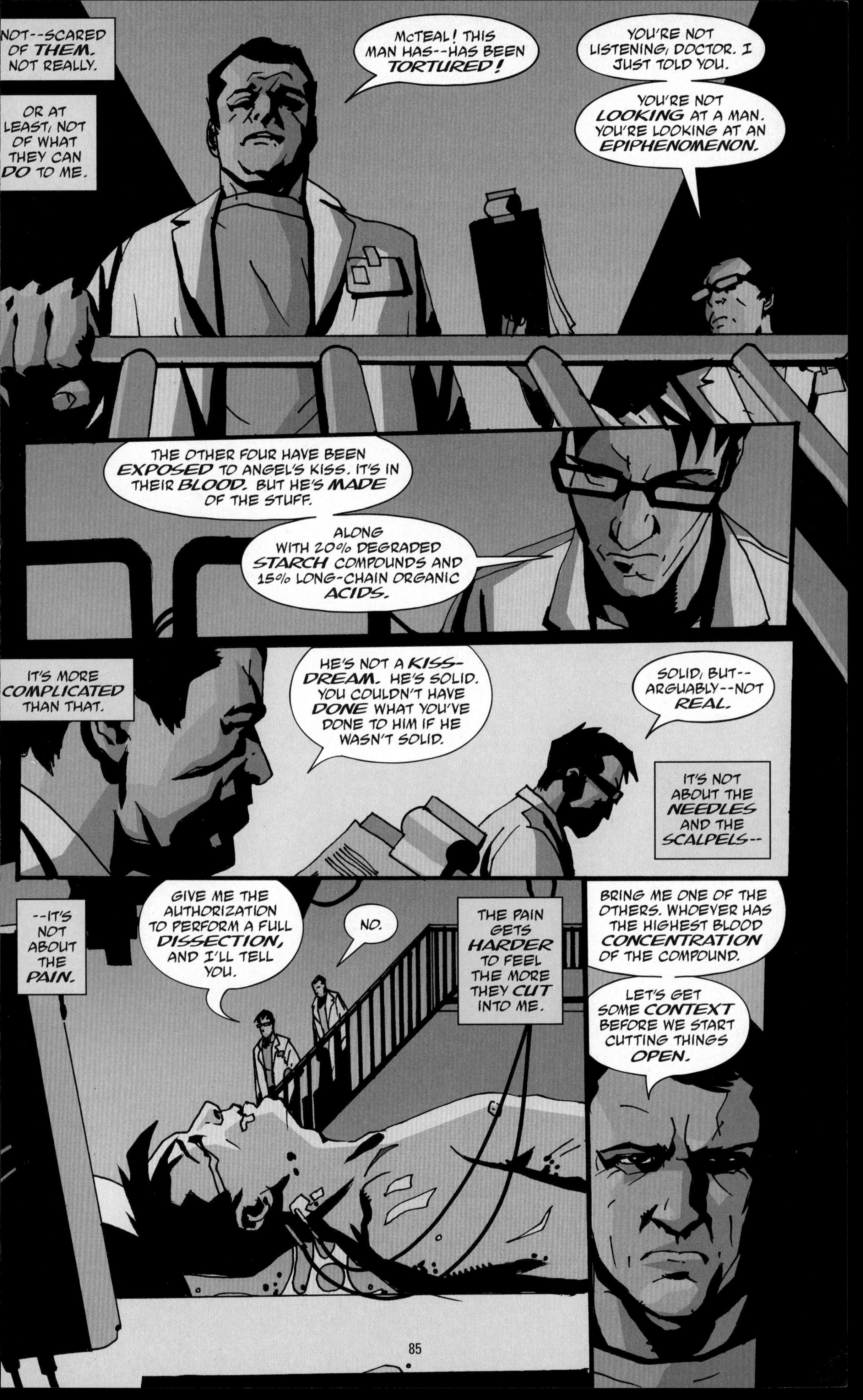
NOT--SCARED OF THEM. NOT REALLY.
OR AT LEAST, NOT OF WHAT THEY CAN DO TO ME.
McTEAL! THIS MAN HAS--HAS BEEN TORTURED!
YOU'RE NOT LISTENING, DOCTOR. I JUST TOLD YOU.
YOU'RE NOT LOOKING AT A MAN. YOU'RE LOOKING AT AN EPIPHENOMENON.
THE OTHER FOUR HAVE BEEN EXPOSED TO ANGEL'S KISS. IT'S IN THEIR BLOOD. BUT HE'S MADE OF THE STUFF.
ALONG WITH 20% DEGRADED STARCH COMPOUNDS AND 15% LONG-CHAIN ORGANIC ACIDS.
IT'S MORE COMPLICATED THAN THAT.
HE'S NOT A KISS-DREAM. HE'S SOLID. YOU COULDN'T HAVE DONE WHAT YOU'VE DONE TO HIM IF HE WASN'T SOLID.
SOLID, BUT--ARGUABLY--NOT REAL.
IT'S NOT ABOUT THE NEEDLES AND THE SCALPELS--
--IT'S NOT ABOUT THE PAIN.
GIVE ME THE AUTHORIZATION TO PERFORM A FULL DISSECTION, AND I'LL TELL YOU.
NO.
THE PAIN GETS HARDER TO FEEL THE MORE THEY CUT INTO ME.
BRING ME ONE OF THE OTHERS. WHOEVER HAS THE HIGHEST BLOOD CONCENTRATION OF THE COMPOUND.
LET'S GET SOME CONTEXT BEFORE WE START CUTTING THINGS OPEN.

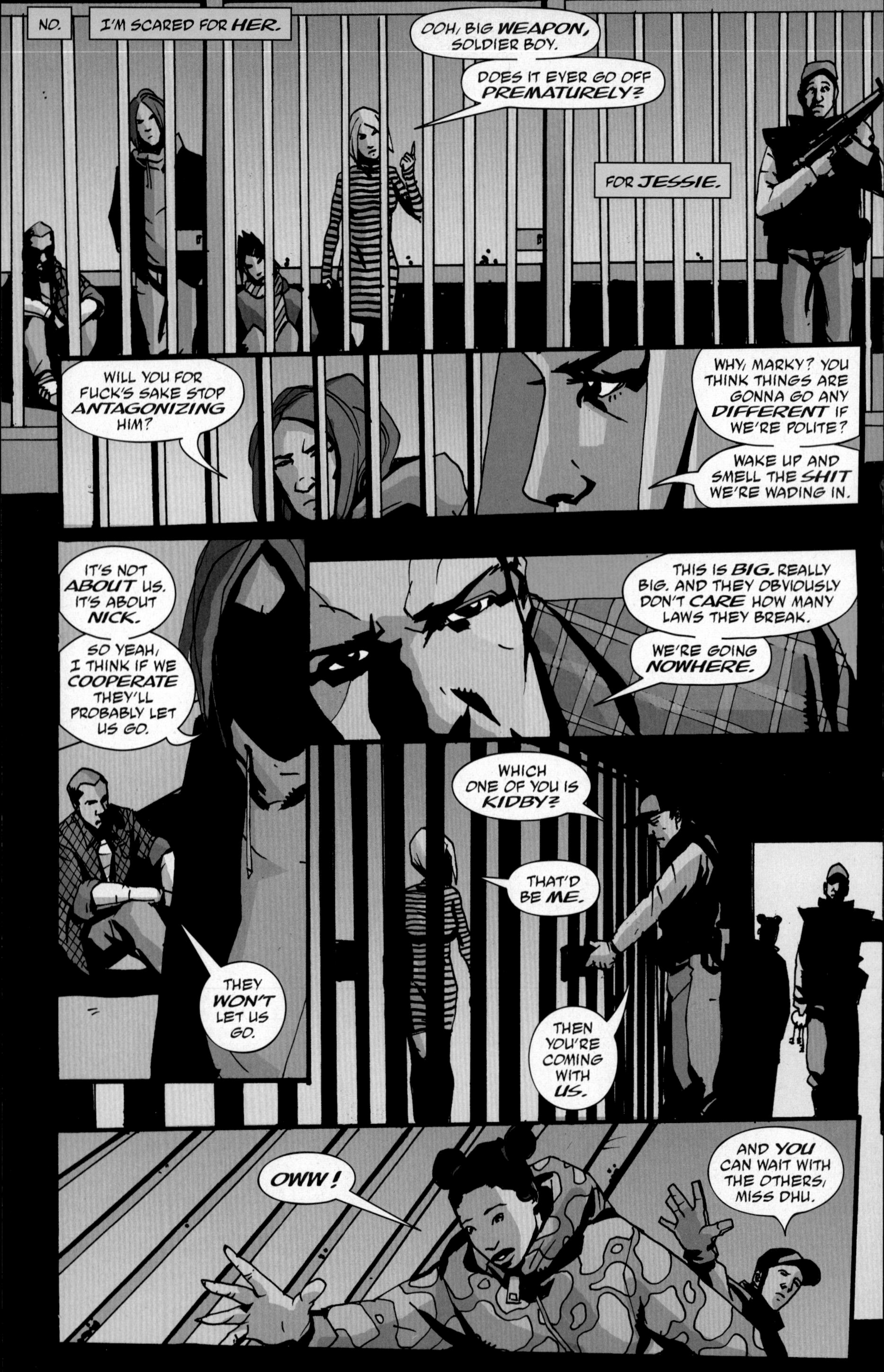
NO.
I'M SCARED FOR HER.
OOH, BIG WEAPON, SOLDIER BOY.
DOES IT EVER GO OFF PREMATURELY?
FOR JESSIE.
WILL YOU FOR FUCK'S SAKE STOP ANTAGONIZING HIM?
WHY, MARKY? YOU THINK THINGS ARE GONNA GO ANY DIFFERENT IF WE'RE POLITE?
WAKE UP AND SMELL THE SHIT WE'RE WADING IN.
IT'S NOT ABOUT US. IT'S ABOUT NICK.
SO YEAH, I THINK IF WE COOPERATE THEY'LL PROBABLY LET US GO.
THIS IS BIG. REALLY BIG. AND THEY OBVIOUSLY DON'T CARE HOW MANY LAWS THEY BREAK.
WE'RE GOING NOWHERE.
THEY WON'T LET US GO.
WHICH ONE OF YOU IS KIDBY?
THAT'D BE ME.
THEN YOU'RE COMING WITH US.
OWW!
AND YOU CAN WAIT WITH THE OTHERS, MISS DHU.

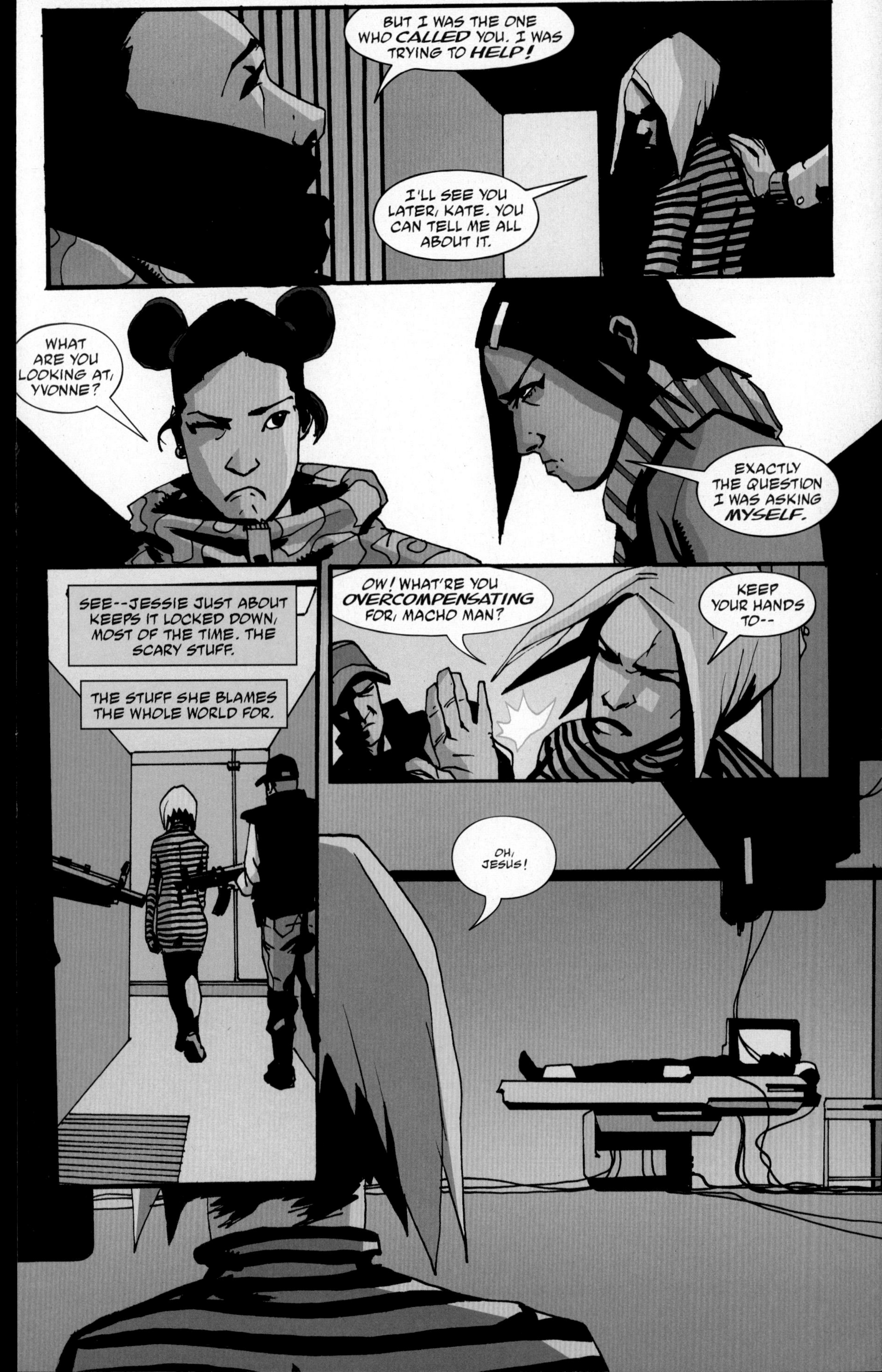
BUT I WAS THE ONE WHO CALLED YOU. I WAS TRYING TO HELP!
I'LL SEE YOU LATER, KATE. YOU CAN TELL ME ALL ABOUT IT.
WHAT ARE YOU LOOKING AT, YVONNE?
EXACTLY THE QUESTION I WAS ASKING MYSELF.
SEE--JESSIE JUST ABOUT KEEPS IT LOCKED DOWN, MOST OF THE TIME. THE SCARY STUFF.
THE STUFF SHE BLAMES THE WHOLE WORLD FOR.
KEEP YOUR HANDS TO--
OW! WHAT'RE YOU OVERCOMPENSATING FOR, MACHO MAN?
OH, JESUS!

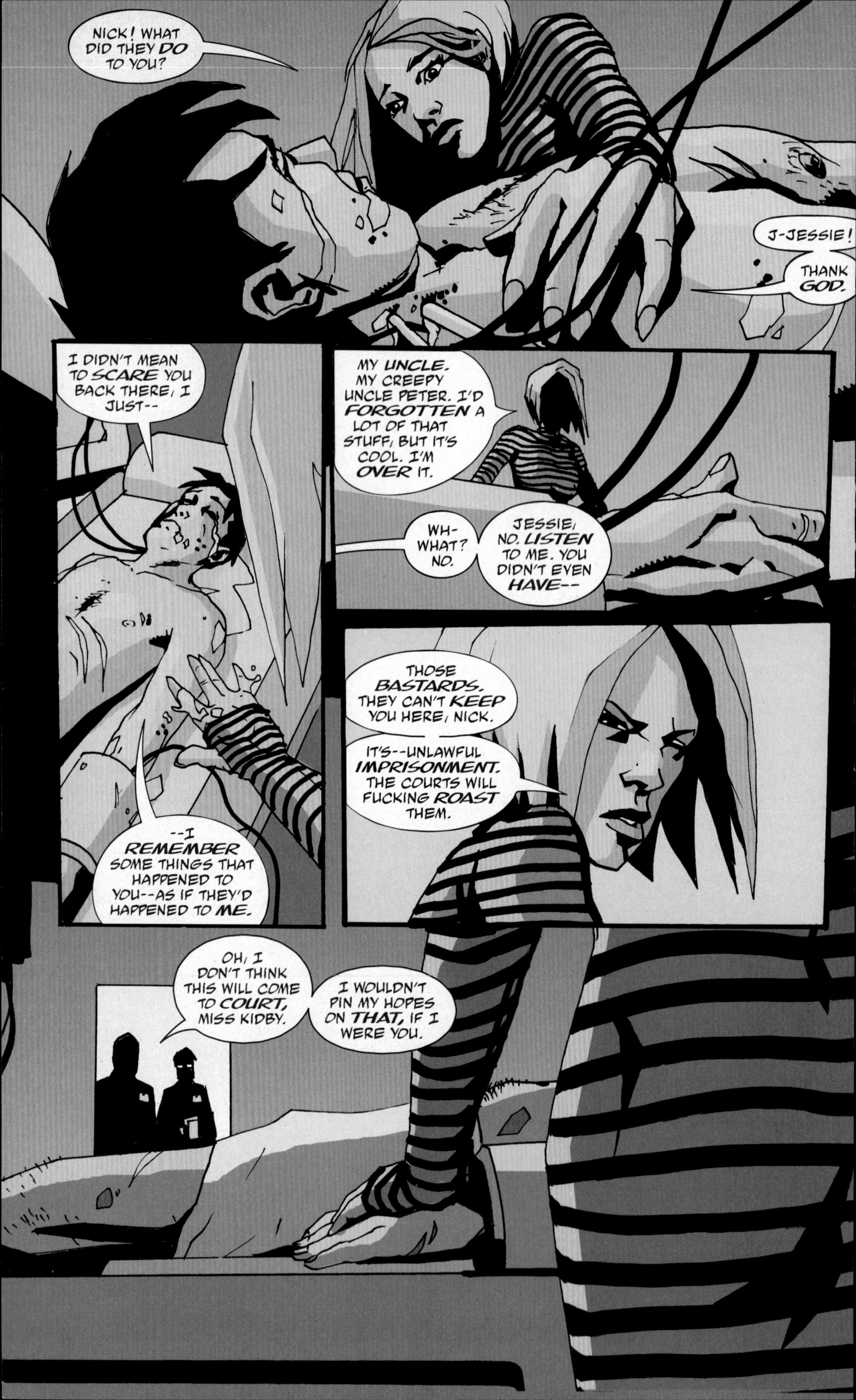
NICK! WHAT DID THEY DO TO YOU?
J-JESSIE!
THANK GOD.
I DIDN'T MEAN TO SCARE YOU BACK THERE, I JUST--
--I REMEMBER SOME THINGS THAT HAPPENED TO YOU--AS IF THEY'D HAPPENED TO ME.
MY UNCLE. MY CREEPY UNCLE PETER. I'D FORGOTTEN A LOT OF THAT STUFF, BUT IT'S COOL. I'M OVER IT.
WH-WHAT? NO.
JESSIE, NO. LISTEN TO ME. YOU DIDN'T EVEN HAVE--
THOSE BASTARDS. THEY CAN'T KEEP YOU HERE, NICK.
IT'S--UNLAWFUL IMPRISONMENT. THE COURTS WILL FUCKING ROAST THEM.
OH, I DON'T THINK THIS WILL COME TO COURT, MISS KIDBY.
I WOULDN'T PIN MY HOPES ON THAT, IF I WERE YOU.

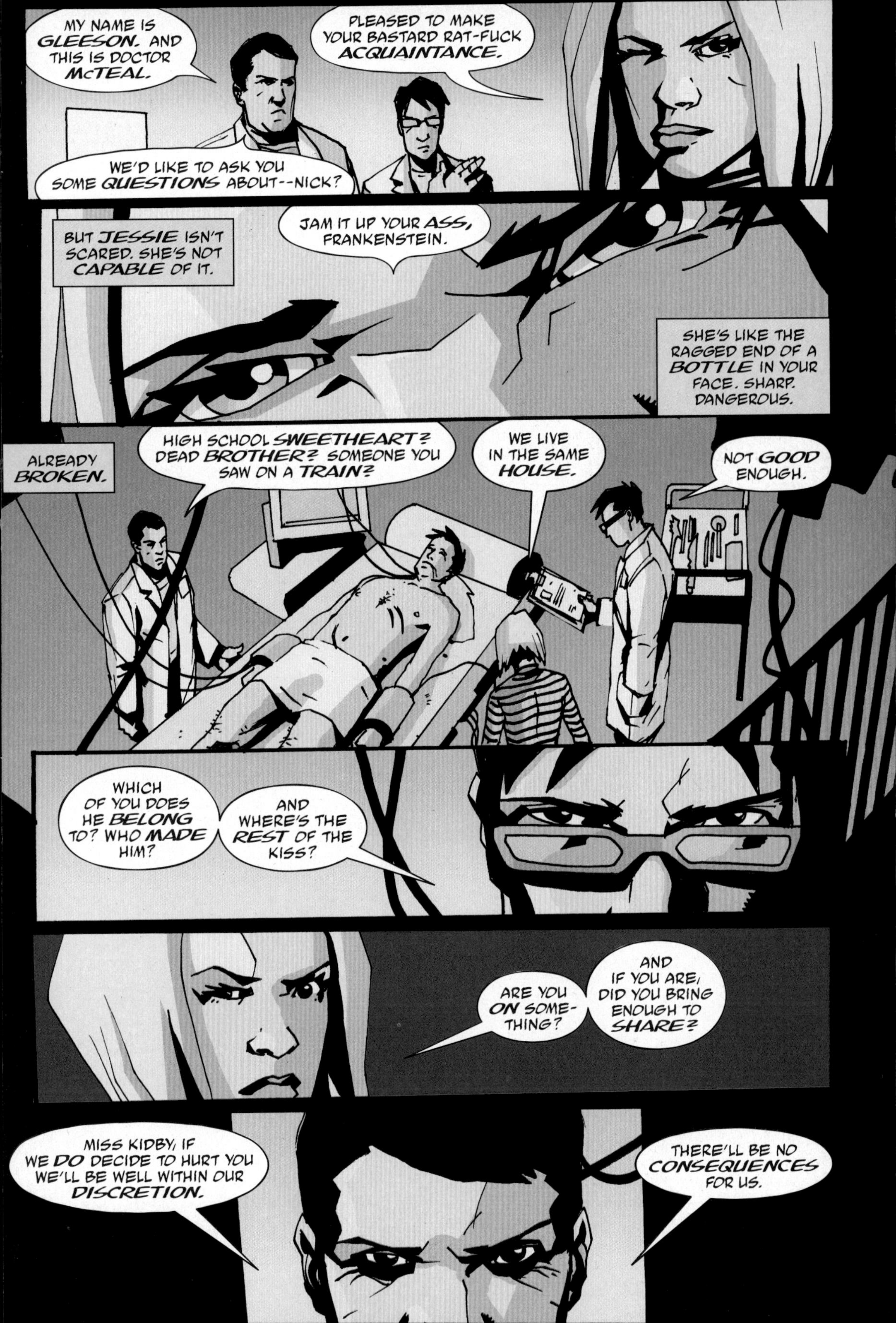
MY NAME IS GLEESON. AND THIS IS DOCTOR McTEAL.
PLEASED TO MAKE YOUR BASTARD RAT-FUCK ACQUAINTANCE.
WE'D LIKE TO ASK YOU SOME QUESTIONS ABOUT--NICK?
BUT JESSIE ISN'T SCARED. SHE'S NOT CAPABLE OF IT.
JAM IT UP YOUR ASS, FRANKENSTEIN.
SHE'S LIKE THE RAGGED END OF A BOTTLE IN YOUR FACE. SHARP. DANGEROUS.
ALREADY BROKEN.
HIGH SCHOOL SWEETHEART? DEAD BROTHER? SOMEONE YOU SAW ON A TRAIN?
WE LIVE IN THE SAME HOUSE.
NOT GOOD ENOUGH.
WHICH OF YOU DOES HE BELONG TO? WHO MADE HIM?
AND WHERE'S THE REST OF THE KISS?
ARE YOU ON SOME-THING?
AND IF YOU ARE, DID YOU BRING ENOUGH TO SHARE?
MISS KIDBY, IF WE DO DECIDE TO HURT YOU WE'LL BE WELL WITHIN OUR DISCRETION.
THERE'LL BE NO CONSEQUENCES FOR US.

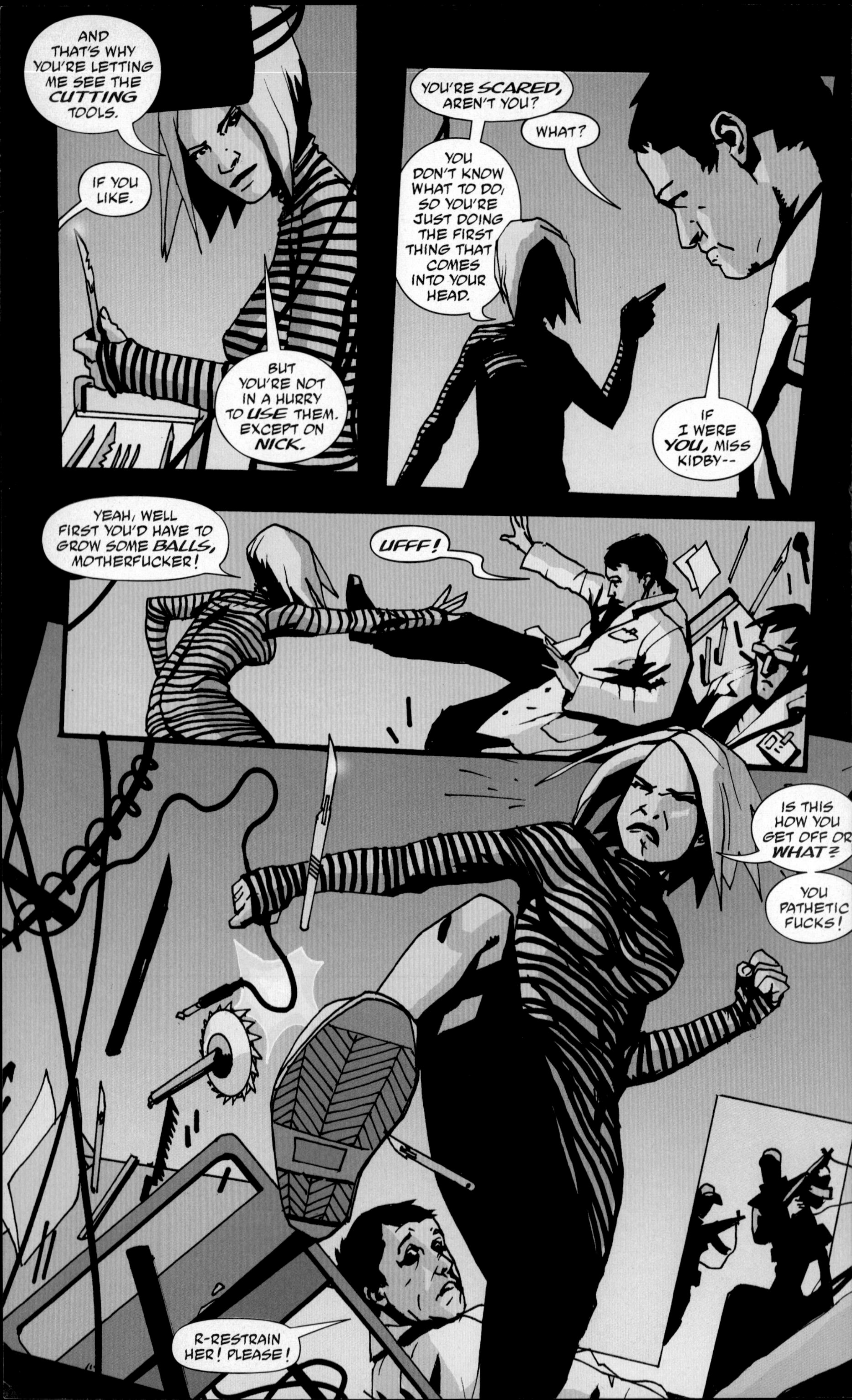
AND THAT'S WHY YOU'RE LETTING ME SEE THE CUTTING TOOLS.
IF YOU LIKE.
BUT YOU'RE NOT IN A HURRY TO USE THEM. EXCEPT ON NICK.
YOU'RE SCARED, AREN'T YOU?
WHAT?
YOU DON'T KNOW WHAT TO DO, SO YOU'RE JUST DOING THE FIRST THING THAT COMES INTO YOUR HEAD.
IF I WERE YOU, MISS KIDBY--
YEAH, WELL FIRST YOU'D HAVE TO GROW SOME BALLS, MOTHERFUCKER!
UFFF!
IS THIS HOW YOU GET OFF OR WHAT?
YOU PATHETIC FUCKS!
R-RESTRAIN HER! PLEASE!

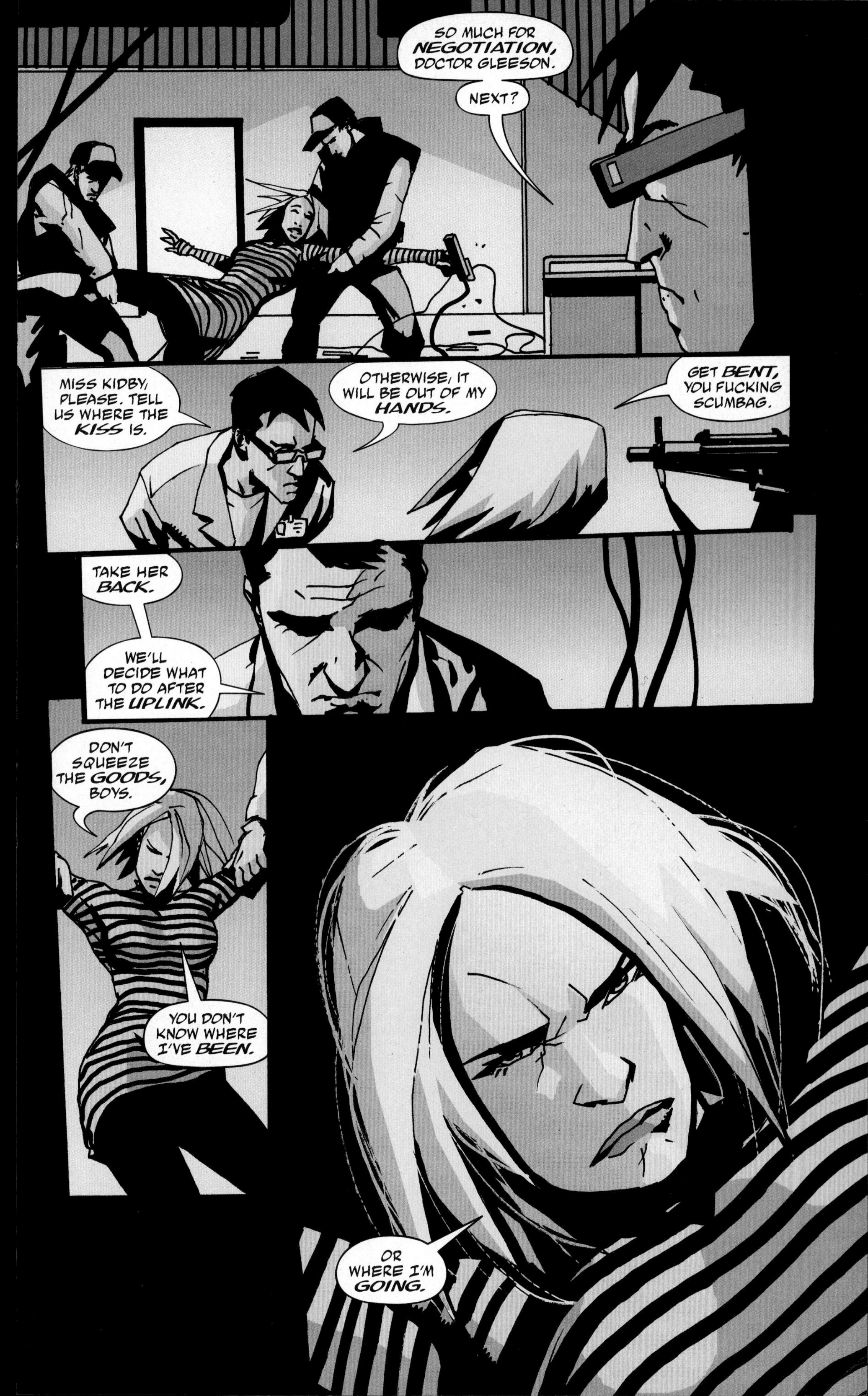
SO MUCH FOR NEGOTIATION, DOCTOR GLEESON.
NEXT?
MISS KIDBY, PLEASE. TELL US WHERE THE KISS IS.
OTHERWISE, IT WILL BE OUT OF MY HANDS.
GET BENT, YOU FUCKING SCUMBAG.
TAKE HER BACK.
WE'LL DECIDE WHAT TO DO AFTER THE UPLINK.
DON'T SQUEEZE THE GOODS, BOYS.
YOU DON'T KNOW WHERE I'VE BEEN.
OR WHERE I'M GOING.

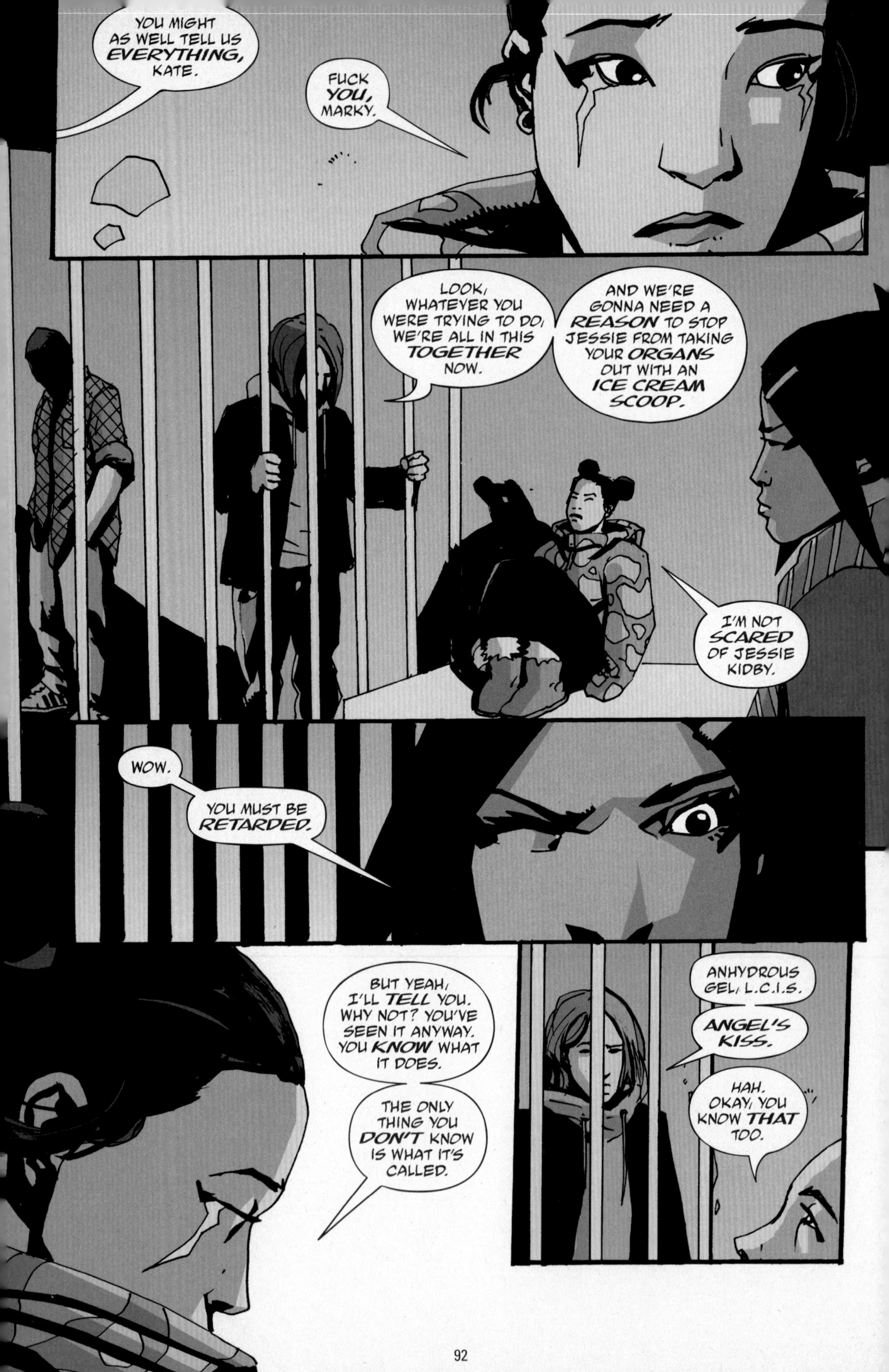
YOU MIGHT AS WELL TELL US EVERYTHING, KATE.
FUCK YOU, MARKY.
LOOK, WHATEVER YOU WERE TRYING TO DO, WE'RE ALL IN THIS TOGETHER NOW.
AND WE'RE GONNA NEED A REASON TO STOP JESSIE FROM TAKING YOUR ORGANS OUT WITH AN ICE CREAM SCOOP.
I'M NOT SCARED OF JESSIE KIDBY.
WOW.
YOU MUST BE RETARDED.
BUT YEAH, I'LL TELL YOU. WHY NOT? YOU'VE SEEN IT ANYWAY. YOU KNOW WHAT IT DOES.
THE ONLY THING YOU DON'T KNOW IS WHAT IT'S CALLED.
ANHYDROUS GEL, L.C.I.S.
ANGEL'S KISS.
HAH. OKAY, YOU KNOW THAT TOO.

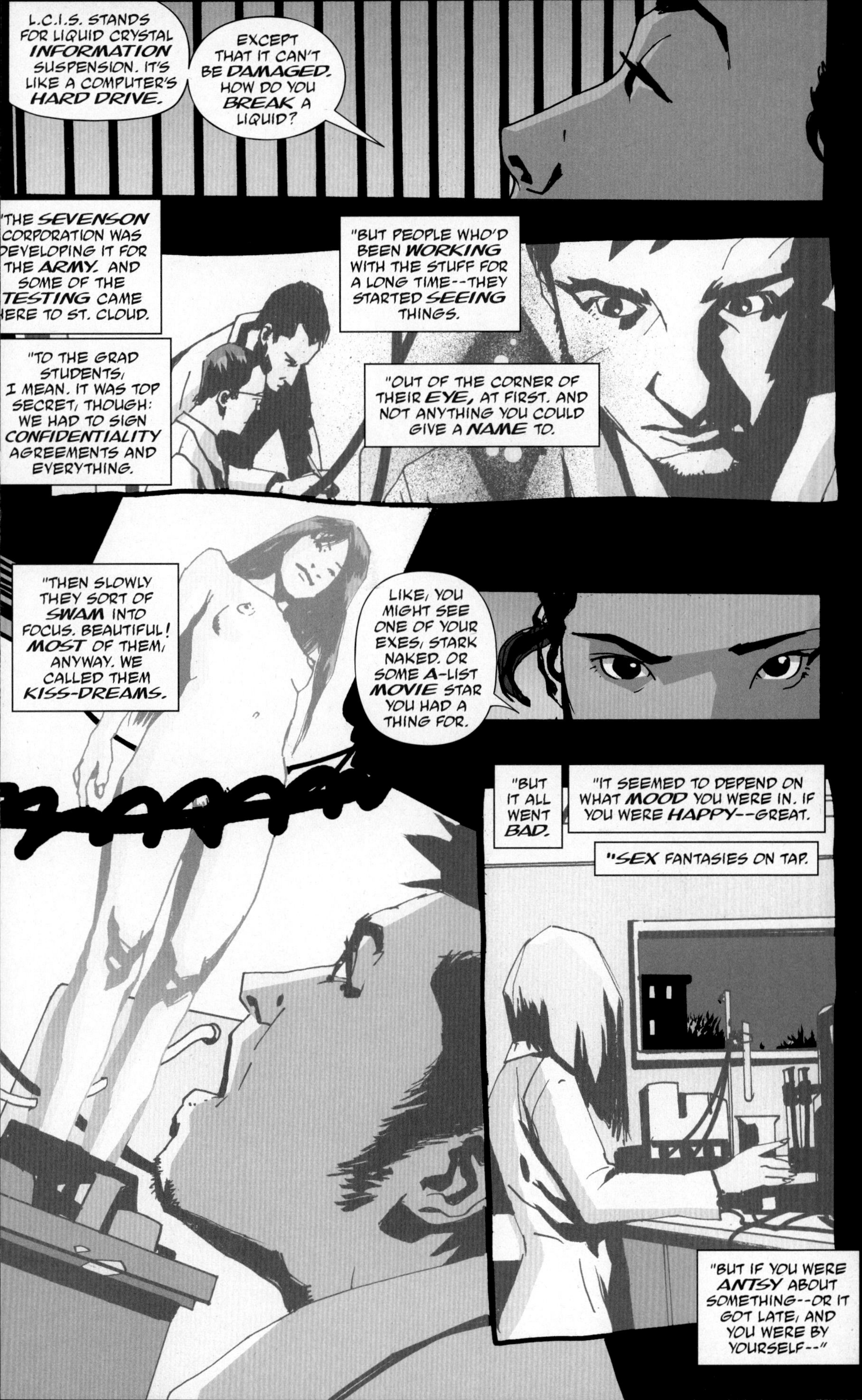
L.C.I.S. STANDS FOR LIQUID CRYSTAL INFORMATION SUSPENSION. IT'S LIKE A COMPUTER'S HARD DRIVE.
EXCEPT THAT IT CAN'T BE DAMAGED. HOW DO YOU BREAK A LIQUID?
"THE SEVENSON CORPORATION WAS DEVELOPING IT FOR THE ARMY. AND SOME OF THE TESTING CAME HERE TO ST. CLOUD.
"TO THE GRAD STUDENTS, I MEAN. IT WAS TOP SECRET, THOUGH: WE HAD TO SIGN CONFIDENTIALITY AGREEMENTS AND EVERYTHING.
"BUT PEOPLE WHO'D BEEN WORKING WITH THE STUFF FOR A LONG TIME--THEY STARTED SEEING THINGS.
"OUT OF THE CORNER OF THEIR EYE, AT FIRST. AND NOT ANYTHING YOU COULD GIVE A NAME TO.
"THEN SLOWLY THEY SORT OF SWAM INTO FOCUS. BEAUTIFUL! MOST OF THEM, ANYWAY. WE CALLED THEM KISS-DREAMS.
LIKE, YOU MIGHT SEE ONE OF YOUR EXES, STARK NAKED. OR SOME A-LIST MOVIE STAR YOU HAD A THING FOR.
"BUT IT ALL WENT BAD.
"IT SEEMED TO DEPEND ON WHAT MOOD YOU WERE IN. IF YOU WERE HAPPY--GREAT.
"SEX FANTASIES ON TAP.
"BUT IF YOU WERE ANTSY ABOUT SOMETHING--OR IT GOT LATE, AND YOU WERE BY YOURSELF--"

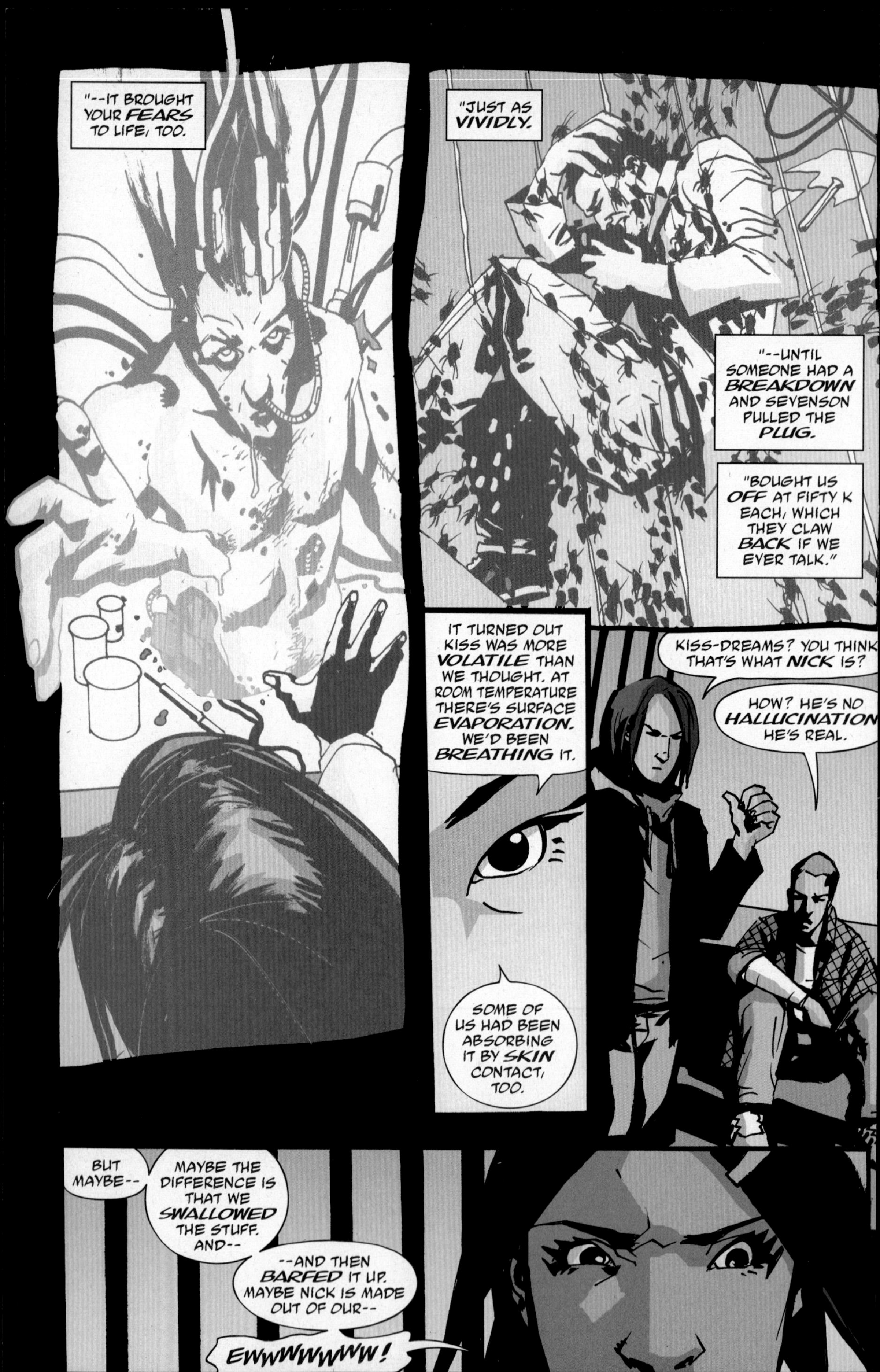

"--IT BROUGHT YOUR FEARS TO LIFE, TOO.
"JUST AS VIVIDLY.
"--UNTIL SOMEONE HAD A BREAKDOWN AND SEVENSON PULLED THE PLUG.
"BOUGHT US OFF AT FIFTY K EACH, WHICH THEY CLAW BACK IF WE EVER TALK."
IT TURNED OUT KISS WAS MORE VOLATILE THAN WE THOUGHT. AT ROOM TEMPERATURE THERE'S SURFACE EVAPORATION. WE'D BEEN BREATHING IT.
SOME OF US HAD BEEN ABSORBING IT BY SKIN CONTACT, TOO.
KISS-DREAMS? YOU THINK THAT'S WHAT NICK IS?
HOW? HE'S NO HALLUCINATION. HE'S REAL.
BUT MAYBE--
MAYBE THE DIFFERENCE IS THAT WE SWALLOWED THE STUFF. AND--
--AND THEN BARFED IT UP. MAYBE NICK IS MADE OUT OF OUR--
EWWWWWWW!

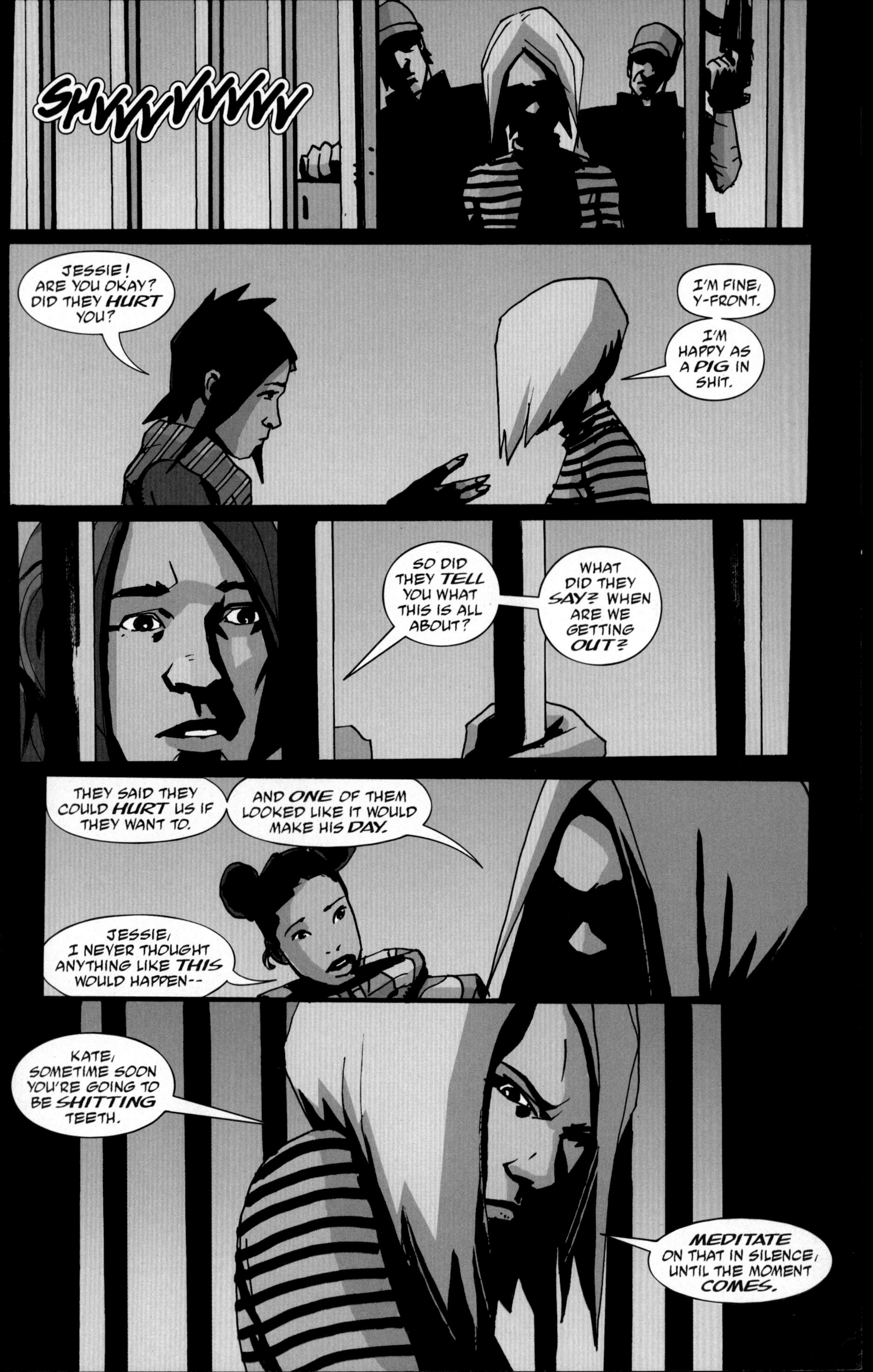
SHVVVVVVV
JESSIE! ARE YOU OKAY? DID THEY HURT YOU?
I'M FINE, Y-FRONT.
I'M HAPPY AS A PIG IN SHIT.
SO DID THEY TELL YOU WHAT THIS IS ALL ABOUT?
WHAT DID THEY SAY? WHEN ARE WE GETTING OUT?
THEY SAID THEY COULD HURT US IF THEY WANT TO.
AND ONE OF THEM LOOKED LIKE IT WOULD MAKE HIS DAY.
JESSIE, I NEVER THOUGHT ANYTHING LIKE THIS WOULD HAPPEN--
KATE, SOMETIME SOON YOU'RE GOING TO BE SHITTING TEETH.
MEDITATE ON THAT IN SILENCE, UNTIL THE MOMENT COMES.

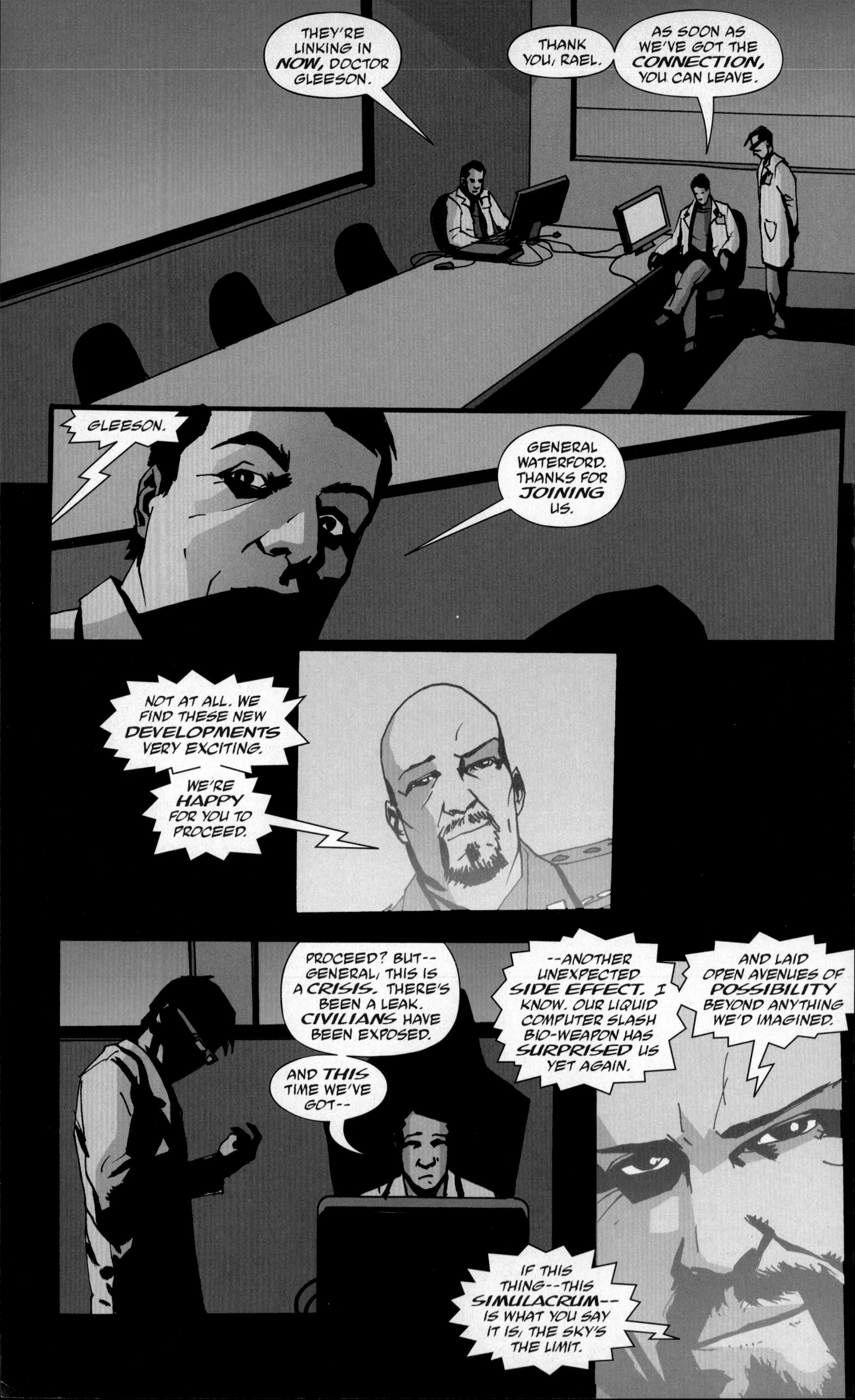
THEY'RE LINKING IN NOW, DOCTOR GLEESON.
THANK YOU, RAEL.
AS SOON AS WE'VE GOT THE CONNECTION, YOU CAN LEAVE.
GLEESON.
GENERAL WATERFORD. THANKS FOR JOINING US.
NOT AT ALL. WE FIND THESE NEW DEVELOPMENTS VERY EXCITING.
WE'RE HAPPY FOR YOU TO PROCEED.
PROCEED? BUT-- GENERAL, THIS IS A CRISIS. THERE'S BEEN A LEAK. CIVILIANS HAVE BEEN EXPOSED.
AND THIS TIME WE'VE GOT--
--ANOTHER UNEXPECTED SIDE EFFECT. I KNOW. OUR LIQUID COMPUTER SLASH BIO-WEAPON HAS SURPRISED US YET AGAIN.
AND LAID OPEN AVENUES OF POSSIBILITY BEYOND ANYTHING WE'D IMAGINED.
IF THIS THING--THIS SIMULACRUM--IS WHAT YOU SAY IT IS, THE SKY'S THE LIMIT.

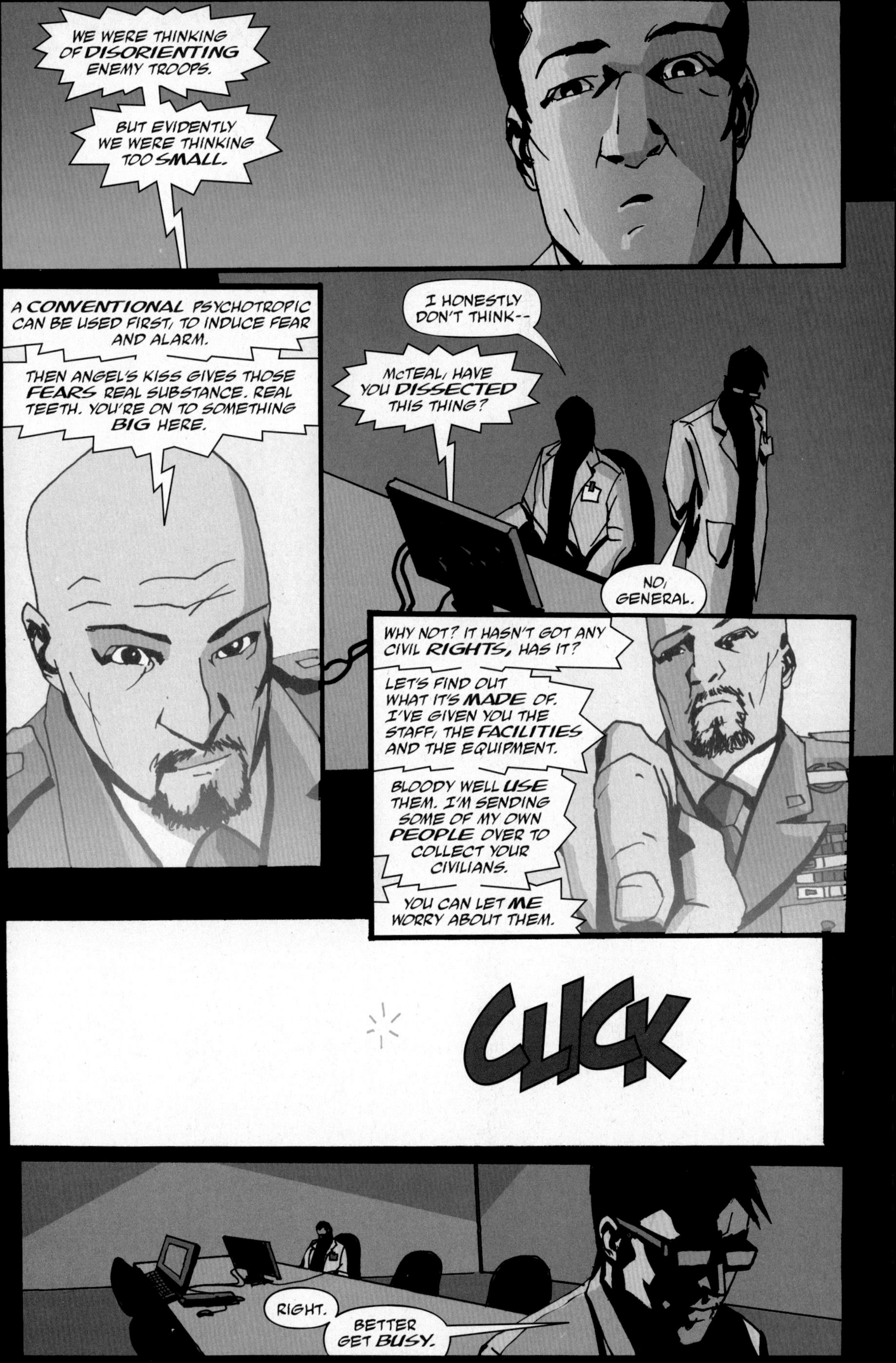

WE WERE THINKING OF DISORIENTING ENEMY TROOPS.
BUT EVIDENTLY WE WERE THINKING TOO SMALL.
A CONVENTIONAL PSYCHOTROPIC CAN BE USED FIRST, TO INDUCE FEAR AND ALARM.
THEN ANGEL'S KISS GIVES THOSE FEARS REAL SUBSTANCE. REAL TEETH. YOU'RE ON TO SOMETHING BIG HERE.
I HONESTLY DON'T THINK--
McTEAL, HAVE YOU DISSECTED THIS THING?
NO, GENERAL.
WHY NOT? IT HASN'T GOT ANY CIVIL RIGHTS, HAS IT?
LET'S FIND OUT WHAT IT'S MADE OF. I'VE GIVEN YOU THE STAFF, THE FACILITIES AND THE EQUIPMENT.
BLOODY WELL USE THEM. I'M SENDING SOME OF MY OWN PEOPLE OVER TO COLLECT YOUR CIVILIANS.
YOU CAN LET ME WORRY ABOUT THEM.
CLICK
RIGHT.
BETTER GET BUSY.

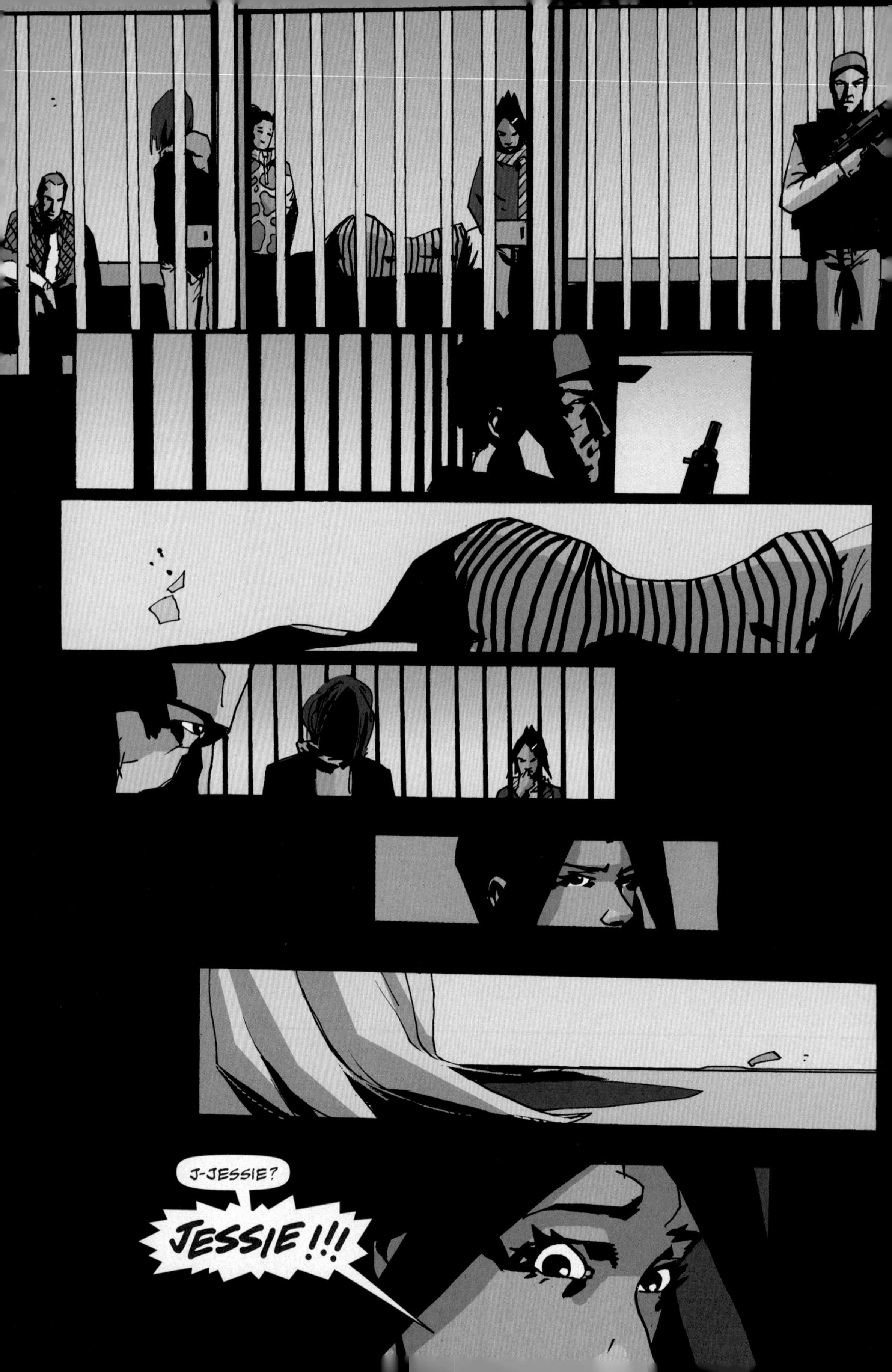
J-JESSIE?
JESSIE!!!

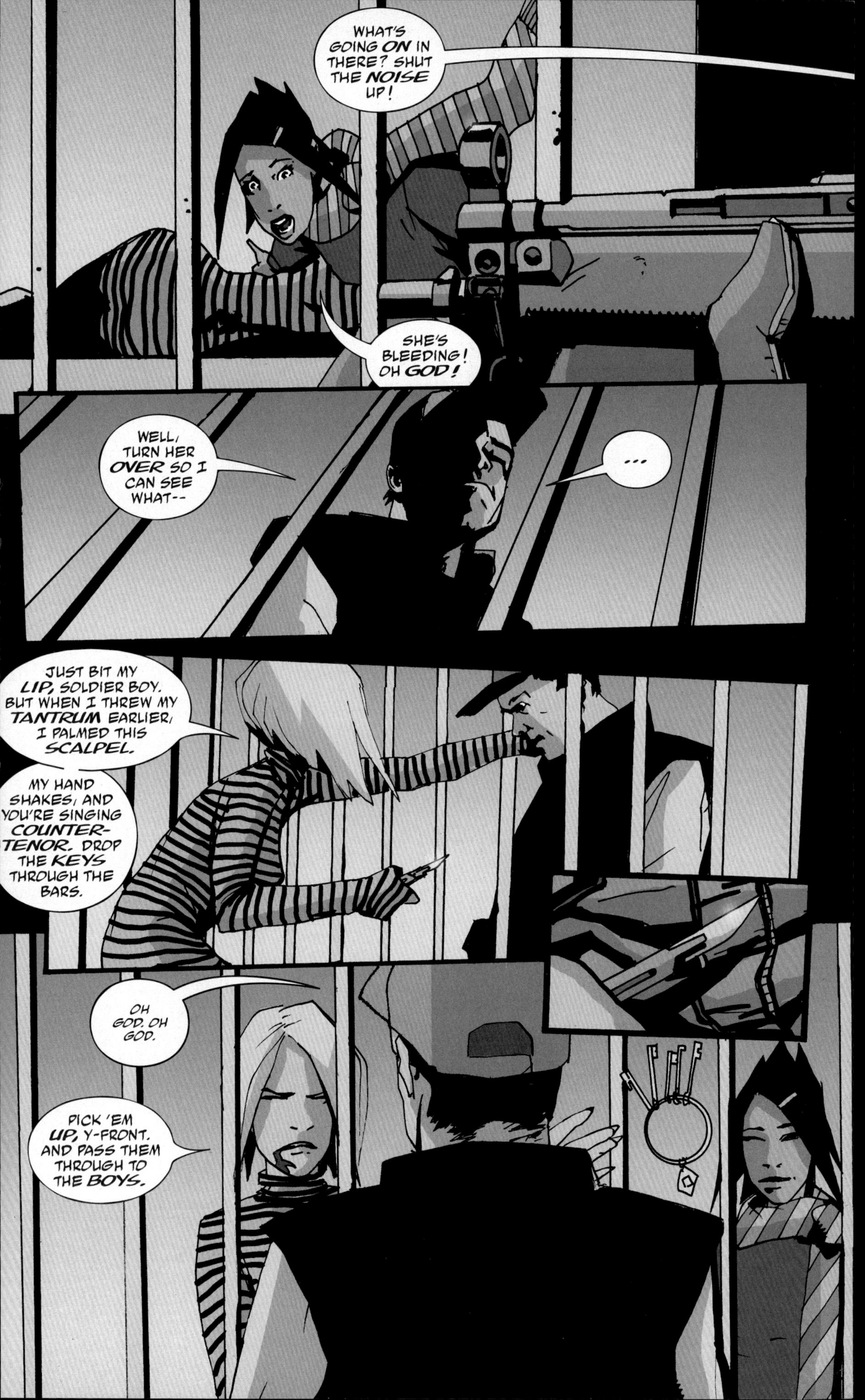
WHAT'S GOING ON IN THERE? SHUT THE NOISE UP!
SHE'S BLEEDING! OH GOD!
WELL, TURN HER OVER SO I CAN SEE WHAT--
...
JUST BIT MY LIP, SOLDIER BOY. BUT WHEN I THREW MY TANTRUM EARLIER, I PALMED THIS SCALPEL.
MY HAND SHAKES, AND YOU'RE SINGING COUNTER-TENOR. DROP THE KEYS THROUGH THE BARS.
OH GOD. OH GOD.
PICK 'EM UP, Y-FRONT. AND PASS THEM THROUGH TO THE BOYS.

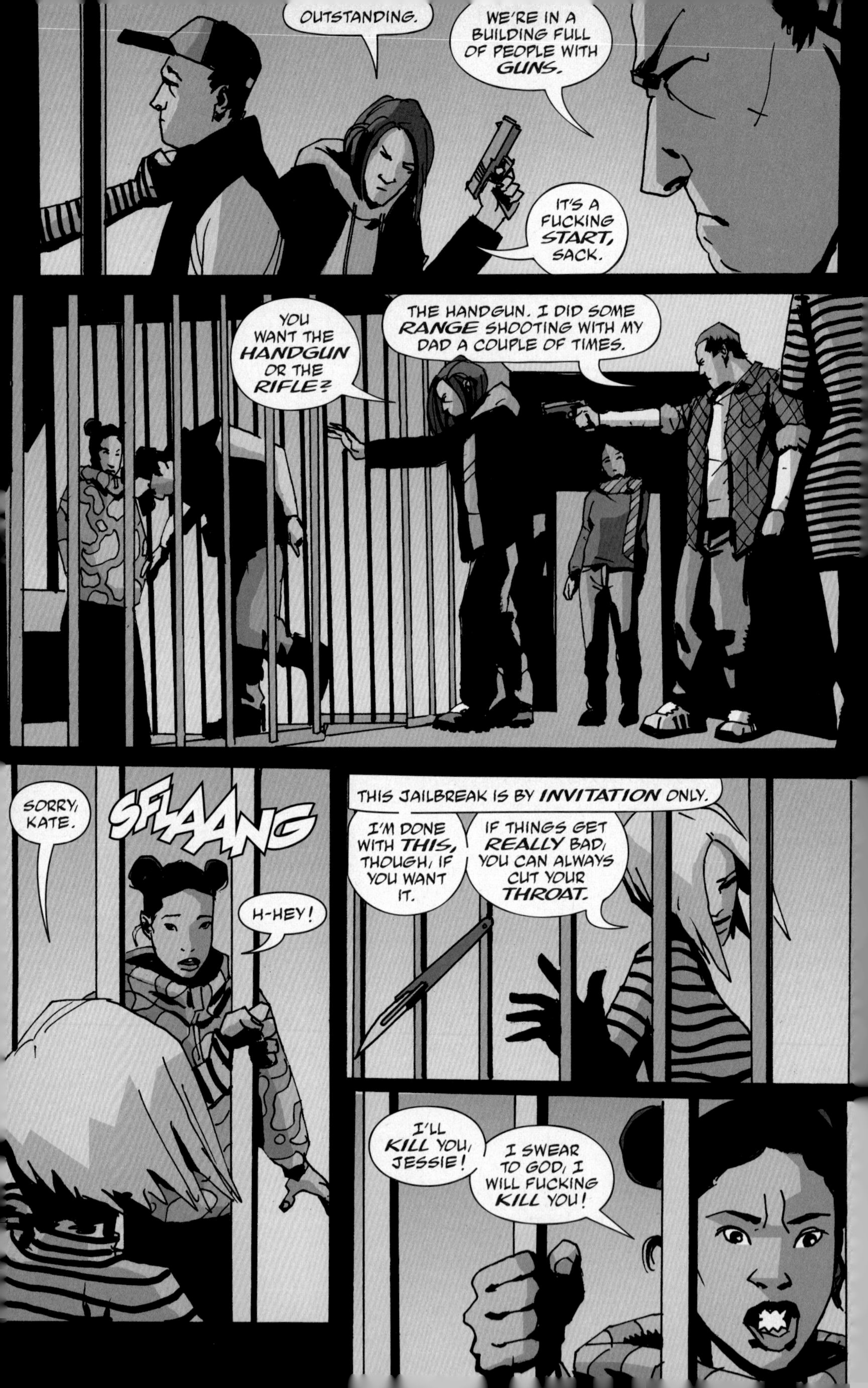
OUTSTANDING.
WE'RE IN A BUILDING FULL OF PEOPLE WITH GUNS.
IT'S A FUCKING START, SACK.
YOU WANT THE HANDGUN OR THE RIFLE?
THE HANDGUN. I DID SOME RANGE SHOOTING WITH MY DAD A COUPLE OF TIMES.
SORRY, KATE.
SFLAANG
H-HEY!
THIS JAILBREAK IS BY INVITATION ONLY.
I'M DONE WITH THIS, THOUGH, IF YOU WANT IT.
IF THINGS GET REALLY BAD, YOU CAN ALWAYS CUT YOUR THROAT.
I'LL KILL YOU, JESSIE!
I SWEAR TO GOD, I WILL FUCKING KILL YOU!

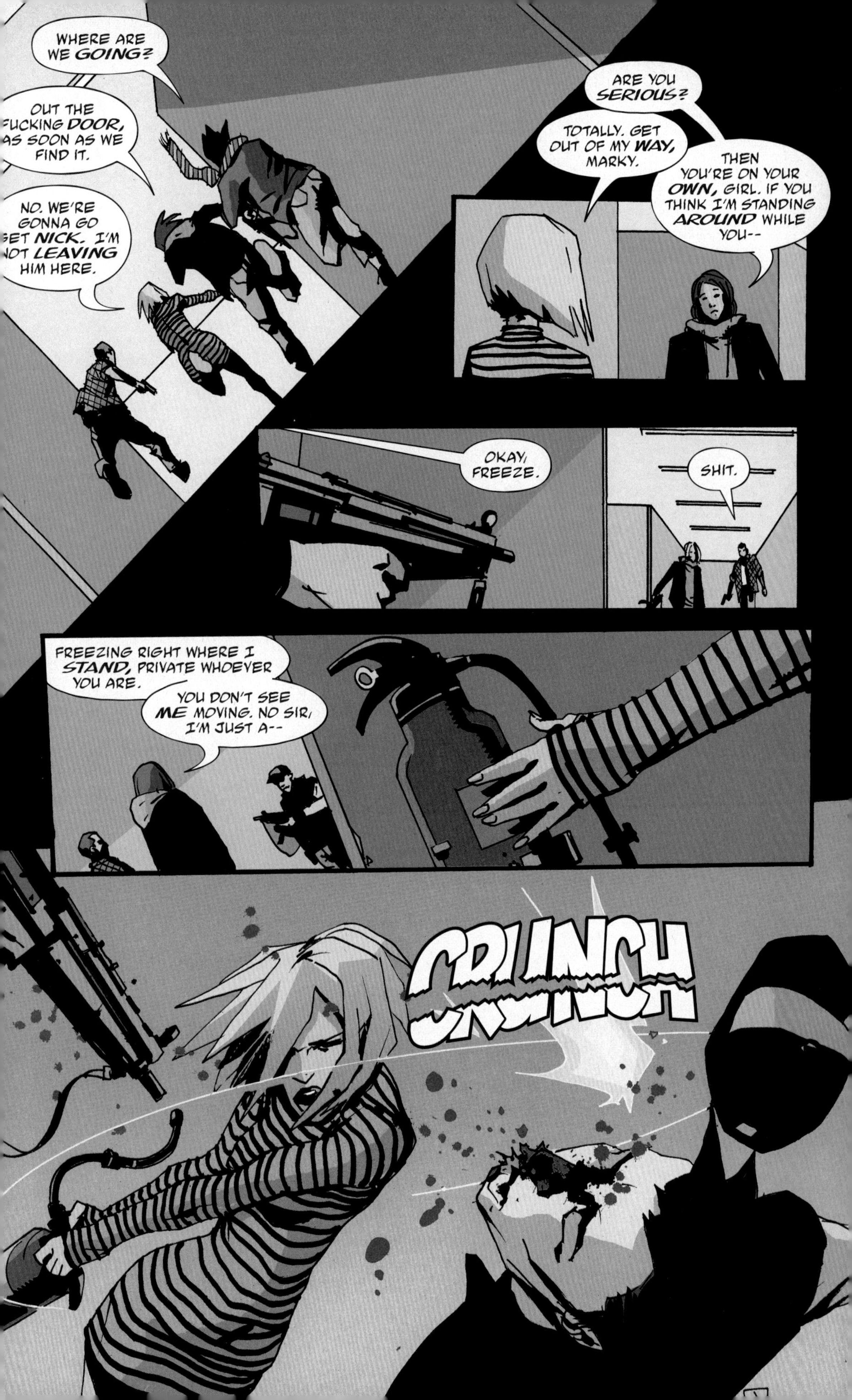
WHERE ARE WE GOING?
OUT THE FUCKING DOOR, AS SOON AS WE FIND IT.
NO. WE'RE GONNA GO GET NICK. I'M NOT LEAVING HIM HERE.
ARE YOU SERIOUS?
TOTALLY. GET OUT OF MY WAY, MARKY.
THEN YOU'RE ON YOUR OWN, GIRL. IF YOU THINK I'M STANDING AROUND WHILE YOU--
OKAY, FREEZE.
SHIT.
FREEZING RIGHT WHERE I STAND, PRIVATE WHOEVER YOU ARE.
YOU DON'T SEE ME MOVING. NO SIR, I'M JUST A--
CRUNCH

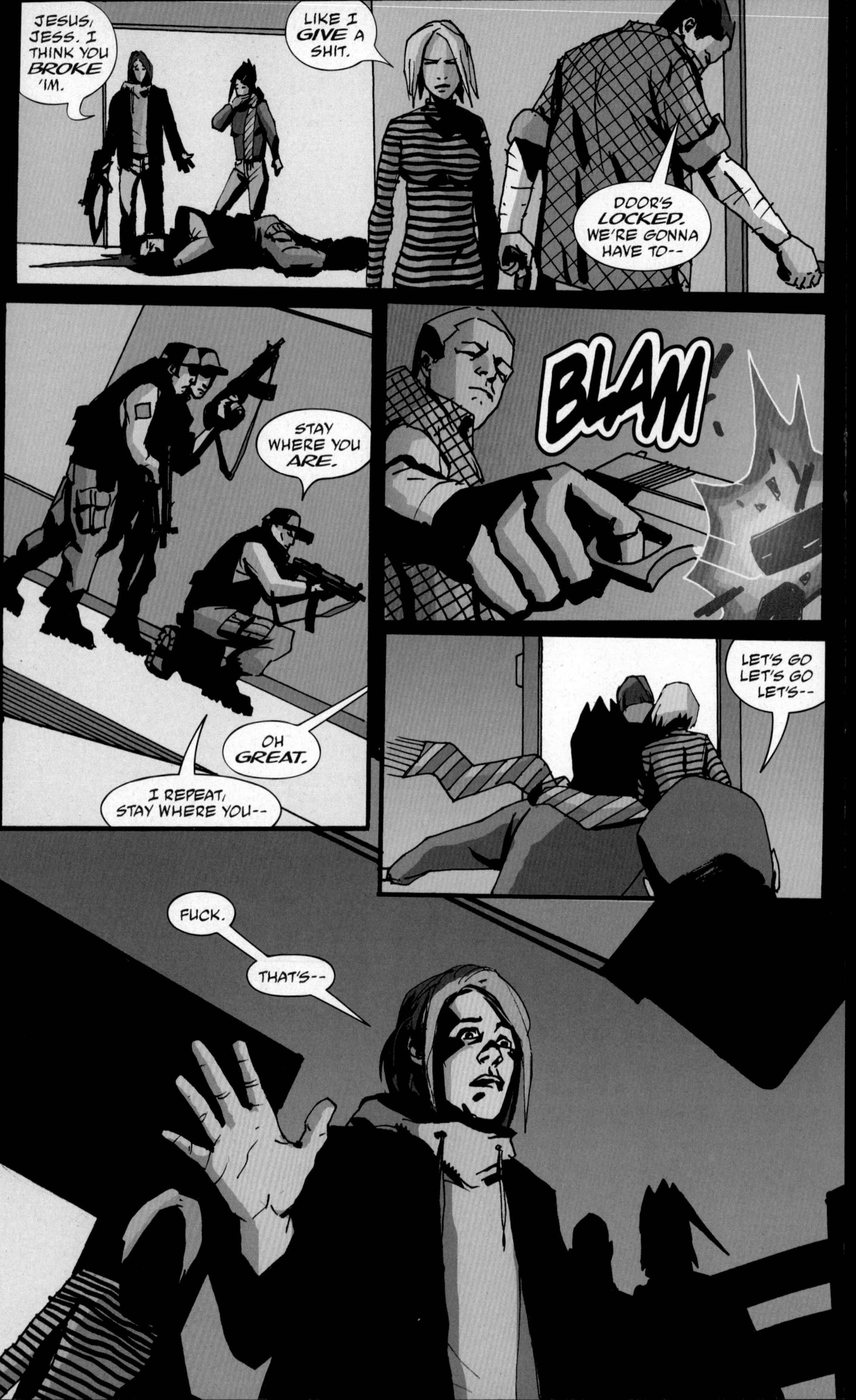
JESUS, JESS. I THINK YOU BROKE 'IM.
LIKE I GIVE A SHIT.
DOOR'S LOCKED. WE'RE GONNA HAVE TO--
STAY WHERE YOU ARE.
OH GREAT.
I REPEAT, STAY WHERE YOU--
BLAM
LET'S GO LET'S GO LET'S--
FUCK.
THAT'S--

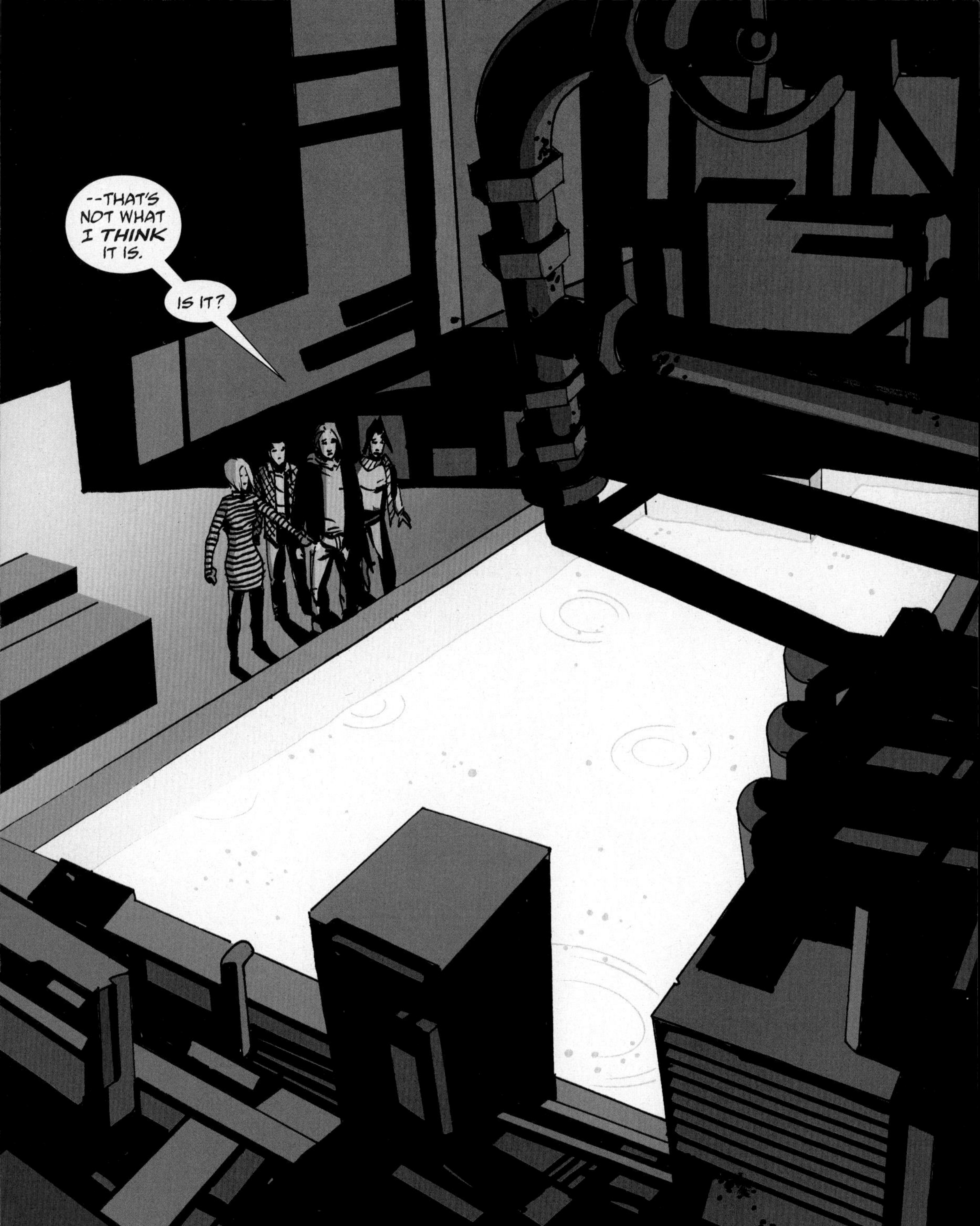
--THAT'S NOT WHAT I THINK IT IS.
IS IT?

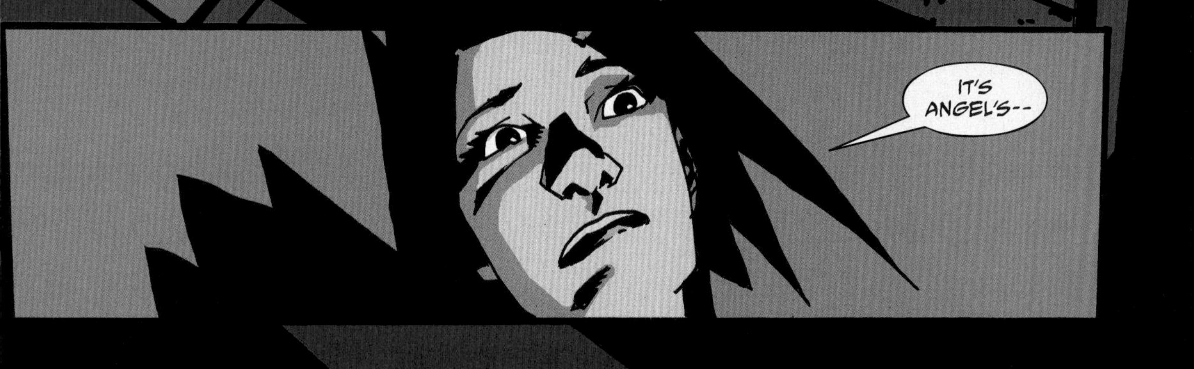
IT'S ANGEL'S--

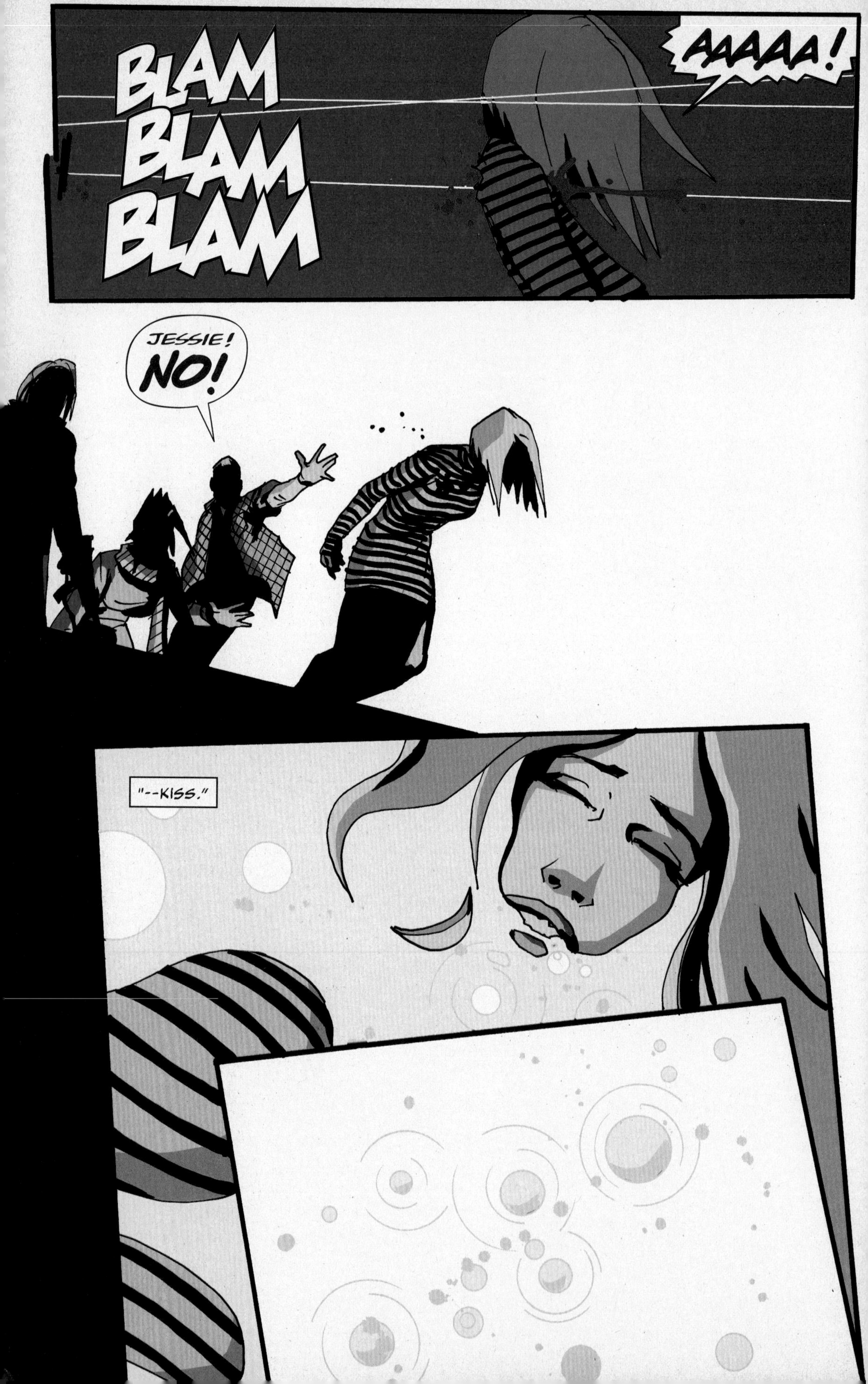
BLAM
BLAM
BLAM
AAAAA!
JESSIE! NO!
"--KISS."

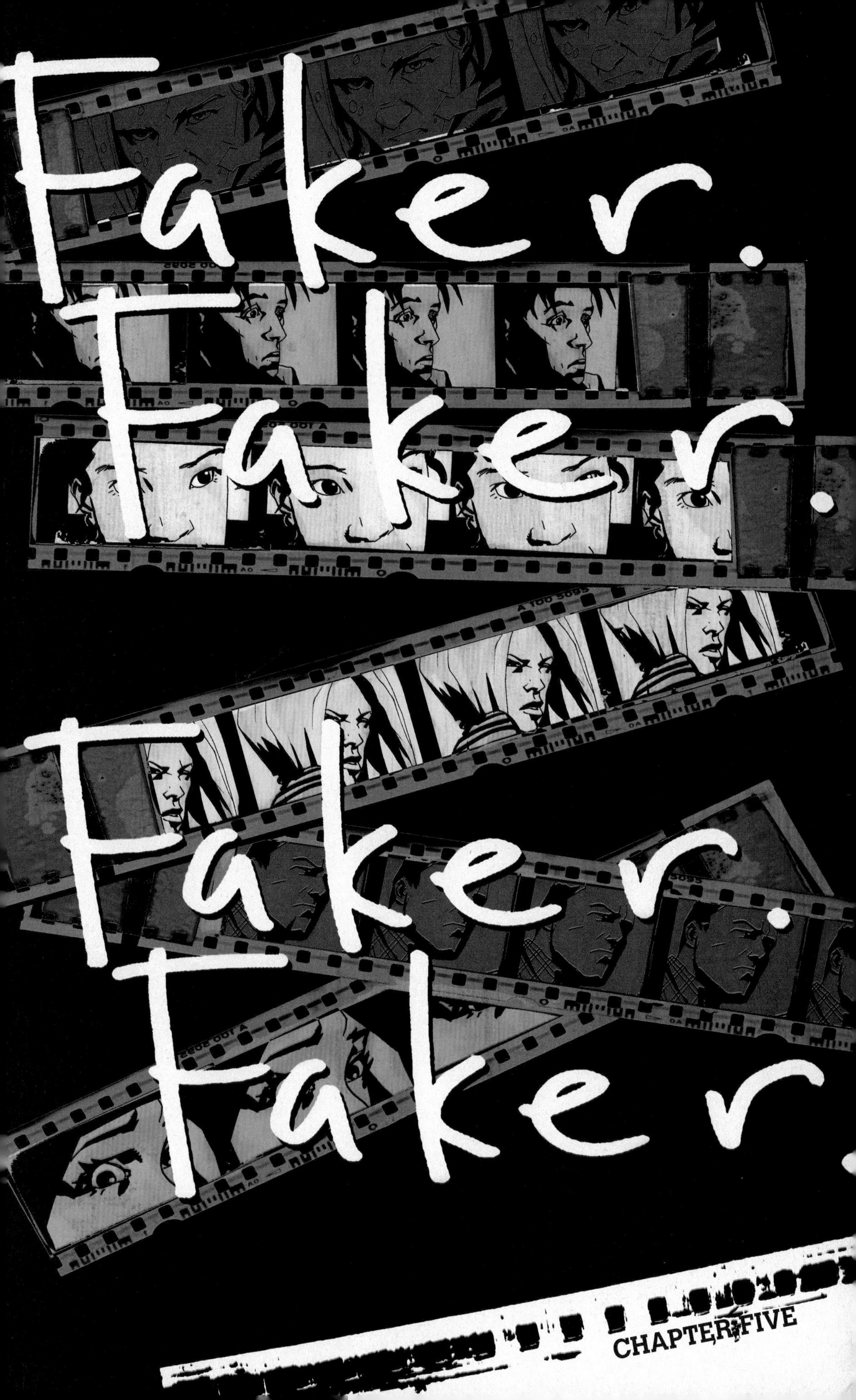
Faker.
Faker.
Faker.
Faker.
CHAPTER FIVE

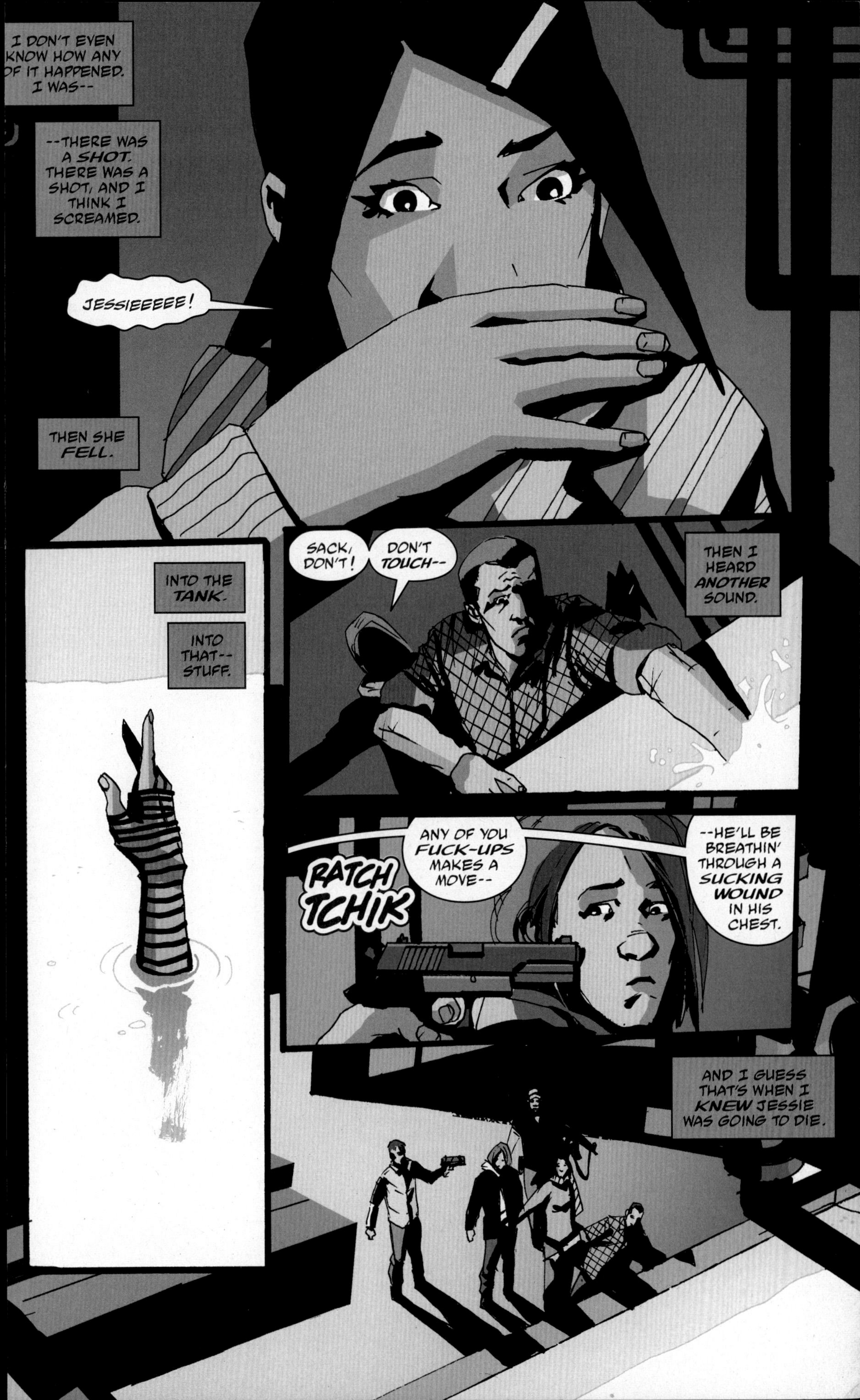
I DON'T EVEN KNOW HOW ANY OF IT HAPPENED. I WAS--
--THERE WAS A SHOT. THERE WAS A SHOT, AND I THINK I SCREAMED.
JESSIEEEEE!
THEN SHE FELL.
INTO THE TANK.
INTO THAT--STUFF.
SACK, DON'T!
DON'T TOUCH--
THEN I HEARD ANOTHER SOUND.
RATCH TCHIK
ANY OF YOU FUCK-UPS MAKES A MOVE--
--HE'LL BE BREATHIN' THROUGH A SUCKING WOUND IN HIS CHEST.
AND I GUESS THAT'S WHEN I KNEW JESSIE WAS GOING TO DIE.

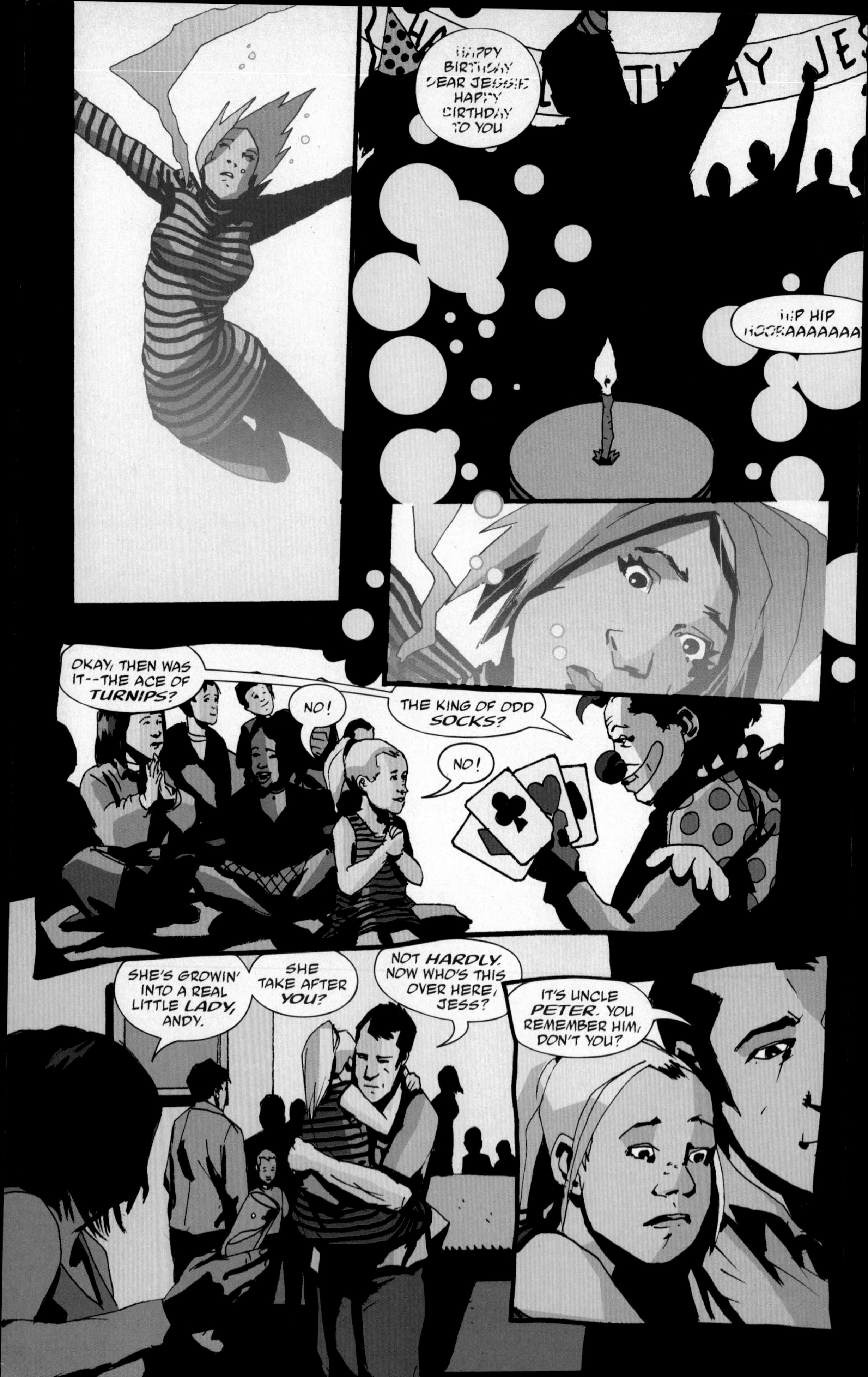
HAPPY BIRTHDAY DEAR JESSIE HAPPY BIRTHDAY TO YOU
HIP HIP HOORAAAAAAAA
OKAY, THEN WAS IT--THE ACE OF TURNIPS?
NO!
THE KING OF ODD SOCKS?
NO!
SHE'S GROWIN' INTO A REAL LITTLE LADY, ANDY.
SHE TAKE AFTER YOU?
NOT HARDLY. NOW WHO'S THIS OVER HERE, JESS?
IT'S UNCLE PETER. YOU REMEMBER HIM, DON'T YOU?

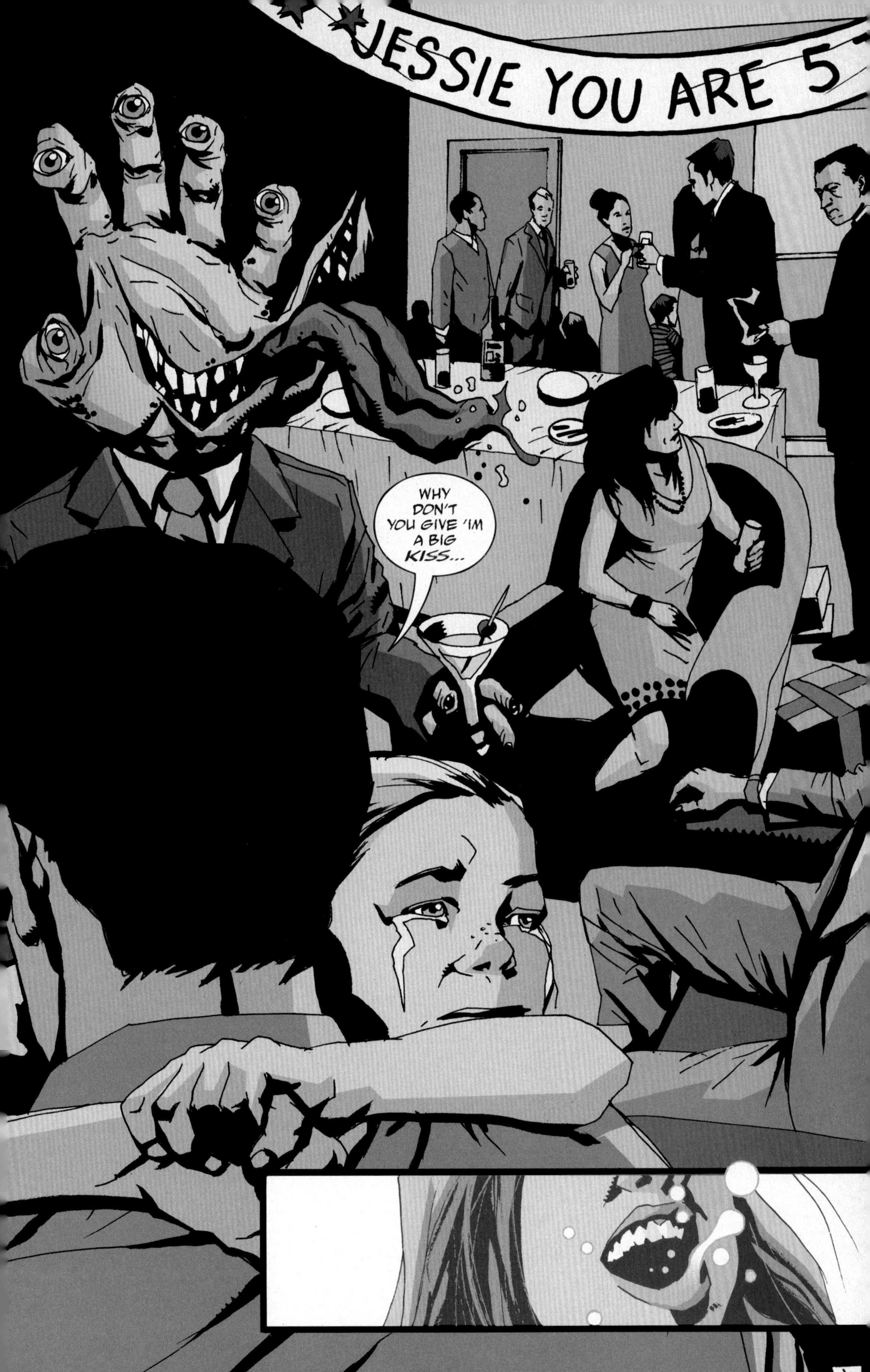
JESSIE YOU ARE 5
WHY DON'T YOU GIVE 'IM A BIG KISS...

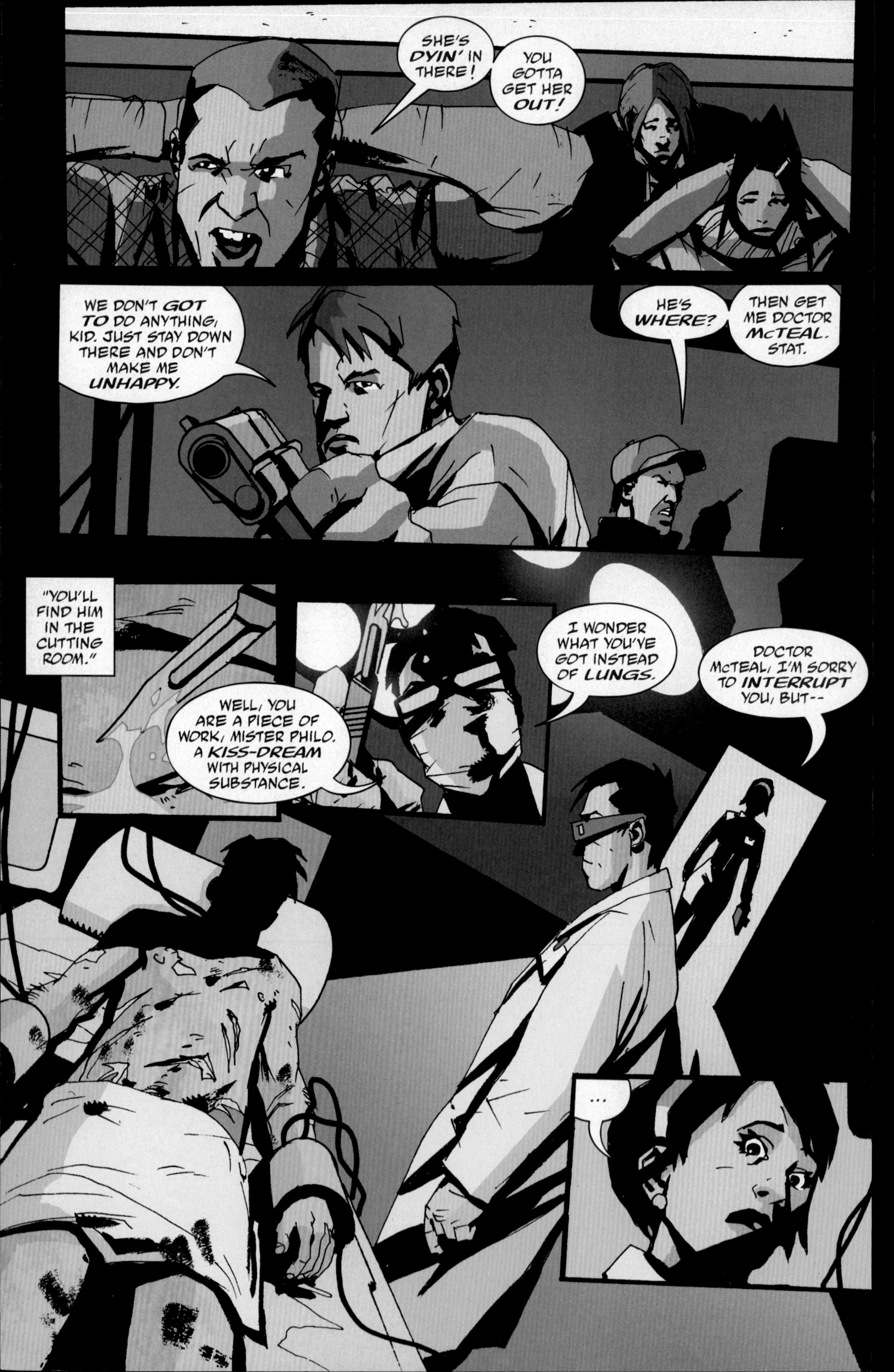
SHE'S DYIN' IN THERE!
YOU GOTTA GET HER OUT!
WE DON'T GOT TO DO ANYTHING, KID. JUST STAY DOWN THERE AND DON'T MAKE ME UNHAPPY.
HE'S WHERE?
THEN GET ME DOCTOR McTEAL. STAT.
"YOU'LL FIND HIM IN THE CUTTING ROOM."
WELL, YOU ARE A PIECE OF WORK, MISTER PHILO. A KISS-DREAM WITH PHYSICAL SUBSTANCE.
I WONDER WHAT YOU'VE GOT INSTEAD OF LUNGS.
DOCTOR McTEAL, I'M SORRY TO INTERRUPT YOU, BUT--
...

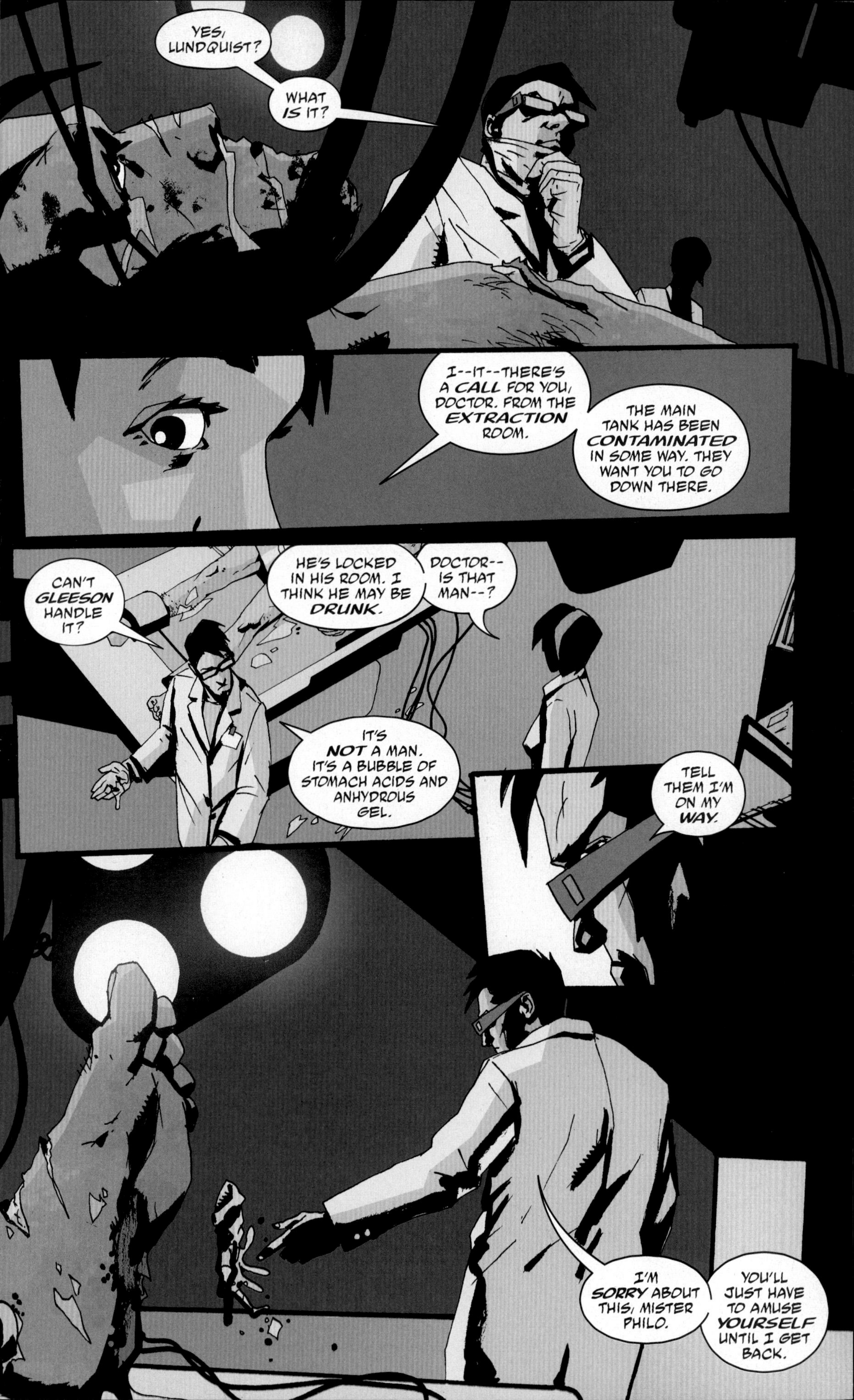
YES, LUNDQUIST?
WHAT IS IT?
I--IT--THERE'S A CALL FOR YOU, DOCTOR. FROM THE EXTRACTION ROOM.
THE MAIN TANK HAS BEEN CONTAMINATED IN SOME WAY. THEY WANT YOU TO GO DOWN THERE.
CAN'T GLEESON HANDLE IT?
HE'S LOCKED IN HIS ROOM. I THINK HE MAY BE DRUNK.
DOCTOR-- IS THAT MAN--?
IT'S NOT A MAN. IT'S A BUBBLE OF STOMACH ACIDS AND ANHYDROUS GEL.
TELL THEM I'M ON MY WAY.
I'M SORRY ABOUT THIS, MISTER PHILO.
YOU'LL JUST HAVE TO AMUSE YOURSELF UNTIL I GET BACK.

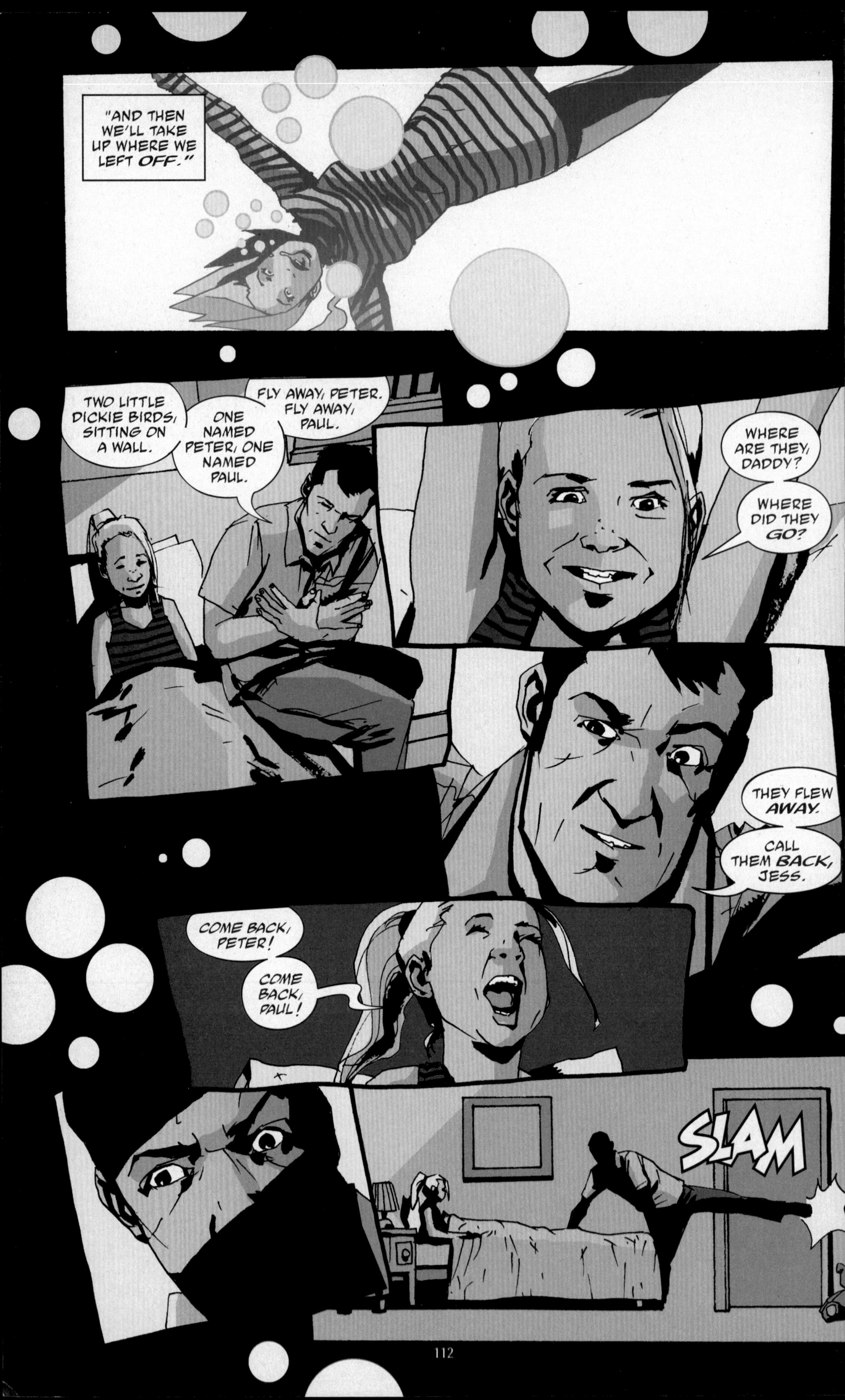
"AND THEN WE'LL TAKE UP WHERE WE LEFT *OFF*."
TWO LITTLE DICKIE BIRDS, SITTING ON A WALL.
ONE NAMED PETER, ONE NAMED PAUL.
FLY AWAY, PETER. FLY AWAY, PAUL.
WHERE ARE THEY, DADDY?
WHERE DID THEY *GO?*
THEY FLEW *AWAY*.
CALL THEM *BACK*, JESS.
COME BACK, PETER!
COME BACK, PAUL!
SLAM

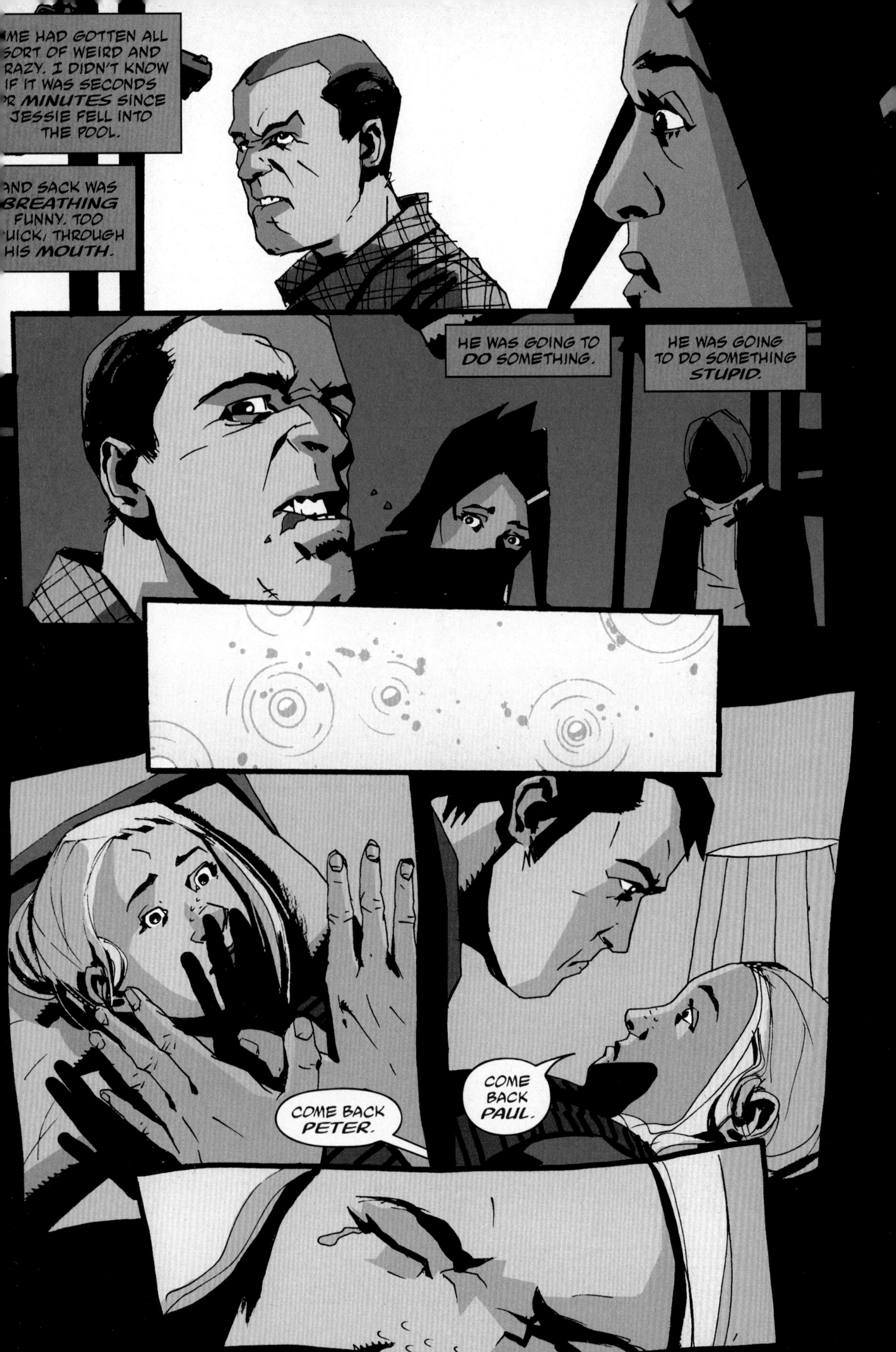
ME HAD GOTTEN ALL SORT OF WEIRD AND RAZY. I DIDN'T KNOW IF IT WAS SECONDS R MINUTES SINCE JESSIE FELL INTO THE POOL.
AND SACK WAS BREATHING FUNNY. TOO UICK, THROUGH HIS MOUTH.
HE WAS GOING TO DO SOMETHING.
HE WAS GOING TO DO SOMETHING STUPID.
COME BACK PETER.
COME BACK PAUL.

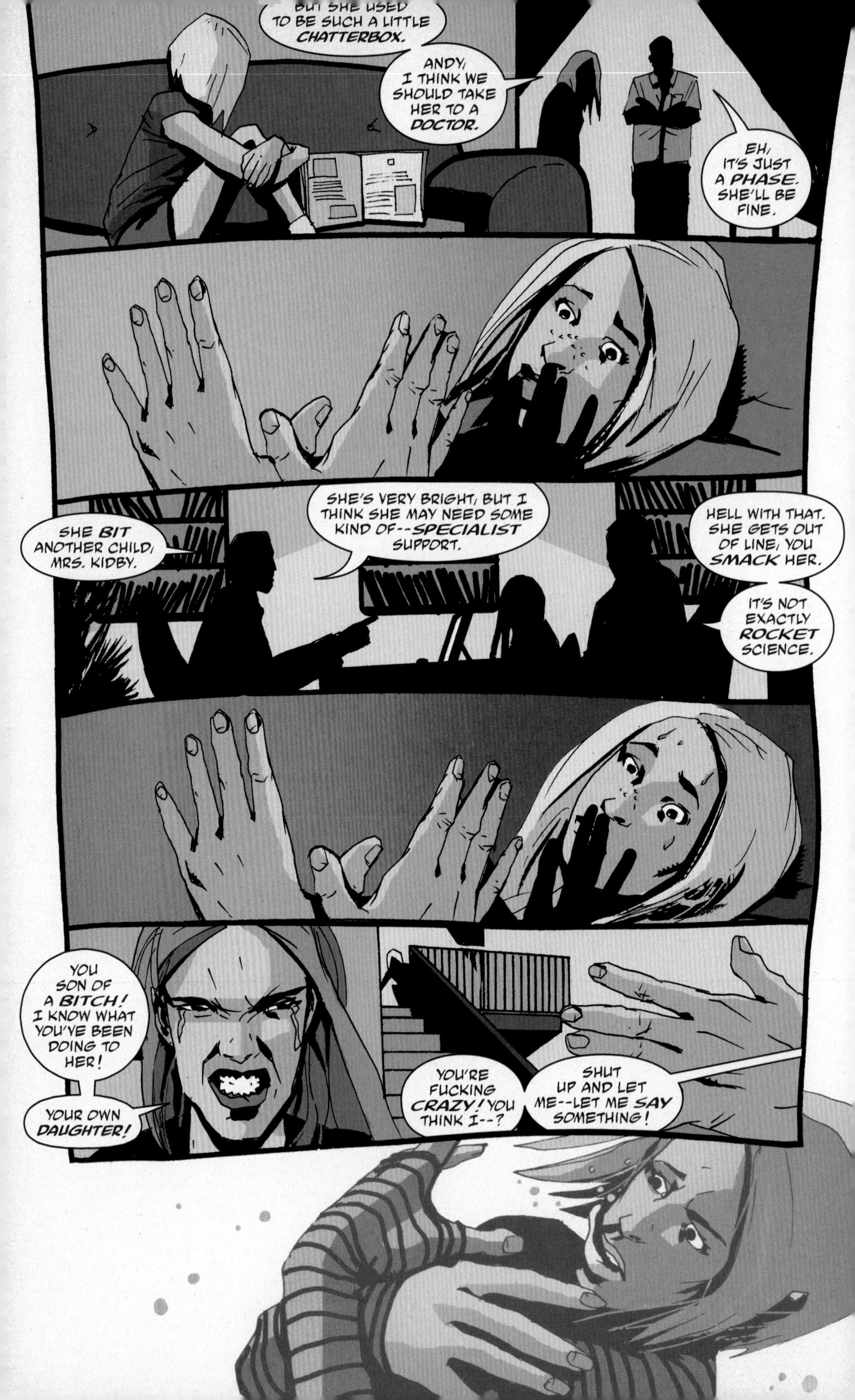

BUT SHE USED TO BE SUCH A LITTLE CHATTERBOX.
ANDY, I THINK WE SHOULD TAKE HER TO A DOCTOR.
EH, IT'S JUST A PHASE. SHE'LL BE FINE.
SHE BIT ANOTHER CHILD, MRS. KIDBY.
SHE'S VERY BRIGHT, BUT I THINK SHE MAY NEED SOME KIND OF--SPECIALIST SUPPORT.
HELL WITH THAT. SHE GETS OUT OF LINE, YOU SMACK HER.
IT'S NOT EXACTLY ROCKET SCIENCE.
YOU SON OF A BITCH! I KNOW WHAT YOU'VE BEEN DOING TO HER!
YOUR OWN DAUGHTER!
YOU'RE FUCKING CRAZY! YOU THINK I--?
SHUT UP AND LET ME--LET ME SAY SOMETHING!

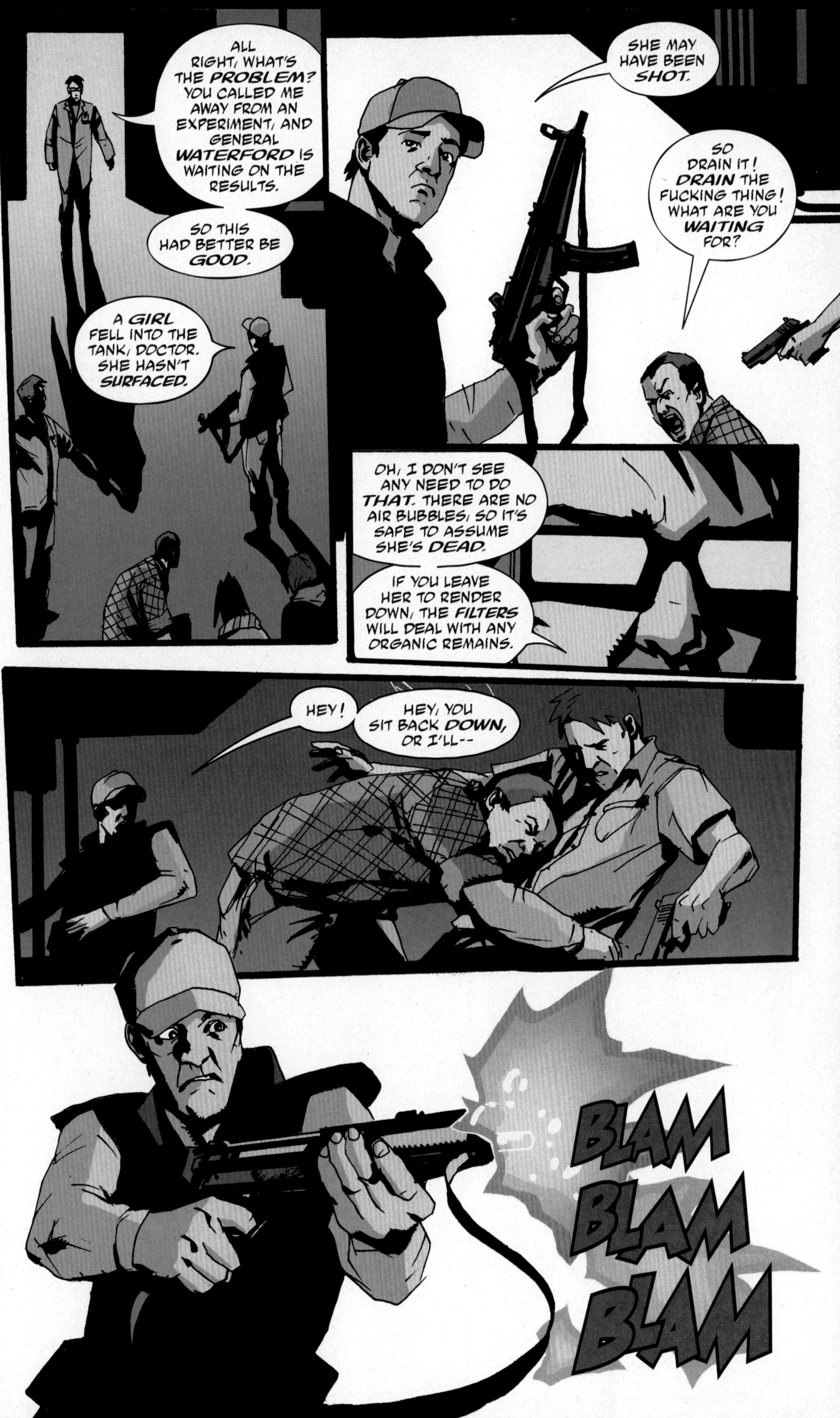
ALL RIGHT, WHAT'S THE PROBLEM? YOU CALLED ME AWAY FROM AN EXPERIMENT, AND GENERAL WATERFORD IS WAITING ON THE RESULTS.
SO THIS HAD BETTER BE GOOD.
A GIRL FELL INTO THE TANK, DOCTOR. SHE HASN'T SURFACED.
SHE MAY HAVE BEEN SHOT.
SO DRAIN IT! DRAIN THE FUCKING THING! WHAT ARE YOU WAITING FOR?
OH, I DON'T SEE ANY NEED TO DO THAT. THERE ARE NO AIR BUBBLES, SO IT'S SAFE TO ASSUME SHE'S DEAD.
IF YOU LEAVE HER TO RENDER DOWN, THE FILTERS WILL DEAL WITH ANY ORGANIC REMAINS.
HEY!
HEY, YOU SIT BACK DOWN, OR I'LL--
BLAM
BLAM
BLAM

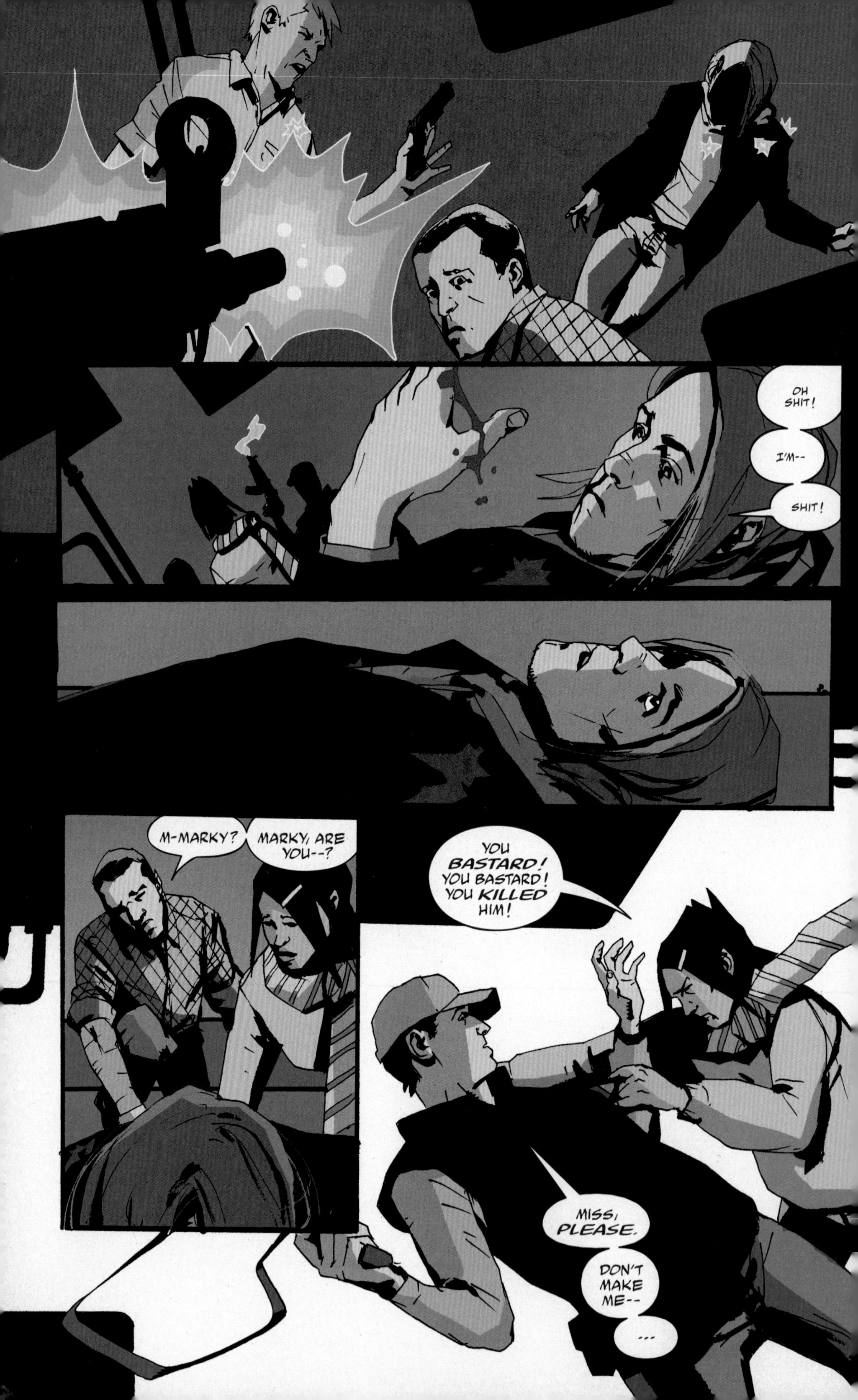
OH SHIT!
I'M--
SHIT!
M-MARKY?
MARKY, ARE YOU--?
YOU BASTARD! YOU BASTARD! YOU KILLED HIM!
MISS, PLEASE.
DON'T MAKE ME--
...

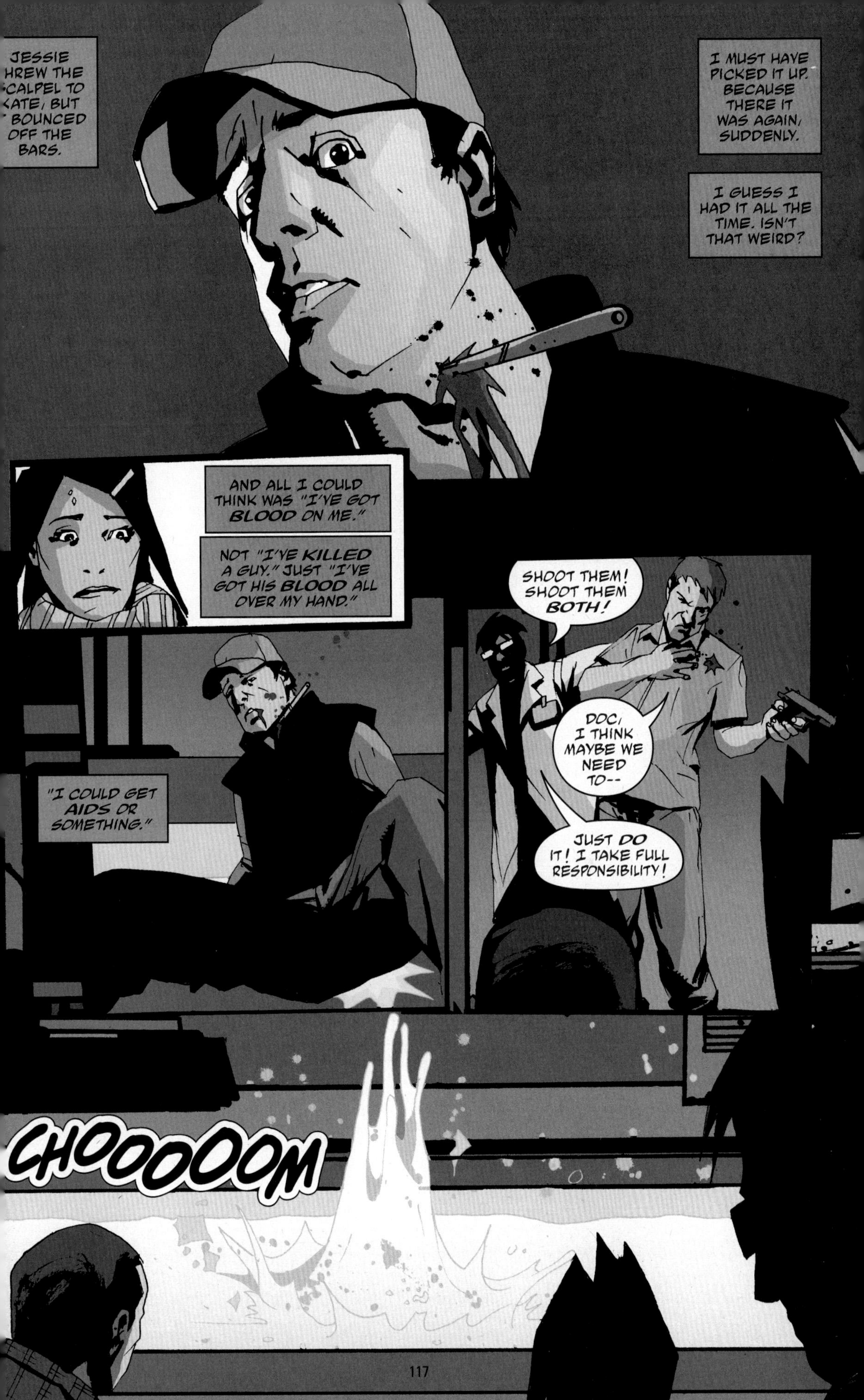
JESSIE HREW THE CALPEL TO KATE, BUT BOUNCED OFF THE BARS.
I MUST HAVE PICKED IT UP. BECAUSE THERE IT WAS AGAIN, SUDDENLY.
I GUESS I HAD IT ALL THE TIME. ISN'T THAT WEIRD?
AND ALL I COULD THINK WAS "I'VE GOT BLOOD ON ME."
NOT "I'VE KILLED A GUY." JUST "I'VE GOT HIS BLOOD ALL OVER MY HAND."
SHOOT THEM! SHOOT THEM BOTH!
"I COULD GET AIDS OR SOMETHING."
DOC, I THINK MAYBE WE NEED TO--
JUST DO IT! I TAKE FULL RESPONSIBILITY!
CHOOOOOM

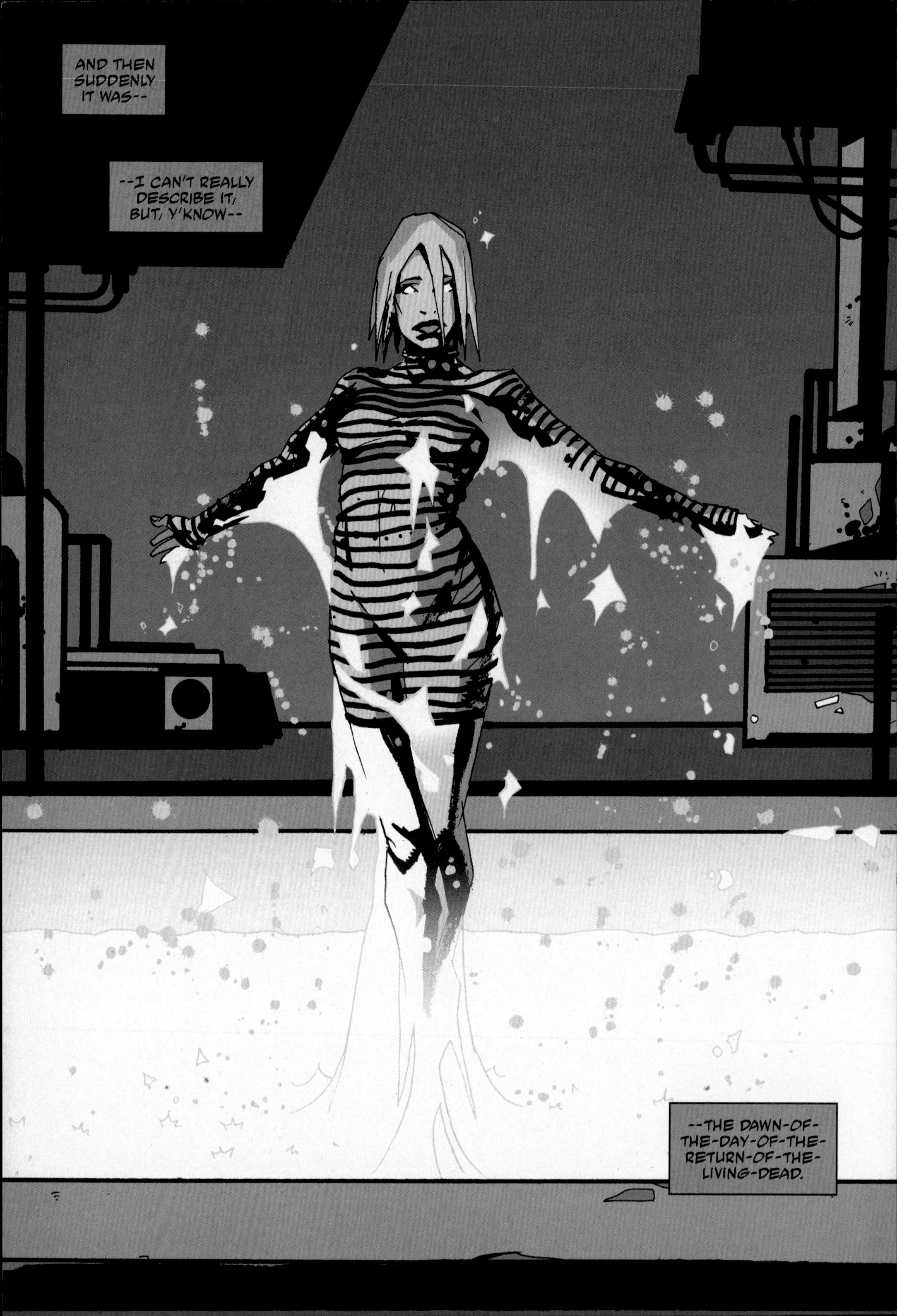
AND THEN SUDDENLY IT WAS--
--I CAN'T REALLY DESCRIBE IT, BUT, Y'KNOW--
--THE DAWN-OF-THE-DAY-OF-THE-RETURN-OF-THE-LIVING-DEAD.

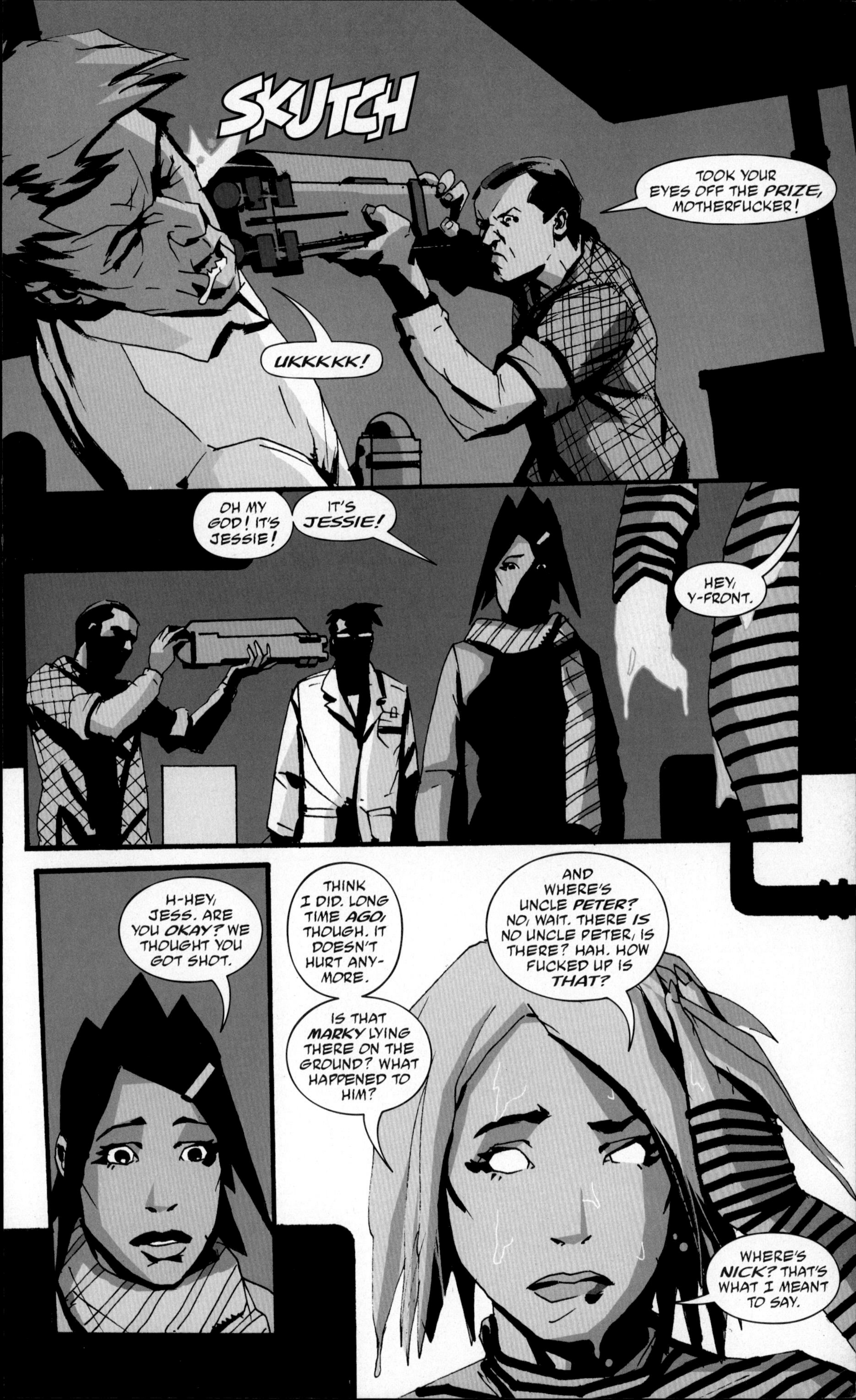
SKUTCH
TOOK YOUR EYES OFF THE PRIZE, MOTHERFUCKER!
UKKKKK!
OH MY GOD! IT'S JESSIE!
IT'S JESSIE!
HEY, Y-FRONT.
H-HEY, JESS. ARE YOU OKAY? WE THOUGHT YOU GOT SHOT.
THINK I DID. LONG TIME AGO, THOUGH. IT DOESN'T HURT ANY-MORE.
IS THAT MARKY LYING THERE ON THE GROUND? WHAT HAPPENED TO HIM?
AND WHERE'S UNCLE PETER? NO, WAIT. THERE IS NO UNCLE PETER, IS THERE? HAH. HOW FUCKED UP IS THAT?
WHERE'S NICK? THAT'S WHAT I MEANT TO SAY.

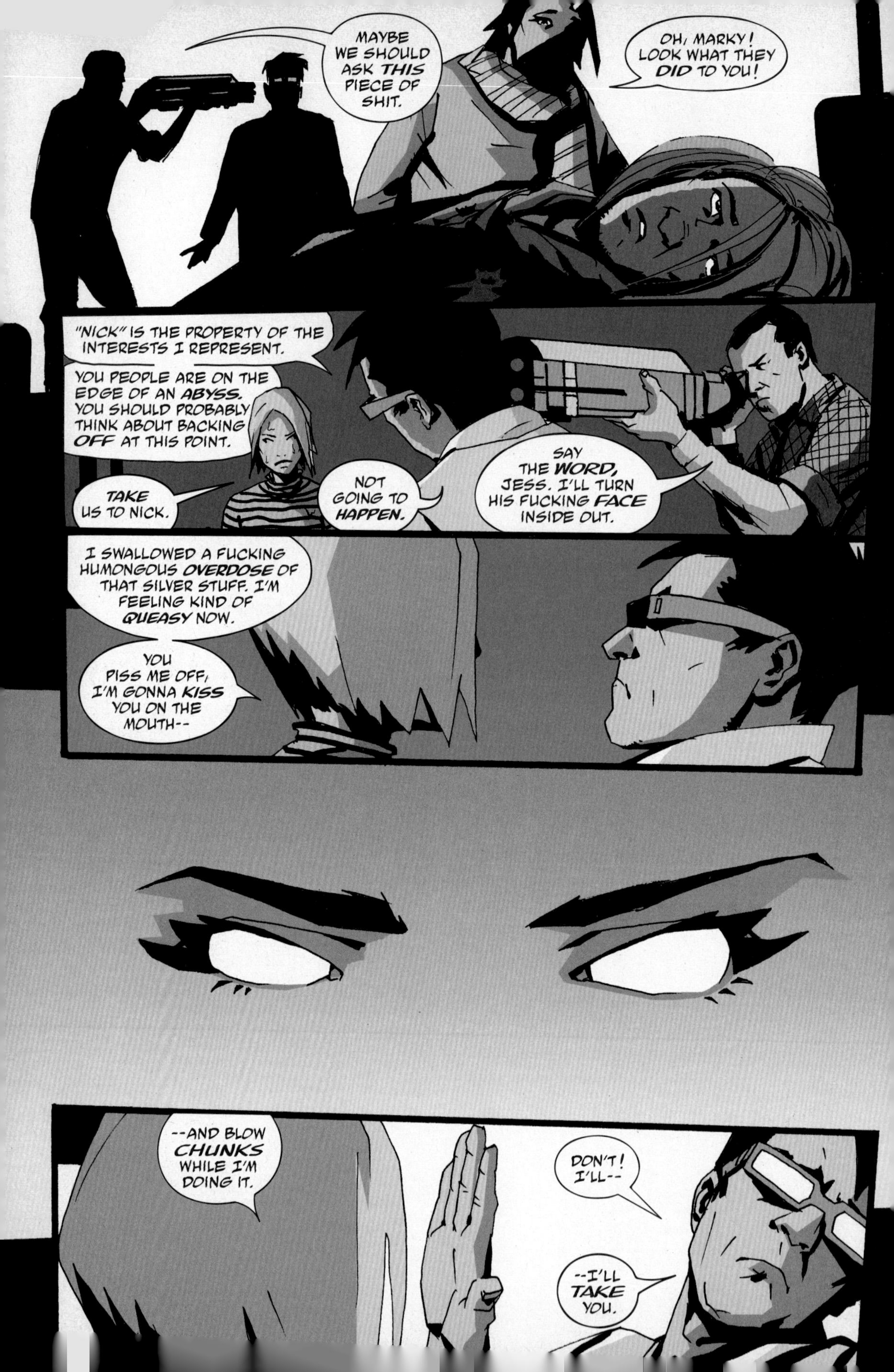
MAYBE WE SHOULD ASK THIS PIECE OF SHIT.
OH, MARKY! LOOK WHAT THEY DID TO YOU!
"NICK" IS THE PROPERTY OF THE INTERESTS I REPRESENT.
YOU PEOPLE ARE ON THE EDGE OF AN ABYSS. YOU SHOULD PROBABLY THINK ABOUT BACKING OFF AT THIS POINT.
TAKE US TO NICK.
NOT GOING TO HAPPEN.
SAY THE WORD, JESS. I'LL TURN HIS FUCKING FACE INSIDE OUT.
I SWALLOWED A FUCKING HUMONGOUS OVERDOSE OF THAT SILVER STUFF. I'M FEELING KIND OF QUEASY NOW.
YOU PISS ME OFF, I'M GONNA KISS YOU ON THE MOUTH--
--AND BLOW CHUNKS WHILE I'M DOING IT.
DON'T! I'LL--
--I'LL TAKE YOU.

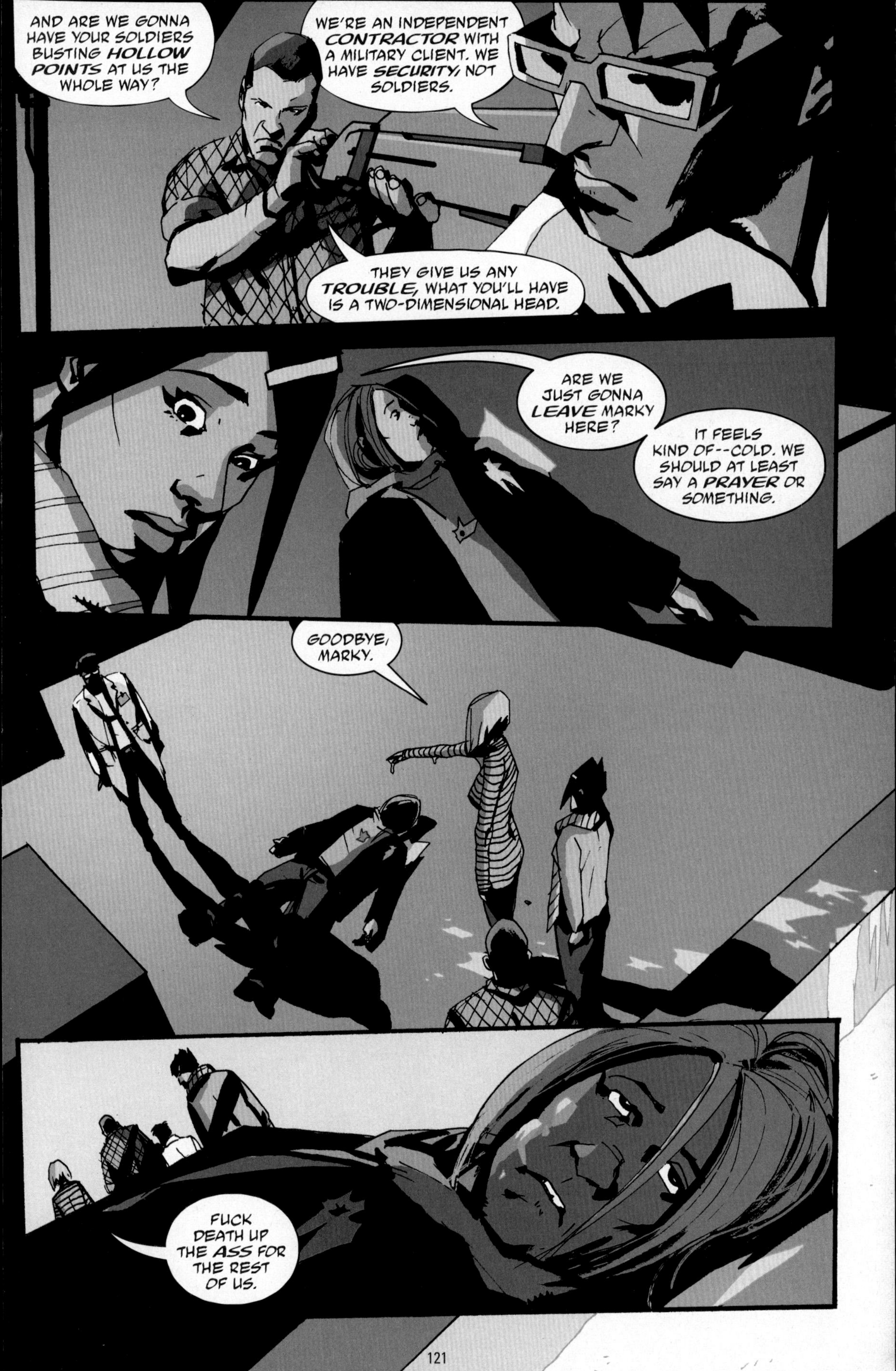
AND ARE WE GONNA HAVE YOUR SOLDIERS BUSTING HOLLOW POINTS AT US THE WHOLE WAY?
WE'RE AN INDEPENDENT CONTRACTOR WITH A MILITARY CLIENT. WE HAVE SECURITY, NOT SOLDIERS.
THEY GIVE US ANY TROUBLE, WHAT YOU'LL HAVE IS A TWO-DIMENSIONAL HEAD.
ARE WE JUST GONNA LEAVE MARKY HERE?
IT FEELS KIND OF--COLD. WE SHOULD AT LEAST SAY A PRAYER OR SOMETHING.
GOODBYE, MARKY.
FUCK DEATH UP THE ASS FOR THE REST OF US.

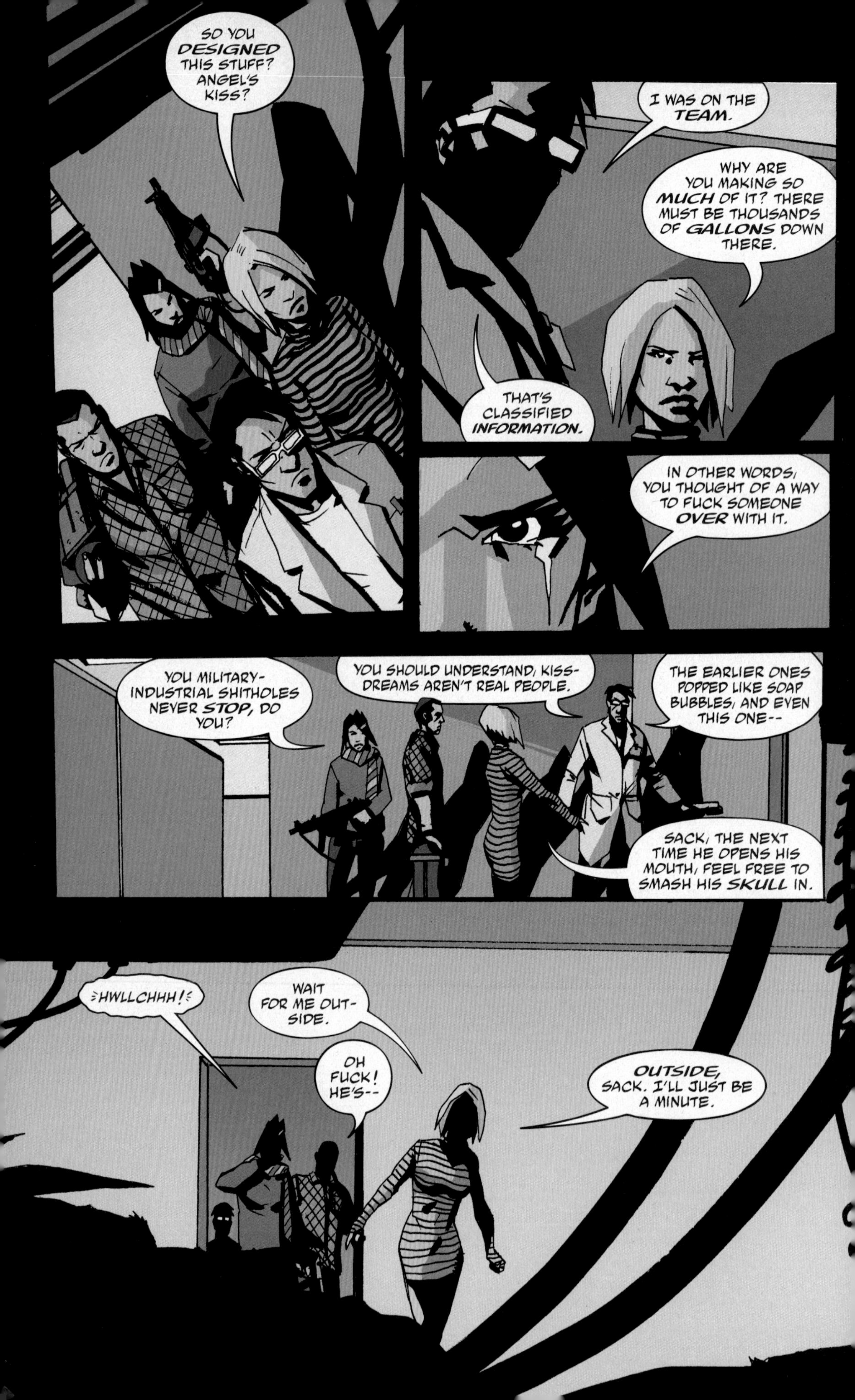
SO YOU DESIGNED THIS STUFF? ANGEL'S KISS?
I WAS ON THE TEAM.
WHY ARE YOU MAKING SO MUCH OF IT? THERE MUST BE THOUSANDS OF GALLONS DOWN THERE.
THAT'S CLASSIFIED INFORMATION.
IN OTHER WORDS, YOU THOUGHT OF A WAY TO FUCK SOMEONE OVER WITH IT.
YOU MILITARY-INDUSTRIAL SHITHOLES NEVER STOP, DO YOU?
YOU SHOULD UNDERSTAND, KISS-DREAMS AREN'T REAL PEOPLE.
THE EARLIER ONES POPPED LIKE SOAP BUBBLES, AND EVEN THIS ONE--
SACK, THE NEXT TIME HE OPENS HIS MOUTH, FEEL FREE TO SMASH HIS SKULL IN.
HWLLCHHH!
WAIT FOR ME OUTSIDE.
OH FUCK! HE'S--
OUTSIDE, SACK. I'LL JUST BE A MINUTE.

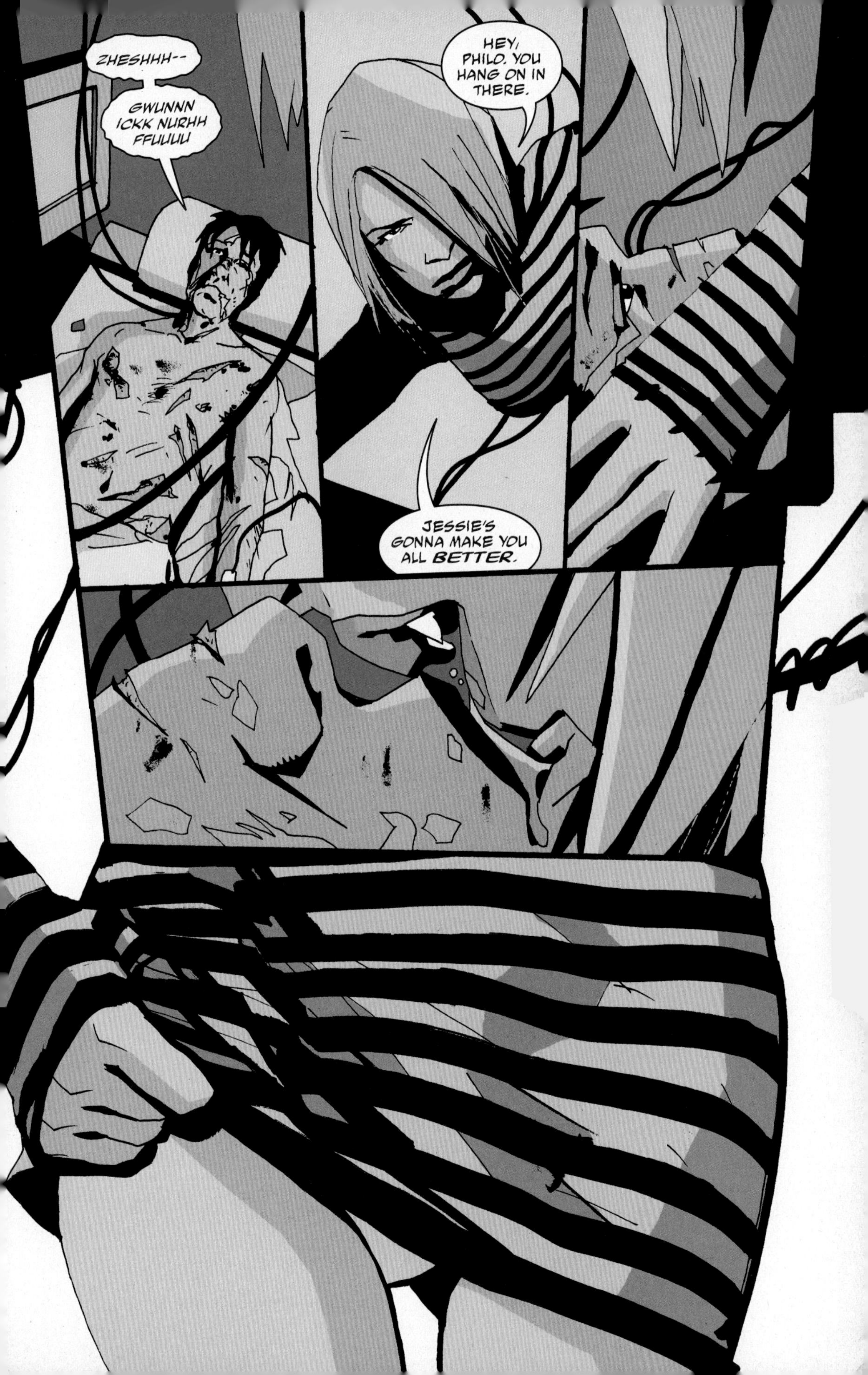
ZHESHHH--
GWUNNN ICKK NURHH FFUUUU
HEY, PHILO. YOU HANG ON IN THERE.
JESSIE'S GONNA MAKE YOU ALL BETTER.

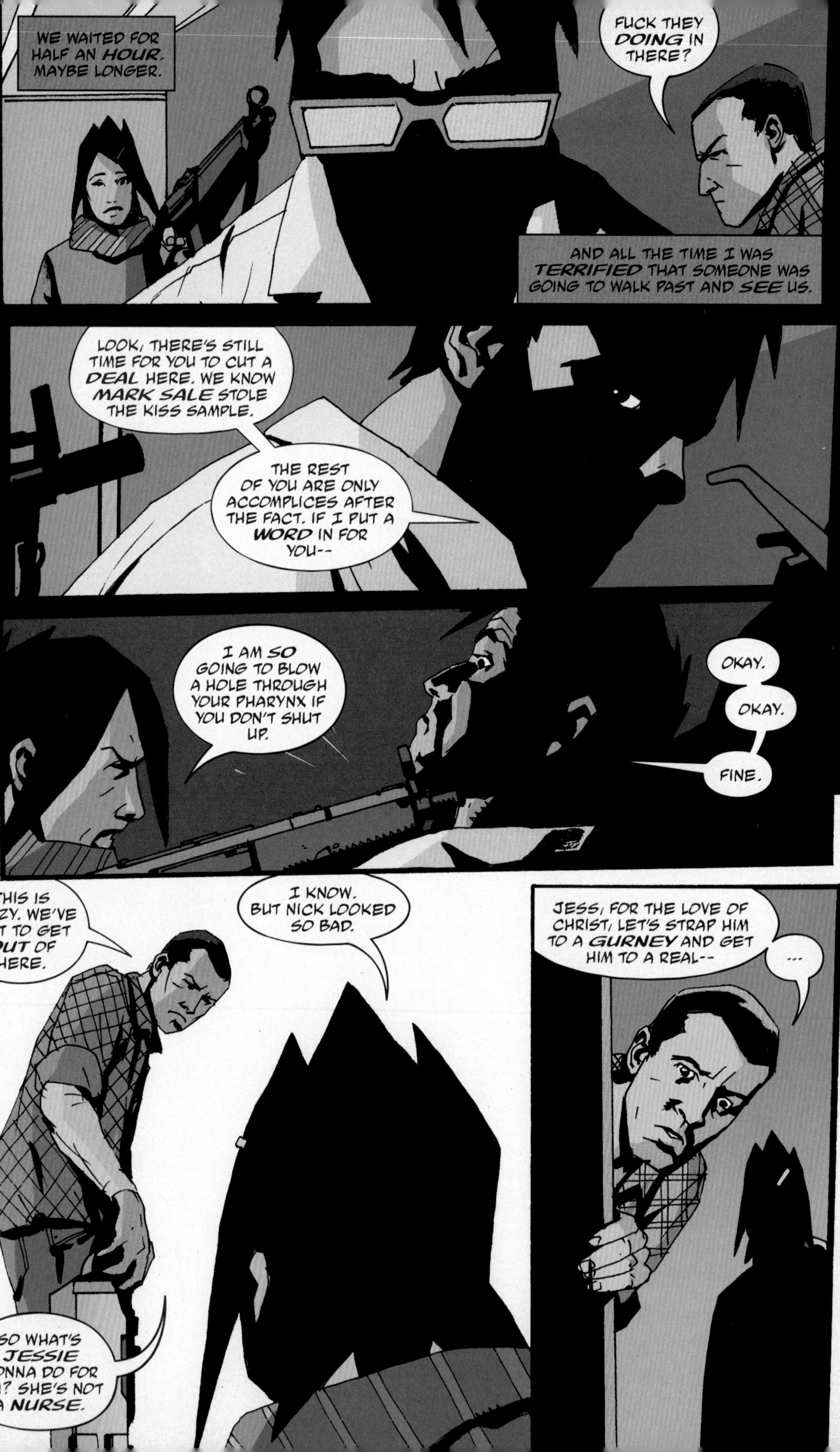

WE WAITED FOR HALF AN HOUR. MAYBE LONGER.
FUCK THEY DOING IN THERE?
AND ALL THE TIME I WAS TERRIFIED THAT SOMEONE WAS GOING TO WALK PAST AND SEE US.
LOOK, THERE'S STILL TIME FOR YOU TO CUT A DEAL HERE. WE KNOW MARK SALE STOLE THE KISS SAMPLE.
THE REST OF YOU ARE ONLY ACCOMPLICES AFTER THE FACT. IF I PUT A WORD IN FOR YOU--
I AM SO GOING TO BLOW A HOLE THROUGH YOUR PHARYNX IF YOU DON'T SHUT UP.
OKAY.
OKAY.
FINE.
THIS IS CRAZY. WE'VE GOT TO GET OUT OF HERE.
I KNOW. BUT NICK LOOKED SO BAD.
SO WHAT'S JESSIE GONNA DO FOR HIM? SHE'S NOT A NURSE.
JESS, FOR THE LOVE OF CHRIST, LET'S STRAP HIM TO A GURNEY AND GET HIM TO A REAL--
...

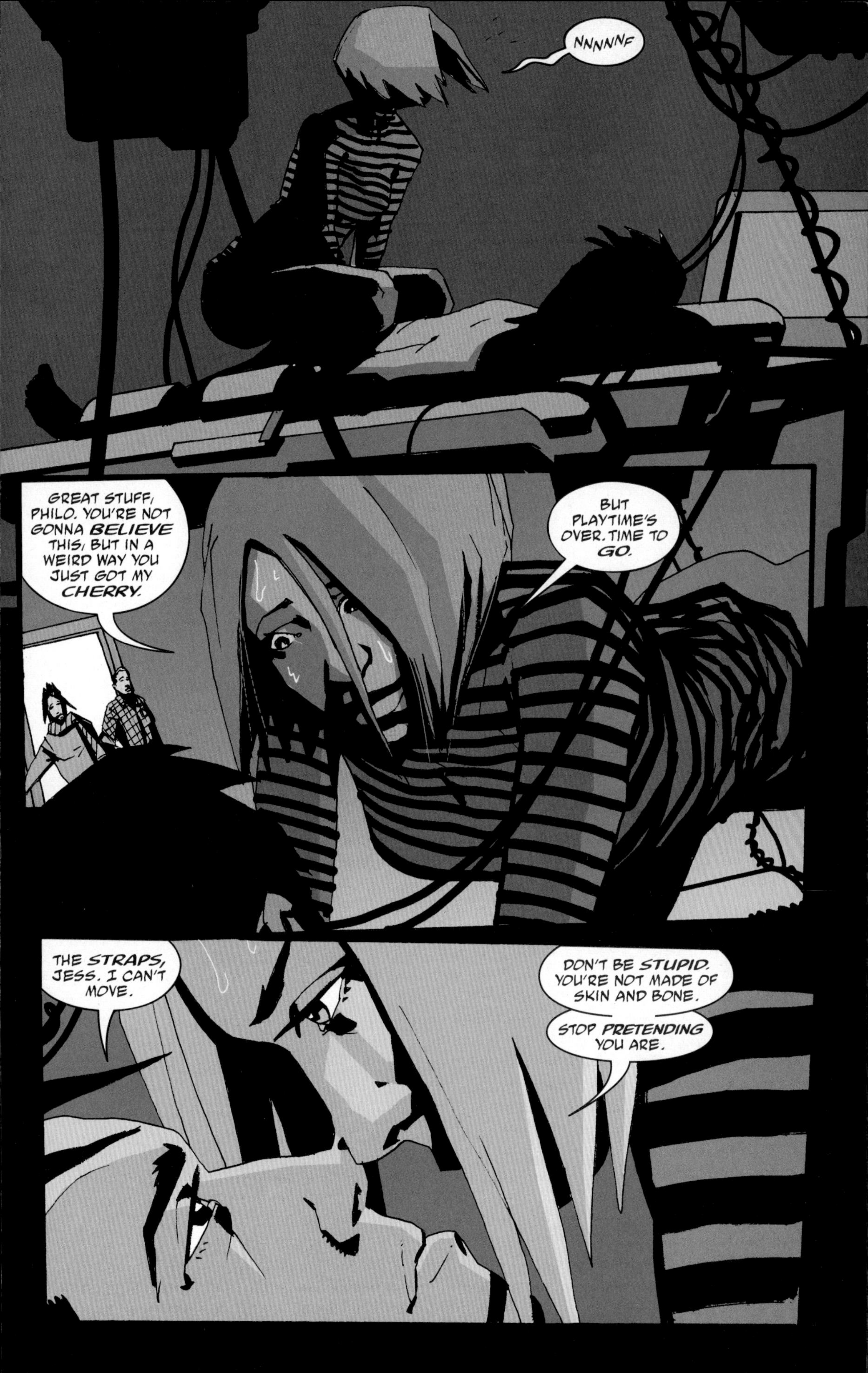
NNNNNF
GREAT STUFF, PHILO. YOU'RE NOT GONNA BELIEVE THIS, BUT IN A WEIRD WAY YOU JUST GOT MY CHERRY.
BUT PLAYTIME'S OVER. TIME TO GO.
THE STRAPS, JESS. I CAN'T MOVE.
DON'T BE STUPID. YOU'RE NOT MADE OF SKIN AND BONE.
STOP PRETENDING YOU ARE.

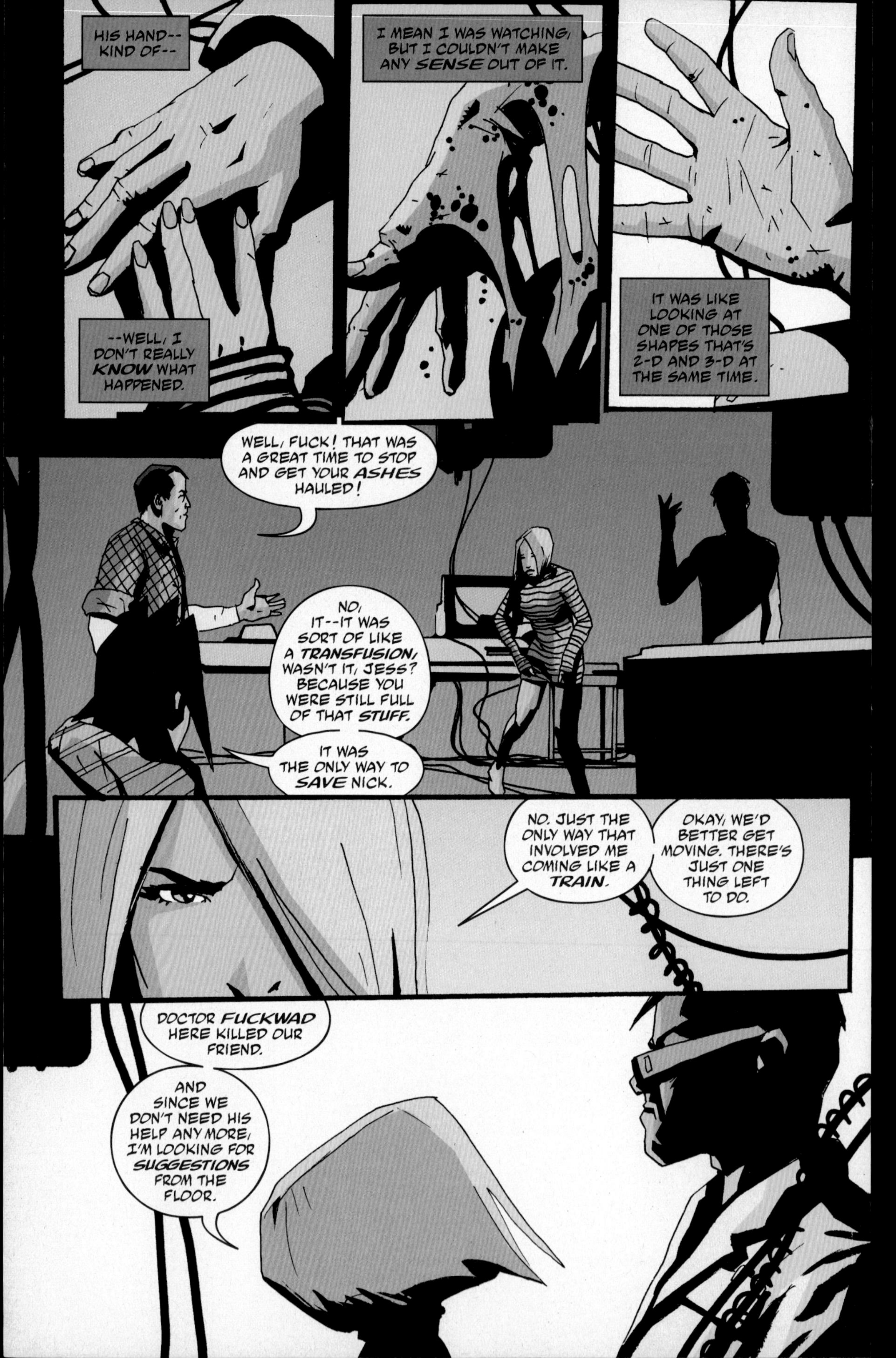
HIS HAND--KIND OF--
--WELL, I DON'T REALLY KNOW WHAT HAPPENED.
I MEAN I WAS WATCHING, BUT I COULDN'T MAKE ANY SENSE OUT OF IT.
IT WAS LIKE LOOKING AT ONE OF THOSE SHAPES THAT'S 2-D AND 3-D AT THE SAME TIME.
WELL, FUCK! THAT WAS A GREAT TIME TO STOP AND GET YOUR ASHES HAULED!
NO, IT--IT WAS SORT OF LIKE A TRANSFUSION, WASN'T IT, JESS? BECAUSE YOU WERE STILL FULL OF THAT STUFF.
IT WAS THE ONLY WAY TO SAVE NICK.
NO. JUST THE ONLY WAY THAT INVOLVED ME COMING LIKE A TRAIN.
OKAY, WE'D BETTER GET MOVING. THERE'S JUST ONE THING LEFT TO DO.
DOCTOR FUCKWAD HERE KILLED OUR FRIEND.
AND SINCE WE DON'T NEED HIS HELP ANY MORE, I'M LOOKING FOR SUGGESTIONS FROM THE FLOOR.

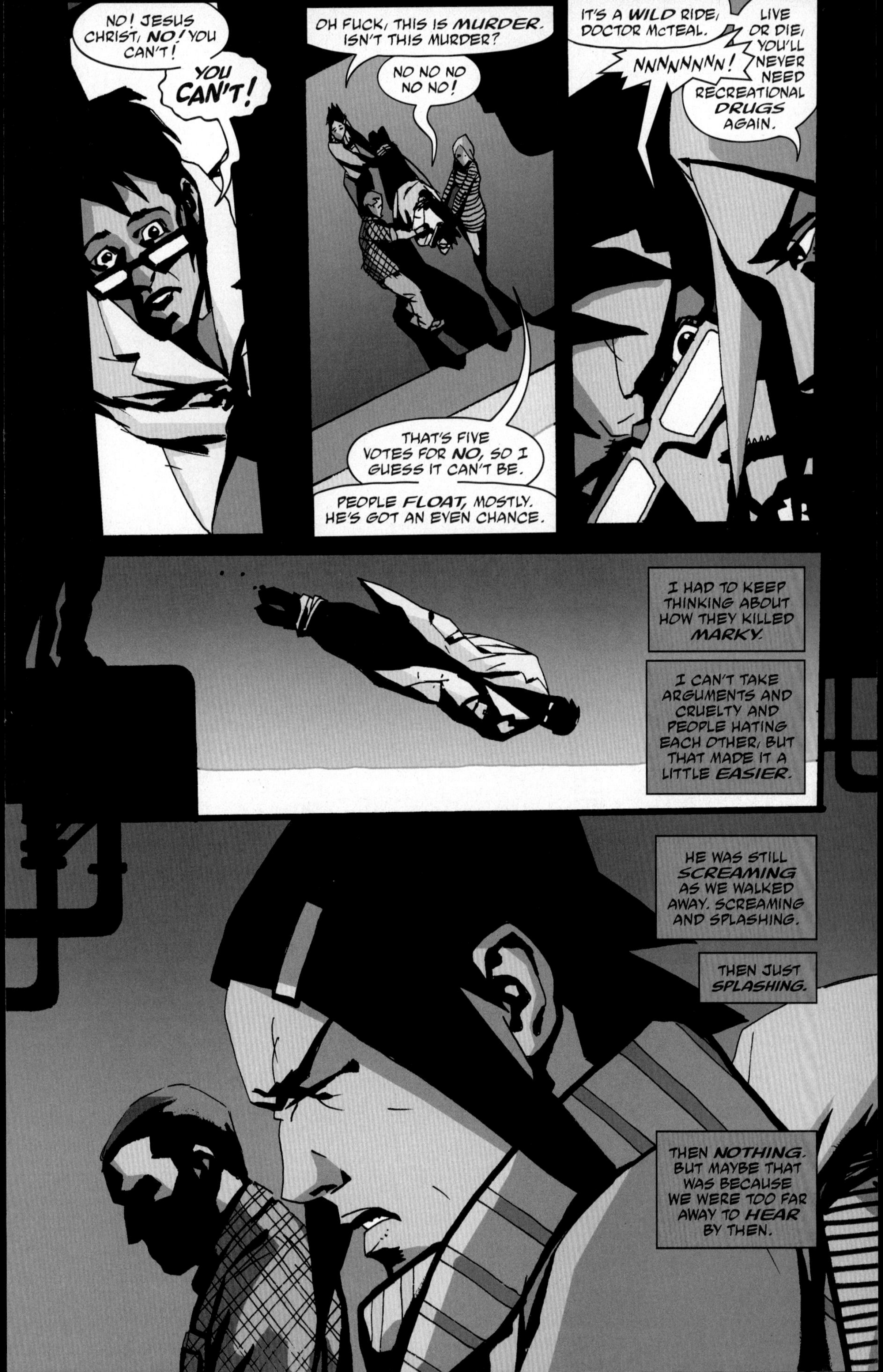
NO! JESUS CHRIST, NO! YOU CAN'T!
YOU CAN'T!
OH FUCK, THIS IS MURDER. ISN'T THIS MURDER?
NO NO NO NO NO!
THAT'S FIVE VOTES FOR NO, SO I GUESS IT CAN'T BE.
PEOPLE FLOAT, MOSTLY. HE'S GOT AN EVEN CHANCE.
IT'S A WILD RIDE, DOCTOR McTEAL.
NNNNNNNN!
LIVE OR DIE, YOU'LL NEVER NEED RECREATIONAL DRUGS AGAIN.
I HAD TO KEEP THINKING ABOUT HOW THEY KILLED MARKY.
I CAN'T TAKE ARGUMENTS AND CRUELTY AND PEOPLE HATING EACH OTHER, BUT THAT MADE IT A LITTLE EASIER.
HE WAS STILL SCREAMING AS WE WALKED AWAY. SCREAMING AND SPLASHING.
THEN JUST SPLASHING.
THEN NOTHING. BUT MAYBE THAT WAS BECAUSE WE WERE TOO FAR AWAY TO HEAR BY THEN.

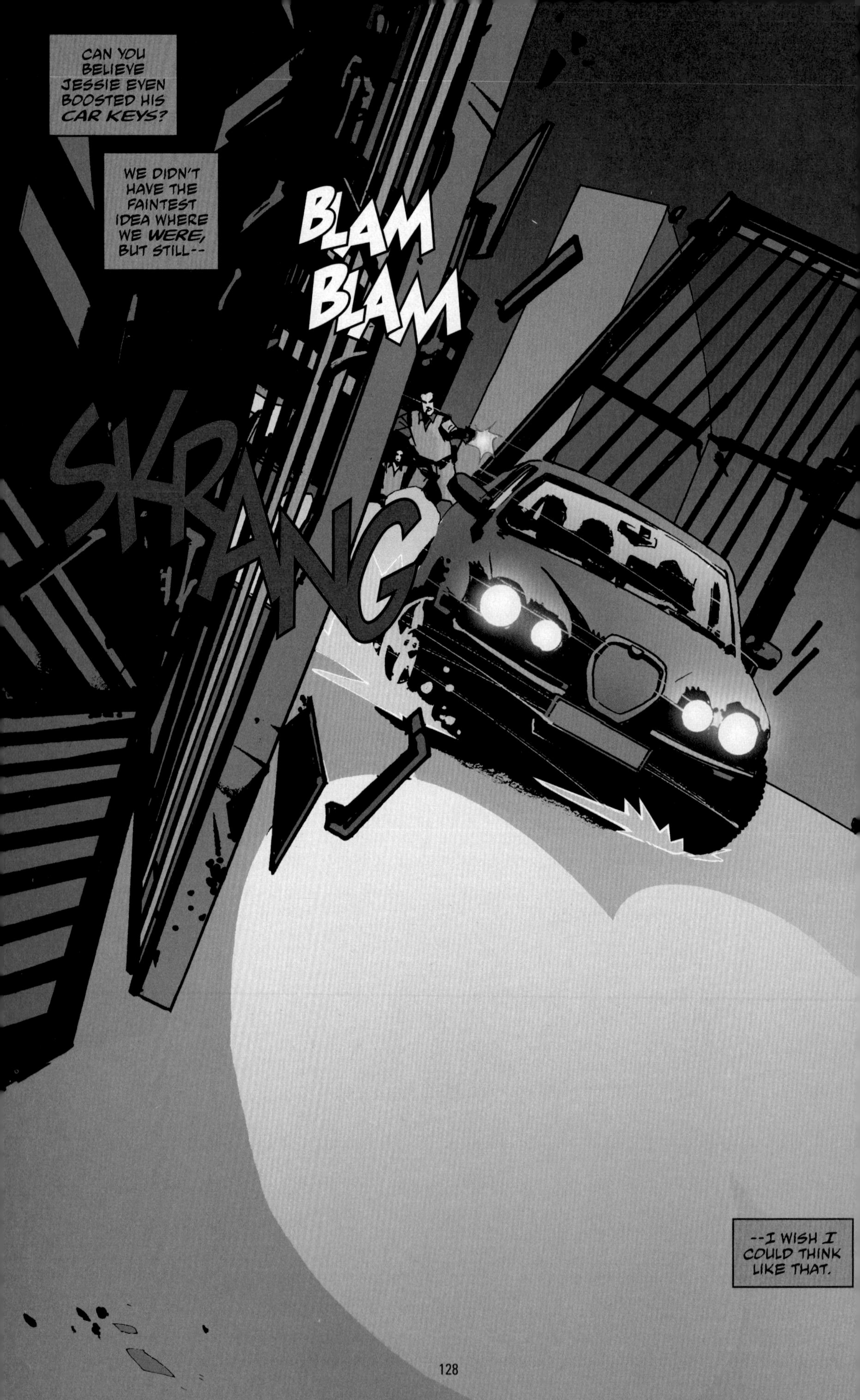

CAN YOU BELIEVE JESSIE EVEN BOOSTED HIS CAR KEYS?
WE DIDN'T HAVE THE FAINTEST IDEA WHERE WE WERE, BUT STILL--
BLAM BLAM
SKRANG
--I WISH I COULD THINK LIKE THAT.

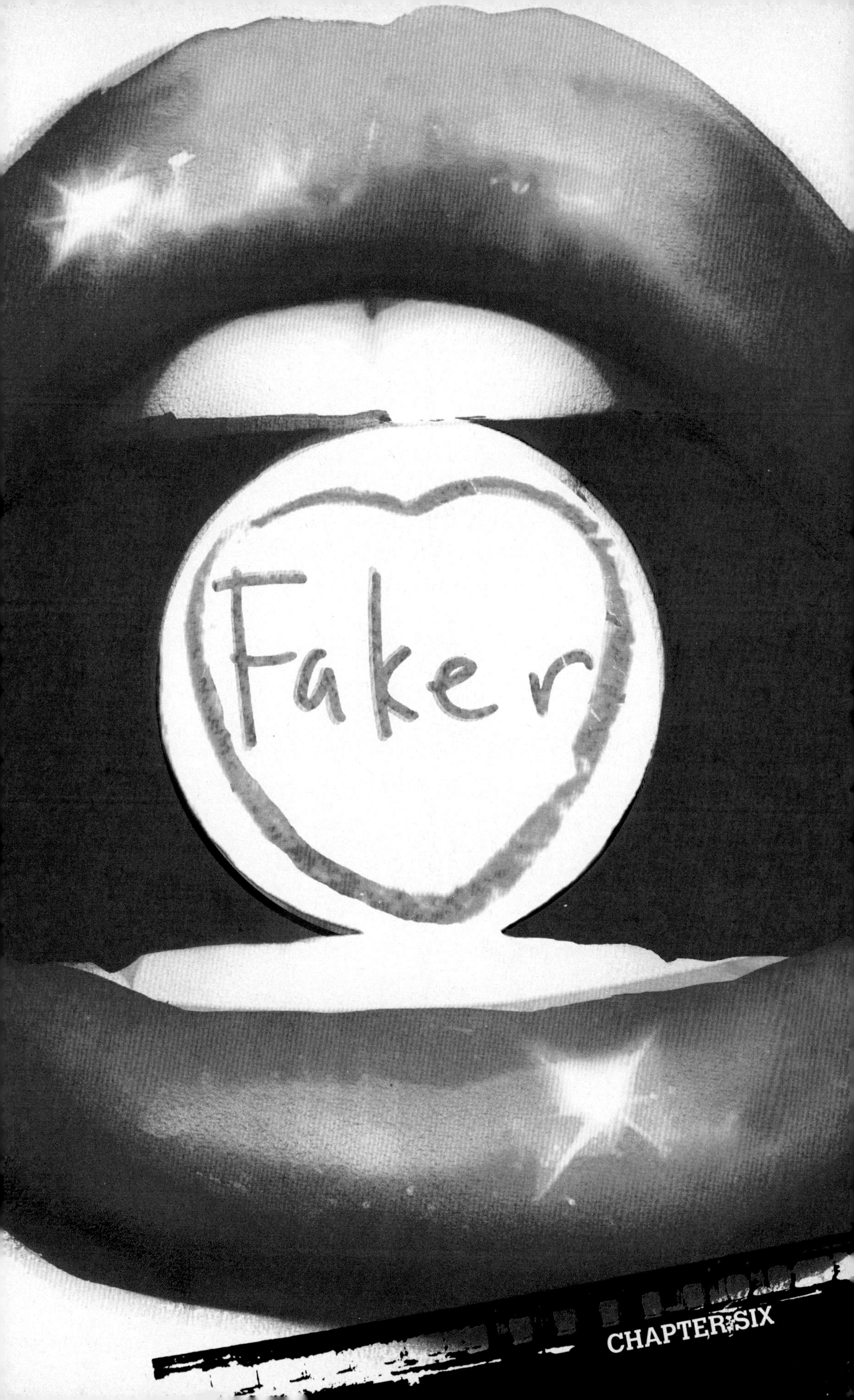
Faker

CHAPTER SIX

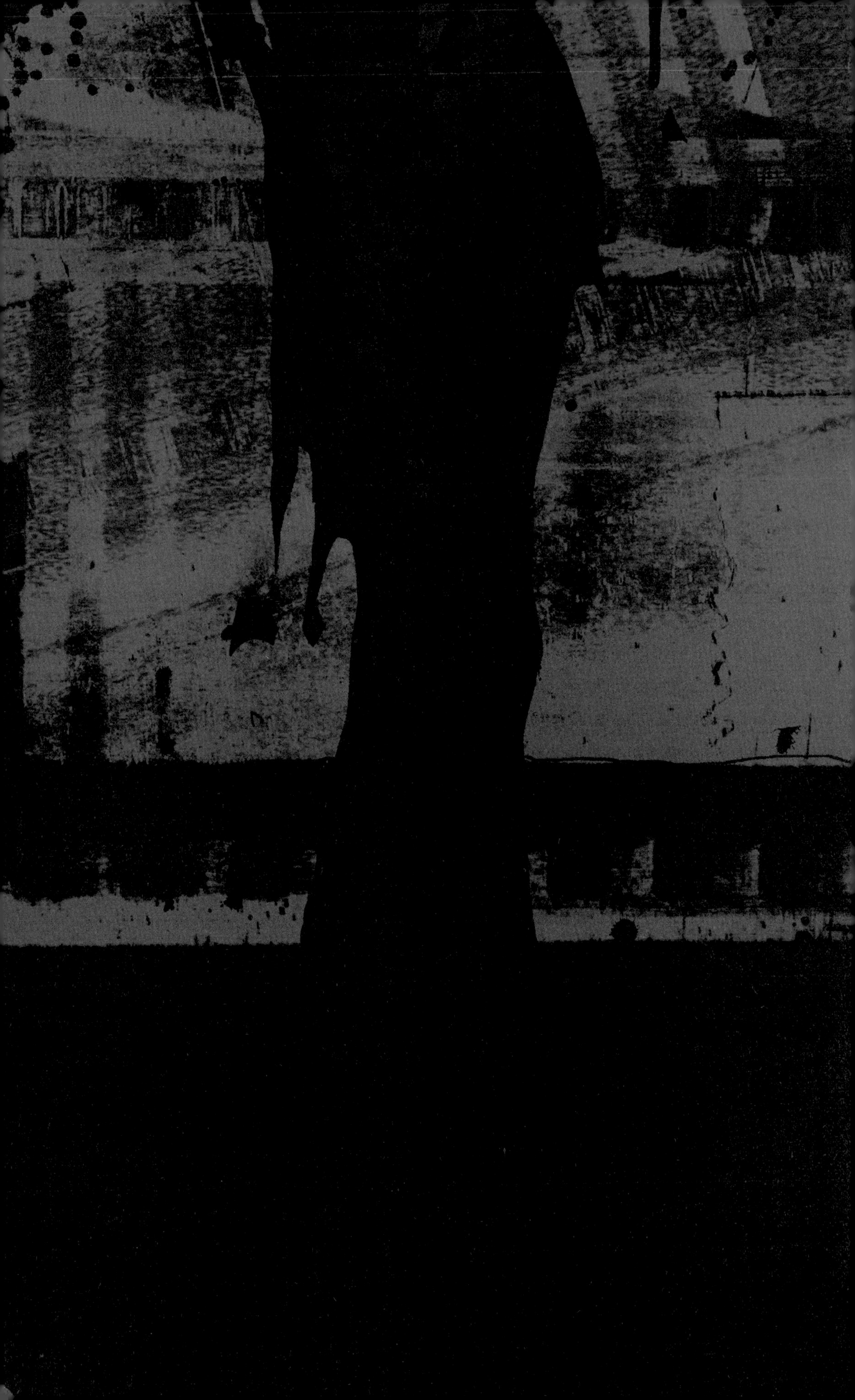

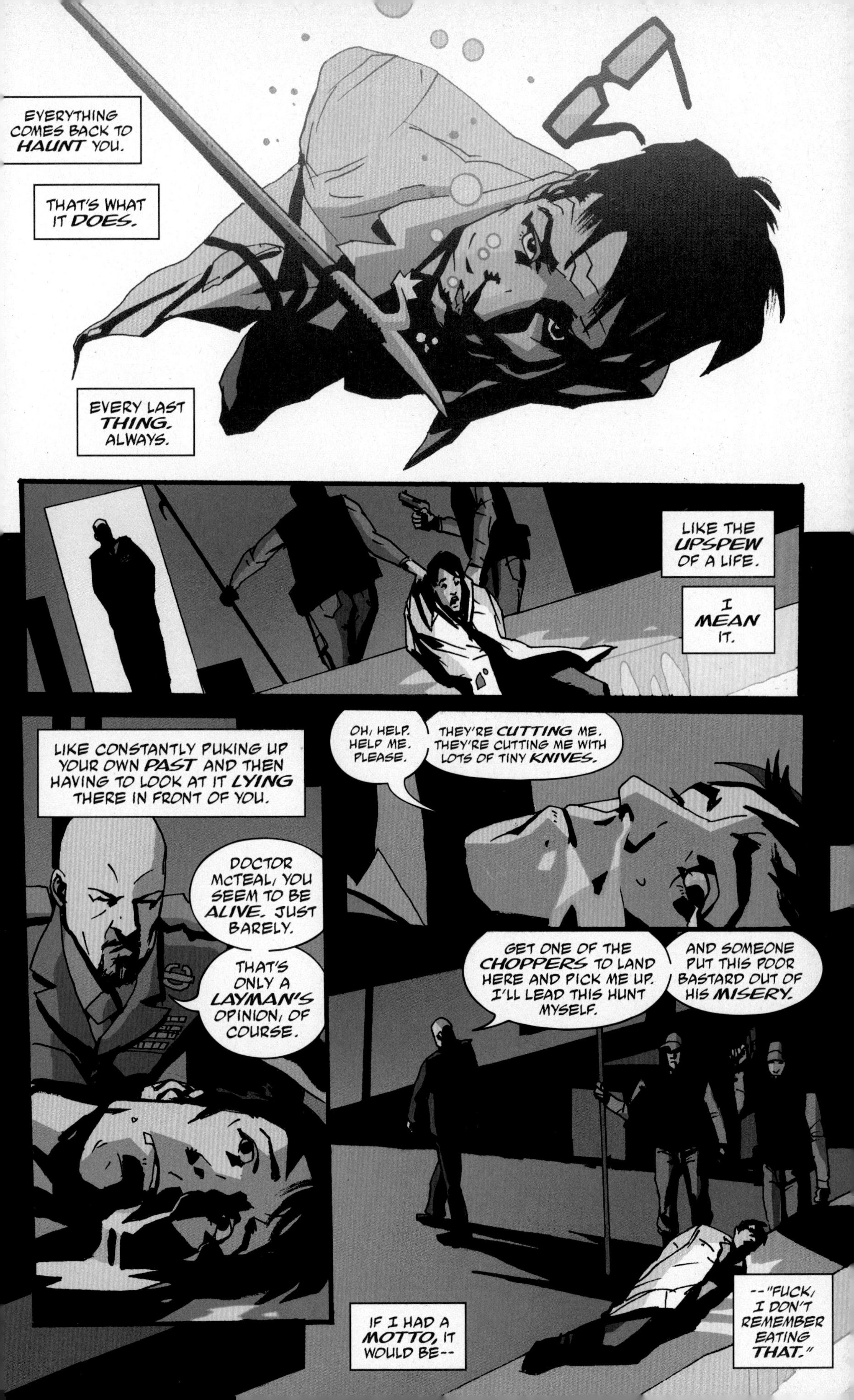
EVERYTHING COMES BACK TO *HAUNT* YOU.
THAT'S WHAT IT *DOES.*
EVERY LAST *THING.* ALWAYS.
LIKE THE *UPSPEW* OF A LIFE.
I *MEAN* IT.
LIKE CONSTANTLY PUKING UP YOUR OWN *PAST* AND THEN HAVING TO LOOK AT IT *LYING* THERE IN FRONT OF YOU.
OH, HELP. HELP ME. PLEASE.
THEY'RE *CUTTING* ME. THEY'RE CUTTING ME WITH LOTS OF TINY *KNIVES.*
DOCTOR McTEAL, YOU SEEM TO BE *ALIVE.* JUST BARELY.
THAT'S ONLY A *LAYMAN'S* OPINION, OF COURSE.
GET ONE OF THE *CHOPPERS* TO LAND HERE AND PICK ME UP. I'LL LEAD THIS HUNT MYSELF.
AND SOMEONE PUT THIS POOR BASTARD OUT OF HIS *MISERY.*
IF I HAD A *MOTTO,* IT WOULD BE--
--"FUCK, I DON'T REMEMBER EATING *THAT.*"

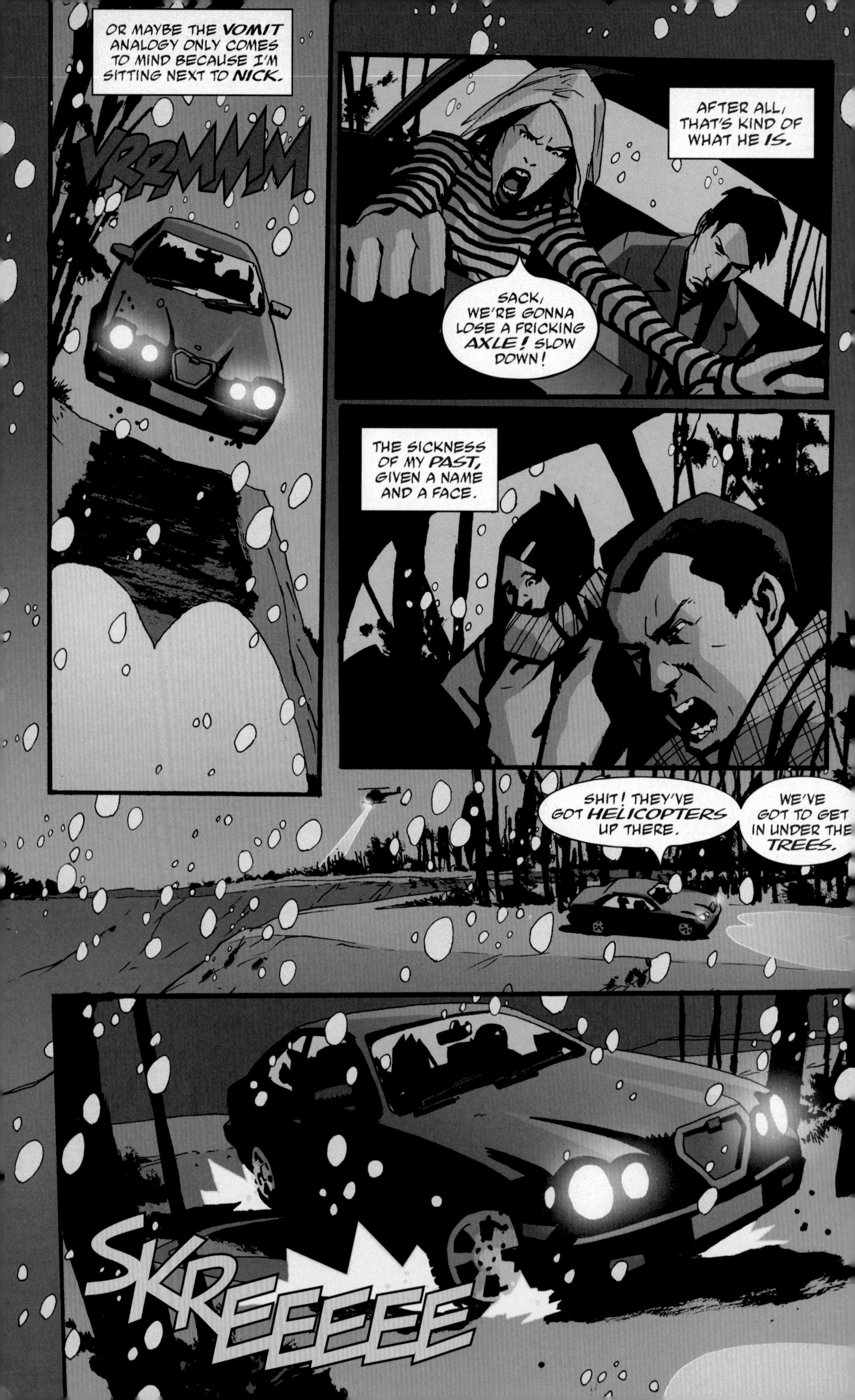
OR MAYBE THE VOMIT ANALOGY ONLY COMES TO MIND BECAUSE I'M SITTING NEXT TO NICK.
VRRMMMM
AFTER ALL, THAT'S KIND OF WHAT HE IS.
SACK, WE'RE GONNA LOSE A FRICKING AXLE! SLOW DOWN!
THE SICKNESS OF MY PAST, GIVEN A NAME AND A FACE.
SHIT! THEY'VE GOT HELICOPTERS UP THERE.
WE'VE GOT TO GET IN UNDER THE TREES.
SKREEEEEE

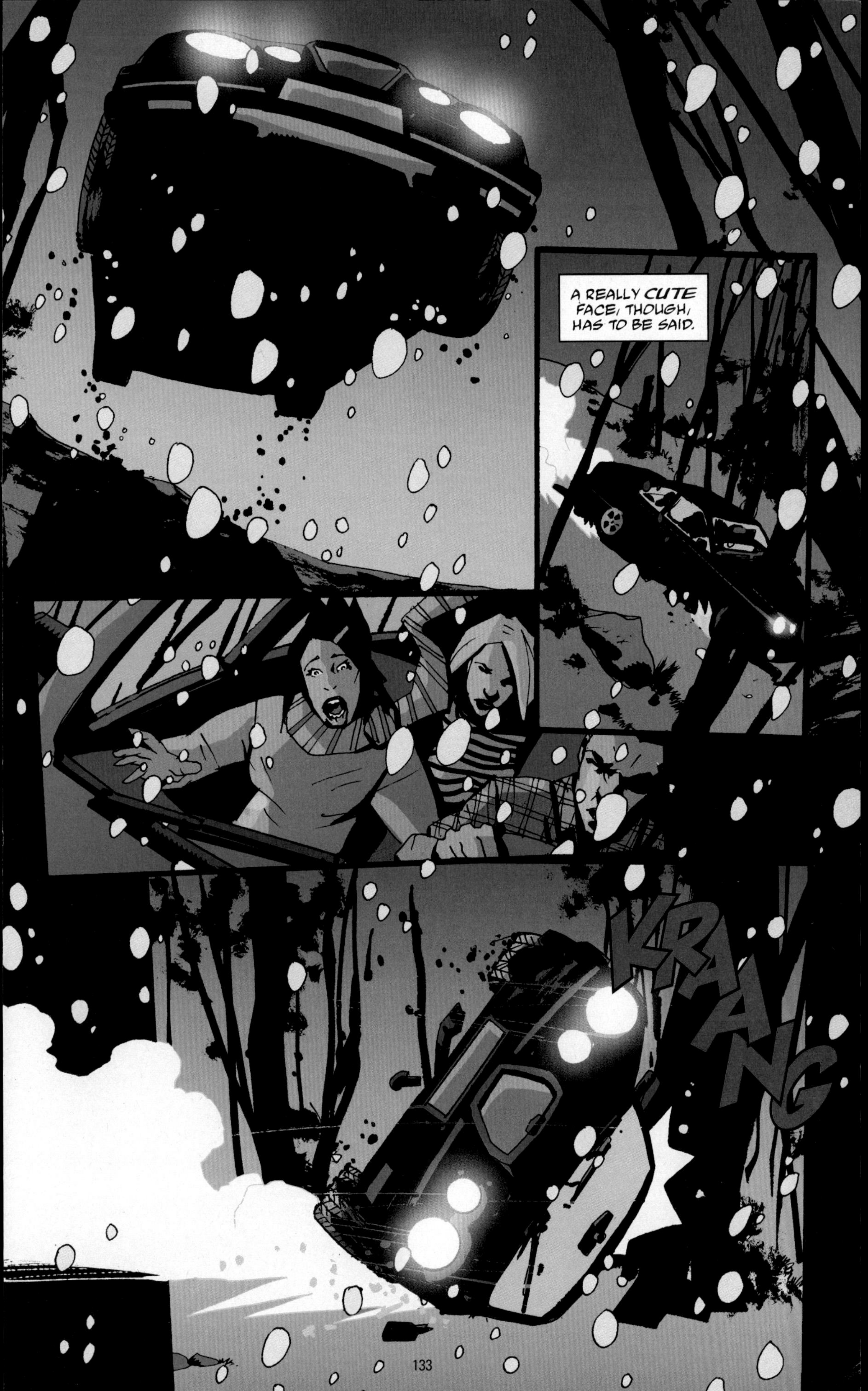
A REALLY CUTE FACE, THOUGH, HAS TO BE SAID.
KRAANG

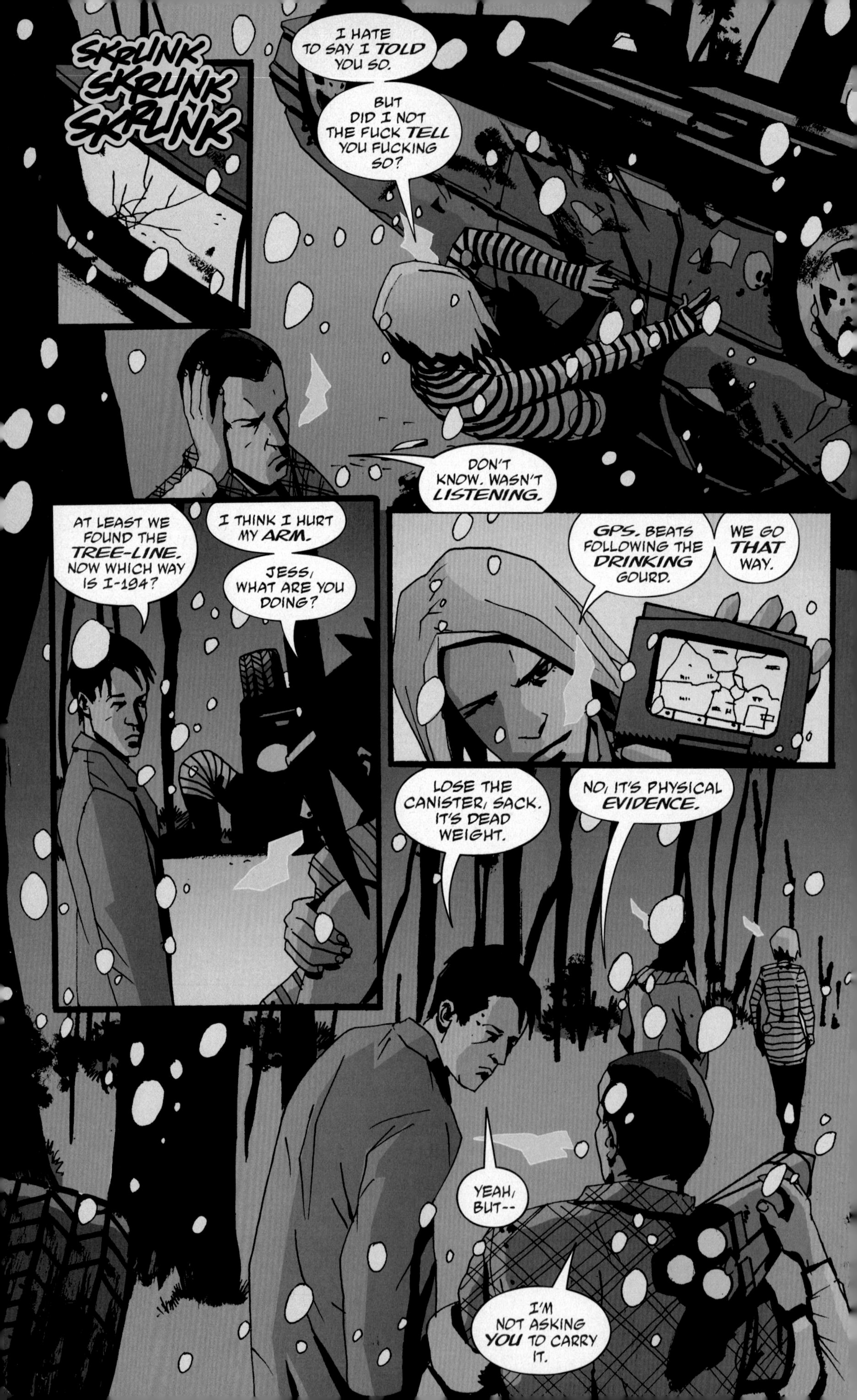

SKRUNK SKRUNK SKRUNK
I HATE TO SAY I TOLD YOU SO.
BUT DID I NOT THE FUCK TELL YOU FUCKING SO?
DON'T KNOW. WASN'T LISTENING.
AT LEAST WE FOUND THE TREE-LINE. NOW WHICH WAY IS I-194?
I THINK I HURT MY ARM.
JESS, WHAT ARE YOU DOING?
GPS. BEATS FOLLOWING THE DRINKING GOURD.
WE GO THAT WAY.
LOSE THE CANISTER, SACK. IT'S DEAD WEIGHT.
NO, IT'S PHYSICAL EVIDENCE.
YEAH, BUT--
I'M NOT ASKING YOU TO CARRY IT.

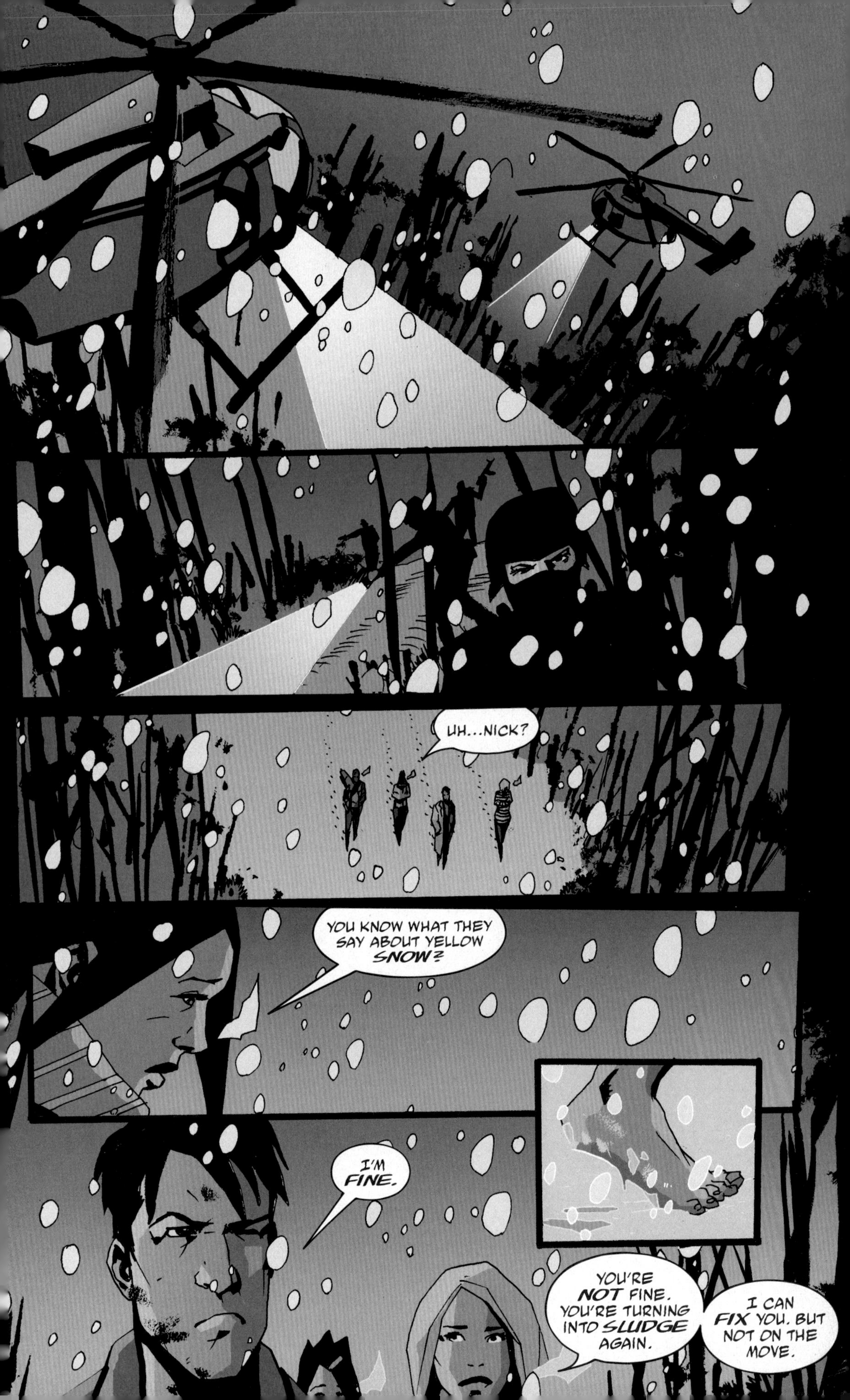
UH...NICK?
YOU KNOW WHAT THEY SAY ABOUT YELLOW SNOW?
I'M FINE.
YOU'RE NOT FINE. YOU'RE TURNING INTO SLUDGE AGAIN.
I CAN FIX YOU. BUT NOT ON THE MOVE.

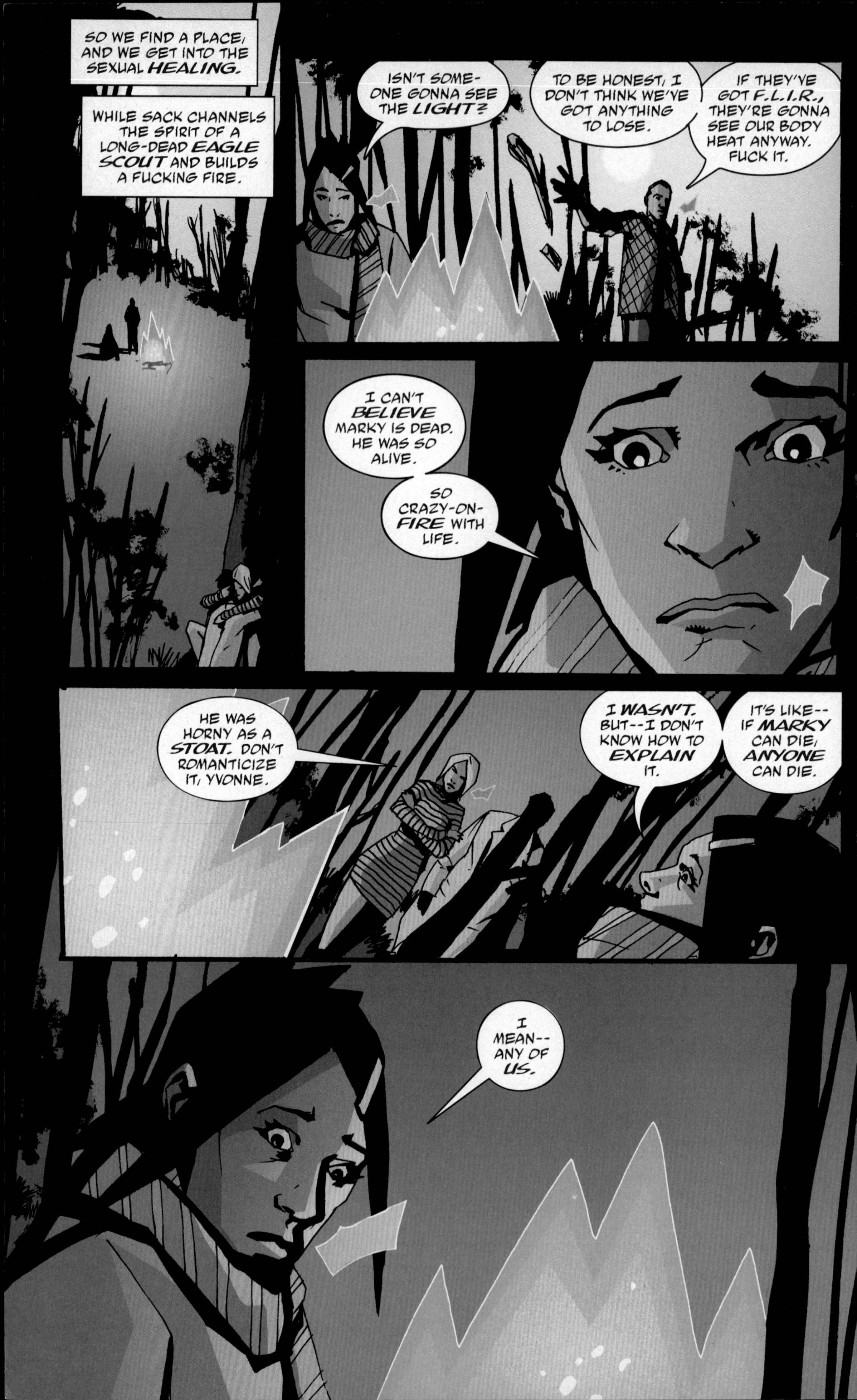
SO WE FIND A PLACE, AND WE GET INTO THE SEXUAL HEALING.
WHILE SACK CHANNELS THE SPIRIT OF A LONG-DEAD EAGLE SCOUT AND BUILDS A FUCKING FIRE.
ISN'T SOME-ONE GONNA SEE THE LIGHT?
TO BE HONEST, I DON'T THINK WE'VE GOT ANYTHING TO LOSE.
IF THEY'VE GOT F.L.I.R., THEY'RE GONNA SEE OUR BODY HEAT ANYWAY. FUCK IT.
I CAN'T BELIEVE MARKY IS DEAD. HE WAS SO ALIVE.
SO CRAZY-ON-FIRE WITH LIFE.
HE WAS HORNY AS A STOAT. DON'T ROMANTICIZE IT, YVONNE.
I WASN'T. BUT--I DON'T KNOW HOW TO EXPLAIN IT.
IT'S LIKE-- IF MARKY CAN DIE, ANYONE CAN DIE.
I MEAN-- ANY OF US.

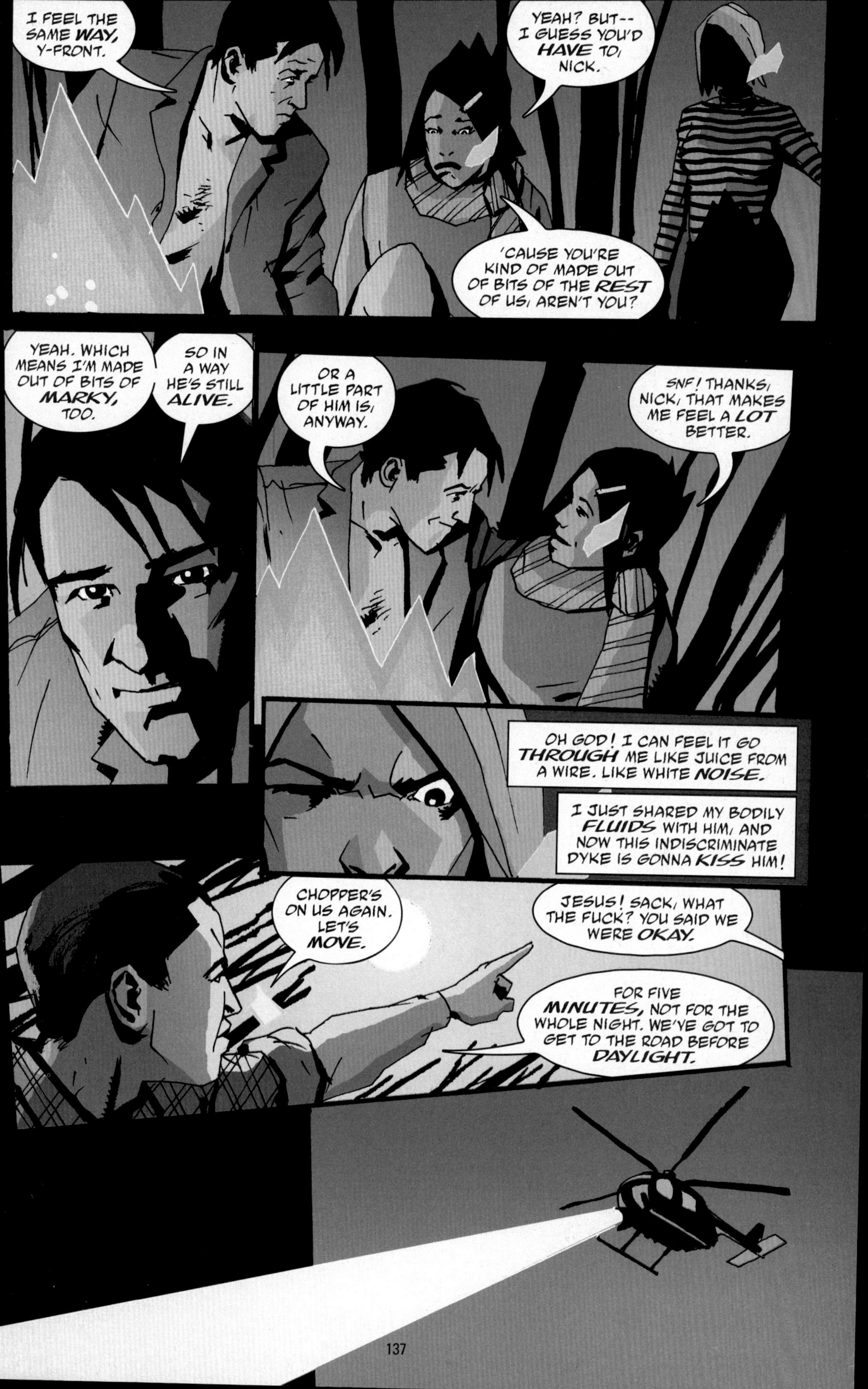
I FEEL THE SAME WAY, Y-FRONT.
YEAH? BUT-- I GUESS YOU'D HAVE TO, NICK.
'CAUSE YOU'RE KIND OF MADE OUT OF BITS OF THE REST OF US, AREN'T YOU?
YEAH. WHICH MEANS I'M MADE OUT OF BITS OF MARKY, TOO.
SO IN A WAY HE'S STILL ALIVE.
OR A LITTLE PART OF HIM IS, ANYWAY.
SNF! THANKS, NICK, THAT MAKES ME FEEL A LOT BETTER.
OH GOD! I CAN FEEL IT GO THROUGH ME LIKE JUICE FROM A WIRE. LIKE WHITE NOISE.
I JUST SHARED MY BODILY FLUIDS WITH HIM, AND NOW THIS INDISCRIMINATE DYKE IS GONNA KISS HIM!
CHOPPER'S ON US AGAIN. LET'S MOVE.
JESUS! SACK, WHAT THE FUCK? YOU SAID WE WERE OKAY.
FOR FIVE MINUTES, NOT FOR THE WHOLE NIGHT. WE'VE GOT TO GET TO THE ROAD BEFORE DAYLIGHT.

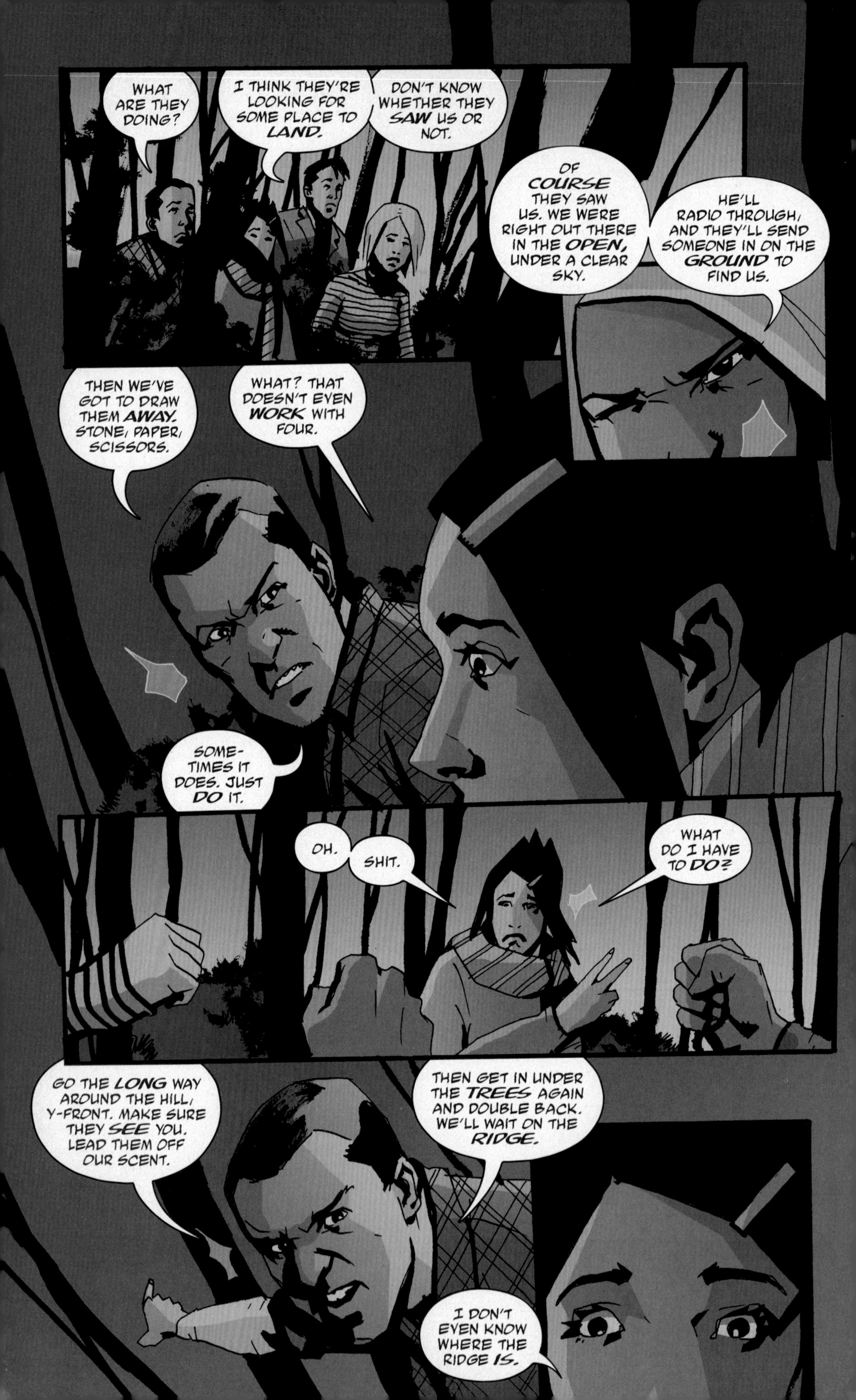
WHAT ARE THEY DOING?
I THINK THEY'RE LOOKING FOR SOME PLACE TO LAND.
DON'T KNOW WHETHER THEY SAW US OR NOT.
OF COURSE THEY SAW US. WE WERE RIGHT OUT THERE IN THE OPEN, UNDER A CLEAR SKY.
HE'LL RADIO THROUGH, AND THEY'LL SEND SOMEONE IN ON THE GROUND TO FIND US.
THEN WE'VE GOT TO DRAW THEM AWAY. STONE, PAPER, SCISSORS.
WHAT? THAT DOESN'T EVEN WORK WITH FOUR.
SOME-TIMES IT DOES. JUST DO IT.
OH.
SHIT.
WHAT DO I HAVE TO DO?
GO THE LONG WAY AROUND THE HILL, Y-FRONT. MAKE SURE THEY SEE YOU. LEAD THEM OFF OUR SCENT.
THEN GET IN UNDER THE TREES AGAIN AND DOUBLE BACK. WE'LL WAIT ON THE RIDGE.
I DON'T EVEN KNOW WHERE THE RIDGE IS.

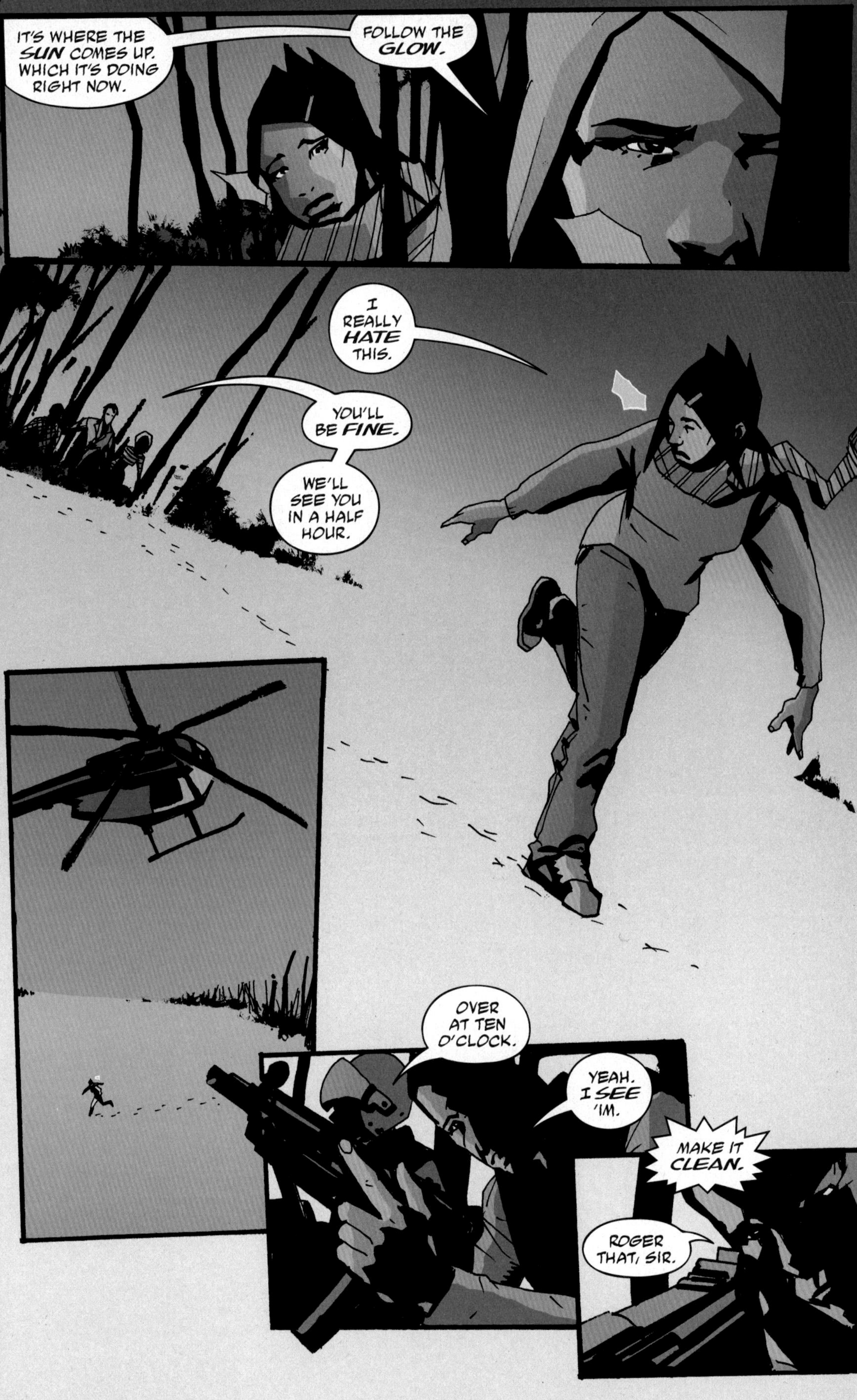
IT'S WHERE THE SUN COMES UP. WHICH IT'S DOING RIGHT NOW.
FOLLOW THE GLOW.
I REALLY HATE THIS.
YOU'LL BE FINE.
WE'LL SEE YOU IN A HALF HOUR.
OVER AT TEN O'CLOCK.
YEAH. I SEE 'IM.
MAKE IT CLEAN.
ROGER THAT, SIR.

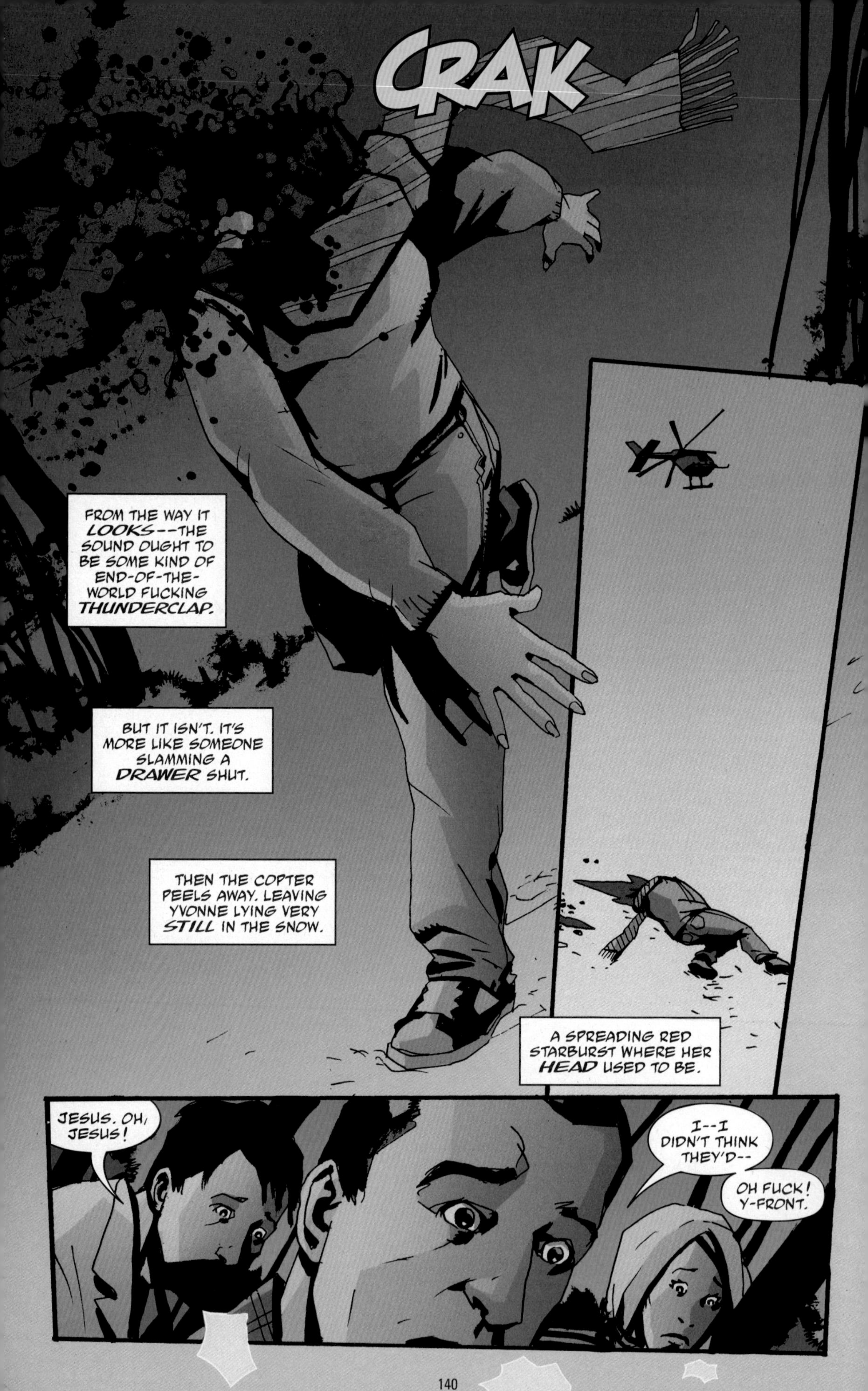
CRAK
FROM THE WAY IT LOOKS--THE SOUND OUGHT TO BE SOME KIND OF END-OF-THE-WORLD FUCKING THUNDERCLAP.
BUT IT ISN'T. IT'S MORE LIKE SOMEONE SLAMMING A DRAWER SHUT.
THEN THE COPTER PEELS AWAY. LEAVING YVONNE LYING VERY STILL IN THE SNOW.
A SPREADING RED STARBURST WHERE HER HEAD USED TO BE.
JESUS. OH, JESUS!
I--I DIDN'T THINK THEY'D--
OH FUCK! Y-FRONT.

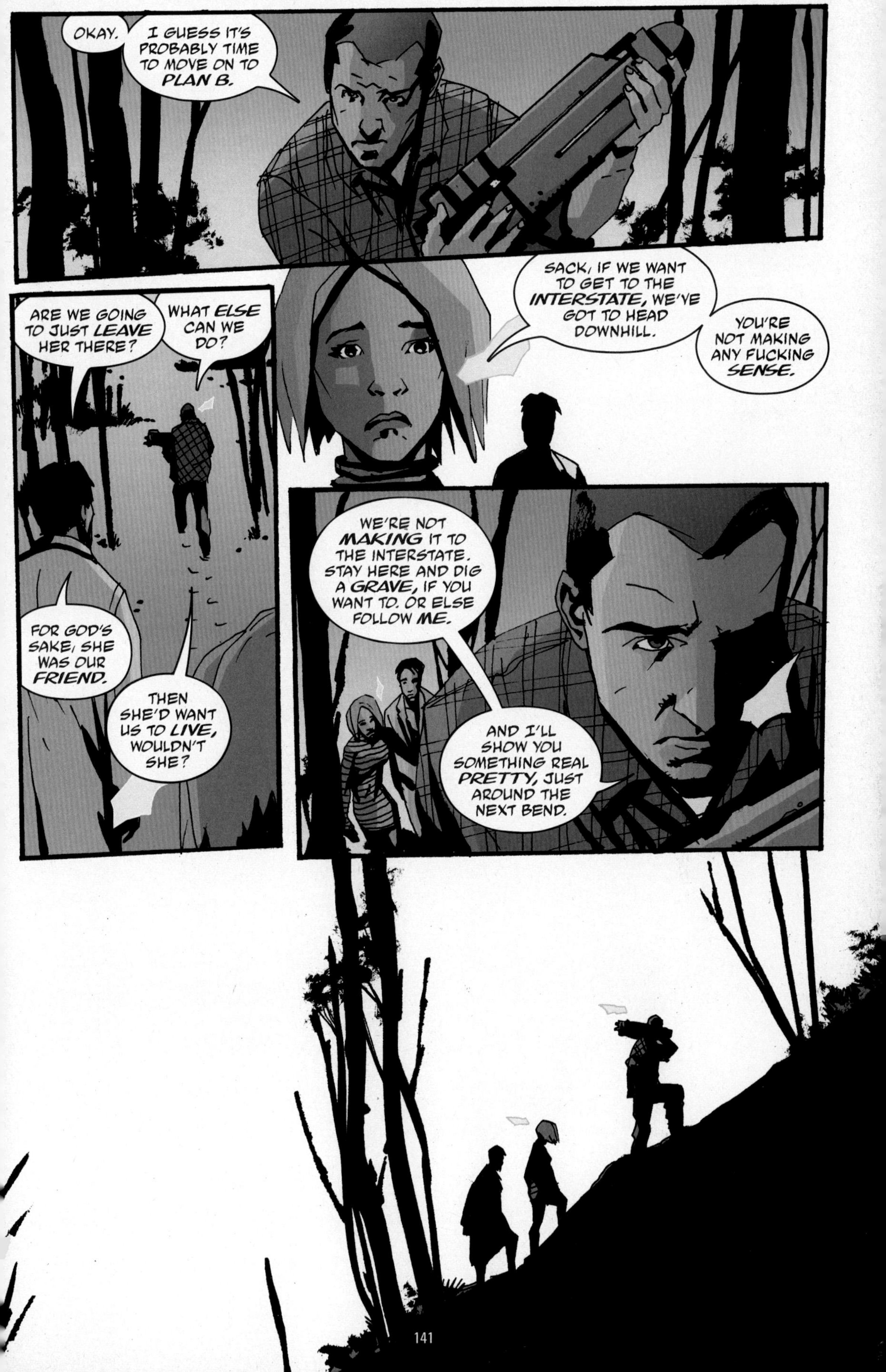
OKAY.
I GUESS IT'S PROBABLY TIME TO MOVE ON TO PLAN B.
ARE WE GOING TO JUST LEAVE HER THERE?
WHAT ELSE CAN WE DO?
SACK, IF WE WANT TO GET TO THE INTERSTATE, WE'VE GOT TO HEAD DOWNHILL.
YOU'RE NOT MAKING ANY FUCKING SENSE.
FOR GOD'S SAKE, SHE WAS OUR FRIEND.
THEN SHE'D WANT US TO LIVE, WOULDN'T SHE?
WE'RE NOT MAKING IT TO THE INTERSTATE. STAY HERE AND DIG A GRAVE, IF YOU WANT TO. OR ELSE FOLLOW ME.
AND I'LL SHOW YOU SOMETHING REAL PRETTY, JUST AROUND THE NEXT BEND.

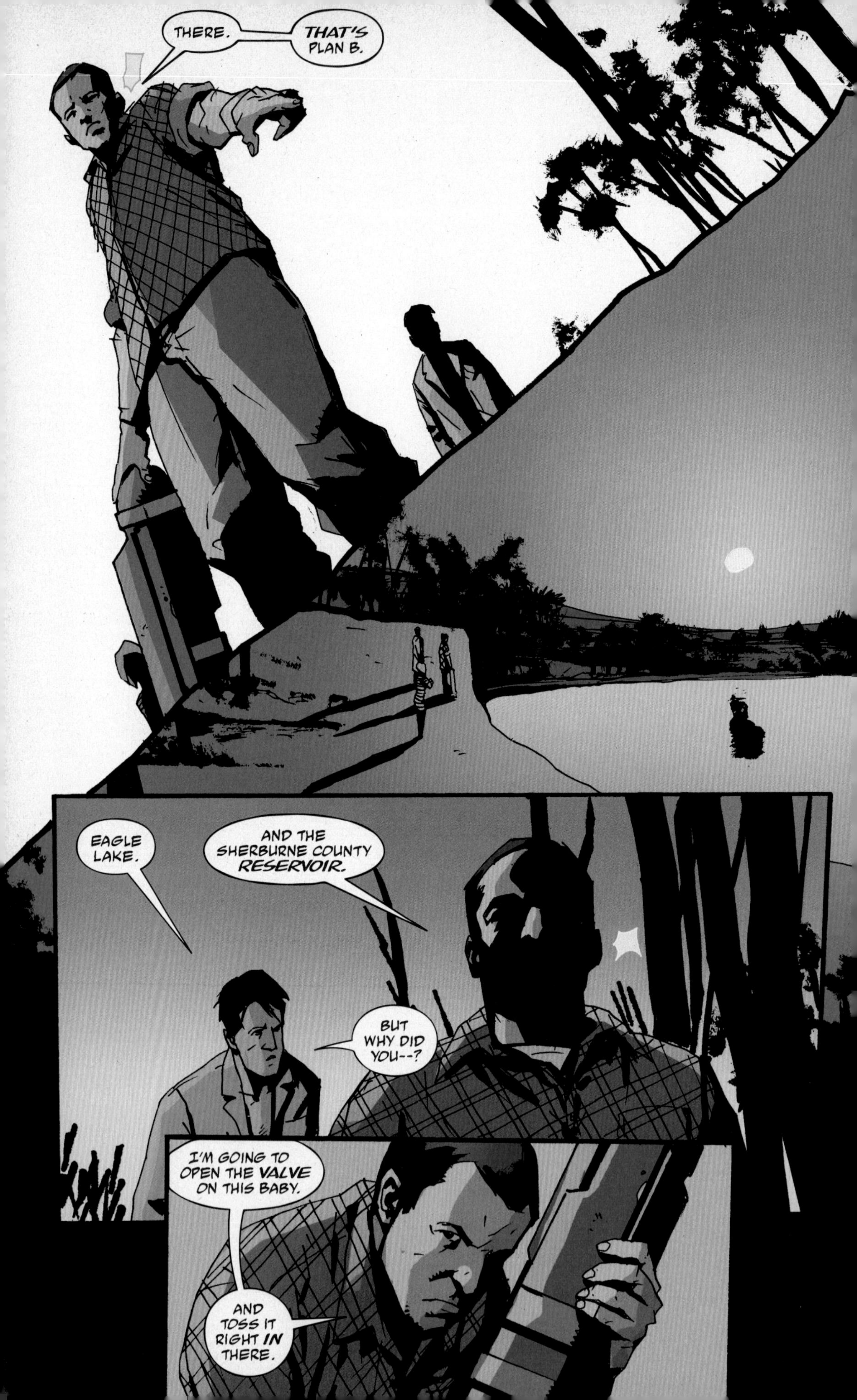
THERE.
THAT'S PLAN B.
EAGLE LAKE.
AND THE SHERBURNE COUNTY RESERVOIR.
BUT WHY DID YOU--?
I'M GOING TO OPEN THE VALVE ON THIS BABY.
AND TOSS IT RIGHT IN THERE.

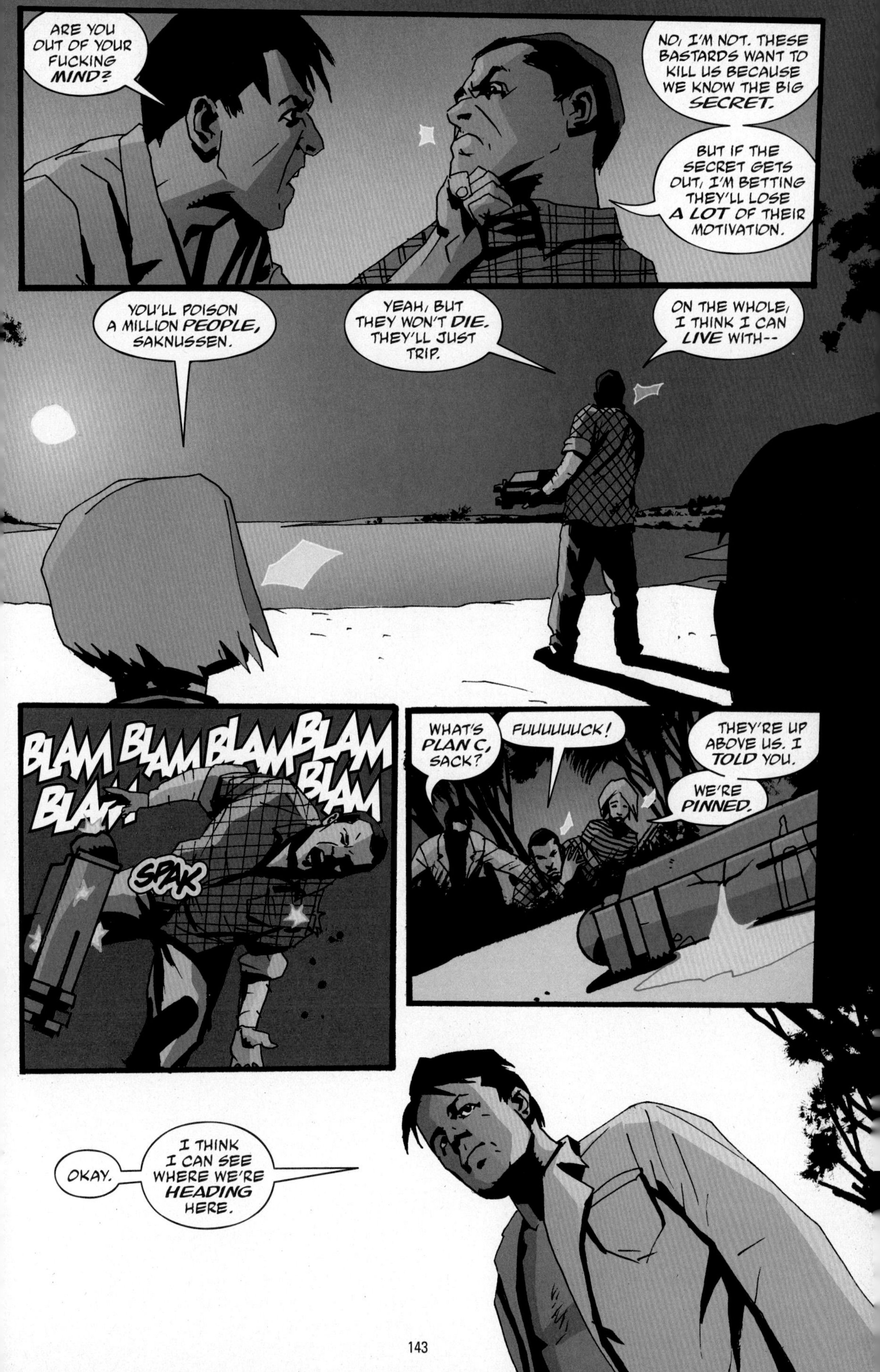

ARE YOU OUT OF YOUR FUCKING MIND?
NO, I'M NOT. THESE BASTARDS WANT TO KILL US BECAUSE WE KNOW THE BIG SECRET.
BUT IF THE SECRET GETS OUT, I'M BETTING THEY'LL LOSE A LOT OF THEIR MOTIVATION.
YOU'LL POISON A MILLION PEOPLE, SAKNUSSEN.
YEAH, BUT THEY WON'T DIE. THEY'LL JUST TRIP.
ON THE WHOLE, I THINK I CAN LIVE WITH--
BLAM BLAM BLAM BLAM BLAM
SPAK
WHAT'S PLAN C, SACK?
FUUUUUUCK!
THEY'RE UP ABOVE US. I TOLD YOU.
WE'RE PINNED.
OKAY.
I THINK I CAN SEE WHERE WE'RE HEADING HERE.

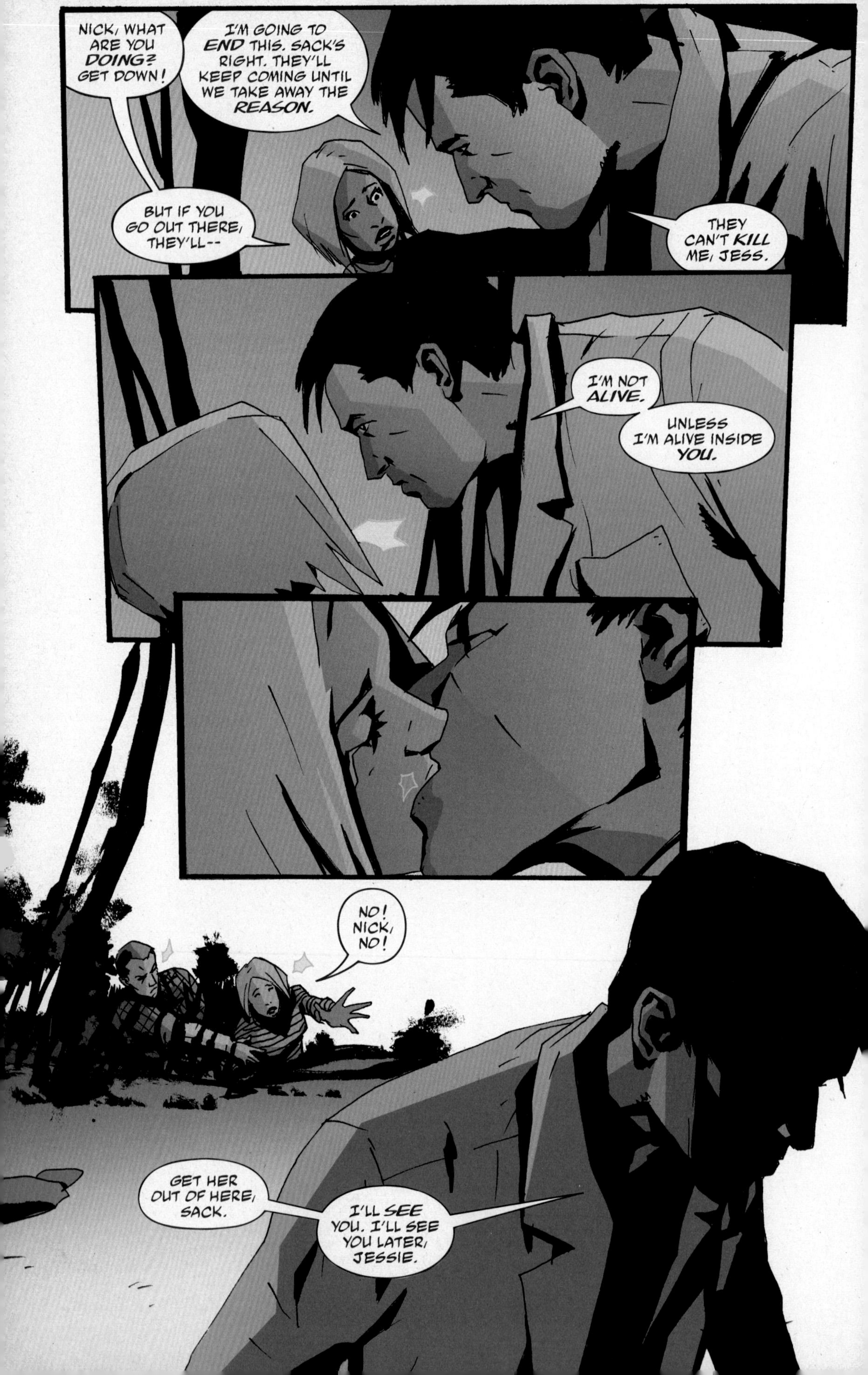
NICK, WHAT ARE YOU DOING? GET DOWN!
I'M GOING TO END THIS. SACK'S RIGHT. THEY'LL KEEP COMING UNTIL WE TAKE AWAY THE REASON.
BUT IF YOU GO OUT THERE, THEY'LL--
THEY CAN'T KILL ME, JESS.
I'M NOT ALIVE.
UNLESS I'M ALIVE INSIDE YOU.
NO! NICK, NO!
GET HER OUT OF HERE, SACK.
I'LL SEE YOU. I'LL SEE YOU LATER, JESSIE.

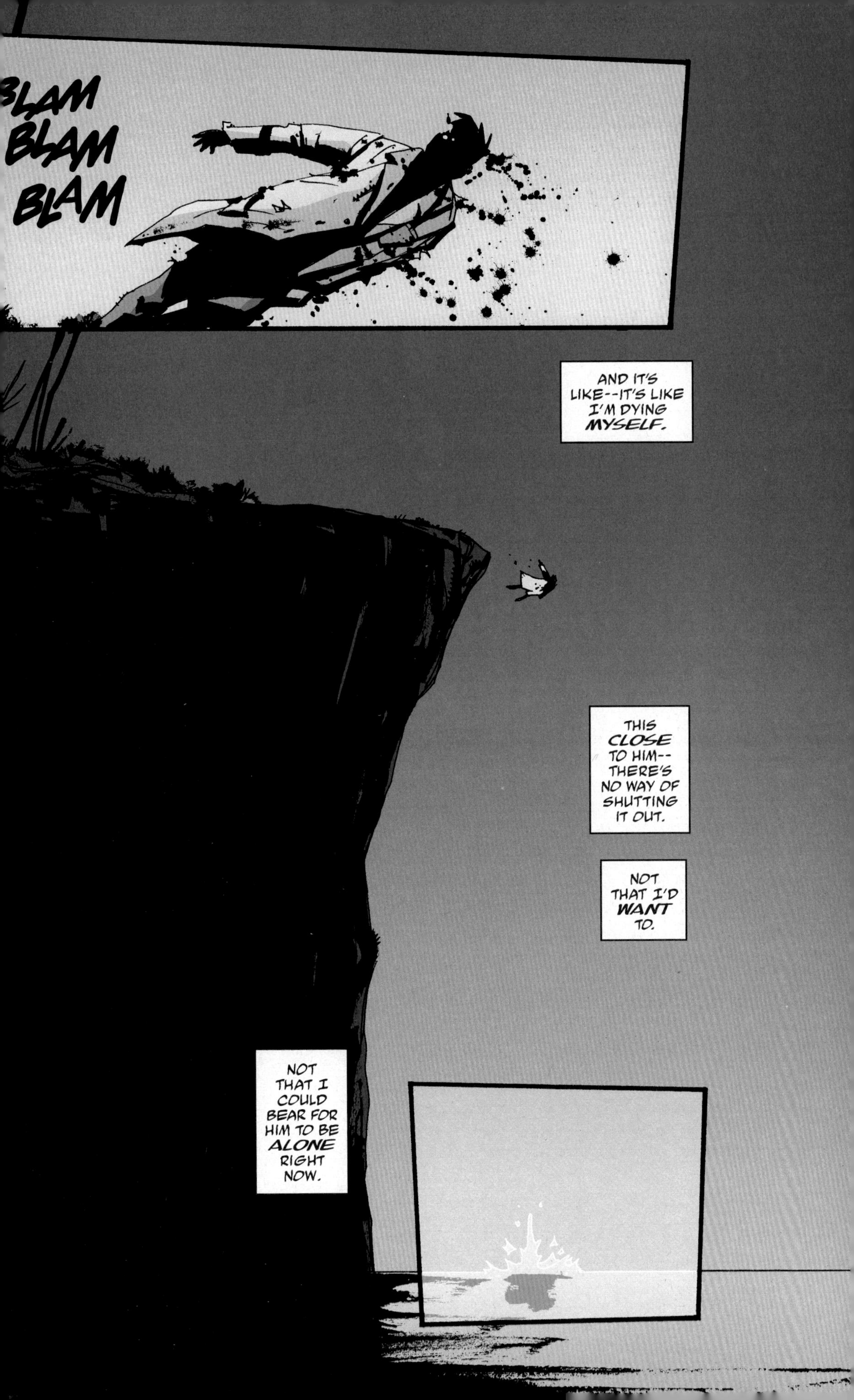
BLAM BLAM BLAM
AND IT'S LIKE--IT'S LIKE I'M DYING MYSELF.
THIS CLOSE TO HIM--THERE'S NO WAY OF SHUTTING IT OUT.
NOT THAT I'D WANT TO.
NOT THAT I COULD BEAR FOR HIM TO BE ALONE RIGHT NOW.

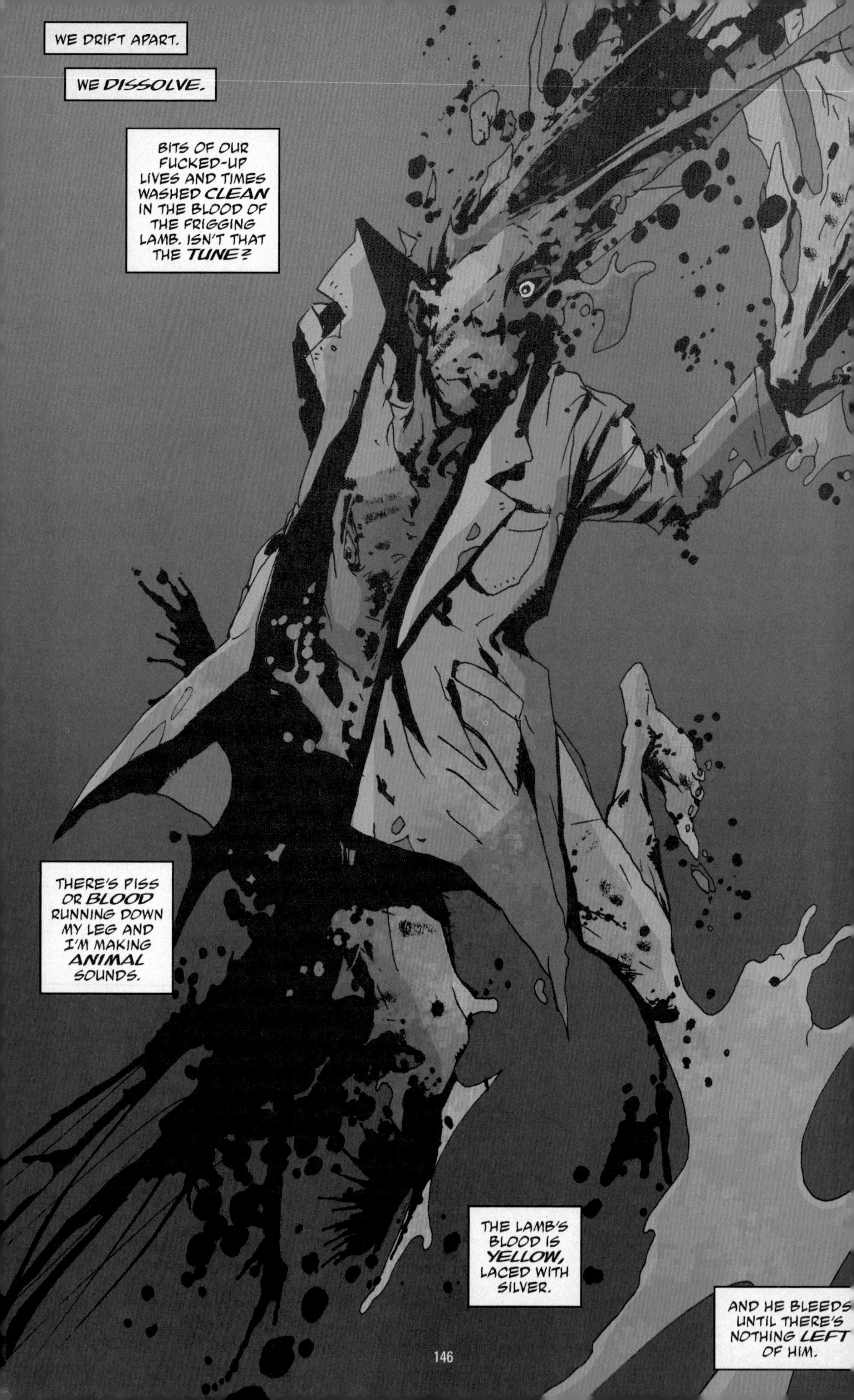
WE DRIFT APART.
WE DISSOLVE.
BITS OF OUR FUCKED-UP LIVES AND TIMES WASHED CLEAN IN THE BLOOD OF THE FRIGGING LAMB. ISN'T THAT THE TUNE?
THERE'S PISS OR BLOOD RUNNING DOWN MY LEG AND I'M MAKING ANIMAL SOUNDS.
THE LAMB'S BLOOD IS YELLOW, LACED WITH SILVER.
AND HE BLEEDS UNTIL THERE'S NOTHING LEFT OF HIM.

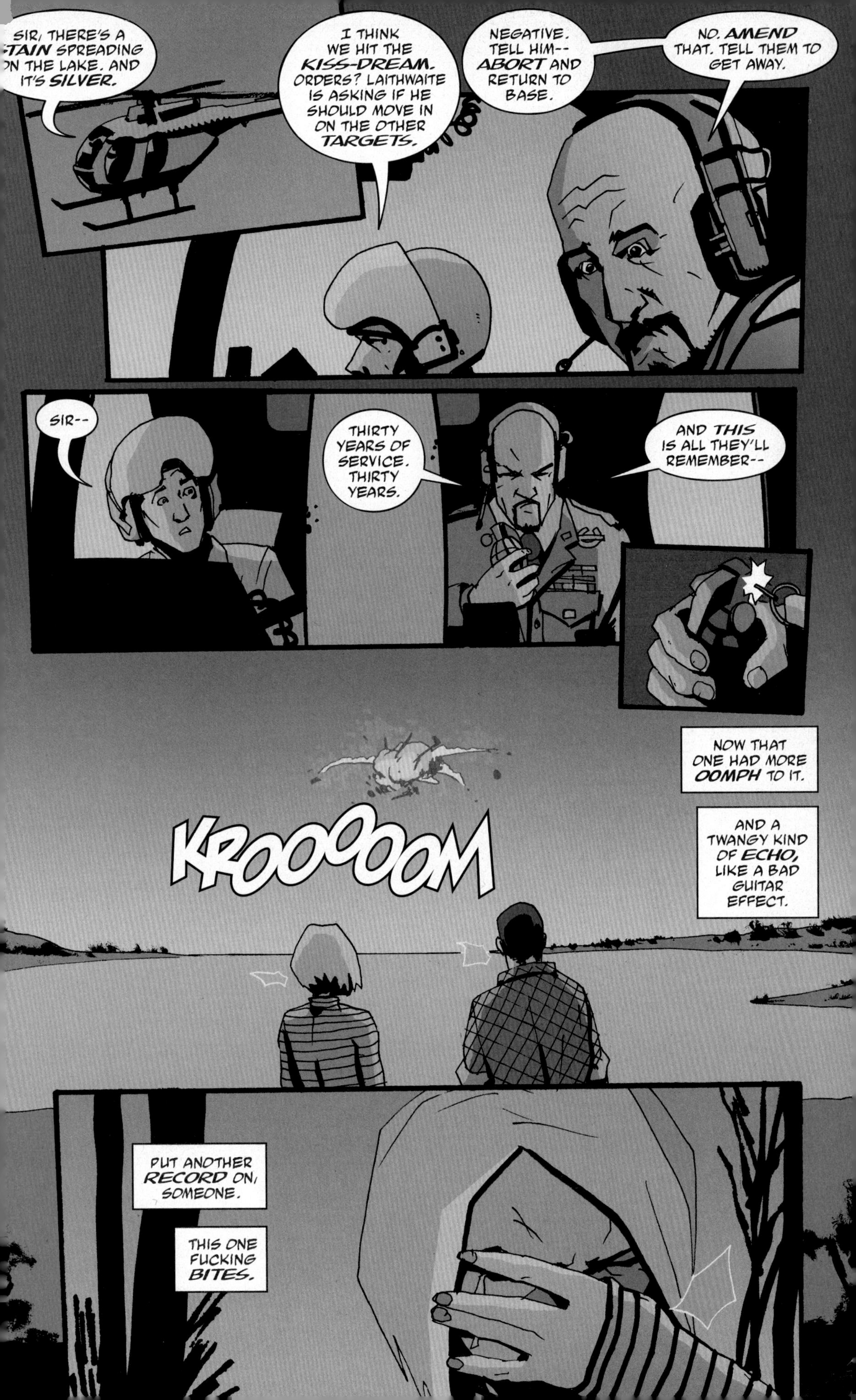
SIR, THERE'S A STAIN SPREADING ON THE LAKE. AND IT'S SILVER.
I THINK WE HIT THE KISS-DREAM. ORDERS? LAITHWAITE IS ASKING IF HE SHOULD MOVE IN ON THE OTHER TARGETS.
NEGATIVE. TELL HIM-- ABORT AND RETURN TO BASE.
NO. AMEND THAT. TELL THEM TO GET AWAY.
SIR--
THIRTY YEARS OF SERVICE. THIRTY YEARS.
AND THIS IS ALL THEY'LL REMEMBER--
NOW THAT ONE HAD MORE OOMPH TO IT.
AND A TWANGY KIND OF ECHO, LIKE A BAD GUITAR EFFECT.
KROOOOOM
PUT ANOTHER RECORD ON, SOMEONE.
THIS ONE FUCKING BITES.

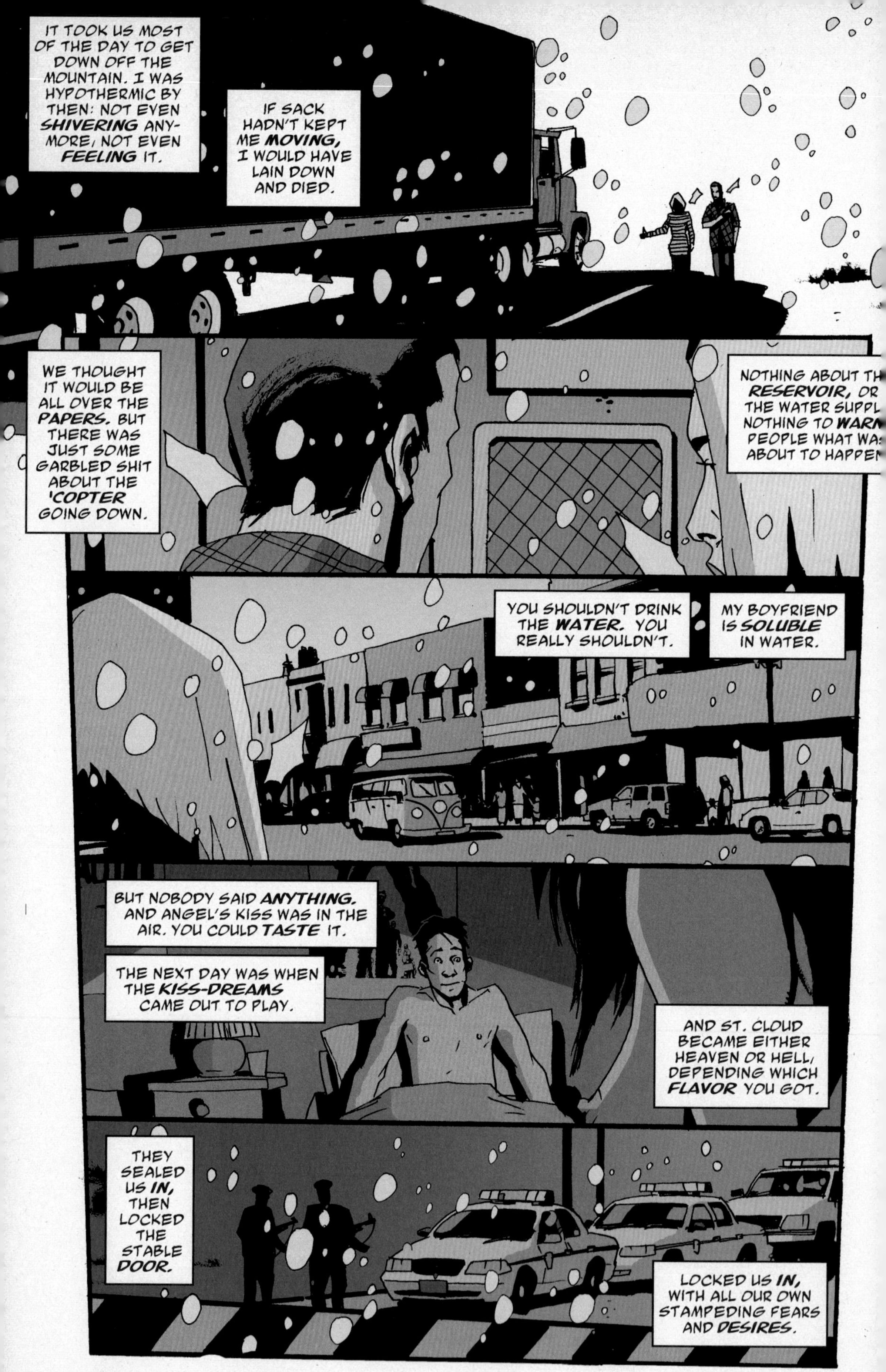
IT TOOK US MOST OF THE DAY TO GET DOWN OFF THE MOUNTAIN. I WAS HYPOTHERMIC BY THEN: NOT EVEN SHIVERING ANY-MORE, NOT EVEN FEELING IT.
IF SACK HADN'T KEPT ME MOVING, I WOULD HAVE LAIN DOWN AND DIED.
WE THOUGHT IT WOULD BE ALL OVER THE PAPERS. BUT THERE WAS JUST SOME GARBLED SHIT ABOUT THE 'COPTER GOING DOWN.
NOTHING ABOUT TH RESERVOIR, OR THE WATER SUPPL NOTHING TO WARN PEOPLE WHAT WA ABOUT TO HAPPEN
YOU SHOULDN'T DRINK THE WATER. YOU REALLY SHOULDN'T.
MY BOYFRIEND IS SOLUBLE IN WATER.
BUT NOBODY SAID ANYTHING. AND ANGEL'S KISS WAS IN THE AIR. YOU COULD TASTE IT.
THE NEXT DAY WAS WHEN THE KISS-DREAMS CAME OUT TO PLAY.
AND ST. CLOUD BECAME EITHER HEAVEN OR HELL, DEPENDING WHICH FLAVOR YOU GOT.
THEY SEALED US IN, THEN LOCKED THE STABLE DOOR.
LOCKED US IN, WITH ALL OUR OWN STAMPEDING FEARS AND DESIRES.

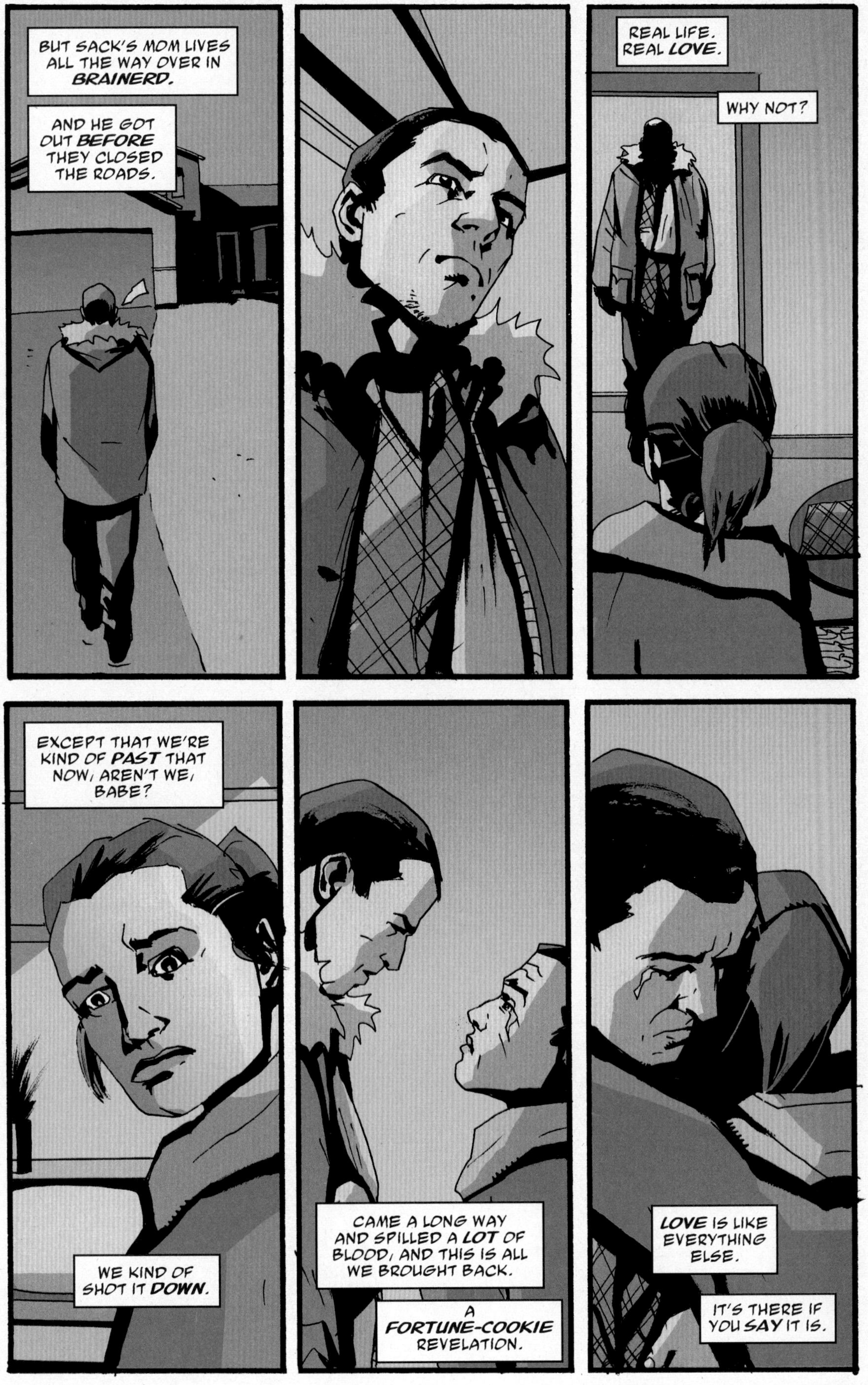

BUT SACK'S MOM LIVES ALL THE WAY OVER IN BRAINERD.
AND HE GOT OUT BEFORE THEY CLOSED THE ROADS.
REAL LIFE. REAL LOVE.
WHY NOT?
EXCEPT THAT WE'RE KIND OF PAST THAT NOW, AREN'T WE, BABE?
WE KIND OF SHOT IT DOWN.
CAME A LONG WAY AND SPILLED A LOT OF BLOOD, AND THIS IS ALL WE BROUGHT BACK.
A FORTUNE-COOKIE REVELATION.
LOVE IS LIKE EVERYTHING ELSE.
IT'S THERE IF YOU SAY IT IS.

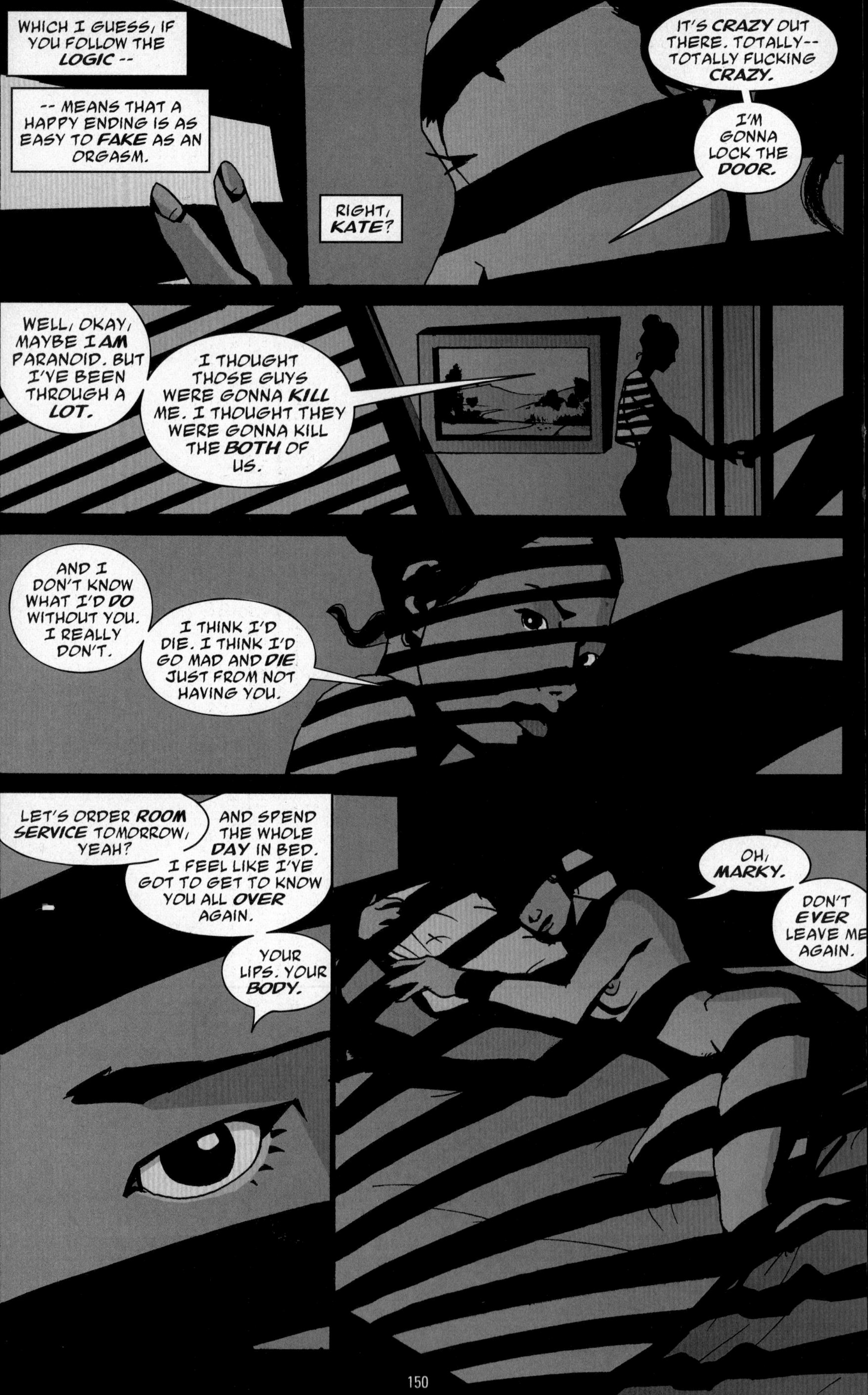
WHICH I GUESS, IF YOU FOLLOW THE LOGIC --
-- MEANS THAT A HAPPY ENDING IS AS EASY TO FAKE AS AN ORGASM.
RIGHT, KATE?
IT'S CRAZY OUT THERE. TOTALLY-- TOTALLY FUCKING CRAZY.
I'M GONNA LOCK THE DOOR.
WELL, OKAY, MAYBE I AM PARANOID. BUT I'VE BEEN THROUGH A LOT.
I THOUGHT THOSE GUYS WERE GONNA KILL ME. I THOUGHT THEY WERE GONNA KILL THE BOTH OF US.
AND I DON'T KNOW WHAT I'D DO WITHOUT YOU. I REALLY DON'T.
I THINK I'D DIE. I THINK I'D GO MAD AND DIE JUST FROM NOT HAVING YOU.
LET'S ORDER ROOM SERVICE TOMORROW, YEAH?
AND SPEND THE WHOLE DAY IN BED. I FEEL LIKE I'VE GOT TO GET TO KNOW YOU ALL OVER AGAIN.
YOUR LIPS. YOUR BODY.
OH, MARKY.
DON'T EVER LEAVE ME AGAIN.

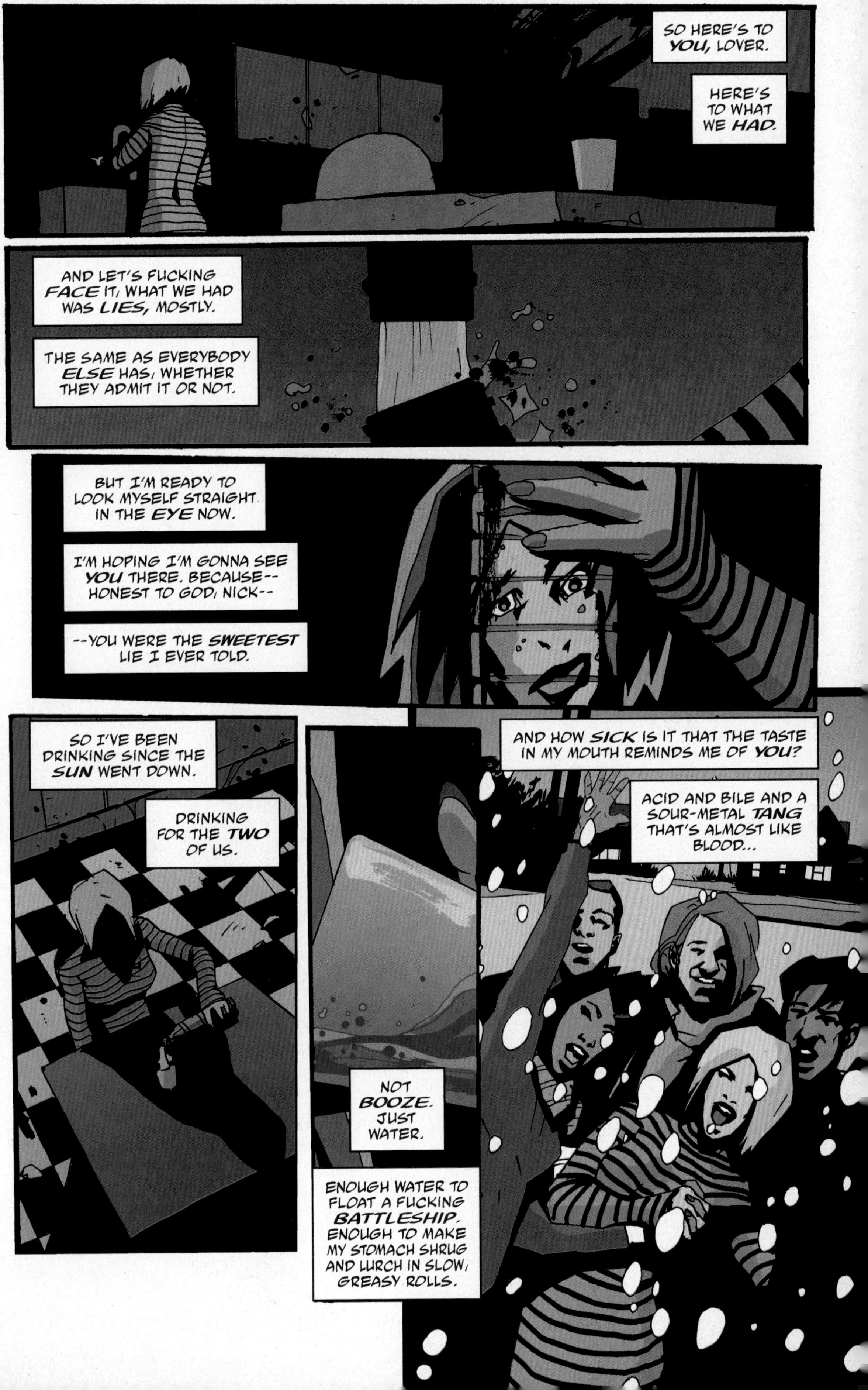
SO HERE'S TO YOU, LOVER.
HERE'S TO WHAT WE HAD.
AND LET'S FUCKING FACE IT, WHAT WE HAD WAS LIES, MOSTLY.
THE SAME AS EVERYBODY ELSE HAS, WHETHER THEY ADMIT IT OR NOT.
BUT I'M READY TO LOOK MYSELF STRAIGHT IN THE EYE NOW.
I'M HOPING I'M GONNA SEE YOU THERE. BECAUSE-- HONEST TO GOD, NICK--
--YOU WERE THE SWEETEST LIE I EVER TOLD.
SO I'VE BEEN DRINKING SINCE THE SUN WENT DOWN.
DRINKING FOR THE TWO OF US.
NOT BOOZE. JUST WATER.
ENOUGH WATER TO FLOAT A FUCKING BATTLESHIP. ENOUGH TO MAKE MY STOMACH SHRUG AND LURCH IN SLOW, GREASY ROLLS.
AND HOW SICK IS IT THAT THE TASTE IN MY MOUTH REMINDS ME OF YOU?
ACID AND BILE AND A SOUR-METAL TANG THAT'S ALMOST LIKE BLOOD...

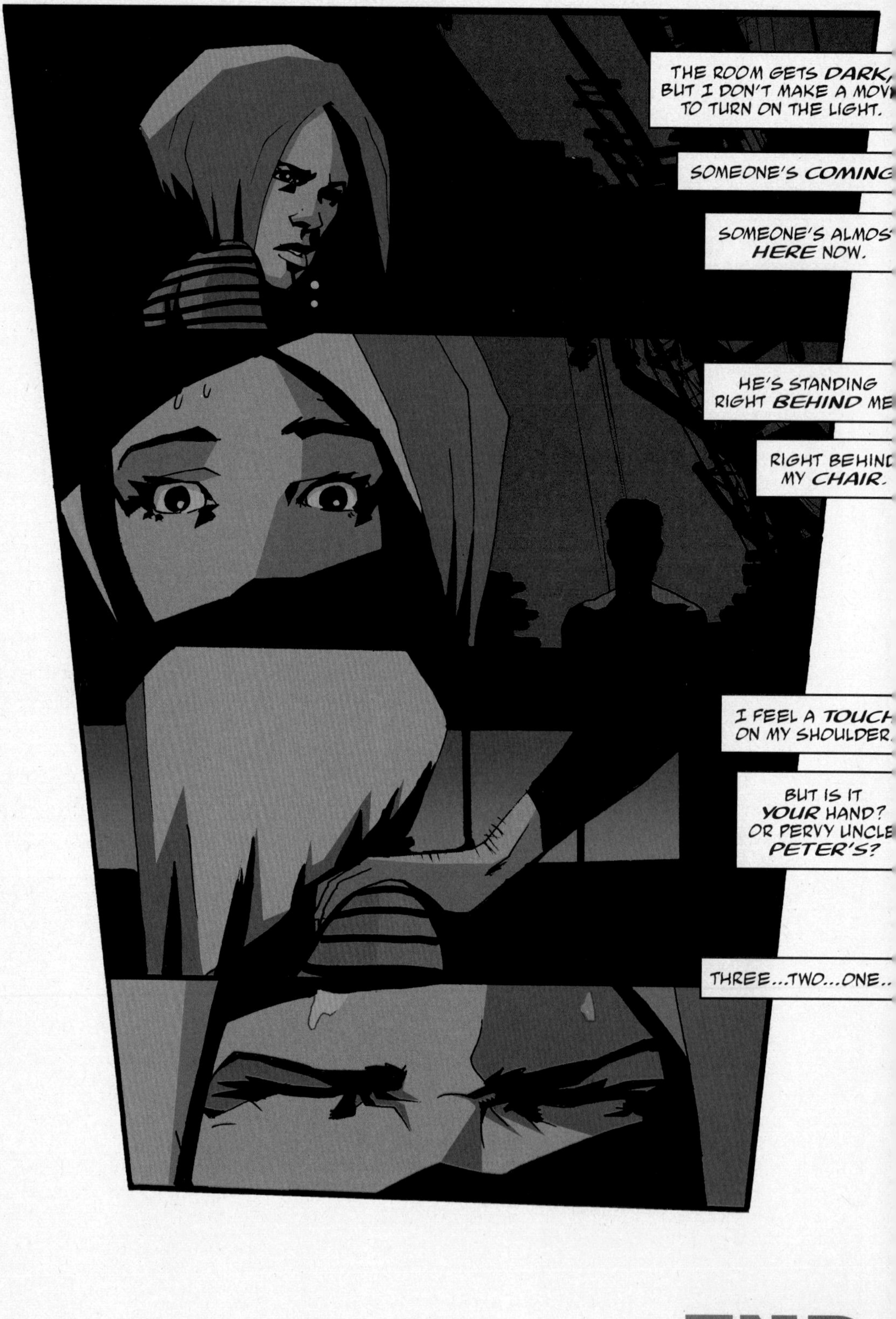
THE ROOM GETS DARK, BUT I DON'T MAKE A MOV TO TURN ON THE LIGHT.
SOMEONE'S COMING
SOMEONE'S ALMOS HERE NOW.
HE'S STANDING RIGHT BEHIND ME
RIGHT BEHIN MY CHAIR.
I FEEL A TOUC ON MY SHOULDER.
BUT IS IT YOUR HAND? OR PERVY UNCL PETER'S?
THREE...TWO...ONE..
END

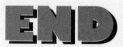

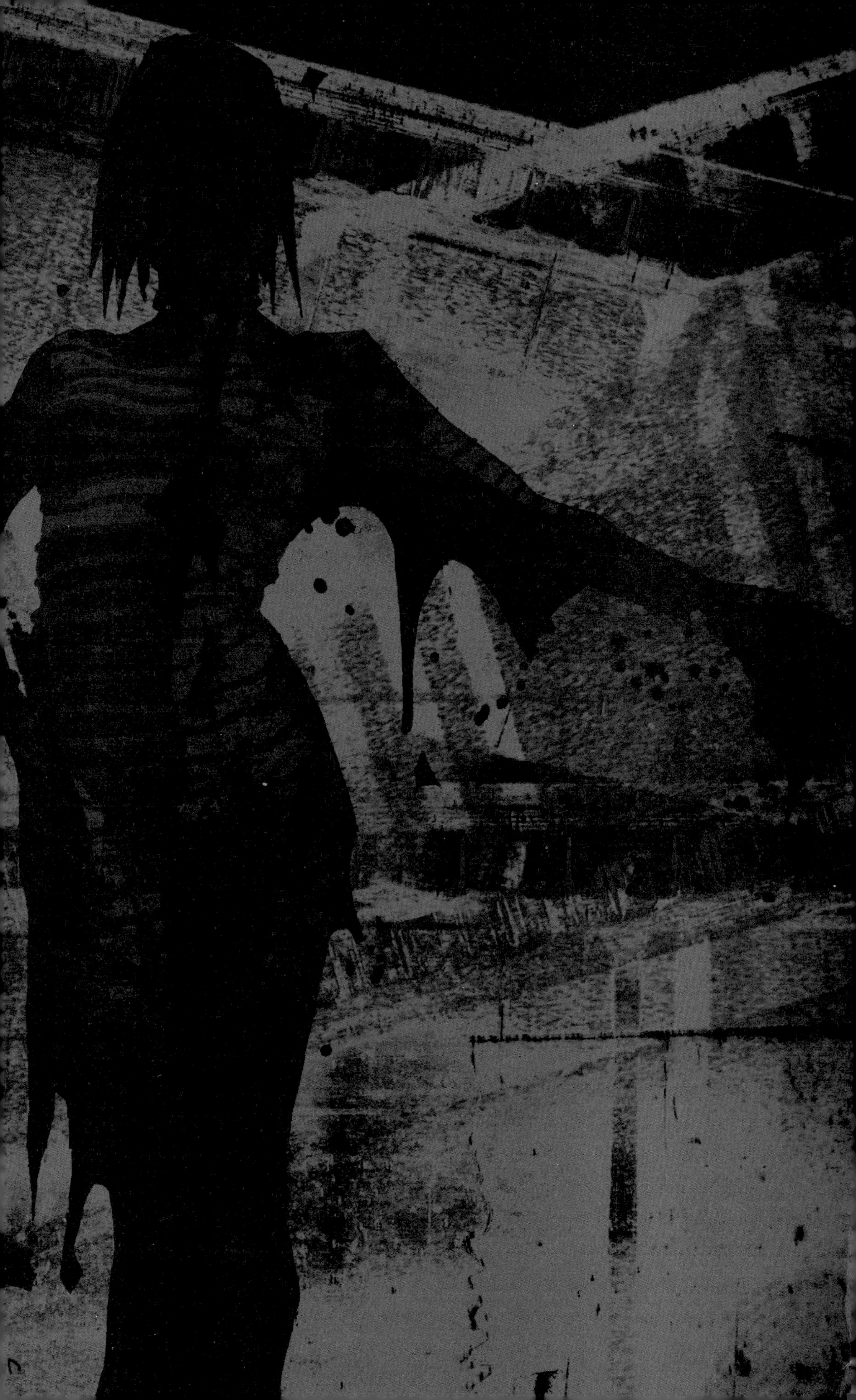

MINNESOTA UNIVERSITY AT ST. CLOUD

ENTRANCE APPLICATION FOR CURRENT ACADEMIC YEAR

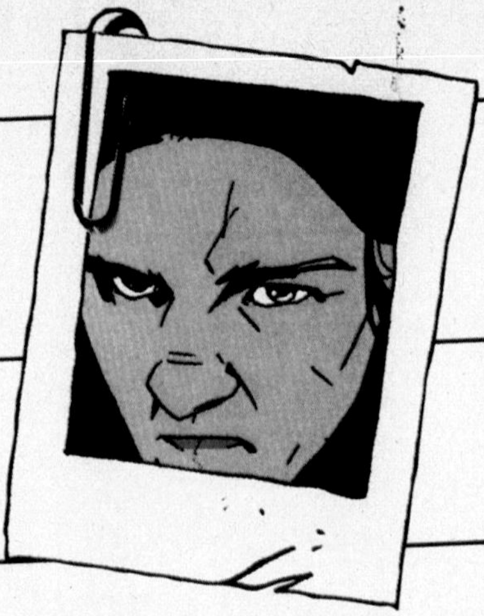

NAME: Mark Alexander Sale

RELEVANT TEST SCORES

Critical Reading	561
Mathematics	568
Writing	594
Literature	587
Biology	600
Physics	598
Chemistry	597

DATE OF BIRTH 06/17/89

HIGH SCHOOL James Sutter Burke High School – Addison, Wisconsin

HIGH SCHOOL ADMISSION CODE: JBWI339

PERSONAL STATEMENT

I made MU St. Cloud my first college choice because I believe that it offers the intellectual climate that I want and need. The science faculty includes leaders in many scientific fields - Peter Leith, Kira Ida Lincoln and John Partington among others - and it is my ambition to study science in an institution which values all branches of human endeavor equally, and doesn't condemn practical applications work in favor of pure theory. MUSC's military tech and blue-sky pharmaceutical research programs are justly renowned, and I would hope to contribute in one of these areas once I reach my senior year.

I consider myself to be first and foremost a serious and committed student. I know that "all work and no play" is a bad formula, but in practice I've found that work for me is a form of play, so I don't really need or look for social distractions when I'm studying.

But at the same time I am an excellent team player, able to contribute to a shared project enthusiastically myself and also to build on the contributions of others. I love exploring new ideas and possibilities with anyone, of any sex, age or background. Teamwork is always productive even if you think you're going up a blind alley. There are no blind alleys in science, or in life.

MINNESOTA UNIVERSITY AT ST. CLOUD

ENTRANCE APPLICATION FOR CURRENT ACADEMIC YEAR

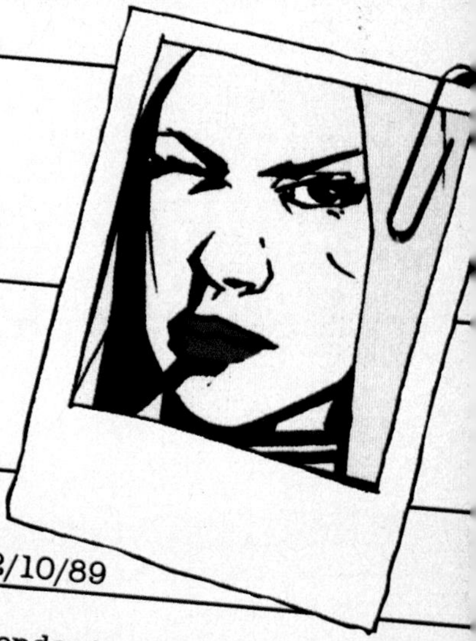

NAME: Jessica Sarah Kidby

RELEVANT TEST SCORES

Critical Reading	538
Mathematics	541
Writing	513
Literature	598
United States History	587
World History	591

DATE OF BIRTH 12/10/89

HIGH SCHOOL Prendergast Senior High School Colfax, Iowa

HIGH SCHOOL ADMISSION CODE: PRIA832

PERSONAL STATEMENT

I would describe myself as a very positive-thinking person, both about myself and about the world. My interests extend into both artistic and scientific areas. I play the cello and am a member of the school chamber orchestra, but I was also a prominent figure in the science club and won third place in the statewide senior science tournament – the only student from an entirely non-selective school to place in the top twelve.

But if I have one interest that comes before all others, it's people. I am a humanist, because I think what human beings can achieve has no limits. I am fascinated by human psychology and by the ways in which even altruism and self-sacrifice can have deep evolutionary roots in our survival needs and our history as a species. Nature has designed us to compete for resources and yet we cooperate and love and help each other and that is what makes us as a species so amazing.

My ambition is to work in the third world in some kind of charitable or developmental role. I know there are no fortunes to be made in work like that, but there couldn't be anything more fulfilling or more inspiring.

Perhaps I am sometimes shy and nervous around people I don't know well, but I'm trying hard to overcome that because self-confidence is a very important thing for me. I know that I have the potential to be a high achiever, but that begins with believing in yourself and then making other people believe in you too.

I am a Silver Ring pledge because the Bible teaches us that chastity is a precious virtue.

MINNESOTA UNIVERSITY AT ST. CLOUD

ENTRANCE APPLICATION FOR CURRENT ACADEMIC YEAR

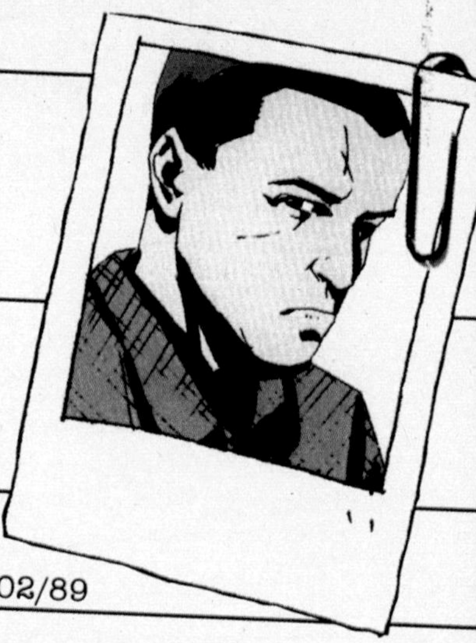

NAME: Paul Saknussen

RELEVANT TEST SCORES

Critical Reading	467
Mathematics	450
Writing	481
Literature	431
United States History	466
World History	490
Combined Science	482

DATE OF BIRTH 07/02/89

HIGH SCHOOL Severn Ridge High School
Brainerd, Minnesota

HIGH SCHOOL ADMISSION CODE: SRMI1212

PERSONAL STATEMENT

I have got a real interest in phisiology and the way human muscle groups work in our bodies so that we can do the things we need to do in our daily lives, whether it is phisical work or shopping or sporting activities or whatever it happens to be. We are all machines desined by nature and it is incredible that this involves so many different systems that do so many different things. This is why I have chosen sports science as my main subject.

Mostly my interests are in sports, by which I include football but also baseball and softball and gymnastics. I am a keen reader, though, and I love movies like those of the Cohen Brothers, Stephen Spielberg and Kuro Sour. Obviously my study is the study of the body, but the mind is important too for perfect health and so I would always want to have academic disciplines in my courses as well as physical ones. Both are as good as each other and both are necessary.

The accompanying letter from my football coach explains my test scores, and he is available if you want to talk to him.

MINNESOTA UNIVERSITY AT ST. CLOUD

ENTRANCE APPLICATION FOR CURRENT ACADEMIC YEAR

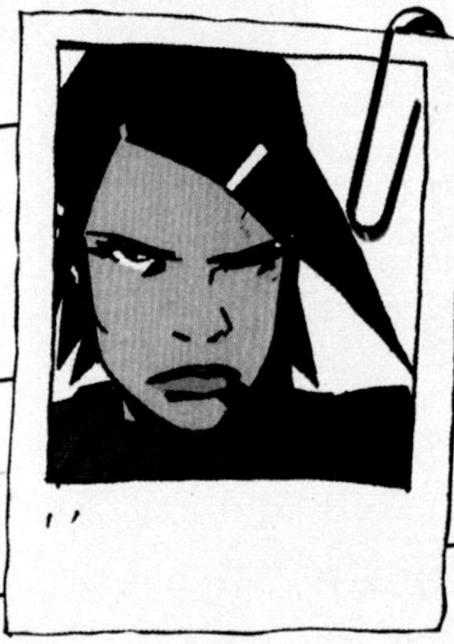

NAME: Yvonne Latimer

DATE OF BIRTH 9/9/89

HIGH SCHOOL Lawton High School
Sheshebe, Minnesota

HIGH SCHOOL ADMISSION CODE: LTMI420

RELEVANT TEST SCORES	
Critical Reading	541
Mathematics	577
Writing	548
Literature	562
World History	591
Combined Science	588
Information Tech	600

PERSONAL STATEMENT

I want to study information technology because information is the future. It makes us what we are, and it allows us to change into whatever we want to be, because it is so flexible and powerful. I also want to study at college because I believe it will help me to pursue my own wider social development.

I am a lively, confident, outgoing young woman with the personal strength to set my own goals and stick to them. I have a strong sense of humor and a strong respect for the beliefs and values of others except when their beliefs and values would take away my freedom to have mine, as with terrorists and extremists of all kinds.

My hobbies include programming and "collecting" computer languages, which I like to learn as a personal challenge. I hope some day to work in the field of copy protection or internet privacy protocols, both of which fascinate me. People must be free to send and receive messages without interception or interference, and intellectual copyright has to be protected. That is the right balance between the individual and the state.

I have chosen Minnesota University at St. Cloud because of its superb facilities and its commitment to academic excellence. My mother is an MUSC alumna, and many of her friends are people she met at MUSC. I look forward to meeting people who will support and fulfill me in the same way.

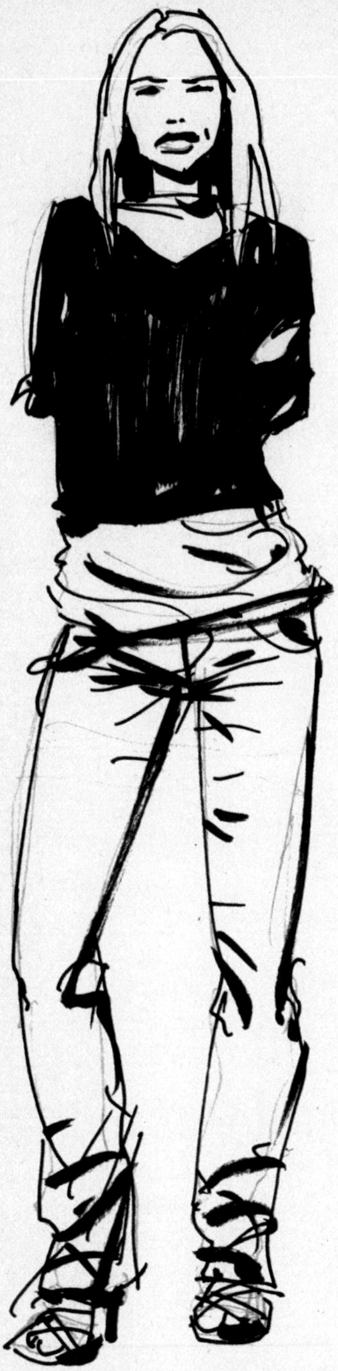

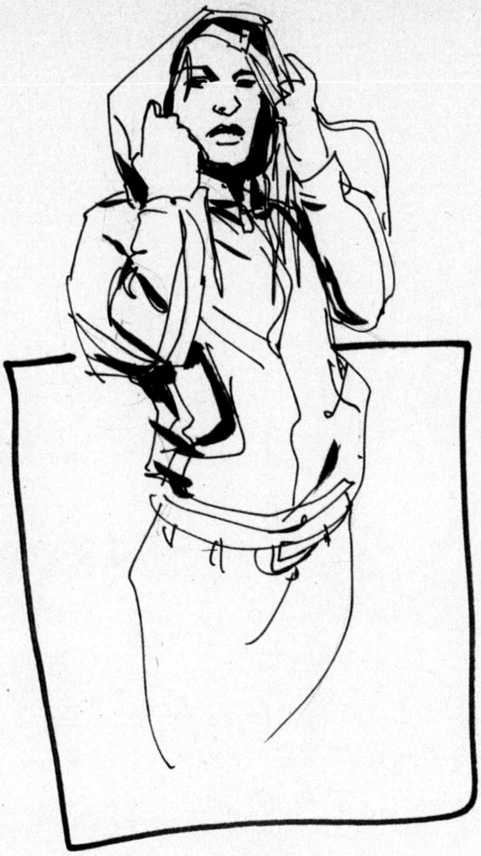

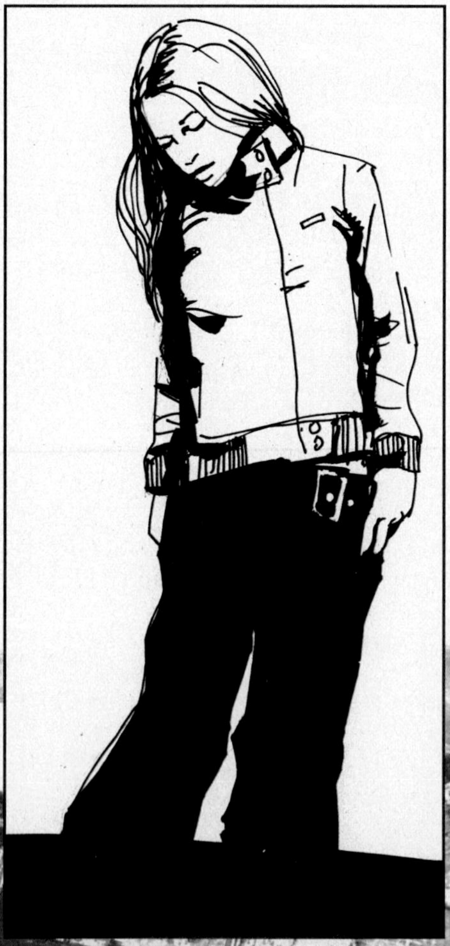

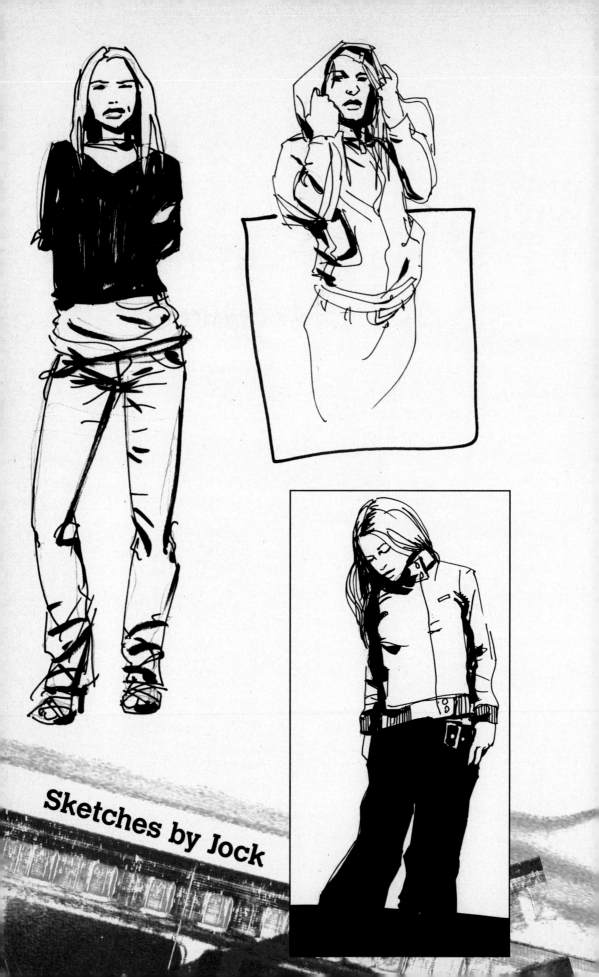

Sketches by Jock

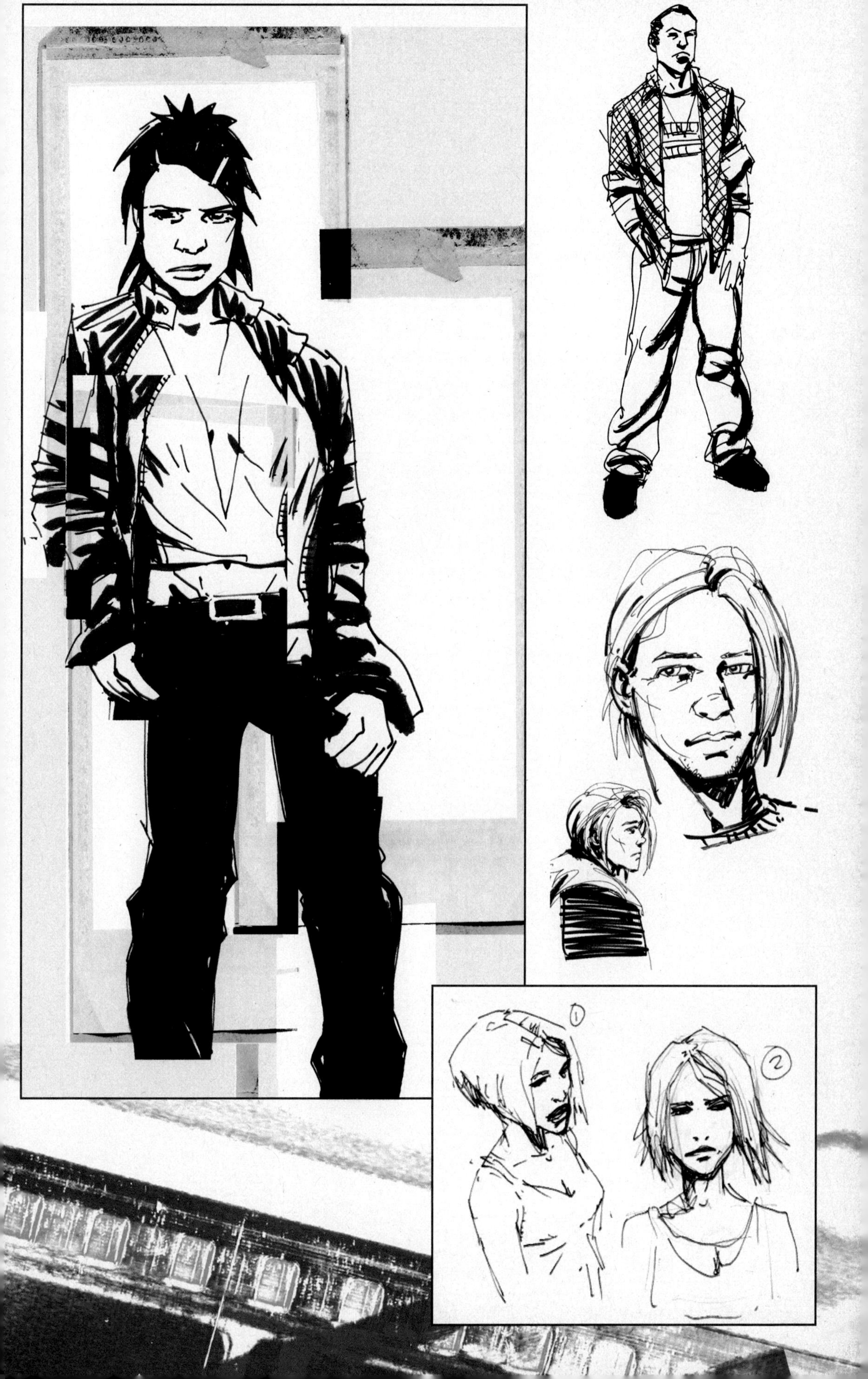
1
2

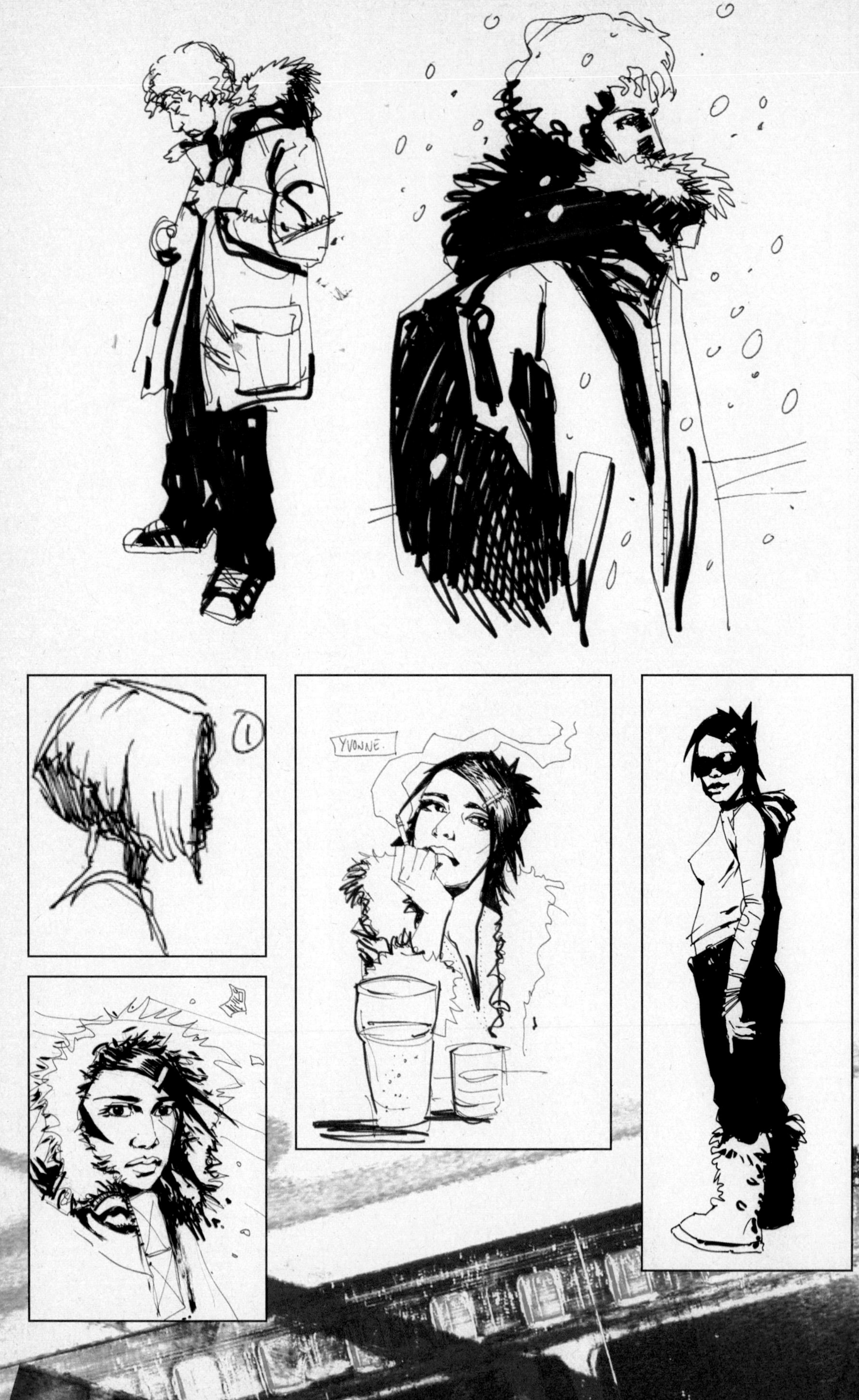
1
YVONNE.